ANALYSIS

OF THE

INTERCHURCH WORLD MOVEMENT
REPORT ON THE STEEL STRIKE

A Da Capo Press Reprint Series

CIVIL LIBERTIES IN AMERICAN HISTORY

GENERAL EDITOR: LEONARD W. LEVY

Claremont Graduate School

ANALYSIS
OF THE
INTERCHURCH WORLD MOVEMENT
REPORT ON THE STEEL STRIKE

BY
MARSHALL OLDS

FOREWORD
BY
JEREMIAH W. JENKS

25287

DA CAPO PRESS · NEW YORK · 1971

A Da Capo Press Reprint Edition

This Da Capo Press edition of
*Analysis of the Interchurch World
Movement Report on the Steel Strike*
is an unabridged republication of the
first edition published in New York and
London in 1923.

Library of Congress Catalog Card Number 73-139199

SBN 306-70082-4

Published by Da Capo Press
A Division of Plenum Publishing Corporation
227 West 17th Street, New York, N.Y. 10011

ANALYSIS

OF THE

INTERCHURCH WORLD MOVEMENT
REPORT ON THE STEEL STRIKE

ANALYSIS

OF THE

INTERCHURCH WORLD MOVEMENT
REPORT ON THE STEEL STRIKE

BY

MARSHALL OLDS

FOREWORD

BY

JEREMIAH W. JENKS, PH.D., LL.D.
*Research Professor of Government and Public Administration,
New York University*

EDITED AS TO THE LAW INVOLVED IN LABOR CONTROVERSIES BY

MURRAY T. QUIGG, B.A., LL.B.
Editor " Law and Labor "

EDITED AS TO DETAILED ACCURACY OF CITATIONS, QUOTATIONS,
AND STATISTICS BY

HASKINS AND SELLS
Certified Public Accountants

———

PART TWO

HISTORY OF THE INTERCHURCH
REPORT ON THE STEEL STRIKE

WITH THE ASSISTANCE OF

NUMEROUS OFFICIALS AND ASSOCIATES
OF THE
INTERCHURCH WORLD MOVEMENT

G. P. PUTNAM'S SONS
NEW YORK AND LONDON
The Knickerbocker Press
1923

Made in the United States of America

ANALYSIS

OF THE

INTERCHURCH WORLD MOVEMENT
REPORT ON THE STEEL STRIKE

FOREWORD

By Jeremiah W. Jenks, Ph.D., LL.D.

Research Professor of Government and Public Administration, New York University

No question at the present day is of greater interest to the public than that of the relations between employers and their working men.   Not only are these two parties interested but the public in many cases loses even more in both financial interests and lack of comfort and public facilities than do either of the parties immediately concerned in the case of a great strike, which suspends an important business like railroading, coal mining, manufacture of steel, the furnishing of milk to a great city, and other similar industries. In consequence the story of a great strike, with its causes and allotment of fault and the results both to the parties directly interested and to the public, is of general concern. And such a story, if it is to do good rather than harm, must be told with absolute impartiality and complete regard for the exact truth.   When the Interchurch World Movement was organized, most people interested in social and moral progress hoped earnestly for its success.   It is generally recognized that no other organization in the civilized world is of so great importance in promoting the welfare of society as a whole as the Christian Church, including all of the various denominations.   It was in consequence the earnest desire of public-spirited men that the work be conducted

v

with wisdom and thoroughness, so that its expressions of
opinion on whatever subject would be received at full value,
and influence social movements accordingly.

Soon after its organization an industrial section was
established, with the thought that it would take charge of
investigations dealing with the various phases of industry
from the moral and religious points of view. I was invited
to attend as a delegate of one of the important social movements, an early conference of this industrial section. This
meeting was held while the steel strike of 1919 was under
way and shortly after Judge Gary had declined to meet
the representatives of the trade union in order to discuss
with them the possible terms of settlement, he feeling it
wiser to deal directly with his own men and with representatives in the employ of the steel corporation whom they
might select. This act of his was condemned openly in this
meeting. One of the members proposed, apparently in
some excitement, that a committee be appointed to investigate and report upon the steel strike. Evidently the
mover of the resolution expected a prompt condemnatory
report.

It has been my fortune to take an active part in a number
of important investigations on industrial subjects. No one
who has not been intimately connected with the management of business or who has not attempted such an investigation can understand its difficulties and the length of time
required to secure impartial information and present it
accurately. From the very nature of their business, ministers of the Christian religion have not the training or the
experience to make such an investigation, or even to plan
and guide such an investigation. Of course there are within
the church organization trained business men and economists who would be especially well equipped for such work.
Generally speaking, experience shows that when ministers
attempt to discuss in detail either practical or business
questions of the day, which are of a partisan nature, they
will inevitably offend a considerable portion of their con-

gregations, because in controverted questions there are usually two sides and an average congregation will be divided in opinion. The minister, therefore, will please one section and offend the other. If, in the discussion of a partisan question, he confines himself to dwelling upon the importance of the truthful and wise solution of the question and to arousing the consciousness of his hearers themselves to make an impartial study of the question and then to act impartially with the welfare of the public in mind, he will usually have accomplished his duty far more effectively than if he attempts to instruct his congregation in the merits of the question itself.

Very many of us felt, therefore, that for the Interchurch World Movement to attempt to intervene in this great strike was probably ill advised. If, however, it seemed best to the managers of the movement to undertake such an investigation, it was of prime importance both to the movement itself and to the public at large that the investigation be made by the best industrial experts, who would follow strictly scientific principles and debar absolutely all partisan spirit. If that could be done the report might be very helpful. If the report were made in any other spirit it was certain to be harmful rather than beneficial to the public and would certainly prove very damaging to the Interchurch World Movement itself.

The investigation was made and the committee in whose charge the investigation had been placed made its report. Shortly thereafter adverse criticisms were made, both by unpartisan reviewers and by prominent church people, on the ground that the report was partisan and inaccurate. As far as I am aware, no detailed analysis of the report has yet been published.

Sometime ago Mr. Olds, the author of this book, came to me explaining that he was making a detailed analysis of the Interchurch report on the steel strike; that he was endeavoring to be absolutely impartial; that he was using the greatest care in verifying his statistics and his statements; that he

was attempting so to present his analysis that it would be
easy for the reader to segregate questions of fact from those
of opinion, and in this way get a really accurate view of this
report, its excellencies and its defects. He also explained
to me that he had the coöperation in his work of some men
who had been active in the preparation of the Interchurch
report; that he was looking up the training and status of all
those who had made the investigations and prepared the
report, and that he hoped his work would prove of service to
the public. I had known Mr. Olds before and believed him
to be sincere in attempting to do an impartial piece of work.

I have since read Mr. Olds' manuscript with care. I have
not had the time and have made no attempt to verify his
figures, his citation of authorities, or his quotations. In-
asmuch, however, as this could readily be done by any party
interested, as Mr. Olds has a reputation as a student of
these questions to sustain, and as he has, I understand,
taken the wise precaution of having all such matter carefully
verified by competent outside assistance, I have no question
that this part of his work has been carefully done.

Considering the very great significance of both the Interchurch Movement and of the steel strike, his study is to
my mind, of decided importance. It should be read by
all who wish to make any use of the Interchurch report, to
quote it or to base any judgment upon it. Especially should
it be read and carefully studied by the leaders in the Interchurch Movement who have loaned their names to the
report, or who were responsible for the investigation. No
honest man can base arguments or conclusions upon a
document whose accuracy he questions, without verifying
by independent study the accuracy of the document. Mr.
Olds' study of the report, impartial as it is in spirit and
generous as it is in its criticism of the motives of those who
have been responsible for making it, is nevertheless such
that it is bound to raise serious question in the mind of any
student of social problems who is interested in the report.
It is to be hoped, therefore, that this study will have a wide

circulation among those who are interested in the relation of the Church to industrial questions, especially those who believe that the Church should take an active part in the direct discussion and solution of industrial problems and particularly those directly connected with the Interchurch World Movement.

STATEMENT BY

HASKINS & SELLS
Certified Public Accountants

Pursuant to engagement, we have reviewed the manuscript of your book *Analysis of the Interchurch Report on the Steel Strike* for the purpose of verifying, by comparison with their stated sources, the citations, quotations, statistics, and figures contained therein; and

WE HEREBY CERTIFY:

That all citations are accurate;

That all quotations, including excerpts in which the sequence of original passages has for clearness or brevity been varied, are accurate as to text and, in our opinion, fairly represent the meaning of their original context;

That all statistics and figures quoted have been verified by comparison with documents from which quoted and those subject to mathematical proof have been so proved; and

That all statistics are presented and used in accordance with generally accepted statistical practices.

(Signed) HASKINS & SELLS.

FOREWORD

STATEMENT OF

REV. WILLIAM HIRAM FOULKES, D.D.

Chairman, Executive Committee Interchurch World Movement

which finally approved for publication the Report on the Steel Strike.[1]

"I fear from what I have heard, after the investigation had been made, that some of the *actual investigators* were not as unprejudiced as they should have been, and that, *personally representing one side of the controversy*, their testimony was therefore, liable to be discounted."

STATEMENT OF

MR. STANLEY WENT

Member Publicity Department, Interchurch World Movement, and original editor of the Interchurch Report on the Steel Strike

Upon the completion of my editing of the original draft of the Interchurch Report on the Steel Strike, I accompanied my editorial notes with a memorandum which was in part as follows:—

June 17, 1920.

From: STANLEY WENT,
To: MR. DENNETT
Re: STEEL REPORT.

In accordance with your wishes, I have edited the accompanying steel report as lightly as seemed compatible with the end in view. That end, as I understand it, was to present the report in a form which should give the least possible *impression* of bias on the part of the investigating committee.

. . . .

[1] Originally Dr. John R. Mott was Chairman, and Dr. Foulkes Vice-Chairman of the Executive Committee. Dr. Mott, however, left for Europe before May 10th, the date on which the Report on the Steel Strike was submitted to the Executive Committee.

I would a great deal rather the Report was published in its original than its present form for the bias of the original seems to me so patent that it would make it a comparatively easy matter to discredit the entire report. My feeling, after editing the report, is that even now I have used the pencil too lightly; but I have rather leaned over backwards in a desire to present the case of the Commission as much as possible in the way the *original writer* thought that it should be presented.

The activities of the Interchurch World Movement came to an end very soon after I had completed that first editing and my connection with the Movement ceased. Subsequent editing was done by other hands. My opinion regarding the merits of the Steel Report was well known at the time to some of my associates in the Interchurch World Movement, and under ordinary circumstances, I should not have expressed it further. Since, however, the Interchurch World Movement has ceased to exist, no possible obligation to keep silent remains, especially since the prestige of the Movement itself is being used, illegitimately I believe, in the dissemination as propaganda of this unfortunate Steel Report.

On that account I welcome Mr. Olds' careful analysis of this Report and of the circumstances surrounding its origin and publication, and have been happy to give him what assistance I was able to afford. Mr. Olds' analysis presents, in detail, facts that speak for themselves. I can only add that in my opinion his treatment throughout is moderate and that I know him to share my own sympathy with the ideals of the Interchurch World Movement.

STATEMENT BY

THE CONTINENT

Leading Publication of the Presbyterian Denomination. The Steel Strike Report Editorial, Nov 4, 1920

"The most unfortunate fact about the Report is that *on its face it is not the work of the Commission which the Interchurch appointed under Bishop McConnell.* The title page says the Commission had 'the technical assistance of the Bureau of Industrial Research of New York' and the style and point of view characterizing the document throughout suggest strongly that this 'technical assistance' extended to the writing of the entire text. Consequently it does not impress the reader as being in any typical sense a Church Report, still less an Interchurch Report. . . . On the contrary it has quite obviously been prepared from the standpoint of some mind convinced beforehand that the United States Steel Corporation is an insincere, oppressive and iniquitous organization . . . the Interchurch protested impartiality and those who saw the inquiry begin certainly expected something like a judicial rendering of opinion—not a brief for the prosecution."

The Second Steel Report Editorial, Oct. 13, 1921

"The reports rest for their real meaning wholly upon the names of their individual authors; their authority is the authority of their respective writers. In no sense can they be looked upon as Church deliverances. The only way in which such matters could be dealt with by the Church even representatively would be thru the official appointment of eminent Church leaders who could and would take the time to carry forward all needful investigation by their personal examination. But the Commission appointed to look into the Steel Strike never even considered that method of procedure; it immediately hired professional 'researchers' none of whom were persons of reputation in the religious world and at least some of whom were totally out of touch with the Church . . . to call it a Church investigation of the Steel Strike was and is preposterous."

STATEMENT BY
The New York Legislative Investigation on Radicalism
(page 1137)

"The most recent proof of the invasion of the Churches by subversive influences is the Report on the Steel Strike by a committee appointed by the Interchurch World Movement. It is not generally known that the direction of this inquiry was not in the hands of unbiased investigators. The principal 'experts' were David J. Saposs and George Soule (Heber Blankenhorn joined the investigation later) whose radical view-points may be gathered from their association with Mr. Evans Clark acting under the direction of Ludwig C. A. K. Martens, head of the Soviet Bureau in the United States, their connection also with the Rand School of Social Science and certain revolutionary labor organization.''

SOURCES OF INFORMATION AND METHOD OF PREPARATION

The facts and information here contained are chiefly from three sources:

First, from officers or members of the Interchurch World Movement or those directly or officially associated with that Movement. The individual or individuals responsible for each such fact or statement is in each case specifically named: This refers particularly to Part Two;—

Second, from the Interchurch World Movement's Report on the Steel Strike and its other reports, resolutions and findings, all of which are published and can be specifically referred to in connection with each such fact or statement here made;—

Third, from public records and public statements, all of which are printed and generally available. Such authority is in each case referred to directly and specifically.

Except for a conversation with one man who was prominently and officially connected with the Interchurch Investigation and who is also active in the "Labor Movement" no one connected with either the steel companies or the Labor Movement was consulted or informed as to the proposed publication of the present analysis until after this analysis had been completed in substantially its present form.

The author's reasons for believing that a detailed analysis of the Interchurch Report should be published and thus made a matter of public record will doubtless become obvious from a reading of the present volume and perhaps can, in the particular circumstances, be more fittingly summarized in an "Afterword" than stated in a Foreword.

Preliminary to the formulation of any definite plan as to how the facts shown in the present analysis should be published, or even if they should be published, such of them as were then available were gone over in the Spring of 1921, with a number of the author's personal friends who had been associated with the Interchurch Movement. As Dr. William Hiram Foulkes had been Chairman of the Executive Committee of the Interchurch World Movement during the time the Report on the Steel Strike was being passed on for publication, and as that Committee is stated in the Report as the final authority to pass on and approve the Report for publication, it was suggested that the facts under discussion and the idea of making them public should be first taken up with Dr. Foulkes.

Shortly thereafter these facts were presented to Dr. Foulkes during a long conversation in which the author stated that while he was convinced that these facts should be presented to the public, he had no fixed plan as to the method by which they should be presented. The author suggested, however, that if, as he was convinced, the Interchurch Report had published as facts many things that were contrary to the facts and was otherwise highly inaccurate, the Interchurch World Movement which had underwritten the Report, and particularly the individual men who had signed the Report, either personally or as members of committees, would be the most fitting medium through which any corrections should come. He stated that he was entirely willing to coöperate with the Interchurch Movement or individual members on any basis they might suggest, provided only that such errors in the Interchurch Report as could be demonstrated and which had received the widest publicity should be publicly admitted and corrected. Dr. Foulkes stated that many of the facts in regard to the Interchurch Report which the author pointed out, had already been called to his attention. He stated that under the circumstances, he personally believed that a careful and impartial analysis of the Interchurch Report should be made. He of course could not, and did not, commit himself in advance in regard to any particular analysis which might be made. He also suggested a plan of operation looking towards such an analysis which included the possible coöperation of certain other gentlemen who had been prominently connected with the Interchurch World Movement.

The point of view on the subject of the various individuals thus named by Dr. Foulkes—as far as they were seen, and with the exception of Dr. Jenks—is stated in Part II of the present Analysis. In general that point of view was that they personally were in no way responsible for the Interchurch Report and they considered it a "dead issue." It was emphasized in regard to the first point that the public had widely accepted the Interchurch Report on its face value largely on the reputation of the Interchurch World Movement and that that reputation had rested largely on the prominence of themselves and other individuals whose names were widely advertised as the leaders of the Movement. It was emphasized in regard to the second point that a second Interchurch Report was at that time being widely advertised as about to appear. Their attitude however remained unchanged.

Dr. Jeremiah W. Jenks had been an invited delegate to represent the public point of view, in the Hotel Pennsylvania conference at which the movement to investigate the steel strike was inaugurated. Doubtless because of his wide reputation as an economic authority he had also been invited to serve as an ex-officio member in an advisory capacity to several of the various committees which were appointed to consider economic questions and was otherwise closely associated with the Movement. His attitude toward the Interchurch Steel Strike investigation and the Interchurch Report has been stated in his foreword to the present analysis. The author saw and talked with Dr. Jenks at the beginning of April and thereafter during the course of the preparation of the present analysis and has followed such suggestions as Dr. Jenks has made in the presentation of the present analysis.

Part I of the present analysis dealing with the Interchurch Report itself was completed in preliminary form by the middle of August. Part II, dealing with the history and personnel of the Interchurch investigation, was not completed until later. Dr. Foulkes was at this time on an extended trip in the West. In his absence the author had had several conversations with Dr. A. E. Cory, then acting head of the Interchurch World Movement. This draft of Part I was at once turned over to Dr. Cory to whom the statement was made that the author was willing to put the material in the hands of the Interchurch World Movement without reserve to go over and analyze as they saw fit and that he would coöperate with them in any use they desired to make of the material so long as that use included either the specific disproving of the facts brought out in the present analysis, or if they could not be disproved specifically, the presentation of these facts to the public. It was further emphasized that irrespective of such coöperation, the author would welcome any specific criticism and would correct any errors in the analysis which could be pointed out.

Two days later (August 18th) the author received a letter from Mr. John A. Fitch, who is listed by the New York Legislative Investigation of Radicalism as having assisted in several capacities the I. W. W. and as being associated with the Bureau of Industrial Research, which organization is specifically stated to have been the technical adviser in the preparation of the Interchurch Report, calling attention to an error in a single obscure sentence in the middle of the manuscript. As this indicated that the Interchurch

Movement's judgment of the present analysis was being formulated by the very group of "technical advisers" whose technical advice in the Interchurch Report itself is the chief subject of criticism of the present analysis, the author immediately called Dr. Cory on the telephone and pointed this out. He urged that the question of whether or not the Interchurch Report is so flagrantly inaccurate and more than merely inaccurate as the present Analysis specifically shows, should be regarded as of sufficient importance to be most carefully considered. He mentioned several Columbia University professors of recognized economic standing who were immediately available and urged that the opinion of some such recognized authority as these should be obtained by Dr. Cory and at least also considered in formulating the Interchurch Movement's opinion on the question. The same day however, Dr. Cory wrote the author stating that the members of the Commission who published the Steel Strike Report or the Executive Committee could avail themselves of the right to answer any inaccuracies in the present analysis after it was published if they so desired.

This first draft was then placed in the hands of Dr. Jeremiah W. Jenks and shortly thereafter, a first draft of Part II was completed and placed in his hands.

Mr. Stanley Went as a member of the Publicity Department of the Interchurch Movement had written the official Hand Book of the Movement, he had written three of their official surveys and had been the original editor of the Report on the Steel Strike and was otherwise intimately informed as to various subjects under discussion in the present analysis. A carbon copy of both parts was therefore also placed in the hands of Mr. Went for his suggestion or correction.

The author had been frequently informed that Mr. Harold C. Reynolds, who had been Superintendent of the Religious Press Division, and Mr. James E. Craig, who had been Superintendent of the Bulletin Division and Superintendent of the Reporting Division of the Interchurch World Movement, were, because of the particular nature of their offices and otherwise, intimately informed in regard to the facts in connection with the investigation of the Steel strike. These gentlemen had both been absent from the city but had returned in the Fall. The preliminary drafts of both Part I and Part II were turned over to these gentlemen who, after going over the manuscript carefully together, agreed to, and did, make voluminous editorial notes and corrections.

In the intervening weeks, Dr. Jenks had gone over the whole manuscript with care, making numerous suggestions. He particularly suggested that special effort should be made to obtain information as to the nature of the "affidavits of 500 steel workers" which the Interchurch Report itself states constituted "the rockbottom" of the findings. At this time also it was announced that the second volume of the Interchurch Report, consisting of evidence on which the first volume was based was about to appear, and it was decided to postpone further editing till this material should be available.

In the meantime also Dr. Foulkes had returned and the first draft of the entire present analysis, including a statement of many of Dr. Jenks' editorial suggestions, was placed in his hands. Some weeks later Dr. Foulkes stated in a letter dated November 1st, that the present analysis "deals with so many alleged facts and conclusions which are out of the range of my observation and knowledge that it does not seem wise for me to attempt to pass any detailed judgement on the statements you have made." He also added at the same time— rephrasing for publication the point of view he had expressed in a previous discussion—his own personal point of view as to the merits of the Interchurch Report, which statement appears at the beginning of the present analysis.

The appearance in the late Fall of the second volume of the Interchurch Report, containing a number of the sub-reports which in turn contained much more of the evidence on which the Report itself was based, and the fact that this volume also contained a small number of the "rockbottom affidavits," on which the Interchurch Report states it is chiefly based, made it then possible to give more detailed consideration to certain sections and particularly to certain arguments and conclusions of the Interchurch Report. Accordingly the section of the present analysis, dealing with the Interchurch Report's allegations as to Social Consequences"—particularly its allegations of the "denial of the right of free speech," of "police brutality," and of discrimination against the strikers on the part of the courts— were considerably enlarged.

As these matters involve many questions of law and facts in regard to labor controvesies, the author secured the assistance of Mr. Murray T. Quigg, editor of "Law and Labor" to collaborate with him on certain parts of these sections and to edit these entire sections.

An effort had been made in September to bring the analysis to the attention of Judge Gary for the expressed purpose of obtaining any criticism or suggestions which he or other representatives of the steel industry might have to offer. His office stated however that the immediate demands on his time were then such that he could not hope to give attention to new or outside matters for at least several months. In December the matter was again taken up and his office agreed to put the manuscript in Judge Gary's calendar of work for his own decision as to whether or not he would read the manuscript, or have it read, with this end in view.

At the end of March, as no reply had yet been received from Judge Gary's office and inquiry revealed that the matter was still merely awaiting his attention, the author urged an opportunity to present the whole matter to Judge Gary personally. In a brief interview the author explained the origin and nature of the present analysis, including the fact that it had been carefully edited and would be still further edited before publication by men who were both impartial and particularly qualified to pass on

the subjects in the present analysis to which they were giving special attention. He urged the desirability, for the
sake of completeness and accuracy, of obtaining the point of
view of the steel industry and if possible Judge Gary's own
opinion on certain specific points. Judge Gary replied
in effect that under the particular circumstances surrounding the Interchurch investigation, and especially because of
the nature of some of the conclusions reached by the present
analysis, he felt that if he went over the analysis in advance
of publication and offered any suggestions that that fact
might be misinterpreted as having unduly influenced some
of the conclusions reached. He believed, therefore, it was
wiser for him to remain in the position of having no detailed
knowledge of the subject matter of the present analysis. He
stated, however, that he hoped that great care would be
exercised in the matter of its detailed accuracy as, in his
opinion, such an analysis would be valuable, from any point
of view, only to the extent that its accuracy could be
absolutely depended on. He added that while no information would be volunteered, Mr. Filbert, the Comptroller of the Corporation, who was present, would supply
any merely detailed figures or facts which he reasonably
could and which the author would take the initiative in
requesting. The few specific figures which were thus
ultimately supplied are in each case accompanied by a footnote stating their source.

As stated the present volume has been prepared in two
parts. The main section—

PART ONE

ANALYSIS OF THE INTERCHURCH REPORT ON THE STEEL STRIKE

consists of a critical analysis of the evidences, arguments
and conclusions of the Interchurch Report on the Steel
Strike as published.

In his foreword to the present volume, Dr. Jenks has,

very properly, emphasized that the story of such an important industrial controversy as the steel strike, if it is to do good rather than harm, must be told "with complete regard for the exact truth." Certainly then an analysis which presumes to criticize the accuracy of such a story must itself be punctilious in this regard. Dr. Jenks had pointed this fact out from the beginning; this was the only suggestion Judge Gary had been willing to make; in all editing it had been kept particularly in mind. But the editing up to this point had been chiefly constructive. In June (1922) Part One was put into type so that copies of the text could be submitted in whole or in part for a wide variety of detailed criticisms.

The statistical sections were thus reviewed with particular care. On the suggestion of certain statistical authorities with whom the author advised, such sections were submitted to Dr. Ernest S. Bradford, Vice President of the American Statistical Association, for the purpose of having them subjected to the most rigid and detailed technical criticism.

Dr. Bradford turned these sections over for this purpose to Mr. Arthur R. Burnet of the American Statistical Association and Mr. W. Herman Greul, M.E., a specialist in Industrial Engineering. Mr. Burnet and Mr. Gruel kindly gave some two weeks of their time to a study of these sections—namely Chapters III to IX inclusive—and offered many valuable suggestions as to simpler and more uniform methods of presenting the various statistics involved. These suggestions have in each case been followed.

As Mr. Burnet and Mr. Greul were not in a position to devote further time to the subject, and as the author had planned from the beginning of the work to have the detailed accuracy of all citations and quotations as well as all statistics throughout the analysis passed on by competent outside authority of recognized impartiality, Haskins and Sells, Certified Public Accountants, were employed for this purpose. Their statement of certification appears on page ix.

FOREWORD

PART TWO

HISTORY OF THE INTERCHURCH REPORT ON THE STEEL STRIKE

consists of a brief outline of the facts and circumstances which led up to the Interchurch investigation and Report on the Steel Strike; statements as to the personnel of the principal committees or other bodies which assisted towards or in the investigation and publication of the Report; together with a brief history of the composition and authorization of the Report.

The facts and circumstances dealt with in Part Two are in general *not* matters of printed or even available written record. The evidence here is thus of an entirely different nature and must be treated on an entirely different basis than that analyzed in Part One.

Moreover the Interchurch Report as a published document can be analyzed and judged on its own merits so that facts as to its origin and authorship must be regarded as secondary.

For these reasons Part Two is treated entirely separately and subordinately.

———

Attention is called to the fact that the summaries to both parts One and Two consist chiefly, not of conclusions but of recapitulations of evidence.

CONTENTS

PART ONE

PART ONE

ANALYSIS OF THE INTERCHURCH REPORT ON THE STEEL STRIKE

Analysis of the Interchurch World Movement Steel Strike Report—as to the accuracy and adequacy of its facts—as to the logic of its reasoning—as to the soundness of its conclusions—as to the adequacy of the bases for its assumptions and speculations. This analysis of the Report is made entirely on the merits of the document itself without any relation to facts presented in Part Two.

CHAPTER I

INTRODUCTION

METHOD OF ANALYSIS ADOPTED

THERE are various possible methods of procedure in attempting to analyze any report of an investigation.

Perhaps the most obvious method is to examine point by point the fundamental evidence on which the report itself is based, to discover if such evidence is adequate and if it fairly leads to the conclusions which the report deduces from it.

The Interchurch World Movement Report on the steel strike states (page 9—line 12):

"The statements and affidavits of 500 steel workers carefully compared and tested constitute the rock bottom of the findings, the testimony of the leaders on both sides being used chiefly to interpret these findings."

Only a comparative few of these 500 affidavits, however, which thus "constitute the rock bottom of the findings," are themselves presented in the Report or otherwise. There is no way, therefore, of making any adequate examination of the fundamental evidence on which the Interchurch Report on the steel strike is based to determine whether or not its conclusions are fair and warranted even by the evidence on which they are based.

Moreover no evidence is presented as to who most of the 500 persons were who made these affidavits except that they were chiefly "of the mass of low-skilled foreigners" (page 9—line 4). No evidence, or even statement, is presented

3

as to why it can be presumed that these 500 men spoke for, or represented the opinion of, the 300,000 other men who the Report says struck, or the 200,000 others who the Report admits did not strike. Not only therefore does the Report itself fail to offer any proof as to the adequacy of the "rock bottom" evidence on which it states it is based but even the most friendly honest critic cannot but question the possibility that 500 affidavits "chiefly of the mass of low-skilled foreigners" could under any circumstances be adequate "rock bottom" evidence on which to determine complex questions involving 500,000 men and the operation of a great basic industry.

With the possibility of analyzing the Interchurch Steel Strike Report from the point of view of the "fundamental evidence" on which it is based thus eliminated, the most obvious alternative is to take up point by point the conclusions of the Report itself, analyzing such evidence as is presented, comparing it with all other available evidence and judging its conclusions accordingly.

Even most casual examination of this Report, however, immediately reveals the fact that it presents 24 "Conclusions and Recommendations" in the "Introduction" (pages 11–19) and 41 "Conclusions and Recommendations" in a separate "Findings" (pages 246–250), which two groups of conclusions and recommendations have little organic relation, as to either specific subject matter or expression, to one another.

Moreover the seven chapters into which the Report itself is divided, while they of course have a general relation to both these separate groups of conclusions and recommendations do not express that relation in any organized form either as to arrangement or wording.

Finally any attempt to follow subject by subject either the "Conclusions and Recommendations" as expressed in the "Introduction" or as expressed chapter by chapter in the main report, immediately reveals the fact that in either case each sub-division deals with a complexity of subjects each one of which has often to be treated on an entirely different basis and each one of which is often referred to in many subdivisions.

The third group of Conclusions and Recommendations—the "Findings"—were written at a different time and by different men than the Report itself including its "Conclusions" and "Recommendations" as they appear in the "Introduction." These "Findings" are arranged with precision and in logical order but their phraseology is so different from that of the Report itself and is often so general that it is difficult, and frequently impossible, to relate it specifically to the evidence in the Report itself.

For instance the first Section of the "Findings" condemns the "Boss system." The phrase "Boss system" does not occur in the index to the Report proper, as far as can be discovered is not discussed in the Report proper, and the phrase itself is so indefinite that it is impossible even to relate it with any assurance to the Report proper.

Again the second Section of the "Findings" recommends "Industrial Democracy." That phrase also does not occur in the index and is not discussed in the Report proper; it is entirely vague in itself and neither the "Findings" nor the Report proper even remotely suggests how it is proposed that men stated to belong to 56 different nationalities with different languages, most of them with only a smattering of English, can be suddenly and arbitrarily formed into any kind of a democracy.

As a matter of logical necessity then, the present analysis discusses the general subjects dealt with in the Steel Strike Report in a somewhat different order than they are discussed in the Report. The particular order chosen and the reason for it are stated in the second chapter.

It will be particularly noted in the following analysis that in certain instances only minor regard is given as to whether particular contentions of either the strike leaders or of the steel companies were more true. The steel strike is long since over and certain of its facts and contentions, as such, have only minor historical interest.

It will be noted, however, that particular attention is given to the attitude and arguments of the Interchurch Report on such points because it is the question of the soundness of the Interchurch Report and its adequacy as an Industrial text-book that is of particular interest in the present analysis.

The Interchurch Report states (page 8, paragraph 7):

"The United States Steel Corporation was the admittedly decisive influence. Whatever the Steel Corporation does, the rest of the industry will ultimately do," and again (page 11, paragraph 3) "The conduct of the Iron and Steel industry was determined by the conditions of labor accepted by the 191,000 employees of the United States Steel manufacturing plants."

Moreover in giving facts, figures and statistics in regard to the steel controversy, the Interchurch Report almost invariably gives such facts and figures as they refer to the U. S. Steel Corporation, undoubtedly because such figures are most available, as well as in keeping with its theory in regard to the determining influence of the Corporation in the industry.

As the present analysis is primarily of the Interchurch Report rather than of the steel situation as such, it follows the Interchurch Report's policy of thus putting major emphasis on facts and figures as they apply to the U. S. Steel Corporation.

For the same reason the present analysis has, in certain cases where the Interchurch Report's own statements or figures reduce its arguments to self-contradiction or other logical absurdity, merely used such statement or figure to this end without going further into the merits of the statements or figures themselves.

Finally the fact that the present analysis is of the Interchurch Report and not of the steel situation and controversy as such, makes it obviously inadvisable to bring up or discuss the right or wrong of any conditions in the steel industry except those brought up by the Interchurch Report or plainly related to those brought up by the Interchurch Report.

The present analysis is built on a careful study of some 8000 pages of original evidence concerning or related to the subjects under discussion. It is seldom possible therefore in quotations to use more than excerpts from the original. Also in quoting from voluminous evidence involving numerous subjects and particularly where one subject is touched on and later returned to—as in testimony which is being cross-examined by several cross-examiners — the present analysis, for clearness and continuity, in a few cases quotes such excerpts in their logical rather than their original order, showing the break of course by the conventional " . . ." Quotations are always, however, accompanied by specific citation of the original by volume, page, and paragraph or line, so that reference can easily be made directly to the original.

The Interchurch Report throughout uses certain terms inaccurately or defines them incorrectly. For instance it continually uses such terms as "all steel workers," the "steel industry as a whole," etc., in connection with facts and figures which apply only to primary production departments. The present analysis when discussing Interchurch arguments in order to avoid confusion generally uses such terms in the same meaning as the Interchurch Report uses them. In discussing the same points on their merits, however, it will often define and use such terms differently.

All italics, unless otherwise stated, are the authors'.

Comment within quotations enclosed in parentheses, i. e., (. . .) is the author's. Such comment inclosed in brackets, i. e., [. . .] is part of the original.

CHAPTER II

THE PURPOSE AND CAUSE OF THE STEEL STRIKE

THE Interchurch Report states the purpose of the Steel Strike (page 15, section 11):

"The organizing campaign of the workers *and the Strike* were for the purpose of forcing a conference . . . this specific conference to set up trade union collective bargaining."

Mr. Gompers in his letter of June 20, 1919, to Judge Gary says:

" . . . The A. F. of L. decided . . . to bring about a thorough organization of the workers in the Iron and Steel Industry . . . we aim to accomplish the purpose of our labor movement . . . *to enter into an agreement for collective bargaining* that is to cover wages, hours of labor, conditions of employment, etc."

That it was the purpose of the unionization efforts that preceded the steel strike to unionize the mills and set up trade unions collective bargaining with the employers, in which the A. F. of L. and its subsidiary unions were to represent the employees, and that the purpose of the strike itself was to enforce this demand for such collective bargaining, was repeatedly emphasized by other strike leaders.

That the Steel Corporation regarded trade union collective bargaining as the basic question at issue is plainly indicated by Judge Gary's statement to the officers of the U. S. Steel Corporation which was published in the Senate Hearings (Part I, page 97):

8

"Not long since I respectfully declined to meet for the purpose of discussing matters pertaining to labor at our various plants a number of gentlemen representing certain labor unions. They claim that this furnishes cause for complaint and have stated that they intend if possible to prevent a continuation of operations at our mills and factories. . . . I entertain no feelings nor animosity toward the gentlemen personally and would not hesitate to meet them as individuals but I did not consider it proper to confer with them under the circumstances . . . first, because I did not believe the gentlemen were authorized to speak for large numbers of our employees; . . . we do not negotiate with labor unions because it would indicate the closing of our shops against non-union labor and large numbers of our workers are not members of unions and do not care to be."

There is no question, then, as to the expressed purpose of the attempted unionization of the steel industry or the steel strike—that it was to establish trade union collective bargaining.

Pursuant to their purpose of establishing trade union collective bargaining in the steel industry, with themselves as the official representatives of the men, after a certain period of unionization work among the men, the strike leaders proposed to Judge Gary a conference which in itself constituted a recognition and initiation of collective bargaining. Judge Gary though stating his willingness to meet the strike leaders as individuals refused to recognize them as representing the steel workers and meet them in such a conference as was proposed.

The union leaders at the time of the strike put great emphasis on this refusal of Judge Gary to meet them in conference and tried to treat it as though it itself were a paramount issue in the controversy and the strike.

Mr. Fitzpatrick, President of the special committee that planned and organized the steel strike testified before the Senate Committee:

" The strike at the present time is brought about by the refusal on the part of Judge Gary to meet a conference. There is nothing else involved in the situation." (Senate Hearings, Part I, page 51.)

Also the other strike leaders specifically declared that the cause of the steel strike was Judge Gary's refusal to recognize them as representing the steel workers and to meet them in conference, and therefore that Judge Gary was the cause of the steel strike.

Such an allegation of course is fairly parallel to the possible allegation that a man who was shot, was shot because he refused to hold up his hands when he was told to. Such an allegation can only be justified if the man who did the shooting was an officer of the law or the circumstances were otherwise such that he had a right to demand and the victim had no right to refuse to hold up his hands.

But whether under the existing circumstances the strike leaders did have a right to insist upon, or whether in view of all the conditions Judge Gary had no right to refuse such a conference is at the least a matter of opinion based on the interpretation of the facts in regard to those conditions and circumstances.

Moreover, considering the known point of view and the express demands of the strike leaders and the known point of view of the steel companies, there is little question that such conference, even if it had been held, would have resulted so unsatisfactorily to the strike leaders that the strike would have been called just the same.

Even if there is assigned, then, as much weight to Judge Gary's refusal of a conference as the strike leaders themselves assign to that refusal as the immediate cause of the strike, the facts which caused the strike leaders to insist on this conference and caused Judge Gary to refuse it, are back of and paramount to this request and refusal, and these circumstances are plainly those in regard to the attempts by the strike leaders to unionize the steel workers and to establish trade union collective bargaining in the steel industry and Judge Gary's reasons for refusing to acquiesce in such collective bargaining in the steel industry.

The reason stated by Judge Gary for his refusal to recognize or coöperate in trade union collective bargaining with the strike leaders as representatives of the A. F. of L. also representing the steel workers, was:

"We do not think you are authorized to represent the sentiments of the majority of the employees of the U. S. steel corporation and its subsidiaries . . . the corporation and its subsidiaries are opposed to the 'closed shop' (the admitted aim of trade union collective bargaining). They stand for the 'open shop' which . . . best promotes the welfare of both employers and employees. . . . In wage rates, living and working conditions, conservation for life and health, care and comfort in time of sickness or old age, and providing facilities for the general welfare and happiness of employees and their families, the corporation and its subsidiaries have endeavored to occupy a leading and advanced position among employers." (Judge Gary's letter of Aug. 27, 1919, to Committee of Strike leaders.)

"The strike was inaugurated by the union leaders not by the men. The union leaders have been attempting all these years to organize the men. The men have not been seeking the assistance of anyone to organize them." (Judge Gary, Senate Hearings, Part I—Page 153, Line 28.)

It was the contention of the strike leaders, on the other hand, that they "did represent the sentiment of the vast majority of the employees in this industry"—were "acting in behalf of the men" and were "selected by duly accredited representatives of the employees" (letter of Strike Committee to Judge Gary, Aug. 26, 1919) and that the vast majority of the employees wanted and required trade union collective bargaining because

"conditions of employment, the home life, the misery in the hovels of, the steel workers is beyond description . . . the standard of life of the average steel worker is below the pauper line" (Letter of Strike Committee to Judge Gary, Aug. 27, 1919).

These points at issue, with their variations, were discussed in detail in the correspondence between the strike leaders and the company, in the testimony before the Senate Investigating Committee, in the Interchurch Report on the Steel Strike, in Mr. Foster's book, *The Great Steel Strike* and in other published discussions either official or from official information. The Interchurch Report also discusses at great length a considerable number of alleged points at issue which had not previously been raised—at least publicly—by either party to the controversy. A careful study of all this documentary evidence indicates that at least the principal points at issue may be summarized as follows:

First, the strike leaders claimed that in their effort to unionize the steel industry on the basis of trade union collective bargaining they represented the great majority of the steel workers and the interests of all the steel workers. The steel companies denied that the strike leaders represented the workers or the sentiment of the workers in general or the interest of the workers, but insisted that the strike leaders were outsiders who had taken the initiative in projecting themselves into the steel industry without invitation from the men and against the wishes of the majority of the men; and that their unionization efforts included "radical" agitation among the foreign workers.

Second, the strike leaders asserted that the workers required trade union collective bargaining because they neither possessed nor were allowed to establish any adequate channels for expressing or negotiating as to any grievances with their employers. On the other hand, the steel companies stated that it was their practice to take the initiative in seeking continually to advance the interests of the workers and that the workers were always free, and had, when the occasion had arisen, frequently availed themselves of that freedom, to present grievances and that it had been the instruction of the companies to all executives to give the utmost consideration to any such complaints.

Third, the strike leaders alleged that trade union collective bargaining was necessary to the workers' interest because the workers were being paid wages below the pauper level. The steel companies stated that steel wages were among the very highest in industry and that it had always been their policy to keep them there.

Fourth, the strike leaders insisted that trade union collective bargaining was necessary to improve the working conditions and particularly to relieve the men of their long oppressive hours of work. The steel companies stated that the majority of their men preferred the longer hours because of the higher pay they brought—that because of automatic machinery and periods of intermission a great part of the work was not unduly hard and that where the work was especially hard and the men had expressed the desire for it the hours had been reduced to eight instead of ten or twelve a day. The Interchurch Report makes very much more of the heaviness and also of the hazard of steel labor than was made by either the strike leaders or the men themselves, who testified as to working conditions.

Fifth, the strike leaders insisted that trade union collective bargaining was necessary for certain other purposes— in order that "the principle of seniority (instead of that of merit) should apply in maintaining and reducing and increasing working forces"—in order that "existing local unions should be abolished"—in order that "physical examination of applicants for employment should be abolished" in order that the "check off system of collecting union dues and assessments" (the system by which the union dues are collected by the union from the company and subtracted from the worker's wages instead of being collected from the worker himself) should be established, and in general that trade union collective bargaining was necessary to change and control other and general conditions of work and the relations between the men and the companies.

It will at once appear from any analysis of the foregoing points at issue that certain of them constitute *direct issues of fact*. In the following analysis, these will be considered first under *Section A*.

It is equally obvious that other points constitute issues of fact as to the opinions of large numbers of men or are based on interpretation of facts or on which of various facts are to be regarded as more important. Any conclusion as to the merits of such points at issue must be determined by the *weight of evidence*. Such points will be discussed second under *Section B*.

Finally it will be noted that certain of these points at issue involve broad general industrial or social considerations which involve to a particular degree *individual opinion*. Such points at issue will be discussed third under *Section C*.

SECTION A

Issues in the Steel Strike and Arguments of the Interchurch Report which are susceptible of being determined on a basis of definite FACTS.

15

CHAPTER III

IN Appendix B of the Interchurch Report on the Steel Strike, pages 265 and 266 are entirely taken up with a table which is itself not discussed or even referred to in the Report proper.

The first figures given, which are stated to be from the U. S. Bureau of Labor Review, October, 1919, are as follows:

Iron and Steel	Earnings Per Full Week
All Employees	$46.78
Common Labor	34.19
Other Labor (including skilled and semi-skilled)	51.74

Below these figures this Interchurch Report Appendix table then gives in considerable detail earnings for ten other general industries. The industries whose wages are thus given are, as will appear from the wage figures discussed later, among the highest-wage, if not the highest-wage industries in the country. In some cases the Interchurch Appendix gives these earnings separately for common labor in the industry and for the industry as a whole, in other cases, it gives them for common labor and for the balance of the industry—that is for skilled and semi-skilled labor.

These figures which the Interchurch Report publishes in its own Appendix as from the U. S. Bureau of Labor Statistics, from the Federal Railroad administration and from

other authoritative sources, but which it does not discuss
or consider in its main argument, show the following:

SKILLED AND SEMI-SKILLED WORKERS

1919

Industry	Earnings Per Full Week
IRON AND STEEL (*skilled and semi-skilled*)	$51.74
U. S. ARSENALS (*skilled and semi-skilled*)	36.53
BUILDING TRADES (*all skilled*):	
Brick Layers	39.47
Carpenters	34.56
Cement Workers and Finishers	36.28
Wiremen (inside)	35.40
Painters	32.61
Plasterers	39.02
Plumbers	40.66
Sheet Metal Workers	35.60
Steam Fitters	40.83
Structural Iron Workers	41.45
NAVY YARDS (*skilled and semi-skilled*)	38.35
PRINTERS Various cities (*all skilled*):	
Linotype Operators:	
Newspapers, day	35.72
Book and Job	30.50
Compositors:	
Newspapers, day	35.59
Book and Job	26.28
RAILROADS (*all skilled*):	
Machinists	34.56
Blacksmiths	34.56
Boiler Makers	34.56
RAILROADS (*semi-skilled*):	
Firemen, Freight	28.80
Firemen, Passenger	26.40
Firemen, Yard Service	24.96
Hostlers	25.49
SHIP YARDS Pacific Coast (*skilled and semi-skilled*)	36.38

There is not a single class of the most highly *skilled*
workers in any of the other representative industries given

whose *earnings* come within $10 a week of being as high as the *average* for *skilled and semi-skilled steel workers.*

These same tables also show the following:

EARNINGS OF ALL WORKERS
Skilled, Semi-Skilled and Common
1919

Industry	Earnings Per Full Week
IRON AND STEEL.............................	$46.78
COAL MINING ANTHRACITE:	
All inside Occupations............................	35.00
COAL MINING BITUMINOUS:	
All inside occupations............................	38.42
(*In both cases, outside occupations bring the whole average much lower—Anthracite to $29.89*)	
BUILDING TRADES, all..........................	37.58
BUILDING TRADES, New York City..............	36.74
SHIP YARDS, Atlantic Coast......................	34.90
STREET RAILWAYS:	
North Atlantic.................................	28.09
South Atlantic.................................	22.45
North Central.................................	27.97
Western.......................................	27.86
The Unweighted average excluding Iron and Steel is...	32.11

The average earnings of all iron and steel workers is thus $8 a week higher than average earnings in the next highest industry—coal mining—even with all the lowest paid classes of coal workers omitted, and is from $10 to $20 a week higher than for all other given industries which are among the highest paid in American industry.

As regards common labor these same tables from the Interchurch Report Appendix show the following:

EARNINGS OF COMMON LABOR
1919

Industry	Earnings Per Full Week
IRON AND STEEL.............................	$34.19
COAL MINING:	
Anthracite inside (outside $21.26)..................	26.90
Bituminous inside.............................	29.90

U. S. ARSENALS................................ $22.08
BUILDING TRADES............................ 22.88
NAVY YARDS................................... 21.36
RAILROADS (footnote 1):
    Section Men....................... 37.2¢ per hour
    Yard Switch Tenders............... 34.7¢ "   "
    Other Yard Employees.............. 37.4¢ "   "
    Engine House Men................. 42.3¢ "   "
    Other Unskilled Labor............. 41.3¢ "   "
SHIP YARDS:
    Pacific Coast..................................... $24.96
    Atlantic Coast.................................... 17.28

It is plain then in regard to common labor also that the steel worker is by far the highest paid in all the industries given which as stated are among the highest paid in the country. The figures given for coal mining include only the highest paid inside and leave out the lower paid outside common labor. They are otherwise higher than the U. S. Bureau of Labor, December, 1919, Monthly Review, from which they are alleged to be taken, actually shows they should be. But taking them as given, steel common labor wages were still $5 to $8 a week higher, and steel common labor wages were $12 to $17 per week higher than common labor wages for all other industries given.

But perhaps the most interesting comparison of all is that between the actual earnings of the *lowest paid steel worker—common labor*, and certain classes of the *highest paid skilled workers* in other of these industries, and between steel common labor and *all workers*—including skilled and semi-skilled—in the other industries given.

Reference to the Interchurch Report's own Appendix figures given above, most of which are stated to be from official government sources—show at once that the $34.19 a week earnings for *steel common labor* is substantially the

---

1 Two classifications listed by the Interchurch table as common labor are here omitted because they are as a matter of fact, and as their wage rate shows, semi-skilled.

same as that for *skilled* carpenters, cement workers, wiremen, painters and sheet metal workers of the building trades. It is substantially the same as the earnings for *all* the *skilled* railroad workers given and is from $6 to $10 higher than the earnings given for *semi-skilled* railroad workers. It is higher than the average earnings of *skilled* printers in large cities where their wages are highest.

The comparison between the $34.19 earned by the *lowest* paid group of *steel* workers and the average earned by *all* workers in all the high-wage industries given, is self-apparent by reference to Table Number 2 above. The Interchurch Report Appendix figures do not in any case give numbers of workers considered so that they cannot be weighted to produce exact statistical averages for exact comparison. The mathematical average of the earnings of *all* classes of workers—including *skilled* and *semi-skilled*—for *all* these other high-wage industries is $32.11. Steel common labor earnings were $34.19.

Moreover the farther this comparison is carried into still other industries, the more it becomes apparent that the *lowest paid steel worker—common labor*, received higher wages than *all* workers—including *skilled* and *semi-skilled*, in the great majority of *all* American industries.

On page 6 the Interchurch Report, in naming its major authorities and those who assisted in the preparation of the Report, lists "the Bureau of Applied Economics in Washington" and elsewhere mentions this organization as one of its authorities. This Bureau of Applied Economics has published in its Bulletin Number 8 (1920) entitled "Wages in Various Industries and Occupations" perhaps the most comprehensive résumé of comparative wages that has yet appeared.

Statistics as to wages are generally given on one of two bases. U. S. Government statisticians, statistical engineers and other technical authorities in this field follow the practise of giving wage figures in terms of *"actual earnings"* which are derived by dividing actual wage pay-rolls for each group of workers by the number of workers in that group. Wage figures in terms of *"earnings"* therefore, represent the wages the workers actually receive. All the figures above given and discussed are, as specified, based on *"earnings."*

The second basis on which wage figures are given is known as *"wage rates"* which represent merely theoretical or *"paper wages."* Wage figures given out by labor unions— particularly in regard to their own industries—are generally in terms of *"wage rates."* *Wage rates* of course may in some cases approximate actual *earnings* but in general they are higher and often very much higher than *earnings*. For instance, Bureau of Applied Economics Bulletin Number 8 on pages 14 to 25 gives detailed figures as to wages in the Building trades partly for 1919 and partly for 1920, which figures were chiefly "furnished by union officials." They are in terms of *wage rates*. It appears from these figures that on the basis of *wage rates* carpenters' wages were $43.97 per week, yet as already shown carpenters' *actual earnings* (1919) were $34.56. Similarly *wage rates* for painters were $42.32 but *earnings* only $32.61. As a matter of fact the *actual earnings* of *steel workers* were so much higher than the wages for all other workers for which authoritative figures for 1919 can be discovered that it makes small difference whether these other wages are in terms of *earnings* or *rates*.

The first fifteen chapters of the Bureau of Applied Economics Bulletin Number 8 are devoted to detailed figures as to earnings or wage rates in industries which, as far as 1919 figures are given, have with a few exceptions already been covered in the preceding tables, and in most of which cases, the figures are either the same or more detailed presentations of original government figures from which the Interchurch Report Appendix figures are also taken. The wage figures given in these chapters which have not already been considered, consist of farm labor wages which averaged in 1919 for the country $56.29 a month or about a third that of steel common labor earnings;

and navy wages which because they include "keep" are so much lower as to be incomparable with steel wages.

Chapter XVI of Bulletin No. 8 is devoted to a detailed study of teachers' wages throughout the country. They were for all schools in the country in 1918, $635 a year or $15.87 a week on the basis of a 40-week year.

Chapter XIX of Bulletin Number 8 is devoted to a study of earnings in various New York State factories. In 1919 the average weekly *earnings* for all workers including skilled, semi-skilled and all office workers as well as common labor in all New York State factories represented, was $23.50 or $11 a week less than the earnings of the lowest class of steel workers.

Beginning with Chapter XX the balance of Bulletin Number 8 is devoted to the detailed study of wages in a wide variety of other principal manufacturing industries. All these figures are based on *actual earnings*. They are for both male and female workers whose earnings are in most cases treated separately. The averages as given are weighted, and where the averages themselves are not given, details are given which make computation of an exact comparable average possible. In a few cases, two sets of figures, representing either different groups or different pay-roll periods for the same industry are given. These actual *earnings* per week as given, or as computed by the weighted average of the detailed figures given, are as follows:

INDUSTRIES FOR WHICH DATA ARE AVAILABLE FOR 1919

For male workers only. In all but three industries given, women workers bring average earnings much lower than these stated.

Averages include skilled, semi-skilled and common labor

Industry	Full Time Earnings Per Week
Boot and Shoe Manufacturing	$25.90
Brick	25.52
Chemicals	25.44
Chemical Manufacturing	26.20

Confectionery	$19.19
Cotton Manufacturing	17.10
Furniture	20.55
Glass	24.46
Hosiery and Underwear	24.66
Leather	26.14
Lumber	20.03
Metal Manufacturing	24.75
Mill Work	20.36
Overalls	27.24
Paper	27.23
Paper Boxes	19.75
Paper Manufacturing	22.40
Pottery	32.04
Pulp	22.70
Rubber	27.62
Rubber Manufacturing	29.35
Silk	23.55
Silk Manufacturing	22.69
Women's Clothing (no common labor included)	36.72
Wool Manufacturing	18.61
Combined Average (weighted and computed by Haskins and Sells)	24.35

All these elaborate wage statistics taken from the Interchurch Report's own authority, show, just as did the Interchurch Report's own figures—which it publishes in its Appendix but omits to consider in its argument and conclusions—that steel wages are not only higher but higher out of all proportion than wages in any other industry given. Out of the 87 occupations of the 17 industries for which detailed figures are given, (in addition to the unspecified occupations for the 8 industries for which only average figures are given) in these last chapters of Bulletin Number 8, only one *skilled* occupation (Pottery kiln placers—earnings $43.49) comes within $10 a week of earning as much as the $51.74 average earnings of all semi-skilled as well as skilled steel workers. The great majority of the *skilled* workers in all the occupations given earn at least $15 per week *less* and great groups of them earn $20 less than the average earnings of all semi-skilled as well as skilled steel workers.

Except for the Women's Clothing industry—whose earnings of $36.72 include no common labor and do not consider the greater part of the employees in the industry who are women workers earning from $15 to $21 a week— and except for the Pottery industry—whose earnings of $32.04 do not include the greatest proportion of the workers who are also women earning in general $15 or $16 a week— there is no other one of the 25 industries given whose average earnings for all workers is within $15 a week as high as the $46.78 average earnings of all iron and steel workers.

But again perhaps the most interesting fact thus shown in regard to iron and steel earnings is that except for women's clothing where the figures do not include any common labor and none of the largest proportion of lowest paid workers in the industry, there is not a single industry here given whose average earnings for all workers including skilled and semi-skilled, are as high as the earnings of steel *common labor* and steel *common labor* earnings were $10 a week higher than the average earnings of *all* workers in *all* these industries.

Turning from wage statistics given by the Interchurch Report itself—but only in its Appendix—or by its own stated authority, to other authorities, the U. S. Bureau of Labor Statistics in its monthly Labor Review for June, 1920, reports on pages 83 to 95 the results of its study as to wages in the Automobile, Freight Car, Electrical Apparatus, Foundry, Machinery, Machine Tool and Typewriter industries, all industries whose labor is predominantly high class, high skilled. The figures published are from actual pay rolls for months from September, 1918, to May, 1919. They are weighted averages of actual *earnings* and so can be exactly compared with figures for steel and other industries already given.

This U. S. bulletin shows that of all the highly skilled labor employed in the Automobile industry only *four* classes of *skilled* labor received as much as unskilled labor in the Steel industry and that all classes in this highly skilled industry averaged $28.22 per week or $6.00 less than the lowest paid, unskilled steel workers.

All workers in car manufacturing plants, also including an especially high per cent of skilled men average $27.98 per week or over $6.00 less than mere unskilled steel workers.

Makers of electrical apparatus are preponderately skilled workers, yet only two groups were paid as high as unskilled steel workers, and all workers averaged $9.00 less a week than the lowest paid steel workers. Similarly all makers of machinery averaged $6.00 a week less, all makers of machine tools $6.00 a week less, and all makers of typewriters $8.00 less than steel common labor.

Judge Gary, Chairman of the Board of Directors of the largest unit in the steel industry, testified before the Senate Committee investigating the steel strike:

"I wish to state Mr. Chairman and Gentlemen that there is no basic industry in this country, nor in the world, in my opinion, which has paid larger wages to its employees than the United States Steel Corporation." (Senate Hearings, Part I, page 147.)

To this general statement, Judge Gary later added (pages 156–158) detailed statements as to average wages.

Finally Mr. John Fitzpatrick, Chairman of the Special Strike Committee, testified before the Senate Committee during the strike (Senate Hearings, Part I, page 74, line 46):

Mr. Fitzpatrick: "We, or at least I, understood that the percentage of increase of the wages of the steel industry was even higher than that."
Senator Wolcott: "Higher than 111 per cent.?"
Mr. Fitzpatrick: "Yes. But it is not a question of wages. The steel industry of course came up with the wages."

Yet the Interchurch Report on the steel strike says:

"That steel common labor has the lowest rate of pay of the trades for which there are separate statistics for laborers." (In italics page 102—line 23.)

"In 1919 the unskilled (steel) workers' annual earnings were more than $109 below the minimum subsistence level and more than $558 below the American standard of living," (page 94—line 8).

"The bulk of unskilled steel labor earned less than enough for the average family's minimum subsistence" (page 13—line 3).

"The annual earnings of 72% of all (steel) workers were and had been for years below the level set by government experts as the minimum of comfort level for families of five" (page 12—line 32).

In other words whereas the United States government statistics and all other authoritative available data, show definitely that all steel workers were paid far higher wages than similar workers in any other industry and that steel common labor actually received from 50 to 100% more than average American common labor, the Interchurch Report by definite statement and by constant repetition and italicizing, attempts to deny these statements and constantly states and insinuates that steel labor is not only the poorest paid in industry but is not paid enough to keep body and soul together.

In view of this definite and sweeping contradiction of what has always been heretofore regarded as evidence of the highest authority, the question naturally arises as to what previously unknown evidence the Interchurch Investigators have discovered or what special methods of analysis they have employed which thus proves that all our government statistics and leading students and economists have for years been entirely wrong in their belief that steel labor is the highest paid, and which justifies the Interchurch Investigators in the opposite conclusion that steel workers are the poorest paid in industry.

The Interchurch Report, as has been remarked, entirely omits any mention or consideration in its wage arguments of the official figures of the U. S. Government as to wages in the steel industry, although it publishes them in detail in its appendix and discusses the tables of which they are a part constantly and in detail in its discussion of steel working hours.   It does not mention or consider the voluminous wage studies of the Bureau of Applied Economics although it specifically mentions this organization as one of the authorities which furnished "technical data" for the Report.

It does however print in some detail (pages 87 and 88) Judge Gary's public statements as to wages and his figures taken from the books of the steel company, not however in any attempt to analyze or refute them, but merely to attempt to cast insinuations and slurs as to their being a source of "popular illusion."

Aside from such continued attempts at argument through insinuation and sarcasm the Interchurch Steel Report attempts to disprove what it calls the "popular illusion that steel is a highly paid industry" in three ways:

These three distinct and different types of argument are not however distinctly organized but on the contrary are rather inextricably mixed. The whole Interchurch argument as to wages begins with a premise which is not developed until after a second argument has been well begun and the conclusions to each, which are quite different, are used or combined quite indiscriminately in each further argument.

The argument in regard to annual wages that is begun second but finished first undoubtedly merits first attention.

The argument in regard to wages per hour which is begun first and concluded last will be considered second.

The third argument here considered, that in regard to the relation between wages and estimated living costs, is the one to which the Interchurch Report gives most space and whose conclusions are most strongly and frequently emphasized.

CHAPTER IV

THE first argument the Interchurch Report advances in regard to steel wages consists of an attempt to estimate the average earnings of different classes of steel employees on an annual basis.

There can, of course, be no question of the average wage of steel employees on a full time daily or weekly basis. The Appendix of the Interchurch Report, quoting the U. S. Bureau of Labor Statistics, gives the wages of *Common labor* as *$34.19 a week.* On page 267 of the Appendix the Interchurch Report itself gives a table of figures (from U. S. Bureau of Labor) which seeks chiefly to emphasize the number of working hours but which states incidentally (but never uses these figures in the main argument) that the "earnings per full week for *common labor* (iron and steel industry) was in 1919 $37.34" for the "Pittsburg District."

It is a matter of the commonest knowledge that at least during 1917 and 1918 and 1919 the steel industry was working at capacity. The Interchurch Report itself spends the whole of Chapter III emphasizing, and emphasizes repeatedly in many other sections, that "the steel industry was speeded up in every direction" (page 55, line 11). It specifically states, in its table on page 71, that *common labor* for the whole steel industry *averaged 74 hours a week—more than 12 hours a day*—in 1919. The Report further states that approximately one half of all steel workers were subject to the 12-hour day and that one half the 12-hour workers were subject to the seven-day week (page 11, Sec. 7)—that the workers only get a Sunday off once in 6 months (page 71—line 1)—and in general emphasizes what is common knowledge that the steel industry during this period worked at least full time.

With these facts as to the amount of time worked a matter of general knowledge and of special complaint by the Interchurch Report, and with earnings per full time week given definitely by the Interchurch Report itself as $34.19, the obvious way to arrive at the average annual earnings of the steel laborer is the simple one of multiplying weeks worked by earnings per week.[1]

If we multiply the average weekly earnings of the 12 hour common laborer in the steel industry as given by the Interchurch Appendix by 50 weeks, which allows each worker a two weeks' vacation each year, the *average annual earnings of common labor is $1709.50.*

If on the other hand we use the Interchurch figures from the appendix (page 267) of *$37.34 a week* and multiply that

[1] In regard to the multiplication of the *hourly* earnings by hour worked as a means of determining earnings, the U. S. Bureau of Labor statistics October, 1919, has itself (page 105) issued the following warning:

"When the rate of earnings *per hour* of an employee has been increased by the addition to his regular earnings of extra pay for overtime or a bonus, it becomes impossible to compute full time earnings by the simple method of multiplying full time *hours* by *hourly earnings.*" In other words, the rate for instance of 46.4¢ an hour, given as full time hourly earnings for common labor is made up on the basis of straight time for 8 hours work and time and a half for the additional four hours work of the 12-hour day. The 12-hour worker therefore received 12 times this 46.4¢ hourly rate per day. The worker whose full time however is 10 hours did not receive 10 times 46.4¢ per day because his hourly wage rate was based on straight time for 8 hours and time and a half for only 2 hours. In all original computations in the present analysis this fact has been carefully allowed for. In the present instance the wage figures used are not on an hourly basis but are the full time *weekly* earnings as specifically stated by the Interchurch Report itself, or to make possible exact comparison, weekly earnings computed on the same basis.

by 50 weeks, still giving the worker a two weeks' vacation which the Interchurch Report insists he didn't get, *the average annual earnings of common labor is $1867 a year.*

Judge Gary states that the average wage paid all common labor on the 12-hour basis was $5.88 a day. If we multiply this by 300 days a year which gives each such laborer all his Sundays and more than all regular holidays off, his wage is *$1764 a year.*

The lowest *"average earnings per hour"* shown by the elaborate U. S. Bureau of Labor Statistics, October, 1919, figures as to steel wages—the authority from which the Interchurch Reports own Appendix figures and the Bureau of Applied Economics figures are both taken—for any class of steel workers for the entire country is 44.9¢ an hour for 68.8 hours a week worked by common labor in the Plate Mill. Plate Mill common labor therefore received $30.89[1] per week of 5⅔ 12-hour days or six 11.5-hour days which is $1606.28 per year.

The lowest paid *common labor* for the entire industry shown by these U. S. Bureau of Labor figures is 161 laborers in Sheet Mills whose earnings were 46¢ an hour for an average of 66.5 hours a week. This is $30.59[1] a week or $1590.69 a year. The *lowest paid* steel workers *of any class* shown by these Government statistics for the whole industry, were 186 Sheet Mill Openers, semi-skilled, whose earnings were 68.5¢ an hour for a 44-hour week. This means that these workers received $30.14[1] a week or $1567.28 a year—but this is for an 8-hour day 5½ days a week.

As has been emphasized, the Interchurch Report does not use or mention in its wage argument these figures for the whole country which it itself publishes in its Appendix and states are from the U. S. Bureau of Labor Statistics.

Although it had spent the whole previous chapter in emphasizing how "the steel industry was speeded up in every direction" during this period, it dismisses in a single brief sentence the obvious method of arriving at at least

[1] Computed on same basis as Interchurch figures above.

approximate annual earnings by multiplying given weekly earnings by approximately full time.

At the bottom of page 98 the Interchurch Report gives a table of weekly earnings for an individual "Open Hearth gang." These earnings for the common laborers among this "gang" are stated as $35.28 a week—substantially the same as the average for the country ($34.19) given in the Appendix. Following this table it states in italics, as indicated[1]:

" . . . if the common laborers *who make up 49 per cent.* of Open Hearth employees, worked this 12-hour schedule for all but 26 of the 365 days in the year, they would still be *nearly $200 below the lowest 'American standard.'*"

The Interchurch Report frequently, through the preceding pages, defines the "lowest American standard" of living as $2024 a year. $200 less than this is $1824 a year. $35.28 weekly (the stated earnings of common labor in this particular "Open Hearth gang") multiplied by 52 weeks is $1834.56. Thus—although entirely indirectly—the Interchurch Report admits that 12-hour common labor which worked full time earned $1800 a year. But immediately after this indirect admission, it hastens to add,

"But few men can stand it and few plants run without a lay-off,— *many are 'down' from 8 to 20 weeks a year, and the year's earnings are never 'full time.'*"

Therefore the Interchurch Report concludes, and emphasizes on page 92 and repeats on pages 93, 94, 97 and elsewhere, that steel common labor received "under $1466 a year."

Of course individual steel workers lay off for sickness or other reasons just as do workers in any other industry. Of course machinery, no matter how busy, must sometimes stop to be repaired. But as has already been shown, 65 days a year may be allowed for such causes and still the 12-hour workers who worked 300 days a year at $5.88 a day—

[1] This table shows plainly on its face a working schedule of 6 days a week yet the Interchurch Report presumes in the next paragraph to use this table as evidence of 7-day work.

the average daily earnings for 12-hour common labor given by Judge Gary and which multiplied by 6 days gives $35.28, exactly the weekly earnings of the "Open Hearth gang" as given by the Interchurch Report—would receive $1764 a year.

But the shut down of "many plants" of "from 8 to 20 weeks" which the Interchurch Report specifically mentions, although it adduces no evidence to support this allegation, means a loss of far more than 65 days a year. An annual wage for all common labor of "under $1466 a year" when the given wage is $34.19 a week, if true, shows that the whole steel industry which was supposed to be operating at full-blast through all this period did not actually so operate an average of more than 268 days a year. This is so entirely contrary to all general evidence and beliefs as to the operation of the steel industry during this whole period as to make an analysis of the argument by which the Interchurch Report presumes to reach such conclusions extremely pertinent.

All the figures and computations on this point as far as they are given, are as follows (pages 91 and 92):

"In 1919 the Corporations wage and salary budget [$255,861,264 for eight months] went to 191,000 employees as follows:

[eight months' budget multiplied by 50 per cent[1] for an annual basis]

58,064 skilled [30.4% of all] got 41.6% or	$159,657,328
60,165 semi-skilled [31.5% of all] got 30.6% or	117,440,320
72,771 unskilled [38.1% of all] got 27.8% or	106,694,145
(191,000)	($383,791,793)

That is individual average earnings were not higher than as follows since the above totals contain administrative salaries:

In 1919:

Skilled annual average earnings averaged under	$2749
Semi-skilled annual earnings averaged under	1952
Unskilled annual earnings averaged under	1466."

[1] Obviously the Interchurch Report means 50% *added to* the figures for 8 months; that is how it has actually made the calculations.

It is at once apparent that the basic figure on which this whole computation rests is the $255,861,264 alleged wage and salary budget for 8 months and the complementary figure $383,791,793 as the wage and salary budget for the year. The annual report of the U. S. Steel Corporation does not give either figure or any similar figure and the Interchurch Report gives no authority for these figures. If this Interchurch Report figure is not accurate all the figures are correspondingly inaccurate.

Again the Interchurch Report divides this alleged annual wage budget by 191,000 employees. But this is the number of employees in one month and is 2450 higher than the average for the year as given by the 18th Annual Report page 23. The average annual wage of all steel workers therefore of $2009 which the Interchurch Report derives from these figures and uses on pages 96, 97 and elsewhere— and all the other averages in the tables above quoted are correspondingly too low.

It will be noted that this Interchurch Report table states in specific and exact figures that in 1919, 30.4% of all steel workers were skilled, that 31.5% were semi-skilled and 38.1% unskilled. It further states that in 1919 the skilled workers got 41.6% of the entire wage budget, the semi-skilled group 30.6%, and the unskilled 27.8%. It also uses exactly the same percentages for its 1918 calculations. In Appendix C at the end of the volume, the Interchurch Report explains that these are based on certain 1910 figures which appear on page 80, Volume III of Senate Document 110.[1]

But on pages 134 and 135 the Interchurch Report emphasize at length the great extent to which the introduction of modern machinery "has revolutionized" the proportions of skilled, semi-skilled and unskilled labor in the industry.

---

[1] Senate Document 110 throughout merely makes this classification according to rate of earnings. The Interchurch Report interprets these figures in terms of skilled, semi-skilled and common labor. (See Appendix C.)

This fact alone, of the known change in steel jobs—which the Interchurch Report itself elsewhere takes such pains to establish, makes it obvious that these 1910 figures not only cannot be depended upon to represent 1919 conditions but are entirely unrepresentative of 1919 conditions.   This much is obvious on the face of the situation.   Reference however to page 80, Senate Document 110 Volume III, from which the Interchurch Report states it derives its percentages, immediately reveals the fact that these figures do not pretend to be for the industry as a whole even in 1910 but on the contrary are merely for one particular plant and are entirely different from the percentages for the industry as a whole which are given in Senate Document 110 on pages xxxi and xxxii.   There it is shown that in 1910 skilled labor constituted 23.6%, semi-skilled 26.71% and unskilled not 38.1% but *49.69%*, of all steel workers.

The Interchurch Report figures show, and it itself states, that the average wage of all steel workers in 1919 was $2009. Now it is obvious that the larger the proportion of unskilled labor the more nearly must the earnings of such workers approach the $2009 average earnings of all workers.   Even on the basis of the actual 1910 figures therefore, the fact that the Interchurch Report by using figures for a single plant instead of for the industry as a whole has placed the proportion of steel common labor 11.6% too low mean that its $1466 is correspondingly too low even if all its other calculations were sound.   But as has been pointed out, it has not only based this whole calculation on an assumption which it itself shows elsewhere is untrue, uses as a basic figure in the calculations one for which it gives no authority, but has made further errors of calculation all of which have worked in the same direction.

The fact, however, that the Interchurch Report's conclusion that steel common labor earnings were under $1466 is based on a self-contradiction and a multiplication of obvious errors, is less important perhaps than the fact that by this conclusion, the whole Interchurch Report is placed definitely and conspicuously in this dilemma of self-contradiction as to its main arguments.

All these wage calculations are made without reference to the strike. There was of course no strike in 1918 and the 1918 and 1919 calculations are made on exactly the same basis. Moreover, in its 1919 calculations, the Interchurch Report specifically bases its figures on the first 8 months before the strike adding 50% to these so that any change brought about by the strike should not be included. Its figures of course apply not to individual workers but to total number of employees.

If then, the average weekly wage of all steel workers was $46.78 as the Interchurch Report itself plainly states in its Appendix on page 265, and the average annual wage of all steel workers was under $2009 a year, then all steel workers worked less than 43 weeks a year and therefore the whole steel industry averaged net less than 43 weeks of operation during the year.

If the average weekly earnings of all steel companies common labor was $34.19, as the Interchurch Report also specifically states in its Appendix on page 265, and the annual earnings of steel common labor was "under $1466" then the average steel common laborer worked under 43 weeks a year and the whole steel industry averaged under 43 weeks of operation during the year. This of course is entirely in keeping with the Interchurch Report's statement on page 99 that "many (plants) are 'down' from 8 to 20 weeks a year."

An average of under 43 weeks worked for all steel workers and so for the industry means that the 7-day worker—who the Interchurch Report insists approximated 25% of the industry—averaged less than 301 days a year and therefore had over 64 days a year off. It means that the 6-day steel worker who must therefore have constituted 75% of all workers—worked under 258 days a year and had over 107 days per year off. It means that all steel workers, including both 6 and 7 day workers and so all departments of the industry averaged only 268 days net out of the year.[1]

But such conclusions are not only entirely contrary to all evidence and information as to steel operation during the war and immediately after the war period, but are entirely contrary to the Interchurch Report's whole argument throughout and particularly in its chapter on the 12-hour day in which it insists "that the steel industry was (so) speeded up in every direction," not merely during the war— "which permitted the steel companies free rein as regards hours," but right into the "months of July, August, and September, 1919," that while "some (workers) got a Sunday off perhaps once in six months . . . most of them . . . do not see the inside of a church more than once in six months because they are forced to work on Sunday" (pages 55 and 71)— that not merely during the war but for the "8 months and 20 days previous to the strike" i.e. from January 1st to September 20, 1919, the employees of a certain Homestead department only got 17 days off out of 244 (page 73) etc., etc.

Attention is also called to the fact that the evidence of these important errors and self-contradictions does not appear in the main argument which shows merely certain very exact looking and otherwise impressive partial calculations and then features the conclusions. Only a careful study of the Appendix, which is not referred to in the main argument, reveals the fact that, and the way that the Interchurch Report in this connection uses as the whole basis of its argument an assumption which it strongly denies and states to the contrary as the basis of a different kind of an argument in a different connection. The other flagrant errors in this argument—the fact that in addition to using 1910 figures as representative of 1919 it takes the 1910 figures for merely one "establishment" which happens to be useful to its argument and ignores the very different figures for the whole industry which refute its argument— are only discoverable by reference to original sources. Again

[1] See foot note page 45.

although the table showing percentages of different classes of workers for the whole industry, but which refute the Interchurch Report conclusions, appear plainly among the main tables at the beginning of Senate Document 110— a section to which the Interchurch Report otherwise frequently refers—it passes this by without comment and uses an obscure table for a single establishment from the third volume, but which does happen to suit its argument. All such facts should at least be noted and borne in mind in the consideration of its further arguments.

CHAPTER V

AFTER stating at length its various conclusions as to wages in the Steel Industry in the beginning of Chapter IV, the Interchurch Report opens its argument to substantiate these conclusions by asserting that there is a "popular illusion that steel is a highly paid industry"—that there is "a public impression that steel may be mighty hard labor but its wages are mighty big." The Report then proceeds in all seriousness to prove that there is no basis for such a public illusion by the very ingenious line of reasoning that if the steel laborer did *not* work so hard his wages would *not* be so big.

There is little question that the Interchurch Report is quite correct in regard to the existence of a general impression that the public has gained from all standard sources of information that the steel worker does work hard or at least long and does make good pay. And there would be little grounds for discussing the Report's ingenious argument that if the steel worker did not work so hard (long) his pay would not be so big, except for the fact that through a less obvious, ingenious series of false analogies, the Report presumes to lead this argument to such conclusions as:

"Steel common labor has the lowest rate of pay of trades for which there are separate statistics for laborers" (in italics page 102, line 23).

"As regards common labor steel is a low wage industry" (page 90, line 21).

"A comparison of common labor earnings of steel with common labor earnings in five other major industries in the Pittsburgh district . . . on the basis of a common standard week shows steel labor the lowest paid of the six" (page 90, line 25).

39

The point was emphasized in the preceding chapter that whereas there exist ample government statistics and other authoritative data which show steel earnings plainly and definitely, the Interchurch Report based its own very different statements as to general wages in the Steel Industry on a complicated compilation of partly doubtful and partly undisclosed figures which attempted to arrive at an actual annual wage on the grounds that because the cost of living is necessarily on an annual basis, wages can only be fairly judged on the same basis (page 98—line 17).

In the present second argument also, in which the Interchurch Report assumes to compare steel wages with wages in other industries, the Interchurch Report again pointedly disregards all reference to standard Government figures, published figures of the Bureau of Applied Economics which it states was one of its technical advisors and other authoritative figures as to such comparative wages, and uses figures as for merely the Pittsburgh district which authoritative data seldom specifically mentions.   Moreover, entirely reversing its former attitude of insisting that steel wages can only be fairly judged on an annual basis because living costs have to be reckoned on that basis, in this second argument, the Interchurch Report not only insists on basing its figures on an artificial and untrue weekly basis but insists on making its comparison with other particular industries where weekly earnings are *least* representative of actual annual earnings.

The hypothesis of this argument is that if steel workers did not work such long hours they would be poorly paid rather than well-paid workers.   The alleged evidence it presents to justify that conclusion and the statement of that conclusion particularly emphasized in italics are as follows:

TABLE FROM PAGE 102, INTERCHURCH REPORT

"Comparative earnings for 44-hour week at prevailing hourly rates (Pittsburgh district 1919):

Common Labor:

Iron and Steel.......................	$21.12 (48 ¢ per hour)
Bituminous Coal......................	25.30 (57.5¢ " "

Building Trades:

Building Laborers.....................	$22.00 (50 ¢ an hour)
Hod Carriers.........................	30.80 (70 ¢ " "
Plasterers' Laborers..................	30.80 (70 ¢ " "
Average for Laborers..................	27.85

"The comparison makes it plain that *steel common labor has the lowest rate of pay* of the trades for which there are separate statistics for laborers."

On analysis this table and its conclusion become interesting from a number of points of view. In the first place, turning to pages 265–266 (Appendix) of the Interchurch Report itself, it is plainly stated that the rates *per hour* as well as per week for common labor in various industries in 1919 were as follows:

FIGURES FOR COMMON LABOR FROM U. S. BUREAU OF LABOR AND OTHER STATISTICS AS PUBLISHED IN APPENDIX (PAGES 265–266)

INTERCHURCH REPORT

Industry:	Earnings Per Full Week	Average Hourly Rate
Iron and Steel (common labor).............	$34.19	46.2¢
Mining:		
Laborers (anthracite)	$26.90	51.9¢
Laborers (bituminous)	29.90	57.5¢
U. S. Arsenals (common laborers)...........	22.08	46 ¢
Building Trades (common labor)...........	22.88	52 ¢
Navy Yards (common labor)..............	21.36	44.5¢
Railroads:		
Section Men..........................	Earnings	37.2¢
Yard Switch Tenders[1].................	per week	34.7¢
Other Yard Employees.................	not stated	37.4¢
Engine House Men....................		42.3¢
Other Unskilled Laborers..............		41.3¢
Shipyards (east) Laborers.................	$17.28	36 ¢

[1] Here quoted as given in Interchurch table. Interstate Commerce Commission shows different classification and wage rate.

Again, taking the elaborate wage study of the Bureau of Applied Economics, and going through that study, industry by industry, it also plainly appears, according to this authority which is stated by the Interchurch Report to be one of its own authorities, that common labor earnings *per hour* as well as per week for the various industries were in 1919 as follows:

Figures from Bureau of Applied Economics Bulletin Number 8.

Industry	Earnings Per Full Week	Average Earnings Per Hour
Anthracite Coal:		
Outside Labor......................	$21.27	43.4¢
Inside Labor......................	25.43	51.9¢
Brick Making......................	22.72	42.3¢
Chemical...........................	22.39	39 ¢
Confectionery (male).................	17.11	31.8¢
Glass..............................	20.71	35.4¢
Lumber............................	19.23	34.5¢
Mill Work.........................	16.69	32.1¢
Paper Box.........................	18.24	35.9¢
Pottery (male).....................	26.30	47.9¢
Class I Railroads[1]:		
Section Men......................	earnings or	37.9¢
Construction Labor................	number of	39.6¢
Station Service Labor..............	hours	41.7¢
Yard Switch Tenders..............	per week	42.6¢
Other Yard Labor.................	not given	36.1¢
Other Unskilled Labor.............		40.9¢
Rubber (Tire M.)...................	$27.67	54.8¢
Rubber (Other Labor)	20.94	39.5¢
Silk (dye house)....................	22.01	41.4¢

[1] The Interchurch Report's conclusions that,

"The comparison makes it plain that *steel common labor has the lowest rate of pay* for the trades for which there are separate statistics for laborers,"

—is sweeping and unqualified. It will be noted however that previously there had been slipped in, in parenthesis, the qualification, "Pittsburg district." The Pittsburg district obviously covers,—and U. S. Bureau of Labor, October, 1919, Review, page 104 in the introduc-

These tables quoted from official figures of the U. S. Bureau of Labor published in the Appendix of the Interchurch Report itself and from the figures of the Bureau of Applied Economics, specifically accepted by the Interchurch Report as one of its own authorities, show that there are separate statistics for labor in 22 separate trades or industries or occupations. They too show specifically and in detail, as all other competent authorities show, that without question steel common labor received higher wages and in general far higher wages *by the week*, than any other common labor in the country. But these tables particularly show specifically and in detail that in all the 22 trades or occupations for which there are these separate statistics or common labor, except for five—and these are special cases governed by very special circumstances as will be shown later—steel common labor received the highest wages not only per day and per week but also *per hour*— that it received 10 or 12¢ higher wages per hour than was paid to common labor in whole groups of other industries including the Pittsburg district. The Interchurch Table and Conclusion therefore that, "steel common labor has the lowest rate of pay of the trades for which there are sepa-

---

tion to its study of steel hours and wages from which the Interchurch Report Appendix chiefly derives its wage figures, specifically states it to cover, western Pennsylvania, eastern Ohio, and northern West Virginia. With a few exceptions, all the 22 separate industries or trades or occupations listed in the 2 tables above are of course represented in the "Pittsburg district." This district is a particular center of railroading and glass, brick, pottery and chemical manufacturing. Perhaps the largest paper plants in the country and the country's chief center of rubber manufacture are in this district. The figures given above for all these industries are obviously therefore also for the Pittsburg district. This has been particularly checked in the case of the widest variety of common labor rates given for any one industry—railroads; the Comptroller of the Pennsylvania railroad having furnished the author with the *hourly wage rates* paid different classes of common labor *"in the Pittsburg district in 1919."* These rates correspond closely class by class to earnings given above and are from *5¢ to 8¢ per hour lower* than the admitted *hourly* rate for steel common labor.

rate statistics for laborers," is not only utterly and ridiculously untrue but is the opposite of the truth.

From the point of view, however, of an analysis of the Interchurch Report the fact that this important and specially emphasized conclusion is utterly untrue is perhaps the least important fact that a careful analysis of the table and its conclusion actually shows.

There are in these 22 trades or occupations for which there are separate statistics for common labor five in which the earnings per hour—but not per day or week—was higher than the earnings *per hour* in the steel industry. The pottery industry paid male common labor in 1919 a fraction of one cent *less* per hour than was paid steel common labor in the Pittsburg district but throughout the country it paid a little over 1 cent more *per hour* than was paid in the steel industry throughout the country. Common labor in the Rubber industry as a whole earned 39.5¢ an hour—7¢ *less* than steel common labor. But one group in tire making plants, consisting partly of common labor and partly of "helpers" which are low semi-skilled, received more *per hour* than steel common labor. Aside from these, the only common labor thus rated as receiving a higher rate *per hour* than steel common labor was the *inside* coal labor—the outside coal labor received 2½¢ an hour less than the steel laborer—and the laborer in the building trades.

Now it is distinctly shown by the Interchurch Report's own statistics that while the inside coal common labor and the building trade common labor receive a higher wage *per hour* than the steel laborer, they actually receive far less money *per day* or *per week* because of their shorter hours per day. But what is far more significant in connection with a wage comparison in these industries is the fact that the coal industry and the building trades are highly seasonal and therefore can give their workers work only part of the time. For while steel is essentially a continuous industry which over a long period of years has probably given its workers a higher average number of days work per year than any other industry in the country,[1] and while especially during this whole period under discussion the steel worker was working maximum time, the bituminous coal miner in 1919 worked only 191 days and for many years has rarely been able to work as much as 200 days a year. In the same way because of seasonal conditions building operations are often not possible during more than 150 days of the year and it is probably rare for the building laborer to average 200 days a year at his trade. The higher wage rates *per hour* therefore in these seasonal occupations of mining and building are paid fundamentally for the reason that these industries can give labor only limited employment so that during the rest of the year such workers must go without employment or shift for themselves.

Now the first thing to be noticed in regard to the Interchurch Report table on page 102 which presumes to justify the italicized statement that steel common labor wage rates are the lowest for all trades for which there are separate statistics, is that it entirely fails to mention or consider the 18 other trades or occupations which its own authorities plainly show, by separate statistics for common labor, paid *lower* wages per hour than the steel industry, and uses for comparison with steel only the coal industry and the building trades which chiefly because of the general seasonal nature of the employment, pay a higher wage rate per hour than the steel industry.

But this fact—that the Interchurch Report thus carefully handpicks out of a long list of trades for which separate statistics for common labor are plainly given, the only two

[1] During the first half of the past decade (1911–1915) the average number of U. S. Steel Manufacturing employees was 147,932. During this period the country went through a great industrial boom followed by a severe industrial depression with widespread unemployment, yet the average number of such U. S. Steel employees in the worst year fell only 11% below the average for the 5 years. In the last half of the decade (1916–1920) the average number of such employees was 194,914 and in no one of these years did the average vary from the average for the period as much as 4%.

industries which could possibly even be made to appear to justify this utterly false conclusion, and the fact that it thus specifically makes the absolutely false statement that these two industries are the only trades "for which there are separate statistics for common labor"—constitutes only the first way in which the table is flagrantly manipulated and falsified.

Reference to the Interchurch Report's own table will show that under building trades, it specifies three classes of common labor—common labor which receives $22.00 a week of 44 hours or 50¢ an hour; hodcarriers who received $30.80 a week or 70¢ an hour; and plasterers' laborers who received $30.80 a week or 70¢ an hour. It then averages these three alleged classes of common labor and states in its fourth line that the "average for laborers" in the building trades is $27.85 a week.

But it is a matter of the commonest knowledge to anyone familiar with the building trades, and has been especially verified for the present purpose—first, that hodcarriers and plasterers' laborers are not common labor at all but highly semi-skilled labor who, as a matter of fact, generally regard themselves as skilled labor, and second, that they are not two classes of labor but merely two different names for exactly the same labor.

Mr. T. E. Rhodes is Vice President in charge of construction for the Frederick French Construction Company and his extensive building experience includes all parts of the country. Mr. Rhodes states in writing in particular reference to this Interchurch Table that

"Mason's laborers or hodcarriers or plasterers' laborers are at the summit of their trade and are skilled or semi-skilled but never unskilled. This is true in Pittsburg and in all cities where organized labor's established methods exist."

In the same connection, Mr. E. M. Tate, Secretary of the Building Construction Employers' Association in Pittsburg, states (letter to author August 30, 1921):

"Our plasterers' laborers are hodcarriers and they are considered semi-skilled, . . . Common labor . . . has nothing to do with making mortar or tending the mechanics or supplying them with materials" which is the particular function of plasterers' laborers or hodcarriers.

In other words not only is the Interchurch Report's whole table grossly falsified in that its conclusion is false and in that it seeks to justify that false conclusion by hand-picking out of 22 trades for which there are separate statistics for common labor two special trades and representing these as the only trades for which there are separate statistics for common labor, but it is further falsified by adding in semi-skilled labor as common labor and also by counting exactly the same semi-skilled trade twice and counting all the other classifications of building common labor only once in order to make the common labor wage rate seem $6 a week higher than it actually was.

The use of such a flagrantly manipulated and falsified table to make plausible to the casual reader the absolutely false general conclusion which follows it is of course—whether deliberate or only accidental—at least in its effect, precisely equivalent to the use of a weighted scale or loaded dice.[1]

[1] When this and other similar instances of the use of manipulated and falsified figures were specifically called to the attention of certain officials and others prominently connected with the Interchurch Movement during the course of preparation of the present Analysis, one such gentleman replied in substance: "We should not consider the Interchurch Report from the point of view of mere detailed facts and figures. I believe the Interchurch Movement was called of God to challenge the great injustice of the steel industry. We know that God moves in mysterious ways and it is not for us, with our mere finite minds, to question the Infinite." Professor Josiah Royce once replied to a similar argument, "I know that all beings, if only they can count, must find that three and two make five. Perhaps the angels cannot count; but if they can, this axiom is true for them. If I met an angel who declared that his experience had occasionally shown him a three and a two that did not make five, I should know at once what sort of an angel he was."

CHAPTER VI

INTERCHURCH ARGUMENTS AS TO THE RELATION BETWEEN STEEL WAGES AND LIVING COSTS

Among all classes of Americans, our modern American standard of living has been achieved and is maintained because under our modern industrial and commercial system two members of each average family can and do contribute to the family income. This fact is the basis of our modern American spending and enjoying power. It is the basis of our whole industrial and social and commercial organization.

The third argument by which the Interchurch Report seeks to prove steel wages low and on which throughout the wage discussion it puts most emphasis is the argument that the wages of *one* common laborer in the steel industry is not quite sufficient to maintain a standard of living for his family which, in all other industries in the country as a whole, it requires the wages of *two* workers to maintain.

In the 13th United States Census Report, Vol. IV, pages 30 and 31 are devoted to detailed facts and tables as to the distribution of wage earners. These show that 41.5% of our entire population is engaged in gainful occupation—that is, works for wages or profits.

These same U. S. Government statistics show that the average family throughout the country consists of 4.5 individuals. Of this average family of 4.5 persons, 1.868 persons work for wages or profits.

The Interchurch Report on the steel strike for convenience sake, as is frequently done, uses 5 persons as the basis of the average family. According to these U. S. Government statistics therefore 2.075 members of each such family are engaged in gainful occupation contributing towards the family's support.

These are average figures for all classes for the whole country, but the Census Report goes on to say on page 31:

> "The proportion of gainful workers in the population usually is larger for . . . foreign born white than for the native white people, for urban than for rural dwellers, and for manufacturing . . . than for agricultural communities."

Steel workers are urban dwellers—engaged in manufacturing—and at least the unskilled labor, as the Interchurch Report constantly emphasizes, largely consists of foreign born whites.   On all three counts then, there are more than 2.075 members per average family of five steel workers contributing to the family income.

The National Bureau of Economic Research is a research organization whose directors consist of such gentlemen as:

Hugh Frayne "former President of New York Federation of Labor; now organizer for American Federation of Labor, appointed (as director of the National Bureau of Economic Research) by the American Federation of Labor."

David Friday, "economist . . . appointed by the American Economic Association."

Walter R. Ingalls, Consulting Engineer and President of the Metal Statistical Association appointed by the Engineering Council.

J. M. Larkin, "Assistant to the President of the Bethlehem Steel Corporation, appointed by the Industrial Relations Association."

The Director of Research is Wesley C. Mitchell, Ph.D., Professor of Economics of Columbia University. Treasurer of the New School of Social Research.

4

This Bureau was organized for the express purpose of getting together basic economic facts which would be so well founded and accurate that they would be accepted by authorities of such widely different economic belief as the above directors.

Professors Wesley C. Mitchell, Willford I. King, Frederick R. Macaulay and Oswald W. Knauth, working jointly and under the auspices of this Bureau have recently published a study entitled, "Income in the United States." Table 20 on page 102 of this volume shows the average earnings of workers in substantially all industry. These figures *exclude* many part-time workers and *include* pensions, accident compensation, sustenance, etc., and are otherwise doubtless as high as can be justified.

Average Annual Earnings of Employees in Agriculture, Mining, Manufacturing, Transportation, Banking, Government and Other Industries.

1909	$626
1910	656
1911	648
1912	692
1913	723
1914	674
1915	697
1916	831
1917	961
1918	1078

With *two* members of the average family of 5 "gainfully employed" the average *family* income would thus be from some $1252 a year in 1909 to $2156 a year in 1918. This latter figure is *about* what the average *individual* worker in the steel industry earned in 1919. But the point in regard to all these figures is that they show on the basis of average individual income just what the Census states on the basis of nation wide investigation—that throughout the country the average family enjoys "American" standards of living because *two* members contribute towards *producing* the goods and service which go to make up the American standard of living and these *two* members are thereby enabled in turn to *pay for* the goods and service which go to make up the American standard of living.

Yet the Interchurch Report through page after page of statistics and arguments as to wages and family living budgets makes no mention and takes no account whatever of this fact, which is not only statistically incontrovertible but a matter of commonest knowledge; that among every general class in every section of our country Americans enjoy the American standard of living, and all American commerce and industry is built on the buying and enjoying power of American standards of living, because two members of the average American family of five are working and producing and paying for that standard of living.

The Interchurch Report sensationally states and in every section constantly repeats and re-emphasizes that:

" The annual earnings of over one third of all productive iron and steel workers were, and had been for years, below the level set by government experts as the minimum of subsistence. . . . The bulk of semi-skilled workers earned less than enough for the average family's minimum comfort" (page 85—line 6–21).

"In 1919 the unskilled worker's annual earnings were more than $109. below the minimum subsistence level and more than $558. below the American standard of living" (page 94—line 12).

Yet in face of this simple obvious fact of more than one wage earner per family, all these arguments as attempts in themselves to prove low wages, mean absolutely nothing, except perhaps a strange blindness on the part of the investigators as to a fact which must be of the commonest knowledge to them in their own personal experience, yet which for reasons that can only be guessed at, they completely overlooked as a factor in the important national question under their investigation.

The Interchurch Report goes into great detail to establish two different standards of living, one of which is called the "Standard of comfort" level and the other "the Standard of minimum subsistence" level. It may be noted in passing that the costs arrived at to maintain these particular standards of living are taken chiefly from estimates which were based on prices in Washington, D. C., and New York City—undoubtedly the two single cities whose general price levels have been the highest in the country. Again the basis of these figures was the estimated needs of the family of a clerk in government service.   There can be no question that there is a distinct difference between prices in steel communities and in Washington or New York; and also a distinct difference in the requirements of a family of a steel worker and that of a Washington clerk.   There are many other obviously questionable factors in these budgets but these are only details as compared with the fundamental unsoundness of the whole argument itself.

The U. S. Bureau figures, appearing in the Appendix of the Interchurch Report, show as has been stated that for the industries there given common labor earnings were about $22.50 per week.   The figures of the Bureau of Applied Economics, the Interchurch Report's own authority, show as has been emphasized that average weekly earnings for *all* workers—*including skilled*—for 25 leading industries was $24.35.   These rates were for the more developed and organized industries whose earnings are higher than average.   Yet if such workers worked 52 weeks a year, which they did not, they would only earn $1266.20—over $300 below what the Interchurch Report sets as the subsistence level, exactly $200 further below than the Interchurch Report even claims the steel common laborer is. Yet American labor as a whole seemed to subsist pretty well during this period.

The official speaker's manual of the Interchurch Movement on page 27 B under the heading "Talking Points" says:—

"It is a known fact that steel workers receive two and three times as much as ministers. . . . Day laborers receive an average wage *much in excess* of the amounts paid to two thirds of the ministers."

Ministers and their families certainly subsist. It is strange that the investigators, who themselves were, or represented, ministers, should not recognize that something was wrong in their argument that steel workers cannot subsist on earning two or three times as high as ministers' salaries.

Mr. William Z. Foster, Secretary-Treasurer of the Labor Organization that had charge of the steel strike, in his book, *The Great Steel Strike* in a chapter dealing specifically with the living problems of the workers, states:

"The fact is that except for a small impoverished minority the steel workers made their long hard fight virtually upon their own resources" (The Great Steel Strike, page 220 line 21).

The Interchurch Report states frequently that the bulk of the strikers were the lowest paid workers, who, it also states, had not for years been receiving enough wages for mere subsistence. Yet it appears not only obviously on the face of the situation, but from the strike leader's own statement, that at least 99% of these very workers, whom the Report says didn't earn enough to subsist on, actually had enough money saved up to support themselves and the families up to three and a half months without working.[1]

Again on page 244, the Interchurch Report itself, in speaking of the end of the strike says:

"The steel worker went back . . . to earning *under a living wage*" and then in line 28 on same page " *began piling up money* to get themselves out of America."

Mr. Foster, the strike leader, states as above quoted, that there was, as is of course always inevitable, "a small impoverished minority among the steel strikers." The

[1] The strikers' "Commissariat" which supported this "small impoverished minority" during the strike spent $348,509.42 (Great Steel Strike, page 220). Based on this "minimum of subsistence" figure this would have supported just 774 strikers' families for the 15 weeks of the strike. On $\frac{1}{2}$ or $\frac{1}{4}$ or even $1/_{10}$ subsistence rations this could only have supported at most a few thousand strikers' families.

Interchurch Report itself states that "The statements and affidavits of 500 steel workers (which it also explains included chiefly representative cross sections of the mass of unskilled foreigners) constitute the rock bottom of its findings."

Is it possible that these 500 workers (out of the total of 500,000 steel workers) whose affidavits "constitute the rock bottom of the findings," (which findings includes the conclusion that the steel worker "cannot subsist" on wages two and three times as much as ministers' salaries) happen by any chance to have somehow consisted chiefly of the "small impoverished minority" which Mr. Foster refers to as entirely exceptional to the great mass of steel workers who had seemingly enough saved out of past wages to support their families up to three and a half months without work?

This possibility, that its "500 rock bottom affidavits" somehow came to be obtained from the exceptional impoverished, rather than from the average prosperous steel worker is of course one obviously possible explanation as to why the whole Interchurch Report overlooked the simple fact that American standards of living are universally maintained by the earnings of two instead of one member per family—why it overlooked the fact that millions of Americans do subsist on wages far lower than those paid in the steel industry—why it even remained blind to the fact that other arguments and statements in its own Report *ipso facto* reduce this argument to an absurdity.

A close study of the report, however, also reveals one other possible reason why this line of argument was so blindly persisted in and so especially featured.

CHAPTER VII

CHANGING THE WHOLE PRESENT BASIS OF AMERICAN SOCIAL
AND ECONOMIC ORGANIZATION

THE Interchurch Report in its final "Findings" (page 250) *recommends:*

"That a minimum wage commission be established and *laws enacted* providing for an American standard of living through the labor of the natural bread winner permitting the mother to keep up a good home and the children to obtain at least a high school education."

No one questions the desirability of the proposition that every American family should have ample means for all the necessities and comforts of life, including the full, free education of each child. Moreover, the proposition of attempting to bring about such a highly desirable general condition by legislative enactment is not new.

The question therefore is not as to the desirability of such a condition but as to whether or not such a condition can be brought about by mere legislative action and particularly whether it can be brought about by legislation that each *single* worker—irrespective of other conditions and during his entire life—shall receive enough income to pay for all these desirable things for a family of five.

The Interchurch Report spends many pages in the Report itself and goes into much greater detail in Appendix A to show that the minimum American standard of living for an average family of 5 requires a family income of $2025.56 to $2262.47 a year.

This Interchurch proposition is that every head of a

55

family, no matter what his position or ability, should receive a minimum wage of between $2000 and $2200 a year.[1]

But the Department of Industrial Relations which inaugurated the Steel Strike Investigation, in the Report of its "Findings Committee" Document "No. 178—II—10 Nov. 1919" lays down the following basic principle for *"industrial readjustment"* which is emphasized at length but is epitomized in the one phrase that:—

"IV 4. . . The determination of wages on the basis of occupation and service and not on the basis of sex."

And the official Speakers' Manual of the whole Interchurch Movement on page 44, lays down the same general principle in exactly the same words.

But if legislation is to be passed that every man who is the head of a family, and every woman whether the head of a family or not, who does the same work that any married man does, must be paid a minimum wage of $2000 a year, it is obvious that as a matter of practical fact the man who is not married or who is a widower without family must also be paid on this same basis.

In other words considering the constitutional inhibition against class legislation, and the impossibility of minute discrimination in industry, this proposition means that irrespective of position or ability or any other condition, every man and most women in industry must, on the basis of the minimum living costs established by the Interchurch Report, be paid at least from $2000 to $2200 a year.

The National Bureau of Economic Research figures (see page 50 *ibid.*) show that in 1910 the average annual earnings of all wage earners throughout industry were $656. The division of all wages paid, as shown by the 1910 U. S.

---

[1] A clear understanding of the merits of this particular argument is important, not only because of its definite emphasis by the Interchurch Report, but because the union leaders of the coal miners and railroad workers have both widely and strongly advanced the same argument in recent attempts to advance war wages and as part of their advocacy of government ownership.

Industrial Census, by the number of wage earners, gives an annual income for such individual workers of about $600. Such workers are obviously in very large proportion heads of families. Professor Streightoff of Columbia by an analysis of the earnings of 19,658,000 out of the total of 26,000,000 adult male workers indicates that in 1912 the annual wage of such men who were of course preponderately heads of families was about $650. The National Bureau of Economic Research figures show that the average earnings of all wage earners had gone up by 1918 to $1078. This $1078, for reasons already stated, may doubtless be regarded as a maximum figure for the average annual earnings of all American workers.

The Interchurch Official Speakers' Manual states on page 27-B in *1919* that in the

"Baptist church, the average minister's salary outside of some city churches amounts to less than $2.00 a day" (or about $700 a year).

The basic proposition of the Interchurch's argument as to wages and living costs then is that practically every man and woman worker in the country shall arbitrarily by law have their wages approximately doubled.

The principle upon which all American society, including industry, now operates, is that all our people progress most surely and steadily through a sure and steady increase in production proportionate to the population, so that there shall be a continually greater amount of goods of all kinds to be divided and enjoyed either by consuming them or saving their equivalent or enjoying that equivalent in shorter working hours or in some other way.

Production per individual is actually about three times today what it was in 1850, even with everybody working at that time 12 to 14 hours a day, and all our higher present standards of living and our general shorter hours are the result.[1]

[1] M. C. Rorty of the American Statistical Association and President of the National Bureau of Economic Research in his pamphlet "Notes on Current Economic Problems" III, June, 1921, says on page 10:

Modern society also works on the basis that the best, if not the only way to insure production which shall be adequate for a constant general material advancement, is to hold out to each individual, who is the unit of production, the maximum incentive for his individual production.

To this end modern society has organized all production on a system under which each individual worker, if he works at all, is forced to produce enough to supply the necessities to support himself and one or two possible dependents. It forces him to provide for, or itself provides for his children and educates them well and free of charge till they are 16 years old.

Beyond this it holds out to the individual every standard of comfort and luxury as an incentive to greater individual effort and offers each individual at least the freest opportunity that has ever been offered by any major social organization in human history, to achieve whatever such standard of comfort or luxury his own energy and ability are capable of achieving.

The present standard of American living—which is a far higher standard at least as regards material comforts and conveniences than has ever been generally achieved in any other age or nation and which has been brought about entirely on this basis—is one of such incentives. The very fact that such an unparalleled majority in one nation have set and achieved such a standard of living through increased individual efficiency and coöperative family effort is itself a conspicuous demonstration of the adequacy of that incentive.

"The skilled worker's wage, in this country, will buy today over three times as much wheat flour as it would in 1855. Yet he is hardly more capable and works shorter hours than his predecessor of two generations ago. The difference lies almost wholly in the mechanical and scientific developments that have taken place. . . . Careful studies have shown that in the United States the annual production of useful goods increases with remarkable steadiness at a rate between 3 and 4% per annum— while the population increases at the rate of only 2%. . . ."

Moreover, at least so far in human experience every standard of living has in its turn been distinctly an achievement. From the ages of savagery, men have won a bare living, then comfort, then luxury for themselves and their families in proportion to effort and foresight and ability. The whole American people has achieved its present American standard of living on exactly the same basis—through generations of hard productive effort (generally on a 12- and 14-hour day) through generations of foresight in increasing our national margins of production and of ability in using that margin. On no other basis would the enjoyment of our present standard of living and our present shorter working day have been possible.

Exactly the same thing is true of the individual and of the family. It has been the incentive of realizing American standards of family living that has been the chief individual motive for both men and women for a special effort in producing and saving before marriage and for increased effort and better use of ability because of marriage. It has been the incentive of realizing American standards of family living that has been the chief motive for increased coöperative family effort as family responsibilities grew, in which effort older sons and daughters have joined in contributing to the advantages of younger brothers and sisters. Such incentives constitute an asset of paramount value both to the average American and the whole nation.

All the tables and statistics and the whole argument in the Interchurch Report in regard to maintaining an American standard of living have been based on the single short period in family life during which four members may depend entirely on the support of one—a period which seldom lasts more than ten years out of the average individual working life of some 40 years and the very existence of which period offers the maximum incentive for energy and foresight during other periods. Moreover, it is a matter of commonest knowledge that during this period where necessary the family income is frequently contributed to by a father or mother or unmarried brother or sister who for the time being constitute part of the family.

In other words the average worker only has 5 persons, including himself, to support at most for some 20% of his working life. During much more than half of his working life he has no one else or only one other person to support. To give him arbitrarily, irrespective of his ability to earn it, for all or most of his working life enough income to support five persons would not only tax all society to that extent but also to the extent that it would, to a large degree take away all normal incentive.

Yet the Interchurch Report does not suggest or consider these facts, which, if considered, reduce by some 80% the force even of the face value of its argument, and it does not mention or consider the paramount value in industry and in all American life of the incentive which the ambition to achieve American standards of living for the individual and the family exerts in continually raising the whole standard of American life.

The Interchurch Investigation was made among—and its arguments and recommendations based on that investigation refer to—the "mass of low-skilled foreigners particularly in the Chicago and Pittsburg districts."

The majority of "low-skilled foreigners" are from the very facts of their heredity and other circumstances—which facts are beyond the fault or control of any American institution—undoubtedly limited as to their individual possibility of *normal* American economic advancement. But no one who knows the living conditions in the sections of Europe from which most of these foreigners come, can fail to appreciate the very material advances which what is called in America the subsistence level marks over such former conditions of living.

Moreover there is probably no "low-skilled foreigner" in America who is not paid wages sufficient to maintain himself and a limited number of dependents well above the subsistence level. There is probably no foreign labor **in** the country today which is paid as little as the Interchurch Speakers Manual says the average minister is paid. Moreover there are tens of thousands of foreign-born Americans who have become prosperous and wealthy. Also the children of foreigners are in no sense similarly limited and the second and third generations so far have achieved an economic status that is quite on a par with that of average Americans.

In regard to the status of the immigrant worker the Interchurch World Movement in another report—a Special "World·Survey"—Vol. I.—pages 76 and 80 says:

"In their own country they were overshadowed by a state religion which was ritualistic and political in its character. Economically they were compelled to work for starvation wages with no hope for their future. Socially they were handicapped in that they belonged to the lower classes and the possibility of rising to the level of the so-called upper classes was next to hopeless no matter what their natural ability might have been.

"In America they had more to eat. They wore better clothes. They had the right to vote. They had access to free education. They were given better jobs . . . while they discovered that there were classes in America, they had the freedom to pass from one to another according to their character, general ability and personality . . . (and) it is being daily demonstrated in our American life that the children of these very foreigners are taking places of leadership and are rapidly becoming the backbone of America."

In the particular case of the Steel Industry, the unskilled foreign worker received wages per hour far higher than that paid the average of common labor, including the common labor which in many communities is largely or entirely American. And he had the opportunity of long hours and steady work so that in spite of his inherent economic handicaps he was able to earn as much or more than skilled American workers in other industries, by means of which he can at least advance the scale of his children and grandchildren exactly as former generations of Americans, by exactly the same method of long, steady hours of hard work, made possible the present scale of living of their children and grandchildren.[1]

Moreover the Steel Industry as a whole including the U. S. Steel Corporation and the many independent companies have already spent more than a hundred million dollars, in special schools and clubs and playgrounds and otherwise for the express purpose of providing every practical facility to help at least the children of its foreign workers to achieve American standards of living.

Yet the whole Interchurch Report does not discuss pro or con, or otherwise consider, or even mention any of these special inherent circumstances that are the true basis of certain inevitable facts of the unskilled foreign worker's life. Nor has it paid any attention to the large-scale definite and direct work that is being carried on by the steel companies to change these inherent conditions at least as they apply to the next generation.[2]

Yet it proposes, by an argument based on this very partial consideration of certain inherent facts that apply only to a very special class, that we enact laws for the purpose of taking away from all society the chief incentives which Americans have always believed are necessary to the constant advancement that has actually resulted from them.

But this is only the first point to be considered in regard to this "recommendation" that would double average wages.

Throughout all American industry, wages—including the wages of digging or raising the raw material, of transporting it and of carrying it through all the different steps that lead up to its final consumption—amount to between 80 and 90% of the cost of all products. It follows inevitably

[1] A detailed presentation of facts in this connection will be found in Chapter XVIII.

[2] Vol. II which was published a year after the Report proper and has had no such wide circulation or publicity as the Main Report does devote a section to Steel "welfare work."

therefore—and this is recognized as axiomatic by every economic authority as well as every business man—that the doubling of all wages that enter into the production of any product inevitably means practically doubling the cost of the product. And this in turn means that all workers in spite of their double wages would soon be in the same position in regard to their cost of living as they were before. By the same token the possibility of entirely maintaining the high American standard of living for a family of five on the earnings of one individual would be in exactly the same position as it is at present.

The basic fallacy of course of the Interchurch argument, and particularly of this special Recommendation No. 7 in the Findings, is that it entirely fails to distinguish the difference between what economists refer to as "nominal wages" and "real wages." "Nominal wages" may be set at any dollars and cents figure you please but "real wages"—the actual buying power of the wage—remains the same on any given standard of industrial productivity.[1]

The distinction between "nominal" and "real wages" is one that all socialists, I. W. W.'s and other radicals are particularly emphasizing at the present time.

Mr. George Soule, whose connection with the Interchurch Steel Strike Report will be referred to later, in his book *The New Unionism* (page 274) says:

"In the matter of wages a practical limit will before long be reached. If prices continue to rise, wages may rise correspondingly, but 'real wages' must remain almost stationary . . . given a maximum productivity, real wages can rise only by diverting a larger share of the earnings to the workers; but under the present economic régime, this

[1] Dr. Jenks points out that in certain exceptional cases, particularly in the production of luxuries and in production under monopolistic conditions, the burden of higher wages may legitimately be shifted in part to the consumer and that such action limited to such cases, may not effect or effect only slightly, prices in general. Any sweeping advance in wages, however, will inevitably tend to raise prices accordingly unless it is accompanied by a corresponding increase in production.

process cannot go beyond a certain point without driving the employers out of business by making it impossible for them to secure further capital."

Mr. Soule again says in the same volume page 11.

"The time is rapidly approaching as even its conservative (union) officials admit when no further (wage) gains of importance can be made for the members (coal miners) without pressing actively for the nationalization of the mines," and again,

". . . the enunciation of the Plumb plan is a long step toward the acknowledgment of the need for *a new economic order* which can be attained *not* through collective bargaining, but only through combined political and *economic* (the taking over of the railroads by the workers) action."

This basic socialistic program as to the proper solution of our basic wage problem is even more definitely and clearly stated in the preamble to the Constitution of the Amalgamated Clothing workers one of the new "Revolutionary Unions" which states:

"The industrial and inter-industrial organization built upon the solid rock of clear knowledge and *class consciousness* will put the *organized* working class in actual control of the system of production and the working class will then be ready to take possession of it."

In regard to this same problem the *preamble to the Constitution of the I. W. W.* says:

"Between these two classes a struggle must go on until the workers of the world, *organized as a class take possession of the earth and machinery of production.*"

That the same proposition is the fundamental principle of other extreme forms of radicalism including the Bolshevik is too well known to require specific quotation.

The specific relation—undoubtedly entirely unrecognized by the majority of the members of the Interchurch World Movement itself—between the particular wage arguments and "Conclusions" and "Findings" featured in the Interchurch Report and these fundamental theories upon which socialism, I. W. W.ism and other modern forms of radicalism are based, will be specifically discussed in Chapter XXIV of the present analysis.

5

CHAPTER VIII

STEEL WAGES AND STEEL PROFITS

THE Interchurch Report on the Steel Strike states on page 13 line 18—that; "the Commission's investigation did not include analysis of the Corporation's financial organization." Nevertheless, in two sections it brings up specifically and in many other places touches on indirectly "the financial ability of the Corporation to pay higher wages" as an argument by insinuation that because the Corporation could, therefore it should, pay higher wages.

The most definite of such arguments by insinuation (but which are in no case developed) are:

First: that in regard to "net earnings per ton of steel in 1917 and 1918 as against the average since 1910" (page 87 line 16);

Second: that "increases in wages during the war were in no case at a sacrifice of stockholder's dividends" (page 87 line 14—and page 14 line 1);

Third: that the total undivided surplus of the United States Steel corporation was "large enough to have paid a second time the total wage and salary budget for 1918—[$452,663,524] and to have left a surplus of over $14,000,000" (page 13 line 28).

"The net earnings per ton of steel" is stated in the Interchurch Report (page 87 line 18) to have averaged since 1910—obviously from 1910 to 1916—$13.03 and to have been for 1917, $19.76 and for 1918 $14.39.

No authority whatever is given for these figures, or if they were computed from other figures, any suggestions as to how they were arrived at. As a matter of fact they are merely quoted from an equally unsupported statement in a magazine article. Taken at their face value, however, they mean that in 1917 the United States Steel Corporation

66

earned net per ton of steel 51%, and in 1918 just 10%, more than the average earnings for the years 1910 to 1916 which includes the several very poor business years just before the war during one of which, 1914, the income account shows a net deficit of $16,971,983.83 (13th Annual Report).

Against this 51% alleged higher earnings per ton in its best year, must be considered the fact that during the year 1917, in which our entry into the war called for a maximum enlargement of all steel facilities, the U. S. Steel Corporation spent $87,988,000 in extra equipment to meet these war requirements.

Moreover in 1917 and 1918 the dollar was worth very much less than between 1910 and 1916.

Finally, during this period, in which general commodity prices increased 107% and the value of earnings decreased 50%, whereas the Interchurch Report does not even allege that average earnings per ton of steel increased for the two years more than 30.5%, it admits (page 97, footnote 1) that wages increased (1910 to 1919) 150%.

The second argument by insinuation—that wages whould have been further increased "because increase in wages during the war in no case were at a sacrifice of stockholders' dividends"—is repeatedly reiterated in this and similar forms.   This argument is of course on its face obviously untrue because with any given income the more that is paid to workers the less can be paid to stockholders and vice versa.   Moreover, the only possible reason for making such a statement and repeating it is to give the impression that the dividends to stockholders were increased more or at least as much as the increases of wages to labor.   This is specifically not true.   On the contrary, wages to labor were increased very much more than dividends to stockholders.

The cost of living by the end of the war—the period under discussion—had advanced according to the figures of the National Industrial Conference Board (whose figures are regarded as standard and used by the Federal Reserve Banks and the National Railroad administration) 64%.   By

September, 1919, the time of the steel strike, they had gone up 80%. Steel wages on the other hand had during the same time, as the Interchurch Report itself admits (page 97), gone up an average of 150% and in the case of the lowest paid labor had gone up 163%.

The standard dividend on U. S. Steel common stock is 5%. It was 5% in 1910–11–12 and 13. In 1914 because of the $16,971,983.83 net deficit previously referred to, although wages were not cut at all but were paid at the full rate out of the surplus funds as will be shown later, the dividends to stockholders were only 3%, in 1915 1¼%, in 1916 8¾%. In 1917 they were 17%—in 1918 14%—in 1919 and 1920 5%. An exact and detailed comparison of the wages and dividends paid by the U. S. Steel Corporation thruout this period follows. It will be noted that wages are for *all departments* and do *not* include sales and administrative employees. Wages for steel manufacturing departments and for 12-hour workers averaged of course much higher and showed a much greater increase over 1913. Even on this broadest basis of comparison, however, it appears plainly that steel wages were increased far more during this period than steel dividends. Moreover, while steel dividends returned in 1919 to the 1913 level, steel wages remained at the peak level until well into 1921 and in September, 1922, they are at approximately the 1918 level.

COMPARISON OF DIVIDENDS AND WAGES
U. S. STEEL CORPORATION

Year	Rate of Dividends	Dividends 5% = 100	Average[1] Wage Per Day	1913 Wage $2.85 = 100
1914	3 %	60	$2.88	101
1915	1¼%	25	2.92	103
1916	8¾%	175	3.29	115
1917	17 %	340	4.10	144
1918	14 %	280	5.33	187
1919	5 %	100	6.12	214
1920	5 %	100	6.96	244
Average[2]	7.7%	154	$4.67	171.7

[1] Does *not* include selling or administrative salaries.
[2] Weighted averages computed by Haskins and Sells.

The third method by which the Interchurch Report seeks to create the impression that the steel industry can afford to and therefore should, pay still higher wages, is again not by definite straightforward argument or statement, but by insinuations through cleverly coupled facts and vague clever phraseology in regard to the surplus funds of the steel companies.

The Interchurch Report in its conclusions in the beginning of the volume (page 13, line 23), states:—

"Compared with the wage budgets in 1918, the Corporation's final surplus after paying dividends of $96,382,027 and setting aside $274,-277,835 for Federal Taxes, payable in 1919 was $466,888,421—a sum large enough to have paid a second time the total wage and salary budget for 1918 ($452,663,524) and to have left a surplus of over $14,000,000. In 1919, the undivided surplus was $493,048,201.93 or $13,000,000 more than the total wage and salary expenditure."

There is little question that the foregoing statement, because of its particular phraseology would naturally lead anyone not familiar with accounting and the nature of a corporation surplus—which undoubtedly includes the great majority of the readers of the Interchurch Report—to believe that the Steel Corporation's surplus of $466,888,421 in 1918 was the surplus for the one year 1918 after paying that year's dividends, taxes, etc.; and again that the surplus of $493,048,201.93 in 1919 was the surplus for merely *that* year. Unless that impression is to be gathered, why is it stated that the surplus in 1918 could pay "a second time the total wage and salary budget" and leave a balance of $14,000,000, and then in the next year also again pay a second time "the total wage and salary expenditures" and leave a balance of $13,000,000? Moreover, the impression that these figures of $466,000,000 and $493,000,000 represented surpluses for single years is further accentuated by the phraseology of the note which follows at the bottom of the same page which refers to them in the plural as "surpluses."

As a matter of fact, however, the surplus of $466,000,000 in the year 1918 represented the cumulative savings of 18 years and the surplus of $493,048,201.93 in the year 1919 consisted of this $466,000,000 accumulated surplus of 18 years plus $26,000,000 which was the total surplus of the year 1919. If therefore as the Interchurch Report suggests this 18 years' accumulated surplus was used in the year 1918 to double wages, instead of having any surplus at all in 1919, with which again to double wages, all that would have been left of the surplus in 1918 plus all the surplus for the individual year 1919 would not have paid 10% of the annual wages in 1919.

A surplus performs exactly the same function for a corporation as a bank account performs for an individual. It makes it possible to meet any sudden financial contingency without costly sacrifice through sudden curtailment of expenditures—which in the case of a corporation means sudden reduction of wages or suddenly throwing large numbers of men out of work—and it makes it possible to meet a prolonged depression by a gradual readjustment which means a minimum loss to all concerned, including employees.

Attention has already been called to the fact that in the year 1914 the U. S. Steel Corporation had had a net deficit of $16,971,983.83. That same year dividends were decreased from 5% to 3% and the following year to 1¼%. It has also been stated that wages that year were not decreased and the number of men laid off whole or part time was very small as compared with the general unemployment throughout the country. Reference to the table at the bottom of page 13 in the Interchurch Report will also show that the total undivided surplus of the Steel Corporation, instead of being gradually increased as in other years, was in 1914 decreased $16,593,956.99 or by almost the same amount as the net deficit for that year.

In other words during this year of depression and net loss to the Company, dividends were decreased 40% and the following year 75% below the normal rate. But wages were not decreased because the Corporation had a surplus out of which it could meet its losses and maintain its wages and out of which it did meet its losses and maintain its wages.

That this surplus was thus specifically and deliberately used to maintain wages and employment in this period of financial depression is particularly emphasized by certain instructions of Judge Gary to the Presidents of subsidiary companies given in that year and quoted in the Senate Investigation of the Steel Strike, Part I (page 237) as follows'

"Now you will have some occasion perhaps during the immediate future to consider further some of these matters and they may involve considerable cost. If so I should consider the money well expended. It is even possible that there may be some distress among some of your employees or those who have been your employees but who are out of work, or in the families of these men. . . . Some of these families are occupying our houses and while out of work they may be unable to pay rent. In such cases, leave the families in the houses. Suspend the rent until they are able to pay it. The amount of money involved is of slight importance as compared with your duty and your pleasure as big, broad employers of labor. As suggested, you may have to relieve (lay off) more men but do not interrupt their employment unless and until necessary. . . . If you can keep the men at work to some extent around the mills cleaning up, putting your property in condition I would do so. You may expect to meet considerable loss during the coming winter but if in so doing you have added to the relief, benefit and comfort of employees who in the nature of things are more or less dependent upon you, it should be a pleasure."

The whole question of surpluses has been particularly widely discussed in the last few years. Severe criticism has recently been generally expressed of a number of large corporations—particularly the Interborough Rapid Transit Company of New York, the American Woolen Company and other companies—who have been accused of having dissipated all their high earnings of prosperous years in temporary too high dividends or too high wages instead of accumulating a surplus, which would have made sudden large scale unemployment and sudden financial difficulties avoidable. The Kansas Industrial Court has laid down the general rule that employers are in duty bound, as a measure of protection for their workers to lay up during their prosperous years surpluses to meet the contingencies of less favorable business conditions. The Labor Union movement in England is on record in favor of national legislation to compel employers to accumulate surpluses in times of prosperity and to use these surpluses, just as the U. S. Steel Corporation has used its surplus, to insure against sudden widespread unemployment in times of depression. Not only then can there be no question of the fundamental soundness of the accumulation of such a surplus, but there is no question that it is fundamentally unsound business practice not to accumulate such a reasonable surplus as opportunity permits.

The only possible questions therefore in regard to the U. S. Steel Corporation surplus, against which the Interchurch Report goes to such lengths to prejudice its readers, are its size, the rate at which it has been increased and whether or not that rate has seriously handicapped legitimate rates of wages or dividends.

The total assets of the U. S. Steel Corporation as shown by the balance sheet of its 18th Annual Report, December 31, 1919, audited by Price, Waterhouse and Co., was $2,365,882,382.13. The $493,048,201.93 which represents its total of 18 years' accumulative surplus was just 21.7% of these total assets. This 21.7% surplus therefore represents an average increase during 18 years of less than $1\frac{1}{4}$% a year. Certainly no private individual or ordinary business would be criticized for adding to its liquid assets—that is its bank account or its equivalent—at the rate of $1\frac{1}{4}$% a year unless on the ground that the rate was unreasonably small.

The total volume of business of the U. S. Steel Corporation for the year 1918 as reported in its 17th Annual Report (page 24) was $1,744,312,163. Its surplus for the year 1918 as stated in the same Annual Report of the Company (page 6)—and clearly arrived at by a correct interpretation of the table at the bottom of page 13 of the Interchurch Report— is $35,227,617.75.[1] The surplus for the year 1918 then is just 2.02% of the volume of business for that year. Certainly no private individual or ordinary corporation would be criticized for saving a bare 2% of gross income a year unless again perhaps on the grounds that such a percentage of saving was too small.

The total volume of business of the U. S. Steel Corporation for the year 1919, as reported in the 18th Annual Report (page 24), was $1,448,557.835. The surplus for the same year as stated in this annual report (page 6)—which checks with a proper interpretation of the table on page 13 of the Interchurch Report—was $26,159,780,55 which is just 1.8% of gross income. Surely again no private individual or ordinary company would be criticized for saving 1.8% of gross income per year unless again on the ground that such a percentage of saving is too small.

As a matter of plain demonstrable fact then, the Interchurch Report's attempt by insinuations and false or misleading statements in regard to surplus and profits, to argue indirectly that steel wages are low is equally fallacious and otherwise exactly on the same plane with its attempt to justify the same conclusion through a type of direct argument and a misuse of statistics that has already been analyzed and characterized.

[1] This is shown by the financial statement to include some $6,000,000 carried over from the previous year, therefore not to be surplus for the year 1918 only.

CHAPTER IX

THE Interchurch Report begins the chapter in which it discusses steel working hours, and calls "The Twelve Hour Day," with the following specific, emphasized conclusions:

A. "Approximately half the employees in iron and steel manufacturing plants are subject to the schedule known as the 12-hour day [that is a working day from 11 to 14 hours long];

B. "Less than one-quarter of the industry's employees can work under 60 hours a week although in most industries 60 hours was regarded as the maximum working week ten years ago:

C. "In the past decade the United States Steel Corporation has increased the percentage of its employees, subject to the 12-hour day."

These conclusions are largely the same in substance and phraseology as the specially featured conclusions in the Interchurch Report's "Introduction," which consists entirely of conclusions and recommendations, with the following exceptions. Its Introduction states that approximately "one-half the *employees* of the steel industry (without the qualification 'iron and steel manufacturing plants') were subject to the 12 hour day." In addition it is stated that "approximately one-half of these in turn were subject to the 7-day week." It is also stated here that "*much* less than one-quarter had a working day of less than ten hours."

According to the Interchurch Report then, steel working hours are as follows:

(1) "Less" or "much less" than 25% of the men "can work less than 60 hours a week";

(2) Some 25%, although the Interchurch Report does not mention these at all, evidently work something between 10 and 12 hours;

(3) 25% work the 12-hour day 6 days a week;

(4) 25% work 12 hours and also were "subject to the 7-day week";

(5) "*Usually* the shifts alternate *weekly* and the men must work the long turn of 18 or 24 hours—a solid day at heavy labor" (page 47).

In contrast to this picture of steel working hours as presented by the Interchurch Report, Judge Gary testified before the Senate Committee in October, 1919, that the working hours of the United States Steel Corporation were as follows (Senate Hearings, page 157):

(1) 88,994 employees or 34% of all employees worked approximately 8 hours a day.

(2) 102,902 employees or 39.5% of all employees worked 10 hours a day.

(3) 69,284 employees or 26.5% of all employees worked the 12-hour turn.

(4) The 7-day week has been eliminated.

(5) Out of a total of 191,000 employees 82 worked a continuous 24-hour shift once in each month, 344 men worked a continuous 18 hours twice each month. (Senate Hearings page 202.)

"*Employees who can work less than 60 hours a week.*"

There are two things to be noted about the Interchurch Report's conclusion that "less" or "much less than 25% of steel workers *can* work under 60 hours a week."

The Senate testimony as to the working hours of all U.S. Steel Corporation employees stated specifically the number of "approximately 8-hour" workers. The Interchurch Report has this statement and quotes frequently from other parts of the same paragraph but it does not mention or consider these definite figures that 34% of all workers work approximately 8 hours a day. Moreover it itself does not advance any figures as to 8-hour workers or as to 9-hour workers, nor does it as much as mention such workers. It entirely ignores the subject of the 8- or 9-hour workers—just as it leaves a complete blank as to the workers (obviously from its own figures 25%) who work between 10 and 12 hours—except for these two sweeping conclusions that "less" or "much less than one-fourth of the industry's employees can work under 60 hours a week."[1]

There are two principal authoritative sources of information as to conditions in the modern steel industry. The first of these is the figures as to steel wages and steel hours contained in the U. S. Bureau of Labor Statistics, Monthly Review for October, 1919. These figures—at least as far as they apply to 12-hour workers—the Interchurch Report uses constantly.

This government study shows working hours for six principal departments, the hours for one of which were as follows:

U. S. BUREAU OF LABOR STATISTICS

MONTHLY REVIEW, OCTOBER, 1919, PAGES 122–123

Sheet Mill

AVERAGE FULL TIME HOURS PER WEEK

Occupation	1913	1914	1915	1917	"1919"
Pair Heater................	42.8	42.8	42.8	43.7	43.6
Roller...................	42.8	42.8	42.9	43.7	43.6
Rougher.................	42.8	42.8	42.8	43.7	43.7
Catcher.................	42.8	42.8	42.8	43.7	42.8
Matcher.................	42.8	42.8	42.8	43.7	43.7
Doubler.................	42.8	42.8	42.8	43.7	43.6
Sheet Heater............	42.8	42.8	42.9	43.7	43.7
Sheet Heater Helper.......	42.9	42.8	42.9	43.2	43.2
Shearmen................	42.9	42.9	43.0	43.5	43.5
Shearmen Helper..........	42.9	42.9	43.8	43.2	46.6
Openers.................	42.8	42.8	43.6	43.3	44.0
Laborers.................	64.9	65.9	65	61.8	66.5

The second principal authoritative source of information as to conditions in the modern steel industry is the still more comprehensive U. S. Bureau of Labor Statistics Bulletin 218

[1] One brief table presented on page 49 contains one line which says: "on 8 hours 10 per cent."

(October, 1917)—a document of some 500 pages devoted entirely to a most elaborate and detailed study of labor conditions in the steel industry, partly for the decade and partly for the 5 years up to May, 1915.

This study, in its conclusions, groups steel manufacturing throughout the country according to 10 representative departments.   Its conclusions as to hours in each of these departments will be touched on later.   In connection, however, with the Interchurch Report's efforts to hide the existence of the 8-hour day in the steel industry and its statement that "less than one-fourth of the industry's employees can work under 60 hours a week," the summary made by this document as to working hours in *four* of these 10 principal steel-making departments is extremely interesting.

In summarizing working hours in *these departments* U. S. Bureau of Labor Bulletin 218 (October, 1917) says:

PUDDLING MILLS, SUMMARY OF HOURS (Page 186)

"In 1915 (May, nine months after the war began) 24% worked 5 turns per week, 50% worked 6 days one week and 5 nights the next, 11% were employed in 3 shifts in 24 hours, two working five days each only, Monday to Friday, while the third (each shift alternatingly) worked a turn on Saturday, making 6 for the week" (13% worked 6 days per week; 1% 6 and 7 days alternately and 1% 7 days per week leaving 85% working 5 or 5½ days a week).

BAR MILLS, SUMMARY OF HOURS (Page 309)

Hours	*Per cent. of all Employees*
48 to 60......................	48
Over 60 and under 72...........	41
72............................	8
Over 72......................	1

(48% under 60 hours a week, *89% less than 72 hours.*)

SHEET MILLS, SUMMARY OF HOURS (Page 414)

"It will be noticed that the customary working time of the large number of employees in this department was five days, five and six days in rotation. In all except one of the plants covered, the hot mill employees were divided into three groups, each working 8 hours per turn, 5 turns per week, Monday to Friday inclusive, with one crew (alternately) working 1 turn Saturday morning." (40 hours each for two weeks and 48 hours each third week.)

TIN PLATE MILLS, SUMMARY OF HOURS (Page 445)

"It will be noticed that the customary working time of a large percentage of the employees in this department was 5 days, 5 and 6 days in rotation. In all the plants covered the regular turn employees were divided into 3 crews, each working 8 hours per turn, 5 turns per week from Monday to Friday inclusive with one crew (alternately) working an extra turn Saturday morning."

Hours per week, 40 for two weeks and 48 each third week.

The 7-day Week and the 24-hour Shift

After beginning its chapter on steel working hours by the statement of the three conclusions already quoted and making certain further general statements, the Interchurch Report in defining the 12-hour day on page 47 says:

" *Usually* the shifts alternate *weekly* and the men must work the 'long turn' of 18 hours or 24 hours . . . in some plants the 36-hour turn is still not unknown."

In this same connection the Interchurch Report brings up the subject of the 7-day week in regard to which it says in its conclusions that *one-fourth* of the employees "were subjected to the 7-day week."

In regard to the "long turn" the specific Senate evidence already quoted (Senate Hearings, part one, page 202) is that:

"Out of a total of 191,000 employees (of the U. S. Steel Corporation) 82 work a continuous 24-hour shift once in each month. . . . 344 men work a continuous 18 hours twice each month. No other employees work a continuous 18- or 24-hour shift except in emergency times like the war."

Except for reference to it in connection with quotations from diaries or statements of some few individual workers the Interchurch Report makes no attempt to support its conclusion that *"usually"* the 12-hour worker must work the long shift *"alternately weekly"*; makes no specific answer to Judge Gary's statement that out of 191,000 men only 82 per month work a 24-hour shift although it elsewhere quotes the next sentence, and makes no reference whatever to the fact that it was only claimed before the Senate Committee (page 202) that 400 or 500 workers or some $\frac{1}{10}$ of 1% of the workers were subject to such shifts.

As regards the 7-day week there is no question that if it exists, or to the extent it exists, it justifies in the mind of the average American, such condemnation a's the Interchurch Report gives it. The 7-day week is generally regarded as incompatible with modern social standards. But except in connection with war necessity, when it existed in many war industries, the Steel Corporation officials deny its existence in the U. S. Steel Corporation—except temporarily in isolated cases of emergency such as are likely to happen in all kinds of work. In 1911, the Corporation officially declared that: "Whether viewed from a physical, social or moral point of view we believe the 7-day week is detrimental." Positive instructions were issued to all departments of the company that 7-day work was not to be allowed and while it was stated that in any industry, "at rare intervals there may come emergencies that would make absolute enforcement of any exact schedule of hours impracticable," it was also added that "any tendency on the part of any one to disregard the spirit or the letter of such order (against the 7-day week) should be sufficient cause for removal from service." This order is quoted in full in the Senate Hearings, Part I, page 231.

In answer to questions in regard to Sunday and 7-day work under normal conditions—"1914 for example," Judge Gary testified before the Senate Committee (Senate Hearings, Part I, page 179):

Mr. Gary: "Now the war came on and the government was clamoring for more and more steel . . . they were insisting on more and more days of work . . . It was not until after the armistice of November 11, 1918, that Secretary of War Baker through Riley, Adjutant General . . . wrote, 'The Secretary of War directs me to notify you to stop all Sunday work' . . . and we immediately put that into practise just as fast as we could."

Senator Phipps: "Judge Gary, will you kindly give us the practice prevailing in normal times, say just before the war, taken in 1914, what were the hours per day and days per week?"

Mr. Gary: "Sunday work was practically eliminated except as to the blast furnaces which are required to be continuously operated . . . and in those cases we reduced the days per week . . . giving each employee one day (off) during the week whether it was Sunday or another day."

Mr. Clayton L. Patterson, Secretary of the Bureau of Labor of the National Association of Sheet and Tin Plate Manufacturers—among the chief competitors of the United States Steel Corporation—in a published pamphlet[1] in which he admits the limited existence of the 7-day week— from 10% to 14% varying with conditions—in the steel industries with which he himself is associated nevertheless says (page 73):

"The seven-day week has already been eliminated by the United States Steel Corporation and by many independent plants . . . (by using) an extra swing crew, which relieves each regular crew alternately. By this method each crew has one day off each week but that day may be any day in the week."

Now it is to be particularly noted that although no steel man denies the existence of a certain amount of 7-day work in certain "independent" plants of the steel industry— although Mr. Patterson, while emphasizing that the 7-day week has already been eliminated by the United States Steel Corporation, specifically admits its existence to a limited extent in the group of which he himself is an official, the Interchurch Report treats the question of the 7-day week in "independent plants" only incidentally and focuses its effort on attempting to prove that the United States Steel

[1] Review of "The Steel Strike of 1919 by the Commission of Inquiry Interchurch World Movement."

Corporation is chiefly responsible for the continued existence of the 7-day week throughout the industry.

The Interchurch Report particularly quotes the testimony before the Senate Commission in regard to the elimination of the 7-day week in Corporation plants.   In addition it quotes (page 69) from a letter of January 30, 1920 to the Interchurch Commission in which Judge Gary said:

> "As to the 7-day week, however, beg to state that prior to the war *it had been eliminated* entirely except as to maintenance and repair crews on infrequent occasions.   During the war at the urgent request by government officials for larger production, there was considerable continuous 7-day service in some of the departments.   With the close of the war, this attitude was changed and the 7-day service has been very largely eliminated.   At the present time there is comparatively little of it.   We expect to entirely avoid it very shortly."

Using this quotation as its hypothesis, the Interchurch Report begins its discussion of the 7-day week with this question (page 71):

> "What are the simple statistical facts concerning the 'elimination' of 7-day work and the 'reduction' of hours which, according to Mr. Gary, have been the object of such earnest effort by the *Corporation?*"

The Interchurch Report specifically states in its "Conclusions" in the front of the book and elsewhere that one-fourth of all steel workers worked the 7-day week.   It does not attempt, however, to offer any concrete evidence to support that specific figure, but rather depends on building up by "statistics" or otherwise, the impression that a very large number of steel workers work the 7-day week.

The first method by which the Interchurch Report seeks to build up an impression of the large amount of 7-day work in the steel industry is through emphasizing the amount of "Sunday work."

Of course the only reason why 7-day work enters into the problem of the steel industry is because blast furnaces have to be run continuously day and night and Sundays in order to operate the industry.   The only way it is possible to operate and give workers the 6-day week is by a special extra swing crew which alternately takes the place of different men different days, so that while every man gets one day off every week, he only gets one particular day off every six weeks. The existence of a large amount of Sunday work in certain departments therefore, as to which the Interchurch Report adduces much evidence, is no evidence at all as to 7-day work.

Especially on pages 50 through 53 and frequently elsewhere, the Interchurch Report specifies the working schedule of many particular classes of workers as about 84 hours a week and quotes the United States Bureau of Labor Statistics Monthly Review for October, 1919 as its authority. Here and thruout it refers to these figures as though they represent normal working hours in the steel industry. As a matter of fact, however, some of these figures go back to June, 1918 before the Battle of Chateau Thierry and the U. S. Bureau of Labor statement accompanying these figures expressly states (page 1092–104) that:—"It will be seen therefore that the schedules of 64 of the 73 establishments are for payroll periods in the months of December to March"; by far the largest number (27) are for December, 1918, the first month after the war, and over two-thirds are for December or January or earlier. In other words these figures which the Interchurch continually uses as for the year 1919 and as representing normal[1] conditions actually

[1] On page 50 the Interchurch Report says, "Taking the statistics for the center of the industry, the Pittsburg district, by the departments of plant for the last quarter of 1918 and the first quarter of 1919 as compiled by the Bureau of Labor Statistics (October, 1919, *Monthly Review*) we have for the largest department in the industry: stockers, 83.6; larrymen 82.6; larrymen's helpers, 82.3, etc." That is, in relation to this special table, the exact period covered by all the so-called 1919 statistics is specifically mentioned but in this case they are not referred to as 1919 statistics and there is nothing, except that they are occasionally referred to as from the same volume, which would lead any but a close student to recognize or even suspect that all further figures which are stated as 1919 and as normal actually were for the same period.

represent, and themselves plainly state that they represent the period during the war or the *first few months immediately after the armistice*, during which period working hours in all basic industries were in no way near normal. Moreover as regards steel, U. S. Bureau of Labor Statistics Monthly Review June, 1920 (page 152 line 6 and chart) and other authoritative studies all show and state that January, 1919 represented the *peak* of steel war activities and that the return to normal began in February, 1919.

Now as a matter of fact this U. S. Bureau of Labor study published in its Monthly Review for October, 1919 gives detailed figures not merely for "1919" but for 1913, 1914, 1915, 1917, and "1919." When these figures are analyzed as a whole it is possible to see to just what extent "1919" figures were influenced by war conditions and to what extent they do represent the normal trend of hours in the industry. As a matter of fact they show plainly that hours in certain shorter-hour departments increased but that hours in the 12-hour departments shortened during the war. The point to be noted here is that they show certain exceptional and extreme increases due to the war and that it is these extreme war-condition cases which the Interchurch Report chiefly features.

The third argument of the Interchurch Report, however, in regard to the 7-day week, and the one in which it specifically attacks the Steel Corporation as the stronghold of the 7-day week in the industry, is based on figures which apply to 1914, in regard to which period Judge Gary categorically stated that in all continuous operations in the United States Steel Corporation, where furnaces had to be run over Sunday, the workers themselves worked only six days, being given some other one day off during the week.

The Interchurch Report quotes on page 72 as follows:

"Statistics from Bureau of Labor Statistics Bulletin 218 (Oct., 1917) reveal what actual successes were accomplished by the *Corporation* in 'eliminating' 7-day work. Seven-day workers in blast furnaces were (p. 17) 1911, 89%; 1912, 82%; 1913, 80%; 1914, 58%; 1915, 59%. Open hearths during this same period about equally divided among the 7-day; the 7 and 6 day alternately, and the 6-day groups. Even before the war the seven day 'eliminating' waited on what 'steel demand' decided. The best year's figures show that the *Corporation* never achieved even a half reform."

This argument and conclusion which specifically cites the United States Bureau of Labor Statistics for its authority is very interesting. It particularly emphasizes that:

"The best year's figures show that the *Corporation* never achieved even a half reform."

United States Bureau of Labor Statistics Bulletin 218 (October, 1917), page 17, begins:

"A blast furnace from the very nature of its process must be in continuous operation day and night 7 days per week. In 1907 in 20 plants reported for that year for 97% of all employees *in the occupation considered*, the customary working time per week was 7 days . . . but *since 1910 there has been a material reduction in 7-day work. Many plants* having *made provision to lay off each employee in rotation one day in 7* (precisely as Judge Gary described), *thus making a 6-day week for the employee while the plant is continuously in operation 7 days."*

U. S. Bureau of Labor Statistics does not mention the U. S. Steel Corporation by name but Senate Document 110 is specific on this point. It says, Vol. III, page 168, referring to conditions of March, 1912:

"The plan was generally adopted by the Steel Corporation. . . . In all but one of the plants, the plans have *eliminated 7-day work* for all but a very few employees. In the (one) excepted plant, the plan for the elimination of 7-day work has not been completely introduced . . . but in the other blast furnaces the plans were so completely introduced as practically to abolish 7-day work."

Bulletin 218 then gives the table just as quoted in the Interchurch Report for the purpose of showing the decrease in hours in the industry that was brought about by these *many plants* having *eliminated* the 7-day week.

Then follows a summary showing that in Bessemer plants in 1910, 34% of a certain group of workers worked 7 days a week while in 1913 *only 11%* of the same group worked 7 days, at the end of which table the Department of Labor Bulletin emphasizes that, "Throughout the 9-year period (1907 to 1915) the majority of employees in Bessemer Converting departments worked 6 days per week while a few worked 6 and 7 days in alternating weeks." This summary and conclusion the Interchurch Report makes no reference to.

The Interchurch Report does, however, quote and emphasize the next paragraph— that in regard to the "7, 7 and 6 and 6-day groups in open hearth furnace departments" being about equally divided.

The next paragraph in this U. S. Bureau of Labor Bulletin says: "*In all rolling mills the per cent of employees working 7 days a week was very small.*" This paragraph the Interchurch Report also ignores.

Moreover at the end of this section, 4 pages later, the U. S. Bureau of Labor Bulletin recapitulates and again emphasizes: "The very material reduction in working hours" during this period because of the *many plants* which had gone from the 7 to the 6-day week.

In other words, in trying to bolster up its accusations against the United States Steel Corporation in regard to the 7-day week and in a specific effort to seem to disprove Judge Gary's plain detailed statement, the Interchurch Report thus not only misinterprets the obvious meaning of the government figures which it quotes in an attempt to prove the opposite of what is actually indicated; it not only does this in face of the plain, twice-repeated statement of the U. S. Bureau of Labor itself as to what these figures actually show; but it handpicks this U. S. Bureau of Labor evidence paragraph by paragraph, publishing only the figures or quotations which it can misconstrue and entirely leaving out the intervening figures or statements which are so plain they cannot be thus misconstrued.

Number of 12-hour Workers

In regard to the 12-hour day the Interchurch Report begins its whole discussion with the positive sweeping statement of two conclusions; that—

A. "Approximately half of the employees of the iron and steel manufacturing plants are subjected to the schedule known as the 12-hour day [that is, a working day, from 11 to 14 hours long]" and

C. "In the past decade the *U. S. Steel Corporation* has *increased* the percentage of its employees, subject to the 12-hour day."

As the Interchurch Report states these two conclusions in this order and because it is necessary to establish facts before it is possible to establish tendencies, it is desirable to treat these two subjects in this order, irrespective of the fact that in its argument the Interchurch Report itself does not.

In attempting to establish its conclusion as to the proportion of steel workers who work in the 12-hour group the Interchurch Report—as in the case of so many other of its conclusions—immediately finds itself confronted by a plain, definite, official statement of the steel companies substantially to the contrary of those conclusions.

Judge Gary had testified before the Senate Committee that for the U. S. Steel Corporation, the number of 12-hour workers was 69,284 and that these represented 26.5% of all workers.

The Interchurch Report at once points out, and its position up to a certain point is well taken, that the total employees of the U. S. Steel Corporation include the workers in its ore-producing, coal-producing and transportation companies. Although such workers are most certainly engaged in the production of steel they are not in many instances working under the same conditions; do not in general work the same schedule of hours; are not involved in the problem of continuous operation, and particularly were not involved in the issues of the steel strike. If, the Interchurch Report therefore insists, consideration is limited, as it should be, to the "employees of iron and steel manufacturing plants" these 69,284 twelve-hour workers would represent not 26.5% but 36% of all employees that it is fair to include.

By thus establishing with reasonable plausibility the percentage of 12-hour workers in the United States Steel Corporation at 36, the Interchurch Report has brought it within 14% of its own figures as to 12-hour workers throughout the industry. The Interchurch Report then might have considered the fact that the Steel Corporation employs less of its facilities than many other steel companies in producing crude iron and steel—in which processes hours are longer and the proportion of men to output less—and much more of its facilities than many other companies in producing finished products—in which processes the hours are shorter and the proportion of workers to output greater. It is obvious therefore that the United States Steel Corporation may doubtless have a less proportion of 12-hour workers than the industry as a whole.[1]

But the fundamental hypothesis of the whole Interchurch Report, stated as "Summarized Conclusions No. 1" and repeatedly throughout, is that:

"1. The conduct of the iron and steel industry was determined by the conditions of labor accepted by the 191,000 employees of the *U. S. Steel Corporation's* manufacturing plants.

"2. These conditions of Labor were fixed by the Corporation. . . .

"Wage rates in the iron and steel industry as a whole are determined by the rate of the *U. S. Steel Corporation.*"

—and in general the Interchurch Report insists on every occasion that practically every evil in the steel industry

[1] Mr. Clayton L. Patterson on page 64 of his pamphlet on the 1919 steel strike, already referred to, gives the percentage of 12-hour workers for May, 1920 for 20 "independent" plants manufacturing sheet steel (a more finished product) as 24.66%. On the other hand the number of 12-hour workers in 11 "independent" mills manufacturing steel ingots, slabs, billets—the cruder forms of steel—was 39.26%. The aver-

which it mentions is the result of the influence of the U. S. Steel Corporation—even going to the lengths, as has already been pointed out in the present chapter, of expurgating and falsifying the whole meaning of pages of government statistics in order to hide the fact that the United States Steel Corporation took the lead in eliminating the 7-day week.

For the Interchurch Report to admit, therefore, that the United States Steel Corporation had, as evidence and common sense indicate, a somewhat less proportion of 12-hour workers than the industry as a whole, would, at least to that extent, have been to repudiate its first and most repeatedly expressed hypothesis. Instead, therefore, of making any attempt to reconcile its conclusions of 50% of 12-hour workers in the industry as a whole with the different U. S. Steel Corporation figures, it deliberately takes these figures for its text and specifically builds up its 12-hour argument around the attempt to discredit them.

The Interchurch Report seeks to contradict Judge Gary's figures and establish its own in three ways:—first, by elaborate detail quotations and certain deductions of its own from the so-called 1919 figures of the U. S. Bureau of Labor; 2nd, by generalizations from certain alleged figures for 3 particular steel plants; and 3rd, by attempting to show that part of the workers which the Steel Corporation figures specify as 10-hour workers actually worked 12 hours or more on alternating shifts and therefore should be added to the percentage of 12-hour workers.

In regard to the elaborate statistics which the Interchurch Report gives through page after page from the so-called 1919 figures of the U. S. Bureau of Labor Statistics, it need only be pointed out again that these figures are particularly stated to have been almost entirely for the first one or two months after the war, a period obviously entirely

---

age number of 12-hour workers per total of men employed for both groups of plants was 30.75%. These figures show plainly the variation in percentage of 12-hour workers in different types of plants. They are also for a period that is substantially normal.

abnormal in steel as in every other industry; moreover they themselves give no specific facts as to number of 12-hour workers. Whatever these certain extreme figures which the Interchurch Report picks out may or may not show, or whatever may or may not be fairly deduced from them is in no sense conclusive or indicative of working hours even for the same department 8 or 10 months later or under normal conditions.

The second method which the Interchurch Report uses to try to arrive at the percentage of 12-hour workers in the steel industry is to attempt to generalize from three special instances.

In one of these cases—for the Youngstown Sheet and Tube Company—it states it obtained exact figures. This is the only case in which it specifically states it did obtain actual figures. These figures place 12-hour workers at 55%. It next quotes a "verbal estimate of the President of the Carnegie mills," alleged to have been made "to the Interchurch Commission of Inquiry in November, 1919." It states this estimate of 12-hour workers was 60%. Finally, it takes from the Senate Hearings Mr. Oursler's figures as to hours worked by different shifts in the Homestead plant in which the percentage of 12-hour workers is definitely given as 36, and attempts to prove from these figures themselves that the number of 12-hour workers in Mr. Oursler's plant was actually 52% instead of 36%.

In view of the well-known fact, already emphasized, that in certain departments of steel work the percentage of 12-hour workers runs very high, just as in other departments there is only 1 or 2% of 12-hour workers or no 12-hour work at all, the allegation that in three special cases the percentage of 12-hour workers ran between 50 and 60—even if that allegation were entirely true—obviously in no way proves or disproves the specific statement that for the entire United States Steel Corporation the percentage of 12-hour workers was 26.5%, or the corollary of that statement that for the steel manufacturing departments it was 36.2%, which is the particular point the Interchurch Report insists on arguing. By the same token, it proves nothing as to averages in all departments of the "independent" plants that make up the rest of the industry.

Moreover a few isolated figures from both the U. S. Bureau of Labor study for December, 1918, and January, 1919, and the figures for 3 special departments for 8 months later, each obviously represent such special or limited conditions that even taken together they cannot be regarded as supporting each other to show general normal conditions, and certainly not sufficiently to overcome Judge Gary's and Mr. Patterson's very specific and comprehensive figures to the contrary.

The third argument by which the Interchurch Report seeks to substantiate its conclusion that 50% of all steel workers work the 12-hour day is contained in a footnote beginning on page 49 and running through 3 pages. This footnote first quotes 3 brief sentences from a letter of Feb. 13th from Judge Gary to the Interchurch Commission dealing with Mr. Oursler's figures as to working hours in the Homestead mill[1] and a few phrases from another letter of January 30th to the Commission in regard to his own figures for the whole industry.

The classification of all U. S. Steel Corporation employees according to working hours was officially stated as follows:

"12 hour turns....... 69,284.........26.5 %
10 hour   "   ....102,902........(39.39%)
8 hour   "   .... 88,994........(34.1 %)"

These figures do not make any mention of the exceptional worker who works 10 and 14 hours or 11 and 13 hours alternate weeks but averages 12 hours a day. It is to be presumed of course, in face of the obvious facts, that such workers are included in this statement under the 12-hour workers.

[1]Quoted in full in Senate Hearings, page 482, and showing that at that time in that plant 36% worked 12 hours, 16.4% 11 hours, 25.9% 10 hours and 21.2% 8 hours.

The Interchurch Report, however, raises the point that whereas these figures doubtless include the 13 and 14-hour workers among the 12-hour workers, it suspects that they also probably included the group of workers who work 13 or 14 hours on alternating weeks but who happened to be working only 10 or 11 hours the week on which these figures were based, as 10-hour workers, whereas they average 12 hours a week and should be added to the 12-hour workers.   It appears from the afore-mentioned footnote that the Interchurch Commission took this suspicion up with Judge Gary in connection with Mr. Oursler's figures and his own figures. It also appears that Judge Gary answered these letters, discussing this point, with regard to Mr. Oursler's figures and his own figures.   From these letters this footnote quotes a few isolated sentences and phrases from which it seeks to show that Judge Gary became so mixed up in trying to answer this point that the figures which he gives in reply are a self-evident admission that the Interchurch Report suspicions are correct.   Therefore the Interchurch Report argues, a large proportion of his 10-hour workers—it estimates about 15%—should be subtracted from his 10-hour workers and added to his 36.2% (based on steel manufacturing only) of admitted 12-hour workers, making a total of over 50% for the industry.   The merits of such an argument cannot of course be determined one way or the other from a few isolated phrases of otherwise unpublished correspondence.   From the very nature of the case, however, the following is obvious.

The Steel Corporation's figures of course cannot attempt to follow the various changes in hours of the individual worker but doubtless represent the hours being worked by different percentages of all workers at a given time.   The most that is possible therefore is that these figures might represent as 10-hour workers that *half* of the 10 to 14-hour workers (or 11-13-hour workers) which were working 10 hours at the time.   But in order for these to make up its alleged 50% of 12-hour workers, the Interchurch Report must reckon this *half* of uneven shift workers—that is, workers who work 10 hours one week and 14 the next—as 15% of all workers, which would make a total of such uneven shift workers of 30% of all the workers in the industry, reducing the even 12-hour shift workers to 20% or only two-thirds of the odd shift workers. But it is a matter of the commonest knowledge and of plain common sense that the odd shift worker is the exception and not the rule, the odd shift being a bookkeeping and general inconvenience, only due to special circumstances. As a matter of fact, the number of such workers is so entirely negligible that neither the 500-page Bureau of Labor Bulletin 218, entirely devoted to a minute and detailed study of steel hours and which does take up the 7.11,[1] the 9- and the 11-hour classifications, or the U. S. Labor Bulletin of October, 1919, or Judge Gary or Mr. Patterson or any known statistician in regard to steel working hours, give any separate consideration or even mention to such a class.

The strong probability is that the official U. S. Steel Corporation figures included the comparatively small number of such odd shift workers, who are obviously 12-hour workers, in the 12-hour class. As a matter of fact Judge Gary is quoted in one of the sentences from his unpublished letters to the effect that, "The percentage given of 36% is not correct if the percentage was intended to indicate those who work straight 12-hour turns. The number of these straight 12-hour turn men is 26%," which indicates that odd turn men who average 12 hours are included as a matter of course under 12-hour workers. But even if they were not, one-half of such odd turn workers could hardly change the Steel Corporation figures appreciably.

Tendency of Steel Hours

In addition to trying to establish its conclusion that approximately 50% of steel employees worked the 12-hour

[1] 42.8 hours per week.

day by arguments *based on what it alleges were current conditions* the Interchurch Report also makes by far its most lengthy and emphasized argument in regard to the 12-hour day as follows: It states (page 54):

"In May, 1910, the percentage of employees working 72 hours[1] and over per week, i.e. at least 12 hours a day, was 42.58% [ibid. Vol. I p. xlii]." Ibid. refers to Senate Document 110.

With this 42% established for 1910 it then proceeds to argue that steel hours in general and 12-hour workers in particular, had so increased "in a decade" as to make its conclusion that in 1919 50% worked 12 hours an inevitable conclusion.   The Interchurch Report attempts to establish this increase in steel working hours in general and in the percentage of 12-hour workers in particular, by voluminous alleged quotation from Senate Document 110 and U. S. Bureau of Labor Statistics Monthly Review October, 1919.

In its general summary of these alleged statistics, the Interchurch Report says (page 71):

" . . . we have [figures from Senate Document 110 and October Monthly Review U. S. Bureau of Labor Statistics]:

Average steel week—1910 . . . . .67.6 hours
Average steel week—1919 . . . . .68.7 hours

"That is ten years of reduction has *increased* the number of hours. . . ."
"Take the figures for 1914 and 1919:

	1914	1919
Common labor—hours per week	70.3	74
Skilled and semi-skilled—hours per week	57	66
All employees—hours per week	66.3	68.7 "

"In each classification the length of the week has *increased*."
"Take the seventy-nine separate occupations in the steel industry for which statistics are given by the U. S. Bureau of Labor Statistics and

[1] Throughout this section the Interchurch Report's definition of 12-hour workers, i.e. those working 72 hours a week, and its use of the term "all employees," etc., in connection with figures which actually represent only primary production departments, is necessarily adopted.   It will be noted that in the independent discussion of steel working hours in Chapter XI a different basis is used.

compare 1914 and 1919. In eighteen classes, hours have decreased; in four remained stationary; *in fifty-seven of the seventy-nine classes hours per week have increased. . . .*" (Italics those of the Interchurch Report.)

These tables, under analysis, show on their face, without reference to the original figures which they allege to quote that they are entirely false and manipulated. The Conclusions that are stated on the basis of these careful manipulations are provably false from merely a little careful study of the tables themselves just as they are printed. When reference is made to the original sources from which these statistics are specifically quoted, it appears that from the first figure quoted—67.6 hours as the average steel week in 1910, through the last figure quoted—that "in 57 of the 79 classes hours per week have increased," every single figure as given, is either in itself or in its use absolutely false. Senate Document 110 is the source for all 1910 figures. The U. S. Bureau of Labor, October, 1919, study is the source for figures from 1913 to "1919." Senate Document 110 (page xliii) gives *69.8* hours as the average steel week in 1910, shows on that page exactly how it arrives at this average and establishes and uses this figure throughout. But 69.8 hours for 1910 is so much higher than any weighting or any manipulation outside of actual forgery can make the figures for "1919" even appear, that to use the official government figure 69.8 for 1910 would at once *ipso facto* disprove the whole Interchurch Report argument that steel hours were lengthening. The Interchurch Report without comment, changes this 69.8 to 67.6 and quotes that as the official figure. The way in which it obviously arrives at this 67.6 is very interesting. Senate Document 110, page xliii, gives its general summary as to steel working hours in 1910 for 14 departments. This table shows average working hours in each of these 14 principal departments, weighted according to the relative number of workers per occupation within the department. At the bottom of the table is given the average—weighted according to the relative number of workers per department for the industry—69.8. This is the only average given or suggested and it is used throughout the original document. By going through those same figures, however, and leaving *in* the weighting by occupations but taking *out* the weighting by departments the result is 67.6—the Interchurch Report figure.

U. S. Bureau of Labor Statistics, October, 1919, study gives the average hours worked per week for 81 occupations throughout the industry in 1913, 1914, 1915, 1917 and "1919." It itself gives no averages for departments or for the industry.

The figures 66.3, given by the Interchurch Report table as the average working hours per week for the industry in 1914, is the straight mathematical average without any weighting whatever of the working hours for these 81 occupations for that year. The unweighted average of the working hours for these same 81 occupations for "1919" is 66.1. But this figure is lower than even the Interchurch Report figure for 1910 and also than its figure for 1914. It shows *ipso facto* that steel working hours were distinctly and consistently shortening. The Interchurch Report by heavily and illegitimately over-weighting these figures (see chapter XI) gets 68.7 and represents that as an official government figure for average steel working hours in "1919." It is of course understandable that those lacking statistical training might take government figures as given and use them incorrectly. But to be able to detect that government figures, which as given refute a particular conclusion may by reweighting of part of the detailed statistics, be so changed as to seem to support that conclusion, obviously shows an intimate knowledge of statistics. What is shown by the fact that the figure thus arrived at is offered without comment as the official government figure, must be left to the judgment of the reader.

In connection with the Interchurch Report's final alleged quotation from the U. S. Bureau of Labor figures, however, the case is not complicated by the question of weighting or any other technical details. The Interchurch Report states that:

"Take the seventy-nine separate occupations in the steel industry for which statistics are given by the U. S. Bureau of Labor Statistics and compare 1914 and 1919. In eighteen classes hours have decreased; in four remained stationary; *in fifty-seven of the seventy-nine classes hours per week have increased. . . .*"

The Interchurch Report thus specifies the figures *by occupations* which is exactly the way the U. S. Bureau of Labor study gives them. The figures as the Interchurch Report alleges to quote them do not in any way remotely resemble the original figures. Not a single figure is the same or near enough the same to be in any way reconciled with the original. As far as their having any relation with the plain detailed U. S. Bureau of Labor figures as to "total" increases and decreases of steel working hours by occupations, which they specifically allege to quote, the Interchurch figures are made out of whole cloth.

The U. S. Bureau of Labor Statistics study in its Monthly Review for October, 1919, to which the Interchurch Report specifically refers, is presented for the express purpose of showing the increases and decreases in working hours for various classes of steel workers from 1913 through the war. The pages are 104 to 126. The majority of the statistics throughout the entire Interchurch Report are taken from these particular pages and a comparison between the Interchurch figures throughout its 12-hour chapter and these original tables shows that those responsible for the Interchurch "statistics" have gone through these U. S. Bureau of Labor figures with a fine tooth comb to pick out and publish each extreme case, and are otherwise thoroughly familiar with them.

The U. S. Bureau of Labor Statistics divides this study into two parts. On pages 107 to 123 it lists the different classes of workers in 6 large representative departments of the steel industry. For each of these 81 (not 79) classes, it gives the full time working hours and the hourly rate of pay for the years 1913, 1914, 1915, 1917, and "1919," i.e. as already explained chiefly for December, 1918 and January, 1919 just at the end of the war and at the statistical peak of steel war activity. It gives these detailed figures for each such class of workers in each section of the country then for the country as a whole.

On pages 124, 125 and 126 the U. S. Bureau of Labor Statistics itself then recapitulates and summarizes the relative increase or decrease of working hours and hourly wage rates for each of these 81 classifications for the whole country, using percentages to make the relative increases or decreases simpler and plainer. Not only are the true facts thus made as plain and simple as they can be made but the results are stated in two different ways—actual figures and percentages—so that they can be double checked.

The Open Hearth department is the one in connection with which the Interchurch Report condemns the 12-hour day most specifically and in regard to which it quotes isolated figures and instances most frequently. The full U. S. Bureau of Labor Statistics figures, showing the relative length of working hours for 1913, 1914, 1915, 1917 and "1919" for all classes of Open Hearth workers for the whole country, are as follows:

U. S. BUREAU OF LABOR STATISTICS

MONTHLY REVIEW, OCTOBER, 1919, PAGE 125

Open Hearth Furnaces

RELATIVE FULL TIME HOURS

Occupation	1913	1914	1915	1917	"1919"
Stockers.................	100	99	99	100	96
Stock Cranemen..........	100	99	98	98	91
Charging Machine Operators	100	99	100	99	94
Malters' Helpers:					
1st "	100	98	98	99	91
2nd "	100	97	97	99	94
3rd "	100	99	100	99	95

Occupation	1913	1914	1915	1917	"1919"
Stopper Setters............	100	97	97	97	92
Steel Pourers.............	100	99	98	99	91
Mold Cappers............	100	99	97	98	94
Ladle Cranemen..........	100	99	98	99	93
Ingot Strippers...........	100	100	100	93	88
Laborers................	100	91	93	98	95

It will be noted that there is not a single class of workers in this entire 12-hour department for the whole country that was not working shorter hours at the height of the war period than it worked in 1913, and only one class which was not working shorter hours at the peak of steel war activity than in 1914.

Figured on the basis of the detailed tables of actual hours given in the first part, and checked with the percentages given in the second part of the U. S. Bureau of Labor Statistics tables, and thus double checked, the increases and decreases of steel working hours in each of the 81 given classifications in the 6 given departments between the year 1913 and "1919" (i.e., chiefly in December, 1918 and January, 1919 the peak of steel war activity) were as follows:

"For all classes of workers given, the hours:
In *Blast Furnace*,

    4 increased;   10 decreased:
In *Open Hearth*,

                        12 decreased:
In *Bloom Mills*,

                        12 decreased:
In *Bessemer*,

    11 increased;   8 decreased:
In *Plate Mills*,

    10 increased;   2 decreased:
In *Sheet Mills*,

    11 increased; 1 remained same:
Total for all classes given,

    36 increased; 1 remained same; 44 decreased.

The United States Bureau of Labor Statistics itself bases its study in both sections on 1913 as the norm.   During the last of 1914, there was a panic; the N. Y. Stock Exchange closed for months; for the latter months of this year work was slack and full time hours in all industry inclined to be shorter. For this reason statisticians generally use either the first part of 1914 or 1913 as norm for this period as does the U. S. Bureau of Labor Statistics in this case. This 1914 depression, however, means that a comparison of hours in any industry between 1914 and the end of the war would show the maximum variation. The Interchurch Report without comment, omits the 1913 figure and uses the U. S. Bureau of Labor Statistics tables with 1914 for the norm. But even on this basis the results are only slightly different and do not in any way resemble the purely fictitious statistics which the Interchurch Report gives and signs with the U. S. Bureau of Labor Statistics' name.

A comparison of length of steel working hours between *1914* and "1919" made and double checked on the same basis as above shows that:

"For all classes of workers given, the hours:
In *Blast Furnaces,*
 5 increased; 1 remained same; 8 decreased:
In *Open Hearth,*
 1 increased; 11 decreased:
In *Bloom Mills,*
 1 increased; 11 decreased:
In *Bessemer,*
 10 increased; 9 decreased:
In *Plate Mills,*
 12 increased;
In *Sheet Mills,*
 11 increased; 1 remained same;
Total for all classes given,
 40 increased; 2 remained same; 39 decreased.

The Interchurch Report states, and signs the Bureau of Labor Statistics' name to the allegation, that:
57 increased, 4 remained stationary; 18 decreased.

There isn't a single Interchurch Report figure even remotely similar to the original and no addition or subtraction or recombination of the component groups of the original U. S. Bureau of Labor figures can make them even approximate those which the Interchurch Report quotes as U. S. Bureau of Labor figures *nor are the figures for any district or group* as given in the stated original. Both the degree of the discrepancy and the nature of the discrepancy is such that there is no possibility that it could have been caused by typographical or mathematical error.

But no study of these voluminous tables of the U. S. Bureau of Labor Statistics can fail to reveal the far more serious discrepancy between the real government figures and the whole 12-hour argument which the Interchurch Report seeks to build up around these very government figures themselves, partly by thus making figures out of whole cloth and signing the government's name to them; partly by picking out the most extreme cases; and partly through an ingenious manipulation and falsification of tables embodying these extreme figures which will be emphasized shortly.

The most obvious thing shown by the real totals of the original U. S. Bureau of Labor figures as to increases and decreases of working hours for all these 6 representative departments is that for the whole 81 occupations given, the number in which working hours *increased*—between either 1913 or 1914 and the peak of steel war activity—and the number in which working hours *decreased*, were about equal. The most obvious thing about the tables themselves—using either 1913 or 1914 for the norm—is that in the first 3 departments the overwhelming tendency was towards *decreased* working hours, in the fourth the increases and decreases about balanced; while in the last two the overwhelming tendency was towards *increased* working hours during the war.

The U. S. Bureau of Labor Statistics in showing the figures for 6 representative departments in the industry, selects as the first two—Blast Furnace and Open Hearth— the chief 12-hour departments of the industry. Its tables for these two 12-hour departments (pages 107 and 110 *ibid.*)

show that for all classes of workers in all parts of the country, the working hours for the years given (1913–1919) increased or decreased as follows:

12-HOUR DEPARTMENTS

	Hours Increased	Remained Same	Hours Decreased
Blast Furnace..........	4		10
Open Hearth..........			12
Total...............	4		22

In thus giving figures for representative departments of the steel industry the U. S. Bureau of Labor Statistics next selects—in the Bloom Mill, Bessemer, and Plate Mill departments—three departments which represent the "middle section" as to working hours, including chiefly 10- and 11-hour workers but including also some 8-hour and some 12-hour workers. Summaries of all the figures given on pages 110 to 121 of the Monthly Review, October, 1919, for these departments, show, for all classes of workers in all parts of the country (1913–"1919"), the following:

"MIDDLE GROUP" DEPARTMENTS

	Hours Increased	Remained Same	Hours Decreased
Bloom Mills............			12
Bessemer.............	11		8
Plate Mills.............	10		2
Totals..............	21		22

These middle group departments, as stated, are made up of 8, 10, 11, and 12 hour workers. Of the 43 occupations of this group, 12 were working approximately 12 hours (70 hours or more per week) in 1913. For all such workers increases and decreases of hours were as follows:

Bloom Mill:	1913	"1919"
Heaters...................	71.2	67.5
Bottom Maker.............	71.9	64.9
" " Helper.......	72	67.4
Laborers..................	73.1	69.6

Bessemer:

Bottom Makers.............	73.8	64.8
Bottom Makers Helpers.....	73.1	70.3
Ladle Liners Helpers........	70.9	71.6
Stopper Makers...........	70.6	70
Laborers..................	75.2	71.1

Plate Mill:

Charging Mach. Oper.......	70.7	71.1
Roll Engineers.............	72.4	72.1
Heaters...................	71.7	70.6

2 increased,   10 decreased

Of all the 81 occupations for which detailed figures as to working hours are thus given by the U. S. Bureau of Labor study, 14 occupations in blast furnaces, 12 occupations in the open hearth, and 12 occupations in the "middle group" departments—a total of 38 occupations—worked approximately 12 hours a day in 1913. Of all these the working hours for *6 increased* in "1919" the peak of steel war activity, while working hours for *32* of the 38 *decreased.*

Moreover among the entire 81 occupations given, there is no case shown of any group of workers which worked less than 12 hours in 1913 having become 12-hour workers even at the peak of steel war activity.

In this connection it is also interesting to note that in all 81 occupations given, in only 6 did hours increase more than 5% even at the height of war activity. The largest increase was that for the Bessemer Stopper Setter who worked 51.6 hours in 1913, 50.7 hours in 1914, 51.5 hours in 1915, 49.6 in 1917, and then jumped to 59.8 at the peak of war activity. The second largest increase—9%—was for blast furnace common labor which had previously worked consistently 12 hours or less a day 6 days a week but which during the height of war activity averaged about half a day on Sunday. Sheet Mill Shearmen Helpers also increased their working hours by 9% going from 42.9 hours per week to 46.6 at the height of war activity. Bessemer Cupola Tappers **and**

Bessemer Vesselmen Helpers increased their hours by 8% and Mold Cappers by 7%, the increases being from 54 to 59 hours, from 56 to 61, and from 57 to 61 hours respectively at the height of war activity.

Finally in giving figures for 6 representative departments of the industry the U. S. Bureau of Labor Statistics selects one of the short hour departments—the Sheet Mill where normal working hours are 42.8 per week. Detailed figures as to working hours for this whole department appear on page 76 of the present analysis.

It is entirely apparent then in regard to this general conclusion of the Interchurch Report, alleging that for the separate occupations in the steel industry for which statistics are given by the U. S. Bureau of Labor Statistics, . . . in eighteen classes hours have decreased; in four remained stationary (and) in 57 . . . increased, that it is not only made out of whole cloth and states almost the opposite of what the U. S. Bureau of Labor figures actually show; but it is equally plain that the whole conclusion which the Interchurch Report seeks to draw from these figures, namely that the percentage of 12-hour workers is increasing, is the opposite of the facts. The facts are that for all the 38 12-hour occupations given for all departments given, in only 6 did hours increase while for *32* hours *decreased.* It is equally clear that the departments whose working hours did increase during the war were the shorter hour departments.

So much for the years 1913 or 1914—to "1919."

It will be remembered, however, that the Interchurch Report in seeking to emphasize the increase in the percentage of 12-hour workers repeatedly insists that steel working hours have lengthened *over a decade.* On page 46 it states:

"Examination of government statistics . . . proves that the hours in the steel industry have actually lengthened *since 1910* . . . (and that the industry has shown an) *unrestricted tendency* toward lengthened hours."

And again (page 56):

"Five years ago the steel week was 2.4 hours shorter; *ten years ago* 1.1 hours shorter. Steel hours have lengthened *in a decade.*"

But this very statement contradicts itself and the Interchurch Report's whole hypothesis that steel hours "have lengthened" and shown an "unrestricted tendency to lengthen," etc., "in a decade" for it itself states that steel hours actually shortened by 1.3 a week during the first half of the decade and right up into the war. Moreover this fact is entirely apparent in every table the Interchurch Report gives in regard to these years.

There are two particular tables it will be remembered which the Interchurch Report uses to attempt to clinch this argument that steel hours in general, and the number of 12 hour-workers in particular, have increased over a decade. They are as follows (page 71):

" . . . we have [figures from Senate Document 110 and U. S. Bureau of Labor Statistics Monthly Review, October, 1919]:

Average steel week 1910...............67.6 hours
Average steel week 1919...............68.7 hours
"That is ten years of reduction has *increased* the number of hours. ...."
"Take the figures for 1914 and 1919:

	1914	1919
Common labor hours per week.........	70.3	74
Skilled and semi-skilled hours per week...	57	66
All employees hours per week..........	66.3	68.7"

"In each classification the length of the week has *increased.*"

The first thing to be noted about these two tables is that, just as in all similar cases, they group statistics for 1910 and "1919" separately from statistics for 1914 and "1919" so that the figures for 1910 and 1914 never appear together. In other cases the Interchurch Report separates by 16 or 18 pages the group 1910 and "1919" from the group 1914 and "1919." In this case it will be noted these two groups are put in an entirely different form. The second is complicated by two other groups of figures and the common denominator in the two tables is called "average steel week" in one, and "all employees" in the other. Taking the figures for this common denominator however, just as they appear in these tables, and putting them in their natural chronological order, the following appears

"Average steel week" "all employees" 1910..........67.6 hours
"Average steel week" "all employees" 1914..........66.3 hours
"Average steel week" "all employees" "1919"........68.7 hours

In other words these very figures which the Interchurch Report itself publishes show on their face that the Interchurch Report's whole argument about the tendency of steel hours to lengthen over a decade is untrue because they show on their face that for the first half of the decade, and up into the war, steel hours actually shortened.

It has already been pointed out that the figure which Senate Document 110 itself gives as the average steel week in 1910 is not 67.6 hours but is 69.8 hours, and that the Interchurch Report obviously arrives at this 67.6 which it gives, by a partial reweighting of the original government statistics. It has also been pointed out that the Interchurch figure of 66.3 hours as the average steel week for 1914 represents a plain mathematical average without any weighting at all, while its figure of 68.7 for "1919" is made two hours higher than the unweighted average by a heavy, illegitimate over-weighting. Fortunately, however, the proof of the absolute falsity of these figures does not depend on technical discussions of involved statistical methods because that falsity becomes entirely obvious the moment the Interchurch Report attempts to use those figures in any detail, as it does in the second table above.

It will be noted that there are two extra sets of figures in the second Interchurch Report table under discussion—those in the first line alleging that in "1919" common labor worked 3.7 hours a week longer than in 1914, and those in the second line alleging that skilled and semi-skilled steel

workers worked 9 hours a week longer in "1919" than in
1914. Common, and skilled and semi-skilled labor of
course make up all the classes of which "all employees" are
composed. The unweighted average between the 3.7 by
which common labor hours are stated to have thus increased
a week, and the 9 hours by which skilled and semi-skilled
hours are thus stated to have increased a week, is 6.3 hours.
But the number of classifications of all workers given by the
U. S. Bureau of Labor statistics, and which enter into the
averages, run from 11 to 18 for skilled and semi-skilled to 1
for common labor. In other words any "weighting" on this
basis must be all in favor of the 9 hours. Also there are of
course more skilled and semi-skilled workers than common.
The Interchurch Report itself insists on page 92 that the
proportion is 61.9% for skilled and semi-skilled to 38.1%
for common. Again any "weighting" must be entirely in
favor of the 9. In other words, the first two lines of this
table show an average increase of working hours for all
classes of steel workers between 1914 and "1919" of something above 6.3 hours a week. Yet the next line of this same
Interchurch Report table specifically says that the increase
for all workers was from 66.3 to 68.7 or just 2.4 hours.
There is no possible average between 3 and 9 that makes 2.

Plainly then these figures, which are specifically quoted as
from the "October Monthly Review U. S. Bureau of Labor
Statistics" are not only fictitious in that they do not themselves appear among the original government figures; in
that they specifically contradict everything that the original
government figures do show, and therefore cannot by any
legitimate means have been derived from the original figures,
but by assuming to show that the average between 3 and 9 is
2 they are fictitious on their face.

The 12-hour argument is the one most emphasized
throughout the entire Interchurch Report. It has been the
most widely emphasized and quoted in connection with the
Interchurch Report. The second volume of the Interchurch
Report, appearing a year and a half after the Report proper,

again particularly stresses its 12-hour allegation. The very great publicity given this argument as well as its own importance warrant particular emphasis being placed on the fact that it is based throughout on the above type of "evidence," presented with a constant, studied ingeniousness in seeking to achieve surface plausibility, and bound together largely with insinuations and sensational anonymous statements.

CHAPTER X

THE NATURE OF TWELVE-HOUR WORK

ON page 64 the Interchurch Report quotes from an individual anonymous steel worker's diary, as follows:

"You lift a large sack of coal on your shoulders, run toward the white-hot steel in a 100-ton ladle, must get close enough without burning your face off to hurl the sack, using every ounce of strength, into the ladle and run, as flames leap to roof and the heat blasts everything to the roof. Then you rush out to the ladle and madly shovel manganese into it, as hot a job as can be imagined." "And this," adds the Interchurch Report, "is not the worst of his daily grind."

The Senate Committee went particularly into the question of the nature of the 12-hour work, and brought out the point strongly through the testimony of various steel officials and 12-hour workers themselves—including strikers—that such work was far from continuous.

"Mr. Gary submitted to the Senate Committee photographs of open hearth laborers at leisure," *says the Interchurch Report on page 64,* "and asserted that they worked but half the time. This hardly accords with the open hearth laborer himself."

It is in specific answer to at least this part of the Senate evidence and to its own question, "What kind of jobs are these 12-hour turns," that the Interchurch Report published this quotation "from a worker's diary" as part of five pages of similar quotations interspersed with generalizations from them in which it seeks to picture the steel mill as a veritable inferno of flaming furnaces and molten metal and of the crash and grind of "man-killing" machines, in the midst of which the worker slaves to the point of "daily exhaustion" and "old age at forty."

In view of the fact that the Interchurch Report devotes much attention to building up such an impression of steel work and largely on the basis of this impression character- izes steel hours as "relics of barbarism" and demands that the church and the public and the government join with "organized" labor in forcing their change, it is particularly pertinent to examine the evidence on which it contradicts much of the Senate evidence and attempts to support its charges.

Throughout this chapter and in fact throughout the whole volume, the Interchurch Report reiterates such charges as that "steel is a man-killer"— that "absentee cor- poration control" tends "inevitably to sacrifice the labor force"—that it is steel policy to "grind the faces of the hunkies," etc., but its "evidence" consists of these five pages of quotations from "workers' diaries."

These "diaries" are presented in 15 separate quotations, spread, with intervening comment and argument, over pages 60 through 64 and it appears upon careful examination that all of them are parts of the diaries of two men. There is no question that taken at face value, these diaries constitute the bitterest arraignment of the conditions they describe. Moreover the first diary is alleged to describe not merely the author's own experience but is expressly featured as "the observations of a keen man on how his fellows regard the job," and the second diary is specifically featured as describing general working conditions. The second alleged author, while stating that the conditions described were in an "independent" and not a Steel Corporation plant, also states that he worked for the Corporation and alleges that conditions there were even more harrowing.

The Interchurch Report especially emphasizes that the first of these diaries "was in the spring of 1919, before the strike or this inquiry and selected here because no charge of exaggeration could be made concerning it" and repeats again in regard to both of them that "these workers' records were made before the strike began and are open to no possible charge of bias." But of course the strike agitation was at its height during this period.

The Interchurch Report also especially emphasizes that— "both of these workers were distinctly critical of labor organizers." The Interchurch Report, however, in other sections emphasizes that many of the strikers were distinctly critical of their leaders as too conservative. The Interchurch Report does not state that these alleged authors were not strikers or in any way connected with the strike movement which would be the simplest way of stating as a fact what it tries to convey as an impression. In view of the fact that these five pages of quotations constitute the chief evidence which the Interchurch Report produces to show that 12-hour steel work is a "relic of barbarism," which the church and the public and the government should unite in abolishing, and particularly in view of the fact that not only statements but quotations of the Interchurch Report have already been shown, when compared with the actual facts or with the sources of the quotation, to be highly misleading, meticulous inquiry into the actual value of such major "evidence" can hardly be regarded as unjustified.

Again these diaries are anonymous. This fact may be explained on the ground of protecting the authors. On the other hand it is well known that strike agitators were busy both before and during the strike, creating or highly exaggerating and coloring "evidence" of all kinds for prop-aganda uses. When many of the "statements and affidav-its of 500 steel workers [which] constitute the rock bottom evidence of the [Interchurch] findings," as these are pub-lished in the Second Volume, are analyzed, it appears, as will be shown later in detail, that they consist in large part of such doctored propaganda "evidence," originated and circulated for such propaganda purposes, yet published by the Interchurch Report as "rock bottom evidence," even in some cases after the "author" under oath and cross-examination by the Senate Committee had admitted the essential falsity of his whole previous statement.[1]

Moreover in certain very significant particulars the second of these diaries closely parallels other standard propaganda "evidence" that was widely circulated in preparation for and during the strike in that it gets a large part of its effect through vivid insinuation rather than direct statement that can be directly controverted. One of the most widely circulated strike propaganda documents, for instance, contains the statement that the author "personally walked out into the middle of the street *to stop these men* (police) and ask them what did they mean *by clubbing peaceful worshippers* leaving the church" and one of the Interchurch Report's own "rock bottom affidavits" declares: "there was no provocation for (the police) . . . riding over women and children." Yet under oath and cross-examination it was admitted that the first man never saw anybody clubbed and only knew of one man being clubbed during the strike and in the second case, it was admitted that no women or children were actually ridden over or hurt at all. This Interchurch "diary" keeps repeating, "it is easy for a man to get badly burned"—"it is easy to burn your face off"—"operations if performed in wrong order, stove tender will break his stove and kill himself"—"unless tremendous pressure is first blown off the opening of another valve will blow operators to bits," etc., etc., without even alleging that any man ever did actually get "his face burned off" or "get blown to bits," etc. To any one who has read the "statements" and "affidavits" after "statements" and affidavits in the Interchurch second volume which consist of the most harrowing insinuations and exclamations but which carefully avoid actually alleging a single fact this similar method of getting an impression without any direct statement cannot pass unnoticed.[1]

Again the Interchurch Report quotes the "author" of this "diary" as insisting that in a "former job" "last spring"—

[1] See chapter XXIII present analysis.

"everyone in the department works 14 working days out of every fourteen calendar days, on the 13-hour night turn, including the 24-hour turn within the 14 days" . . . a "total 104 hours (including dinner), . . . 107 hours under the plant roof in the 168 hours in the week."

Such an allegation as to hours—over 15 hours a day 7 days a week, for a whole steel department, goes so far beyond even any other allegation which has been made public that in spite of the Interchurch Report's insistence that this "diary" "is open to no possible charge of bias," it seems unfortunate that other evidence as to such working hours for a whole department should not have been immediately gathered by some of the 15 Interchurch investigators which would not have had to be presented unsupported and anonymously.

But whatever credence the individual reader may, under the circumstances, choose to place in such evidence, the fact cannot be overlooked that even this bitterly hostile witness admits the highly intermittent nature of 12-hour work. He does this indirectly by complaining that he does not always have "four or five hours to himself" or that cleaning a blast furnace stove, a hot job but one which from the very nature of blast furnace operation is never done more than once in 6 days, takes "from ten minutes to one hour," etc.

As a matter of fact, the evidence is plain that work in the primary departments—where the 12-hour day exists—is inherently intermittent and, from its very nature cannot be "consciously speeded up" because of "war" or "steel demand" or for any other reason.

U. S. Bureau of Labor Statistics Monthly Labor Review for June, 1920 contains a study of "hazard" in the steel industry. This was a study of conditions during war times when of course all the "speeding up" possible was done, yet referring specifically to 1918 this bulletin emphasizes on page 156–1462:

"The operation of such mills as are here grouped—namely, blast furnaces, steel works (open hearth and Bessemer furnaces) and rolling mills—are *necessarily* of a rather *leisurely character* and *cannot in the nature of the case be hurried* sufficiently to increase greatly the hazard of the individual man."

—by exactly the same token these processes are *"neces-sarily"* of such a *"leisurely character"* that they *"cannot in the nature of the case be hurried* sufficiently to" change greatly the leisurely character of the *work* involved.

How "leisurely"—that is how highly intermittent, such work actually is, is plain even from the most casual knowl-edge of the operations of these great 12-hour departments[1] and is brought out particularly clearly in the Senate Hearings and other government studies.

Mr. S. E. Wilson, heater in the Gary Mill, testified (Senate Hearings, Part II, page 1046):

> *Senator Phipps:* How many hours a day do you work?
> *Mr. Wilson:* Twelve hours.
> *Senator Phipps:* Is that continuous?
> *Mr. Wilson:* Oh, no, I suppose my work is so I could do it all in four or five hours if it could be so arranged. It is not any physical work I have to do.

[1] The author of the present analysis lived during boyhood in a suburb adjoining the South Chicago plant of the Illinois Steel Company. The older members of a large proportion of neighbor's families worked in the steel mills. Many of his boyhood friends, including his brother, worked during their high school vacations in the mills—his brother, as a com-mon laborer in the open hearth department. The author remembers distinctly that there was great competition for, and every possible pull was exercised by these boys to get on the straight night shift, because they were almost invariably able to get from 3 to 5 hours' sleep on this shift so that after three or four more hours' sleep in the morning they had the rest of the day free. During his last year in high school, the author's brother had the opportunity to continue indefinitely on night shift work and argued with his parents to be allowed both to go to high school and work this shift on the ground that he could get practically enough sleep due to the intermittent nature of the 12-hour night work.

It is notorious that steel towns are great baseball towns, a big extra patronage always being derived from the night shift workers who nor-mally are up by noon, and have the afternoon free. The United States Steel Corporation, as part of its welfare work, has equipped and main-tains 103 baseball fields, one for practically every community in which it has a plant. These fields are extremely popular. Their large use up to five o'clock on week-day afternoons is obviously by the night shift workers.

Mr. Jospeh Smith, a roller in the Homestead Mills, stated (Senate Report, Vol. I, page 455):

"My age is 58 years old . . . I have been standing a 12-hour day for the last 33 years . . . and while I do not work pretty hard at times, at times I do work pretty hard . . . but we do not actually work the 12 hours. We have a rest for lunch at 9: 30 and again at 12: 30 and in the afternoon we stop to adjust things around the mills."

During their personal visit to the steel centers, the Senate Committee carefully interrogated Superintendent August Mann of the American Steel and Wire Works at Denora in regard to this point as follows (Senate Hearings, page 714–715):

"*Senator Stirling:* Is that same thing true with other workmen who work the 12 hours?

"*Mr. Mann:* Well, they work one half hour and they rest one half hour—the roll hands.

"*Chairman:* And do they have anything to do during that half hour?

"*Mr. Mann:* They work a half hour and another man takes their position the other half hour.

"*Chairman:* Can they go outdoors for a half hour if they wish?

"*Mr. Mann:* Yes, sir, the roll hands—the 'sticker-in.'

"*Senator Phipps:* Take the other men that work the 12 hours a day—other than the rollers, they have one half hour of rest and one half hour of work?

"*Mr. Mann:* Yes, sir. Now the other men, they take their spells out at any given time. A great many of them will sit down at nine o'clock and take lunch. A great many of them will go out to the drinking fountain and sit down there. There is no time given for that but they will take their rest.

"*Chairman:* But they are on duty all this time, are they not?

"*Mr. Mann:* They are on duty all of this time.

"*Chairman:* Subject to call?

"*Mr. Mann:* Yes, sir."

Even Mr. Oscar Edward Anderson, President of the Hustler Lodge Number 36 of the Amalgamated Association of Iron Steel and Tin Workers, and Chairman of the Allied Iron and Steel Workers' Council in Gary, which had charge of the strike in Gary, though he tried to evade and qualify on this point, finally admitted under cross-examination (Senate Hearings, page 959):

Mr. Anderson: But a guide setter does his work whenever he gets a chance—whenever the mill stops rolling for a few minutes or something like that and the rest of the time he would be continually there and watching so that if anything happens he can immediately attend to it.

"*Senator Phipps:* Yes, it is not continuous but is variable according to the conditions of the operation?

"*Mr. Anderson:* Yes, sir."

This statement of Mr. Mann was made to the Senate Committee while it was in the strike area, visiting the different mills and taking a far greater volume of testimony —often on the same points—from workers or strikers than from their employers. It is hardly possible, therefore, for even the most hostile critic to doubt that Mr. Mann's statements were accurate at least as regards conditions in his own plant. Mr. Anderson's statement is of course the admission of a hostile witness. The question remains as to how far conditions thus described are representative of conditions throughout the industry.

Mr. Mann's statement referred specifically to a 12-hour rolling mill *in 1919.* Senate Document 110, Vol. III., page 361, gives two tables for two typical 12-hour rolling mills of the *hand type* which then prevailed, showing in detail the amount of time each class of workers actually worked *in 1910.* Bottom Makers in the first mill actually worked 3 hours and 17 minutes or 28% of their 12 hours on duty. Such workers therefore, had 72% of their time largely to themselves. Chargers worked about 5 hours and had about 7 hours largely to themselves. Roughers and Pitcranemen worked about 7 hours and had about 5 hours of leisure. The various roll-hands however,—which class of workers Mr. Mann stated worked just 6 hours a day in alternating reliefs in 1919—averaged about 10 hours, and in one case 11 hours work out of the 12 in 1910. Moreover, Senate Document 110 refers to these hand rolling departments—obviously meaning these roll-hand occupations—as being most subject of all in the steel industry to the criticism of speeding-up. Just after this however, on page 363, it states:—

" Within the last few years small mechanical rolling mills of the continuous type have been installed in a number of plants throughout the country . . . *in these mills the severe manual labor is almost entirely eliminated,* the work consisting almost entirely of handling levers . . . it is certain that within the next few years small rolling mills of the continuous type will supplant a great many of the hand mills. . . ."

This is precisely what has happened. These "small mechanical rolling mills" have been both enlarged to perform the heaviest rolling and developed to perform the widest variety of rolling, till today they are in almost universal use.   Take the rolled output of the U. S. Steel Corporation for 1920 as an example (see 19th Annual Report, page 15); all steel rails, blooms, plates, heavy shapes, tubing and pipe, and car wheels, as is well known, and 70%[1] of merchant shapes and 50%[1] of wire rods—constituting 8,937,934 tons out of 11,529,955 tons, or 77.5% of rolled products, are rolled in "mechanical mills" in which "*severe manual labor is almost entirely eliminated,* the work consisting almost entirely of the handling of levers."

Of the remaining 22.5% of rolled products two thirds consist of sheet and tin plate which cannot be rolled by the mechanical mill. But the whole department producing such products has for years, as has already been emphasized, worked on a three shift 8 hour schedule of 42.8 hours a week.

There remain certain mills making rod and miscellaneous merchant shapes, to a total of 8.5% of rolled production, which are still of the old fashioned "hand-rolling" variety. In these the other occupations actually work, as shown by Senate Document 110 tables already referred to, only about half of their 12 hours on duty, and for the more continuous roll-hand occupations all such mills now employ 2 men for each occupation who "spell" each other every hour or half hour as described by Mr. Mann.

This, then, is what the U. S. Bureau of Labor Statistics means specifically when it refers to the rolling mills—which together constitute the greater part of the industry—as among the departments where, even in 1918 at the height

[1] Percentages furnished by U. S. Steel Corporation.

of war activity, the work was "*necessarily of a rather leisurely character.*" Moreover the facts are equally plain and specific as to what the U. S. Bureau of Labor Statistics means when it refers to the work in the *furnace departments* which make up the balance of the industry (the term "industry" being used as the Interchurch Report consistently uses it, to mean the primary production departments) as of a "*leisurely character.*"

Mr. Clayton L. Patterson, in discussing the intermittent nature of 12-hour work in furnace departments says, on page 65 of his pamphlet, "Review of the Steel Strike,"—

"Time studies made in the Corporation (U. S. Steel) plants indicated that all employees were actually working an average of 30 to 40% of their time in the *blast furnace* departments and an average of 40 to 55% in the *open-hearth* departments."

In its four pages of quotations from steel workers' diaries, through which the Interchurch Report seeks to build up its specific detailed picture of the awful conditions under which the steel worker "labors to daily exhaustion" and "to old age at forty," it makes its definite references chiefly to the open-hearth departments.

On page 316, Volume III of Senate Document 110, as part of a detailed description of the work performed by all different open hearth workers, appears a detailed table as to the amount of time each different kind of worker has to work under a temperature above normal. It is particularly stated that this study was made during summer when heat was naturally most oppressive and the outside temperature is specifically stated at 84 degrees.

One man[1] in such a department has to work under a temperature of 98 degrees for 8 hours and 45 minutes out of the 12 hours. Two men have to work under a temperature of 126 degrees for 7 minutes at a time, ten times at regular intervals, for a total of one hour and ten minutes

[1] This man is the foreman, no other man in the department has to work as much as 8 hours out of the 12-hour day.

out of the 12 hours. Three men have to work at a temperature of 126 degrees for a period of about 7 minutes three times at intervals or for a maximum total of 30 minutes out of the 12 hours. One man has to work at a temperature of 112 degrees 20 minutes at a time 10 different times or for a total of 3 hours and 20 minutes out of the 12 hours. Two men have to work at a temperature of 112 degrees 20 minutes at a time 6 different times or for a total of 2 hours out of the 12 hours. Three men have to work at a temperature of 108 degrees for 15 minutes at a time 8 different times for a total of 2 hours out of the 12 hours.

Page 355 of Volume III Senate Document 110 shows that for all these different groups of 12-hour workers in an open hearth department, the average time actually spent at *work* is 40.2% while the time actually spent at *rest*—most of which the workers have to themselves, to sleep if it is the night shift, or as the Senate Investigation described, to go out to the fountain and eat or smoke or talk—is 59.8% as follows (last column and unweighted averages computed):

DIVISION OF WORKING DAY INTO ACTIVE TIME AND
IDLE TIME IN THE OPEN HEARTH DEPARTMENT
OF A LARGE STEEL PLANT

Occupations	Hours Per Day			Per Cent. of Time Active	Per Cent. of Time Idle & Observ.
	Total	Active	Idle or Observation		
		H. M.	H. M.		
Charging Machine Operators..........	12	5 06	6 54	43	57
First Helpers..........	12	3 16	8 44	27	73
Second Helpers.........	12	5 31	6 29	46	54
Third Helpers.........	12	4 26	7 34	37	63
Ladle Cranemen........	12	6 12	5 48	52	48
Steel Pourers..........	12	3 36	8 24	30	70
Brake-Men Engineers...	12	5 58	6 02	50	50
Stripper Cranemen.....	12	4 25	7 35	37	63
Average.............	......	4 49	7 11	40.2	59.8

THE problem, as such, of determining what the working hours in the steel industry actually are, or what working hours in industry as a whole actually are, is of no concern in the present analysis whose interest is merely in determining the accuracy of the Interchurch Report. But the Interchurch Report particularly emphasizes that steel working hours are "relics of barbarism . . . which must be compared with hours in other industries of the country" (page 55)—that the steel worker is "being un-Americanized by the 12 hour day" in "scores of thousands" (page 84) and otherwise insists that steel working hours are so different and so much more harmful to the worker than working hours throughout the country that:

"The church and every other American institution has a duty to perform" which "duty cannot be fulfilled till the 12 hour day is abolished" (page 84).

Moreover it here and elsewhere calls upon the church, the public, and the government to force a change in steel working hours which shall bring them down to what it alleges are average American working hours.

It is necessary, therefore, in judging the validity of this very important Interchurch Report charge and demand to determine as accurately as possible under the circumstances what steel working hours actually are and how they compare with the actual working hours of average American workers.

There are four principal sources of information in regard to working hours in the steel industry.

First, Senate Document 110—a 4 volume report of a

most exhaustive study of the steel industry made by the government's own experts which gives detailed figures as to wages and hours of work for each production occupation in 14 steel departments by sections of the country and for the entire industry. This report also goes in the greatest detail into conditions of labor and accident hazard, into methods of operation, into the nature of each different type of job, into the reason for the variation of hours, etc. These figures are for 1910.

Second, U. S. Bureau of Labor Statistics Bulletin 218 published October, 1917. This is a 500 page study as to wages, hours and incidentally working conditions, chiefly for 10 principal representative departments of the industry, giving this information by sections of the country and for the industry as a whole, partly for the 9 year period and partly for the 5 year period up to and including May, 1915. This study is particularly interesting for its own discussion and summaries based on conditions of May, 1915.

Third, U. S. Bureau of Labor Statistics Monthly Review October, 1919 giving first detailed figures as to full time hours per week and earnings per hour for the 81 occupations in 6 representative steel departments for each section of the country and for the industry as a whole, and second, recapitulating this same information in percentages based on 1913 as norm. It gives these figures for 1913, 1914, 1915, 1917 and "1919"—the so-called "1919" figures representing pay roll periods running from June, 1918 to May, 1919 but about two thirds of which were for the months December, 1918 and January, 1919. Except for a brief foreword this study does not itself discuss these figures or give totals or averages except occupation by occupation for the country.

Fourth, the official figures for the U. S. Steel Corporation presented before the Senate Hearings in September, 1919, giving the number of employees and the percentage of employees working different groups of hours for all employees of the U. S. Steel Corporation, the biggest unit in the steel industry.

Of the six representative steel making departments for

which figures are given by U. S. Bureau of Labor statistics October, 1919, study it will be remembered that the Bessemer department is one of what was referred to in Chapter IX as the middle group—in which working hours averaged about 65 a week but which included a certain proportion of 48 hour and 72 hour workers. It will also be remembered that this is the one department given in which increases and decreases in working hours about balanced—between either 1913 or 1914 and "1919," the peak of steel war activity.

By merely setting down each official government figure as to hours per occupation, without any averaging, weighting or other change but just as they are given in the first and third government documents above referred to, it is possible to get such a table as the following:

BESSEMER CONVERTERS

	1910	1911	1912	1913	1914	1915	1917	"1919"
Stockers	65.3			58.1	55.5	55.6	55.3	64
Cupola Chargers	74.8							
Cupola Melters	64.5			62.7	59.5	59.3	61.7	59.4
Cupola Tappers	63.9			54.3	56.9	55.8	54	58.9
Blowing Engineers	74.6							
Blowers	69.7			63.3	64	64	64	63.1
Regulators 1st	67.2			66.4	63.8	64.7	66.8	68.2
" 2nd				68.3	66.5	66.6	67.4	64.4
Vessel Scrapers	71.4							
Vesselmen	59.4			57.8	55.6	56	61.9	60.3
Vesselmen Helpers	58.3			56.4	54.3	55.5	56.5	61.1
Cinder Pitmen	72.6			67.8	71.9	72	72	71
Bottom Makers	70.6			73.8	73	73	72	64.8
Bottom Makers' Helpers	69.2			73.1	72.4	72.6	72	70.3
Ladle Liners	68.3			68.7	68.6	68.8	71.2	69.7
Ladle Liners' Helpers				70.9	69.1	69.5	71.3	71.6
Stopper Makers				70.6	70.2	69.7	67.8	70
Stopper Setters	55.6			51.6	50.7	51.5	49.6	59.8
Steel Pourers	56.6			55.7	52.5	53.5	52.7	58.5
Mold Cappers				56.9	60.8	60.9	54.6	61.1
Ingot Strippers	66.3			69.9	66	66.2	68.7	64.2
Laborers	74.3			75.2	74	74.3	73.4	71.1
Other Occupations	—							
Average	69.5							

It will be noted at once that there are no hours given for the last group of workers listed as "other occupations" at the bottom of the 1910 column. Reference to the original source of these figures (Senate Document 110 pages xliii and 74) show that these "other occupations" consist of electricians and engineers who maintain power, bricklayers who reline furnaces, tool makers, repair men, etc., who constitute 25.3 per cent of the workers of the department. The working hours of these classifications, because of the special technical reason that many of such classes of workers in other industries belong to labor unions, are analyzed separately by Senate Document 110 and not included in the average of working hours for the department. These same or similar classes of occupations in all other departments are also treated separately in Senate Document 110. Therefore the exact extent to which they influence average working hours in each department is not indicated.

Again it will be noted that there is a stated average— 69.5 hours—at the bottom of the 1910 column. This is the government statistician's own *weighted* average of the working hours of the department. Similarly weighted averages are given by Senate Document 110 as to average working hours in each of the 14 departments given and for all these departments.

These 1910 figures given by Senate Document 110 are homogeneous—the result of a single investigation. They are for 14 different departments, much more representative of the industry than 6 departments can be. These 1910 figures therefore, can be fairly weighted and averaged and an approximately accurate figure computed from them as to average working hours throughout at least that part of the whole steel industry which they represent.

The 1913 to "1919" figures on the other hand, are a composite of three different investigations, not only made at different times but involving different proportions of departments, different plants, and different numbers of workers. The figures for 1913, 1914, and 1915 are borrowed from U. S. Bureau of Labor Bulletin 218, a study based on 10 different departments. The 1917 and "1919" figures are based on two other studies each involving but 6 departments. Take the Blast Furnace figures for instance. Those for 1913 are based on pay rolls from 33 plants; those for 1914–1915 from 35 plants; for 1917 from 14 plants; and for "1919" from 20 plants. Yet while the 35 plants in 1915 employed only 878 Blast Furnace Stockers, the 20 plants in "1919" employed 988 stockers. Again while the 8 Bessemer plants in 1917 employed 30 Regulators, 9 Bessemer plants in "1919" employed 23 Regulators. This same discrepancy in the average number of workers per occupation—due chiefly to the fact that the figures represent different plants, appears throughout. Again figures are given for three times as many Blast Furnaces as for Sheet Mills whereas at least the Steel Corporation, for which definite figures are available, have more Sheet Mills than Blast Furnaces.[1] The Bureau of Labor figures give specifically the average hours worked each different year by each of 81 representative *occupations*—that is they say definitely that Bessemer Blowers throughout the country worked 64.1 hours in 1914 and 63.1 hours in "1919," that Sheet Mill Shearmen worked 42.9 hours in 1914 and 43.5 hours in "1919," etc., etc. But because of the facts above emphasized, to weight figures so limited and so non-homogeneous to attempt to arrive at an actual working week for the theoretical average individual worker for the whole industry would be so subject to error that it cannot fairly be done and the government statisticians themselves have refused to do it. There are therefore no government figures as to working hours in terms of the average individual worker since 1910, and no figures from which such an average can be fairly computed.

Moreover these various government figures are based on 6 departments, 10 departments and 14 departments. But

[1] Average number employees per Blast Furnace (1919) 314; per Sheet Mill 397.

the 14 departments do not include either Sheet Mill or Tin Plate Mill which are included in the studies based on the lesser number of departments. Thus even the most extensive government report makes no pretence of being more than a study of a limited number of representative iron and steel making departments. How limited these studies are is at once evident from reference to any Annual Report of the U. S. Steel Corporation. The 1919 Report, page 46 for instance, shows that in this single unit in the steel industry, over 40 various iron and steel making departments are listed.

Again while in the U. S. Bureau of Labor, October, 1919, study Blast Furnaces are listed as 1 of 6 departments and their extremely long hours influence any averages accordingly, in the case of the U. S. Steel Corporation, not only do Blast Furnaces represent merely 1 out of 40 odd different types of departments but in the total of departments of all kinds there are only a total of 124 Blast Furnaces out of a total of over 1400 iron and steel making departments. Again the U. S. Bureau of Labor, October, 1919, study lists the long hour Blast Furnace and the short hour Sheet Mill departments equally as one each of 6 representative departments. Moreover it gives figures for three times as many Blast Furnaces as Sheet Mills. But the Corporation records show that its 124 12-hour Blast Furnace departments, are much more than offset by its 155 "Sheet Jobbing and Plate Mill departments" and 222 "Hot Mills Black Plate for Tinning" in which departments the 7 and 8 hour day prevails.

Finally the last U. S. Industrial Census (1914) shows (Abstract page 96), 1,061,058 iron and steel workers in the country of which 29,356 Blast Furnace workers represent only about 3%. At the time of the steel strike the term iron and steel industry was generally used to mean that half of the industry which both produces and manufactures steel and which employes about 500,000 workers. Even if Blast Furnace workers increased 50% during the war they still represented less than 10% of the industry so inter-preted.

In other words it is plain that in an industry in which the smaller units have at least a dozen different departments, the largest unit over 40 departments and the industry as a whole at least 50 or 60 departments (see footnote); in which working hours vary from 42 to 72 per 6-day week, no approximation of average working hours for the industry as a whole is possible without an interpretation of what is included in the industry.

Because of this and because the Interchurch Report continually confuses 12-hour workers with 12-hour depart-ments, a clear understanding of the relation between the different iron and steel making departments and the rela-tion between the working hours of the various departments and the working hours of many groups of employees in these departments, which are frequently very different, is corre-spondingly necessary.

Iron and steel making departments may be roughly divided into two groups—the primary departments which through a series of carefully synchronized operations smelt the ore and process it in a continuously hot state into various semi-finished iron and steel products,—and the finishing departments which take up these semi-finished products cold and convert them into their finished forms.

Blast Furnace

The basic key department in all primary iron and steel making is the Blast Furnace which converts iron ore by use of coke and limestone into pig iron. To shut down and relight a Blast Furnace costs up to $50,000 and takes two weeks' time. This department must operate therefore day and night 7 days a week. As has already been shown

[1] In the official list of its 40 principal kinds of departments the Steel Cor-poration does not show Puddling Mills, Garret Rod Mills, or Crucible Fur-nace departments, all listed among the 14 representative departments, used by Senate Document 110. There are numerous other such iron and steel making departments not represented in the Corporation activities.

however, since 1911 the U. S. Steel Corporation and the larger units in the industry have employed a swing crew in Blast Furnace operation so that the men themselves only work 6 days a week. The government figures however indicate that at least up to 1919 this has applied only to about half the Blast Furnaces in the industry as a whole. Twenty-four hour operation means of course that the workers must work on a 2-shift 12-hour schedule or on a 3-shift 8-hour schedule. The stocking of a blast furnace is a regular and continuous hour by hour operation. However since the work is chiefly performed by automatic machinery the operator does not actually work much more than 50 to 60% of the time. The iron is drawn off every 6 hours or 2 times each 12-hour turn. In 1910 before much of the modern automatic machinery was installed, all Blast Furnace workers only actually worked, according to Senate Document 110, Volume III, page 361, about 70% of their hours on duty. With modern machinery they actually work less than 50% of their time on duty or less than 6 hours out of the 12, for which of course they receive 12 hours' pay. If Blast Furnace work was put on a 3-shift 8-hour schedule the average worker would actually work less than 4 hours a day, and because pourings are generally every 6 hours, the work could not as at present be evenly divided among the shifts.[1]

The molten iron goes from the Blast Furnace into Mixers which are in reality merely great reservoirs in which the molten metal is temporarily stored to be drawn off as required for use in the Open Hearth and Bessemer Furnaces which convert it into steel.

Open Hearth

The Open Hearth is today the principal and by far the most rapidly expanding department in steel making. The

[1] This is general practice. It is practicable, however, and some furnaces are tapped 6 times per day. In such cases the work could be evenly divided between 3 shifts.

capacity of the average Open Hearth furnace runs from a
normal of 12 to 14 to a maximum of 18 "heats" a week.
That is, such furnaces are charged with a combination of
molten iron and scrap steel and this product converted into
Open Hearth steel under normal conditions about every 12
hours. Except for cleaning up and minor jobs the work of
the department is done in preparing and charging the
furnaces at the beginning of the "heat" and in pouring the
steel at the end of the "heat," the men in the meanwhile
having their time largely to themselves. Senate Document
110, Volume III, page 355, shows in detail as already quoted
that the average Open Hearth worker in 1910 actually
worked only 40.2% of his time or 4 hours and 49 minutes
out of his 12 hours on duty and had 59.8% of his time or 7
hours 11 minutes out of his 12-hour turn to himself. If this
work were put on the 3-shift 8-hour basis, it would obviously
mean that instead of preparing a furnace at the beginning
of a turn and pouring the steel at the end of the turn—thus
being responsible for one complete operation—part of the
crews would have to pour a "heat" for which the previous
crew had been responsible, and prepare and change a "heat"
for which a succeeding crew would have to be responsible,
while each third crew would have a turn between charging
and pouring during which it would have practically nothing
to do.[1]

   The fact that the Blast Furnace must operate 7 days a
week and that the Open Hearth uses the iron molten, years
ago led to the practise of 7-day operation in the Open
Hearth department also. If this department operates only
6 days and the Sunday production of Blast Furnace iron is
allowed to cool, it must be remelted at the cost of about a
dollar a ton. For this reason some of the smaller plants,
which find it necessary to take advantage of every opportunity to meet the competition of their larger and better

   [1] This again refers to normal practice and operation. In times of
great steel demand when furnaces are pushed to 18 heats a week, or 3 a
day, the work could be equally divided among 3 shifts.

equipped rivals, continued to run their Open Hearth departments 7 days a week. The "1919" government figures, however, show average Open Hearth hours of 72.6 weighted or 71.9 unweighted per week for the whole country.

Bessemer

The second and older method of steel making is the Bessemer process which requires only from 20 to 30 minutes to convert pig iron into steel. Although for many of the occupations in this department the nature of the work is as inherently leisurely and intermittent as in Blast Furnace or Open Hearth work, the mere rapid nature of the process makes the work in many of the occupations in this department entirely different. This difference in the nature of the work is plainly indicated in the table of Bessemer hours already given. The work of the Stopper Maker for instance is leisurely and intermittent and is therefore on a 2-shift basis. The work of the Stopper Setter however while only for a few minutes at a time with 10 or 15 minute rest periods is in close proximity to be the molten metal and hours for this occupation throughout the country except at the peak of war activity when they were 59 a week averaged 51, 50 and 49 which means that in all but a few plants they are on a 3-shift 8-hour basis. Other occupations in this department are similarly on a 2-shift or 3-shift basis largely according to the nature of the work. The government figures also plainly show that this whole department throughout the country works 6 days a week and in a large part of the plants but 5 and a half days a week.

The molten steel from both the Open Hearth and Bessemer departments is poured into ingot molds and these ingots, of from 1 to 5 tons each, are carried to the "soking" pits where they remain under a high even temperature for from 2 to 5 hours before they are passed on to the Bloom Mills—the first of the Rolling Departments.

Rolling Mill

Of the Rolling Mills which take the steel while hot from the furnace departments—the Bloom Mill rolls the raw ingots turning out the product in billets or slabs or sheet bars of various sizes according to further use. The average working hours for all occupations in the Bloom Mills were 66.5 a week weighted and 64.6 unweighted in "1919" at the height of steel war activity. This means that the department as a whole averages 5 and a half days a week on a 2-shift basis.

From the Bloom Mill, the product in these various forms passes still hot into other rolling departments such as Rod Mill, Bar Mill, Structural Mill or Plate Mill which make various semi-finished products which are allowed to cool and finished or fabricated in other departments.

In the Sheet Mill where the product is rolled cold and thin and flexible it requires a considerable amount of physical handling. Therefore as has already been shown on page 76 by detailed U. S. Bureau of Labor statistics, Sheet Mill work throughout the country has for years been on a 3-shift 8-hour basis 5 and one third days a week or 42.8 hours a week.

In the Bar Mills also a certain amount of physical handling of the product is necessary. Detailed statistics from U. S. Bureau of Labor statistics have already been quoted on page 72 showing that 48% of the workers in this department work less than 60 hours a week and 89% less than 72 hours a week.

As regards the bulk of the Rolling Departments however, it will be remembered that U. S. Bureau of Labor Statistics Monthly Review, June, 1920, includes these among the departments whose work is referred to as "necessarily of a leisurely character." Senate Document 110, Volume III, page 361, shows the exact amount of time worked and the amount of time spent in resting in the 14 different occupations of two typical U. S. Steel Corporation Rolling Mills in

1910. These 2 mills worked 5 and and three fourths days and 5 nights on a 2-shift basis. Bottom makers in the first mill worked 3 hours and 17 minutes and had nearly 9 hours to themselves out of their 12-hour turn. Chargers worked 5 hours and had 7 hours out of the 12 to themselves. Roughers and Pitcranemen worked 7 hours and had 5 hours to themselves. The great bulk of Rollers however at this time worked 10 and a fraction hours out of the 12-hour turn. In plant number 2, hours actually worked and hours idle per occupation varied from plant number 1 but the average for both plants was practically the same—74% of time working and 26% of time resting. Since 1910, however, the "mechanical rolling mills" described by Senate Document 110 as then coming into use and thru whose use it states "severe manual labor is almost entirely eliminated" have been generally adopted and in processes where they cannot be used either the entire department has been put on an 8-hour schedule or extra roll-hands are employed so that this harder or more continuous work is now done by two men relieving each other every hour or half hour. Thus the average worker thruout the 12-hour rolling departments now actually works about half his time on duty. (See page 116.)

All these departments are engaged in the manufacture of *steel*. In the manufacture of cast iron, the product goes in pigs directly from the Blast Furnace to the Foundries which are finishing departments for the manufacture of iron castings. In the manufacture of wrought iron, it goes to the Puddling Mills in which the hours in 1910 averaged 55 a week or 9 a day (Senate Document 110, page xliii) and for 1915 are summarized in detail on page 77 of the present Analysis.

It is plain then that the question of working schedules in these great primary iron and steel producing departments involves 3 problems which are more or less unique to the steel industry.

First, the necessity of continuous operation leaves no alternative except a 2-shift or a 3-shift system. In other words, it has never been possible for the steel industry to arbitrarily set or gradually reduce its general working hours as has been possible in other industries.

Second, in many of the occupations in the primary production departments the fact that the only human labor involved comes only at long intervals when furnaces are charged or poured or rolls changed, etc., means that the work is so highly intermittent that if hours on duty were reduced to 8, the only alternative of 12, the men in these occupations would only average from 2 to 5 hours actual work a day.

Third, the fact that periods of work cannot be arbitrarily set but are determined by the time it takes the metal to heat and the fact that these periods in the 2 principal departments are normally 6 or 12 hours apart means that the work could not under ordinary conditions be evenly divided between 3 shifts and that in the largest department—the Open Hearth—the crews which happened to be on duty only the 8 hours between charging and pouring would have practically nothing to do.

In occupations or departments on the other hand in which the work is not inherently intermittent or is particularly hard either the work is actually on a 3-shift 8-hour basis or else such worker is periodically relieved.

In regard to this whole subject of the variable working hours in primary production departments, U. S. Bureau of Labor Statistics Bulletin 218 (page 27) in its general conclusions says:—

"It will be seen therefore, that there is no *standard* turn for the iron and steel industry as a whole, and even if one were created arbitrarily to attempt to conform all the odd turns to it would present insuperable difficulties."

Finishing Departments

The other great group of steel making departments—the Finishing Departments—which make tin plate, galvanized iron, horse shoes, woven fence, nails and a host of other steel products from car wheels to tacks, are in most cases not under the necessity of continuous operation but are in general straight manufacturing departments whose hours are on practically the same basis as those of other ordinary manufacturing industries.

The proportion of the iron and steel industry as a whole which is devoted to primary production, i.e., "crude iron and steel and rolled products," and the proportion devoted to finishing departments according to the last government figures (U. S. Abstract of Census of Manufactures, 1914, page 96) is as follows:

	Wage Earners Average Number
Blast Furnace....................................	29,356
Steel Works and Rolling Mills...................	248,716
Total Crude Iron and Steel and Rolled Products....	278,072
Other Iron and Steel Products...................	782,986
Aggregate......................................	1,061,058

According to the U. S. Census interpretation of the term iron and steel industry then, the primary production departments, in which, because of continuous operation and highly intermittent work, the 12-hour day is a problem, constitute just 26.2% of the industry. Thus the 12-hour steel worker constitutes something less than 40% of 26.2% of all iron and steel workers.

But while wire, steel tubes, nails, horse shoes, nuts, bolts, screws, barrelhoops, and a host of other such products are commonly made in finishing departments of companies which also produce the steel itself, much primary steel production is finished in plants which ordinarily do not produce the iron and steel which they consume. Steel plate, for instance, is largely bought from primary production departments and finished in stove plants or in boiler factories or steel car works. But again this is not necessarily the case and in many instances primary producers of steel also make such finished products. In other words, it is plain, as already emphasized, that the problem of establishing even approximate average steel working hours depends primarily on the definition of what is to be included in the term iron and steel industry.

The 24 International unions conducting the 1919 steel strike interpreted the industry to include departments which employed about 500,000 men or about the same departments which are included in the U. S. Steel Corporation outside of its shipyards, by-product and transportation departments.

The average working hours for U. S. Steel Corporation employees as given in the Senate Hearings, page 157, were in 1919 as follows:

12-hour workers................	69,284 or 26.5 %
10-hour workers................	102,902 or 39.39%
Approximately 8-hour workers.....	88,994 or 34.1 %

These figures are based on a 6-day Blast Furnace week instead of a 6½ day week which the U. S. Bureau of Labor figures show to be the average for the whole industry in "1919." They also include such workers as electricians, engineers, repair men, etc., whose hours are not considered in the U. S. Bureau of Labor figures but who are very necessary factors in steel operation and who were distinctly involved in the steel strike. They include of course the Corporation's finishing departments. They also include about 20% of workers in mining, transportation and by-products departments not generally considered a part of the steel industry. In spite of this last fact, however, they are very obviously the most representative figures for the industry as a whole that are available.

On their face these figures show an average working day of 9.85 hours or an average 6-day working week of 59.1 hours.

Because the Interchurch Report has characterized the steel workers' hours in general and the 12-hour day in particular as a "barbarism without valid excuse penalizing the workers of the country," as "preventing Americanization of the steel workers" and otherwise made the most bitter arraignments against them, there remains the problem of checking the steel workers' hours against such information as we have in regard to the working hours of Americans as a whole.

Now while the idea that the 12 hour day is more or less unique to the steel industry has been strongly impressed on the public mind through constant discussion of the 12 hour day in connection with the steel industry, and while the fact that in certain conspicuous industries the 8 hour day prevails has been so played up as to give a general impression that the 8 hour day is more or less standard in American industry, neither of these impressions fits the facts.

Five hundred thousand bituminous coal miners, although their labor leaders have been talking voluminously about a 6 hour day, still according to the figures of the Interchurch Report (page 56) "work a 52.9 hours' weekly schedule."

Street railway men, according to the Interchurch Report (page 55), work 56.4 hours a week—27 minutes a day less than the U. S. Steel worker. "These are," the Interchurch Report emphasizes, "the nearest competitors to steel hours in the list of principal industries compiled by the Bureau of Applied Economics of Washington, D. C."

Bulletin No. 8 of the Bureau of Applied Economics, however, shows on page 62 that—

In the brick-making industry which is not handicapped by the necessity of continuous operation, the average employee works 57.1 hours a week or just 20 minutes a day less than the average United States Steel employee.

In the chemical industry, according to the same authority and on same page, the average worker works 56.54 hours a week, only 26 minutes a day less than the average U. S. Steel worker.

In lumbering, a non-continuous industry, the average worker, according to this same bulletin, No. 8, page 59, works 56.1 hours or just 30 minutes a day less than the average

U. S. Steel worker, and the tables on each side of this show that furniture makers work about the same length of time and mill workers only a few minutes a day less.

Turning, however, from particular industries to industry as a whole the U. S. Census, and particularly the industrial census of 1914, offer most comprehensive figures as to average working hours or from which average working hours may be estimated.

The last U. S. Census (13th Census Vol. IV p. 57) shows 30,091,564 male workers gainfully employed as follows:

"Agriculture......................	10,760,875
Professions......................	1,151,709
Domestic and Personal Service......	2,740,176
Trade and Transportation...........	6,403,378
Manufacturing and Mechanical......	9,035,426 "

The 1914 industrial census indicates that between 5% and 10% should be added to some of these groups and gives exact figures and detailed information in regard to the last group.

Every one knows that these 10,000,000 farmers—whether in 1910, 1914 or today work 12 to 14 hours a day 6 days in the week in addition to a good half day's work on Sunday. Moreover no one relieves the farmer on his harder jobs every half hour and if he worked as intermittently as the 12 hour steel worker, even in his slack seasons, he would go to the poor house.

There are of course no figures possible as to average working hours for doctors, lawyers, ministers, etc., because the very nature of their work generally makes it necessary for them to be available at all hours. When Senator Kenyon remarked to Mr. Gompers (Senate Hearings, page 429) that Senators "have no 8 hour day at all," Mr. Gompers replied, "Me too," and it is probable that for at least the successful professional man in all lines—including the labor leaders—a day's work means much nearer 12 hours than 8.

Domestics and Personal Service includes barbers, restaurant keepers, cooks, waiters, and other such workers, in restaurants and hotels as well as in homes, policemen, firemen, night watchmen, etc., by far the largest proportion of whom work 12 hours.

Trade and transportation include a million retailers who the public demand shall keep open 12 hours and on Saturdays and special seasons for longer. It includes perhaps as many more retail clerks. It includes a million railroad workers who under threat of strike during the war obtained from the government the "basic" 8 hour day that was given the steel workers, but they work more than 8 hours a day. It includes street car operators whose working hours are 9½. It includes all sorts of draymen, cabmen, pedlars, etc., whose work probably averages over 12 hours a day. It includes most office workers whose hours probably average 9.

"Manufacturing and mechanical" are divided into two classes—office workers and proprietors, whose hours probably average 9 for the former and more for the latter, and wage earners whose weekly hours are specifically given (1914 Census Abstract, page 482) as follows:

48 and Under................	11.8%
48 to 54....................	13.4%
54.........................	25.8%
54 to 60....................	22 %
60.........................	21.1%
60 to 72....................	3.5%
72.........................	1.5%
Over 72....................	.8%

Weighted average (taking middle point of variables) 55.65 or 9.27 hours a day.

When steel working hours are compared in detail with the figures for this last group of "industrial wage earners" whose hours are the shortest of all groups of American workers, two facts are at once apparent:

First, steel had a far greater percentage—the Steel Corporation in 1919 three times as many 8 hour workers as this whole group (1914) which is the only group in all American industry which emphasizes the 8 hour day and which has in general by far the greatest percentage of 8 hour workers.

Second, steel has an entirely disproportionate number of 12 hour workers.

But steel faces an entirely different problem from most manufacturing industries in that many of the departments must be continuously operated. This is its reason for the large per cent of 12 hour workers. In manufacturing as a whole, on the other hand, the necessity of continuous operation is negligible and this is doubtless a chief, if not the chief reason, for its negligible per cent of 12 hour workers.

If we make the comparison on the basis of the figures as they stand—without allowing for the fact that steel faces the big disadvantage in its labor problems of continuous operation which average manufacturing does not—it appears that the average daily working hours of the U. S. Steel Corporation (1919) of 9.85 is *35 minutes longer,* than the daily working hours (9.27) of the average "industrial wage earner" in 1914.

Whether as a mere matter of fairness, steel working hours as a whole—including the 12 hour day—should be compared only with the working hours of general manufacturing industries which do not have the same big problem of continuous operation, or whether they should be compared with the working hours of other industries which do have the same or other special problems, must perhaps be left to individual opinion. But certainly it is not fair or even reasonably possible to characterize steel working hours as a whole or the 12 hour day in particular, as "relics of barbarism," "un-American" and "un-Americanizing" without comparing them with the working hours of the great and conspicuous bulk of other American workers in industries which have to face the same or other special conditions as the steel industry.

When steel working hours are compared with those of the **first** great industrial group enumerated by the census, it at once appears that whereas less than 40% of some 300,000[1] steel workers work the 12 hour day, of 10,000,000 farmers practically 100% are forced by the special nature of their occupation to work more than 12 hours a day at both harder and less intermittent work than the steel worker. It is plain that well over 50% of the 2,740,176 workers comprising the third great census group work 12 hours or more a day, it is plain that 60% to 80% or more of the largest class (retailers and assistants) in the next census group are forced by public demand to work 12 hours or more a day. Taking all these groups as enumerated by the last census it is plain that average steel hours (including all departments) were substantially the same as average working hours for all Americans; and it is particularly plain that the *8 hour day* was worked by a greater percentage of steel workers than of all American workers and the *12 hour day* by a considerably *less* percentage of steel workers than of all American workers.

The question of the 12 hour day in the steel industry has a social side, as a matter of fact, several social sides, and there is much to be said for each of them. From the way in which it has been so frequently presented it has been, and doubtless will continue to be, discussed from a sentimental point of view. But the facts cannot be determined by social or sentimental arguments and social and sentimental arguments at least ought to be determined on the facts.

The facts very plainly are that if steel working hours are "inhuman" and "relics of barbarism without valid excuse" —if 12 hour workers are being "un-Americanized" in "scores of thousands," the same indictment, and in some particulars a worse indictment will have to be brought against working conditions throughout the country, for steel working hours

---

[1] As already emphasized this percentage of course becomes correspondingly less in proportion as the industry is interpreted to include various steel finishing departments.

represent a little better than a cross-section of average American working hours as they were in 1914—not to mention the working hours on which America and Americanism were built.

CHAPTER XII

THE Interchurch Report in its "Conclusions" (page 12, line 13) states:

"Steel jobs were largely classed as heavy labor and hazardous."

It generalizes on page 98 and elsewhere in regard to the steel workers'

"Exhaustion due to overwork."

It says on page 67 that:—

"It was surprising in view of the reputation which the Steel Corporation had been accorded for safety to find so large a number of strikers complaining about hazards. They described with specificness menaces to limb or life, concerning which they had complained to foremen *and superintendents* month in and month out without avail."

It states later on the same page that:—

". . . it was inadvisable to pay great heed to the number of crooked-legged men always seen in the streets of a steel mill town."

It emphasizes on page 66:—

"The Steel Corporation set up a Safety Department which has been the recipient of many medals. Only statistics can determine to what extent the safety campaign is adequate. Statistically steel still ranks with mining for fatal accidents"

—and makes similar statement either directly or by insinuation in many other places throughout the Report.

There is no question that certain operation in steel production involve hard work just as certain operations in every other basic industry involve hard work. Plowing is hard work. Pitching hay is hard work. The handling of heavy merchandise in transportation is hard work. Driving railroad tunnels through great mountains or subway tunnels under New York City involves hard work. Lumbering, mining, firing engines on railroads or steam ships and a hundred and one other jobs—whose regular performance is absolutely necessary to the very existence of modern society—all involve hard work.

Again there is no question that certain operations in steel production involve hazards just as mining, lumbering, railroading, fishing, building construction and many other operations involve hazards. Almost every act of living involves hazards, of which taking a bath is the single most hazardous common act of all, for 30% of all accidents in and around a home result from slipping on the modern porcelain bathtub.

On the other hand it is equally unquestionable that one of the major efforts and one of the most conspicuous achievements of modern progress has been the effort and achievement in reducing the extra hard labor and the extra hazards in both modern industry and in all modern life. From the thrasher to the tractor scores of machines have reduced the physical labor of farming. The automatic shute for loading and the automatic dumping device for unloading are typical of similar conspicuous achievements in reducing the hard manual labor in railroading. And both these are typical of the extent to which industry has been able to go in reducing both the hard work and the hazard of many of its operations. Nevertheless, handling a four gang plow 12 or 14 hours a day with a tractor is still hard work. Firing a locomotive, pitching hay, mining coal or copper, loading a steamship, cutting and rafting timber, no less than any operation in the steel industry, are all hard and sometimes hazardous work. Yet every one of these is so necessary to the whole functioning of society that **to** eliminate them would largely reduce all modern society to the primitive individualistic basis where every man would be subject to the even harder labor and often even greater hazards of primitive existence.

Given the facts of the laws of nature—that molten metal burns, that speed involves risks, that heavy objects require heavy effort to handle—on the one hand; and on the other hand that modern society demands to be heated and fed and transported, there inevitably exists the absolute necessity that men work hard and face hazards. The only basis of progress therefore is to reduce such hard work and such hazards as much as possible under the circumstances.

The pertinent question therefore, in regard to hard work and hazards in the steel industry, or any other industry is whether or not men are forced to work harder than is necessary or have to face hazards that may be made unnecessary.

Unless the Interchurch Report means that "steel jobs were largely classed" as *heavier* labor than average or necessary, or as *more* hazardous than average or necessary, its whole statement in regard to hard work and hazards in the steel industry means nothing at all. That the Interchurch Report does mean to give the impression that most steel work is far harder than average or necessary and far more hazardous than average or necessary, is entirely plain from its statements above quoted and from the whole nature of its arguments and conclusions on this point.

The Interchurch Report makes its most specific argument as to the hardship of steel labor in connection with the twelve-hour day—resting its case, as has been pointed out, chiefly upon a large number of quotations from the alleged diaries of two anonymous 12-hour workers. The actual facts as to the nature of 12-hour work however, have already been sufficiently emphasized.

In addition to its specific argument as to the hardship of 12 hour work, the Interchurch Report attempts to build up an impression of the hardship of steel work in general by mere constant repetition of such phrases as that "steel is a man killer"—that the men work "to the point of daily exhaustion"—to "old age at 40," etc., etc.

Some ten years ago, Mr. John A. Fitch, who also wrote the foreword to Mr. William Z. Foster's book *The Great Steel Strike*, and who is listed by the New York legislative investigation as per footnote,[1] published a magazine article, entitled, "Old Age at Forty" in which he particularly emphasized the hard nature of steel work. Although this article referred only to conditions of ten years and generally longer ago, before much of the present automatic machinery had been installed, the Interchurch Report particularly dwells on this phrase, "Old Age at Forty" and on the facts which Mr. Fitch then alleged. This same article was also several times referred to in the testimony before the Senate Investigating Committee.

As direct evidence on the accuracy of this talk about "Old Age at Forty" while at the Homestead plant, the Senate Committee obtained statistics (Page 529, Part II of the Senate Hearings), showing the ages of all the different employees in that plant. This table shows that 4 of the workers in this mill are over 70—24 between 65 and 70—64 between 60 and 65—132 between 55 and 60—216 between 50 and 55—and that 27.6% of the entire working force were men over forty years old which, even without considering the fact that 60% of the entire working force here was

[1] The New York Legislative Investigation on Radicalism in its index lists:

"FITCH, JOHN A.
  Assistance in preparation I. W. W. pamphlet. Page 1093.
  Industrial editor *The Survey.* Page 1093.
  Member I. W. W. defense committee. Page 1094.
  Lecturer Bureau of Industrial Research. Page 1121.
  ('Technical Advisors' to the Interchurch Commission.)
  National Committee American Civil Liberties Union. Page 1101-1989."

Special attention is called to the full context of the pages referred to.

unskilled common labor with their large labor turnover, is a remarkably high average for any industry.

The Senate Committee also interrogated a number of witnesses either specifically in regard to the hardship of steel work or generally as to the nature of steel work and the attitude of the men toward the work.

Mr. T. J. Davis who had formerly been for 14 years a member of the Amalgamated Association (labor union) who was a delegate to the 1902 Union convention and was for a time National Deputy Vice President of the Union, in testifying for the steel companies emphasized (Senate Hearings, Part I, page 439) the hard nature of his own work but stated that men in such processes only worked the 8 hour shift and actually seldom more than 7 hours a day, for which he received $17 a day. Mr. Davis also stated that he had been in the rolling mills 34 years and had been doing that particular kind of work for 18 years and yet was still hardy enough at 55 years of age to have spent 15 months with the A. E. F. in France.

Mr. Edward M. Lynch of the McKeesport Mills, also formerly a union man, stated he was 50 years old and had worked for the company "34 or 35 years." He also stated that he had "what is termed the hardest job in the mills where I work—the heaviest job," but he stated it with pride rather than as a complaint. He worked ten hours and ten minutes on day turn and 12 hours on night turn "for $11 a day" (Senate Report, Part I, page 459).

Mr. Richard Raymond, an Englishman by birth, who was a day laborer at $6.03 a day in the Vandergrift Sheet and Tin Mill testified (Senate Hearings, Part II, page 691):

The Chairman: Do you want to work 12 hours a day yourself?
Mr. Raymond: Yes, sir, I can stand 12 hours a day.
Senator McKellar: Why do you want a 12-hour day?
Mr. Raymond: I am like the rest, I want to get what money I can.
Mr. Ashmead: How old are you, Mr. Raymond?
Mr. Raymond: Sixty-seven.

Mr. Ashmead: Have conditions been improving in the steel company's plants among the laboring classes?

Mr. Raymond: It has been improving in regard to money matters and I am certain of one thing which has been improving—that men certainly do not work nearly so hard as I had to when I first came here.

Among the strike leaders special witnesses were many ex-workers who were obviously most disgruntled. Yet among the many complaints of such strikers a careful reading of the whole Senate evidence does not reveal that even these particularly hostile witnesses made any specific complaint concerning the hardships of steel work.

The Senate Committee, also in the course of the investigation, personally visited numerous mills and talked with a large number of representative employees of all types who were at work and a large number of strikers whom they met haphazard on the street.

The testimony thus adduced was taken entirely from men chosen at random by the Senators themselves. The interviews were taken down verbatim and reported in full in the Senate Hearings. A large number of these men did not know who it was that was interviewing them. They all seemed to talk with the utmost freedom and frequently with a profanity that indicated anything but restraint or intimidation on their part. All the evidence was given during the strike when grievances are naturally exaggerated and multiplied. Yet among all the strikers thus interviewed, except for one man who admitted he was sickly and who remarked—but merely incidentally—that he "had to work like a mule," no worker or striker as far as can be discovered either mentioned, or directly or indirectly referred to his work as being either hard or hazardous.

As regards hazard, it is a fact that has received the widest publication that the steel industry in general and the U. S. Steel Corporation in particular have made a most conspicuously successful effort in the installation of safety devices and the organizations of safety systems among employees. In competition with every other industry in every nation in the world, the U. S. Steel Corporation has received the highest award for its exhibit of safety devices and of its special systems for promoting safety among its employees at practically every prominent safety congress held in this country or abroad in recent years. This single corporation has 7000 of its employees organized into special safety committees with ex-committee men to the number of 35,000 as ex-officio members. It has organized an elaborate system of competition for prizes awarded for the prevention of accidents or for ideas that will contribute to lessening accidents. These facts too have been given the widest publication and are emphasized in detail in the Senate Hearings.

The Interchurch Report recognizes the U. S. Steel Corporation's safety efforts in this way. It says, page 66:

". . . the Steel Corporation set up a Safety Department which has been the recipient of many medals. *Only statistics can determine to what extent the safety campaign is adequate. Statistically steel* still ranks with mining for *fatal accidents.* The 1918 report of *compensable accidents* for the State of Pennsylvania gives the four largest hazardous industries as follows:

	Number	Per Cent of Total
Mines and Quarries.................	23,161	33.12
Metals and Metal Products...........	22,222	31.78
Public Service.....................	4,985	7.13
Building and Contracting...........	4,184	5.98"

and then goes straight on to the succeeding page:

"It was surprising, *in view of the reputation which the Steel Corporation had been accorded for safety*, to find so large a number of strikers complaining about hazards. . . . *Without adequate statistics* it was impossible to weigh the value of these complaints, *just as it was inadvisable to pay great heed to the number of crooked-legged men always seen in the streets of a steel mill town.*"

Aside from certain quotations from individual strikers that a certain job was one on which a man if he wasn't careful might be badly burned, or that a worker had fallen from steps which were greasy,[1] etc., the Interchurch Report confines its evidence as to the hazardous nature of steel work to the foregoing—the statement that *"only statistics can determine* to what extent the (U. S. Steel Corporation) safety campaign is adequate,'' followed by a table of "statistics" and in the next paragraph the statement that *"without adequate statistics,"* the conplaints of workers as to hazards cannot be weighed—followed by an obvious and pointed insinuation.

Upon analysis both the "statistics" that are given and the complaint about the lack of statistics become particularly interesting.

Conspicuously featured and in detail in the record of the Senate Investigation (Part 1, page 188) is a table of the official insurance rates of the Prudential Life Insurance Company *on each particular type of steel work based on the hazard or lack of hazard of that work.*

This table shows that while in 1908, steel "blowing" was regarded as hazardous and the insurance rate was $13.22 per $1000, age 35; by 1919, that occupation was regarded as normal and non-hazardous. The insurance rate for "blast furnace keeper" which in 1908 was $13.22 (hazardous) was in 1919 $2.77 (non-hazardous). In the same way throughout the 11 principal processes of steel making which were in 1908 regarded as hazardous, in 1919 all such hazards had become so reduced or eliminated that whereas the average rate for these occupations had been $10.60 in 1908, in 1919 the average rate on the same occupations was less than $4.00.

It is interesting to note that the Interchurch Report refers constantly to the Senate Hearings and refers at least once to the page in the Senate Hearings which faces this conspicu-

---

[1] From the testimony of George Colson, which the Interchurch Report quotes through a full page (67) but whose effect is afterward very much modified by the cross-examination which the Interchurch Report does not quote; for which see Senate Hearings, pages 728-735 and page 374 present analysis.

ous and plainly headed table. Still it complains about statistics not being available.

The first reference to an outside authority made by the Interchurch Report in the chapter in which it discusses "hazard" is to Senate Document 110: "Conditions of employment in the iron and steel industry," and it refers to this document frequently elsewhere. This Document 110 consists of four volumes of which the whole last volume— 341 pages—is devoted to a study of "Accidents and accident prevention in the iron and steel industry." Its conclusions however, are the opposite of those expressed by the Interchurch Report.

Also between 1913 and 1919 the U. S. Bureau of Labor Statistics published in its various Monthly Reviews at least three elaborate statistical studies of accident "frequency" in the iron and steel industry, one of which is specifically referred to in connection with the prominent insurance statistics on page 188 in the Senate Hearings which the Interchurch Report did not see although it found and refers to an obscure sentence on the opposite page. The conclusions of all of these are also the opposite of those of the Interchurch Report.

Undoubtedly the Interchurch Report cites or quotes from the United States Bureau of Labor Statistics Monthly Review for October, 1919 more frequently than from any other document. Even the most casual reference to the U. S. Bureau of Labor Review, October, 1919, shows that the most conspicuous section in this whole document, running through page after page of tables and striking curves and charts, is a most detailed statistical study of accident "frequency," 1913 to 1919, in the iron and steel industry.

At the end of these elaborate detailed government statistics in regard to the specific subject on which the Interchurch Report complains of the lack of adequate statistics, appears the U. S. Bureau of Labor conclusion (page 231-1219):—

"It is obvious that the efforts of the safety organization in these mills were well adapted to meet and control minor injuries. The curve of frequency is a sure index of success or failure in this particular. The organization did not, probably could not, control the tendency to rise during the period of adjustment to war conditions (raw labor was being hircd) but it did prevent a rise above the peak established in the pre-war conditions of 1913. Further, with the establishment of relatively stable conditions, it was able to bring about a *remarkable and continuous decline in frequency rates.*"

Moreover so remarkable did the U. S. Bureau of Labor regard the results achieved by the Safety Organizations in the iron and steel industry in reducing accidents even during the war period that a few months later—but still before the Interchurch Report was published—it devoted pages 151–1457 to 165–1469 of its June, 1920 *Monthly Review* to a further elaborate statistical study of this subject which states in conclusion that:

"1. Whatever form of classification is used [the fundamental departments, production groups, or cause groups] the same trend is shown.

"2. The period just prior to the war was a period of industrial decline . . . accident rates dropped more rapidly than employment.

"3. As soon as the effect of European war orders began to be felt in this country employment began to increase. The accession of inexperienced men increased even more rapidly. Accident rates went up.

"4. The iron and steel industry was alarmed by the increasing accident occurrence and undertook a strenuous counter-campaign.

"5. This was very successful in controlling and finally causing a decline in minor injury.

"6. Major injury was not controlled so perfectly *but was prevented from rising above the level of 1913* (in spite of new labor) *and was finally considerably reduced.*

"This review of the war period strongly supports the contention that *even in the most strenuous times* it is possible to hold in check the tendency to rising accident rates by the application of the three cardinal methods of the safety movement: (1) adequate instruction of the men in skilful methods of work; (2) careful supervision of the well-instructed men; (3) 'engineering revision' by which the safety of work places is increased. . . .

"A considerable number of industrial concerns took the position that the demands of war production were so imperative that they were perfectly justified in relaxing attention to safety measures of all sorts. The result is reflected in the increased accident occurrence registered by most agencies. . . . *It is to the great and lasting credit of the iron and steel industry that it did meet the situation directly and endeavored to combat the inevitable tendency by increased efforts. The final outcome of these various efforts was first to check the rising accident rates (due to new raw labor) and finally to bring them down to points lower than the pre-war level."*

So much—for the time being—as regards the Interchurch Report's complaint as to the lack of adequate statistics for which it substitutes its conclusion by insinuation. As regards the one table of "statistics" which the Interchurch Report itself does discover and quote there are a number of equally interesting things to be noted.

The Interchurch Report leads to and quotes this one table of "statistics" as follows (page 66):

"The *Steel Corporation* set up a safety department which has been the recipient of many medals. *Only statistics* can determine to what extent the safety campaign is adequate. *Statistically steel* still ranks with mining for *fatal* accidents, the 1918 report of *compensable* accidents for the State of Pennsylvania gives the *four largest hazardous industries as follows:*

	Number	Per Cent of Total
Mines and Quarries...................	23,161	33.12
Metals and Metal Products...........	22,222	31.78
Public Service......................	4,985	7.13
Building and Contracting.............	4,184	5.98 "

In the first place this table clearly applies to the metal industry as a whole, including copper and brass smelting and working, and so does not prove anything pro or con about the steel mills or the steel workers who were involved in the strike. This table could therefore mean exactly what the Interchurch Report tries to give the impression it does mean and still prove nothing about hazards in the steel industry. As it is, however, the principal so-called evidence which the Interchurch Report brings forward to supports its conclusion that the steel industry is particularly hazardous and as a further example of the type of "evidence" which the Inter-church Report uses—and therefore as bearing particularly on the question as to whether or not the Interchurch Report is a competent or adequate document—this table is most significant.

As regards the merits of the table itself as being adequate evidence in regard to anything at all it is to be noted that neither the table itself nor any statement in connection with it suggests the fact that there are far more men in Pennsylvania engaged in mining and metal production than in Public Service or Building and Contracting and that therefore the percentages of accidents in these two industries would necessarily be far greater, even though the per cent of accident to men involved—that is the actual comparative hazards of the industry—were less. Giving, therefore, neither the number of accidents in proportion to the number of men employed, nor the number of men among whom the given accidents occurred, this table actually shows nothing whatever as to the comparative hazard even of the industries to which it does apply.

Again it will be noted that this table is not a table of all industrial accidents but merely of "compensable" accidents; which mean accidents to the employees for which the employer is liable under the particular technical rulings of the compensation law. These constituted, as the Pennsylvania Labor Bulletin from which this Interchurch Table is taken (indirectly) plainly states, but 37.8% of all industrial accidents. Moreover the relation between "compensable" accidents and all accidents varies widely in different industries. For instance, comparison of the Pennsylvania figures for "compensable" with the figures for total accidents at once shows that while in the metal trades 39% of all accidents are "compensable," in public service only 15% are "compensable."[1]   In other words

[1] Bulletin Penn. Dept. Labor and Industry, Vol. VI (1919) No. I, pages 237, 268 and 276.

the Interchurch Report is trying to show comparative hazards of different industries by comparing 39% of the accidents in one of these industries with only 15% of the accidents in another industry.

In other words this table, by which the Interchurch Report pretends to show the great hazards of the steel industry—first, does not refer to the steel industry; second, does not show hazard at all because it does not show the relation of accidents to number of men employed; and third, while it includes 39% of all accidents in one of the industries shows only 15% of the accidents in another industry.

But not only does this table in no sense mean what the Interchurch Report gives the impression it means, but the facts are the direct opposite of what the Interchurch Report tries to show from the table.

The 1919 and 1920 Bulletin of the Pennsylvania State Department of Labor and Industry—from which this Interchurch Report Table is (indirectly) taken, shows[1]:

	1918	1919
All Industrial Accidents...	184,844	152,455
Fatal Accidents.........	3,403 or (1.8%)	2,569 or (1.7%)
Serious Accidents........	53,783 or (29.1%)	38,942 or (25.5%)
Minor Accidents.........	127,658 or (69.1%)	111,033 or (72.8%)
"Compensable Accidents".	69,920 or 37.8%	

Now while thus plainly showing the percentage of fatal, serious and minor accidents among all industrial accidents the Pennsylvania statistics for the year 1918 do not show the same facts for each individual industry. But for 1919—for which figures and percentages are in general practically the same as for 1918—the proportion of fatal, serious and minor accidents for the individual industries is given.

Bulletin, Pennsylvania State Department Labor and

[1] 1919 figures from original source, page 49.

1918 figures from indirect source used by Interchurch Report and referred to later.

Industry, Vol. VII, No. 2, 1920, Table 4, beginning page 40 reduced to percentages shows:

ALL INDUSTRIAL ACCIDENTS

	Fatal	Serious	Minor
Building and Contracting........	1.55%	27.7%	70.7%
Metals and Metal Products......	.94%	23.1%	75.96%
Public Service.................	1.84%	26.96%	71.18%

Now it is to be particularly noted that the Interchurch Report quotes without further explanation its small part of Pennsylvania statistics on "Compensable" accidents in metal trades as compared with building and public service immediately after emphasizing the high percentage of *fatal* accidents in the steel industry. But the Pennsylvania figures themselves thus actually plainly show that in the *building trades* the percentage of *fatal* accidents (1.55%) is exactly 60% *higher* than in the metal trades (.94%); and the percentage of *fatal* accidents in *public service* (1.8%) *is just twice as high as in the metal trades.*

Moreover it will also be noted that the percentage of *serious* accidents in the metal trades (23.1%) is *less* than in the building trades (27.7%), *less* than in public service (26.96%) and *less* than in the average industry (25.5%).[1]

But there is still one other point to be noted.

This table as printed in the Interchurch Report appears in a very different form than that in which it is given in the original 1919 (for 1918) Bulletin of the Pennsylvania Department of Labor and Industry—being in fact merely a résumé of pages of tables in the original document. This is of course not significant in itself—but on page 233–1221 of the U. S. Bureau of Labor Monthly Review *October, 1919*

---

[1] The student interested in this subject of comparative hazards *per se* will find much interesting material in the Proceedings of the Casualty, Actuarial and Statistical Society of America 1918–19, Volume v., Numbers 11 and 12 where among other things it is shown that the average accident insurance premium for the four iron and steel classifications given is .57 while for "house construction" it is .78.

there appears a résumé of the 1918 Pennsylvania state figures as to compensable accidents.   This table plainly states that these figures are a special class of 37.8 of all the industrial figures.   It makes no pretense of showing comparative hazards (which of course it does not show) but plainly states that the value of the table lies in its last two columns—which the Interchurch Report leaves out—showing the comparative amount of *accident compensation* and the comparative per cent of *accident compensation* the different industries paid in 1918.

Except that the Interchurch table leaves out some of the industries and all of the figures that give this table any meaning and omits all the careful explanation as to what it does mean, this special U. S. Labor October, 1919 résumé of the complex original Pennsylvania figures and the Interchurch Résumé are exactly identical.

Moreover this table in U. S. Bulletin, October, 1919, is *part* of the conspicuous section already referred to of page after page of statistics and charts in regard to accident "frequency" in the iron and steel industry.   It appears on the page opposite and facing that study.

The Interchurch Report may not have noticed that the whole 341 pages of Vol. IV of Senate Document 110, to which the Interchurch Report frequently refers, is devoted to elaborate statistics on steel accidents in regard to which the Interchurch Report complains of the lack of statistics.   The conclusions of this Senate Document, however, are the opposite of its own.   It may have overlooked the several detailed statistical studies of the same subject appearing in U. S. Bureau of Labor Bulletin between 1913 and 1919 whose conclusions are also the opposite of its own.   Even though it found an obscure sentence to refer to on the next and facing page, it may also have overlooked the detailed insurance statistics in regard to steel hazards on page 188 of the Senate Hearings.   But these also plainly show that its own conclusions are false.   However, there does not seem to be a single table in a'l these studies which can be expurgated or otherwise twisted out of its true meaning. The plainly stated conclusions of the U. S. Bureau of Labor Review, *October, 1919* statistics are also the opposite of its own, but in connection with the October, 1919, study there is this one table which if partly expurgated and taken out of its context can be so featured as to seem to show the opposite of what all other statistics plainly show and state.

The Interchurch Report takes this one table, expurgates all the figures in regard to percentage of compensation, leaves out the statement that the table represents only a special 37.8% of all industrial accidents and is used only to show percentage of *compensation*, and then so introduces and features this expurgated table as to make it seem to bolster up a conclusion which is the opposite of the truth.

CHAPTER XIII

THE Interchurch Report says (pages 15 and 11):

"11. The organizing campaign of the workers and the strike were for the purpose of forcing a conference *in an industry where no means of conference existed.*"

"2. These conditions of labor were fixed by the Corporation without collective bargaining or *any functioning means of conference also without above board means of learning how the decreed conditions affected the workers.*"

"3. . . . . machinery of control gave . . . but negligible information of working and living conditions."

"In normal times the Steel Corporation had no adequate means of learning the conditions of life and work and the desires of its employees" (page 22 line 15).

"In practice grievances which drive workers out of the steel industry are effectually stopped from getting higher than the first representative of the company reachable by the workers—the foreman" (page 26, line 17).

Moreover in many other places throughout the Report it is stated and emphasized that the steel companies had little or no practical interest in the lives or working conditions of their men—that there not only existed no "functioning machinery" through which steel officials could learn of the living or working conditions of their men or through which the men could express their grievances or other feelings as to working and living conditions to the employers who controlled these conditions, but that on the contrary the "system of control" so worked that all expressions of grievance were arbitrarily prevented from getting any higher than the foreman who had no authority to remedy them.

The Interchurch Report in its discussion of this whole question rests the issues chiefly on the relationship between the United States Steel Corporation and its employees.

In regard to the first point raised—that the steel company has no real interest in the lives or working conditions of its employees—it is a matter of general information that the United States Steel Corporation had up to the time of the strike spent nearly $80,000,000 in providing shower baths (3,016), insurance, old age pensions, churches (26), rest rooms (260), tennis courts (105), baseball fields (103), night and technical schools, etc., free for the workers themselves —playgrounds (138), special schools (50), with exceptional teachers (215), and other special facilities for the workers' children—community clubs (19), practical housekeeping centers (20), special educational classes, etc., free for the workers' wives—doctors (359), nurses (292), etc., etc.   In addition to this $80,000,000 spent outright for such purposes, the Corporation had loaned further millions of dollars, practically without security, at 5% interest, to enable the employees to build their own homes.   Such loans were made to practically any worker who wanted to build and own his own home and at the time of the strike the Corporation had actually thus built for rent or purchase by its workers 27,000[1] such homes of a value of some $100,000,000.

It is equally well known that this policy of improving the employees' working and living conditions was originated years ago during a time when there was no question of labor trouble and money has been appropriated for such purposes in just as large amounts and often larger amounts during years when labor was plentiful and the labor problem far more a problem to labor than to the employer.

An interest in the better living and working conditions

[1] According to U. S. Steel Corporation Bureau of Safety, Sanitation and Welfare Bulletin No. 8, the number in December, 1920, was 28,260.

of its employees which has spent $80,000,000 and loaned other millions on such losing terms is so conspicuous a fact that the Interchurch Report could neither have overlooked it nor argued it out of existence.   Therefore, except for a few sarcastic references to it as a "toilets policy" and a policy of "grinding the faces of the hunkies and trusting to welfare to salve the exacerbations," the Interchurch Report entirely ignores this conclusive evidence that the Steel Company has shown a very real interest in the working and living conditions of its employees.[1]

Moreover this expenditure of such immense sums to improve the working and living conditions of the employees in no sense stands alone as evidence of the interest which prompted it but is expressly part of a definite, carefully worked-out policy of the Steel Corporation.

In his letter to the strike committee, in his testimony before the Senate Committee, and elsewhere, Judge Gary specifically stated—which statements have been widely published—that he and the other officials of the Steel Corporation take the greatest interest in the working and living conditions of their employees—that in fact he regards such an interest in, and such treatment of, his employees as will

---

[1] This applies only to the original volume of the Interchurch Report. The second volume which appeared some 15 months later but unlike the original volume has not been widely reviewed or circulated has a chapter signed by Mr. George Soule devoted to a discussion of "Welfare Work."   The mere statement of the nature of this work and of its extent itself constitutes an impressive favorable argument.   Mr. Soule makes such a statement, in general, adequately and fairly.   Unfortunately the same cannot be said for some of his arguments and conclusions.   He complains of the stock subscription plan (page 252) that "it is not a simple business proposition," and complains in his summary of the welfare policy that, "it is a 'business proposition'" (page 259), and is otherwise captious and except in two instances obviously gives praise grudgingly.   This chapter is particularly noteworthy, however, in that, as far as can be discovered, it is the only case in either volume in which any facts in favor of the steel companies are admitted.   In several other respects also this chapter is the conspicuous high water mark of the whole Interchurch investigation effort.

merit and get their loyal support one of the very most important functions of the company's management.

But an "investigation" which can calmly ignore, except for a bit of passing sarcasm, $80,000,000 of evidence of the corporation's interest in the welfare of its employees, can hardly be expected to consider seriously a mere official statement of policy. After garbling part of Judge Gary's testimony in order to be more sarcastic about it (pages 24–25, 122, etc.), the Interchurch Report sweeps the whole statement of policy aside with the insinuation that it is merely for *public consumption*.

It is to be noted, however, that all such statements during the strike are only repetitions of many similar statements made long previous to the strike when there was no question of labor trouble, and that many such statements were made as fundamental principles of management during times when general business conditions were worst, labor was most plentiful, and when there was otherwise no reason why the Corporation should, and many reasons of immediate self-interest why it should not, emphasize such policies and spend its money to carry them out unless the Corporation was entirely sincere in seeking the best good of the workers at the time when the worker needed assistance most.

On May 29, 1911, during a time of general business depression and wage reductions, Judge Gary said to a group of his fellow manufacturers:

"Gentlemen, let us not come to the conclusion of reducing wages until we are compelled to do so. Let us keep them as high as we can just as long as we can . . . (in order that we may) . . . take pleasure in knowing that we are at all times doing all we can for the people in our employ in keeping their wages up and in bettering their conditions." (Senate Hearings, page 236, second paragraph.)

Other employers did reduce wages at that time. The U. S. Steel Corporation did not.

During this same period of depressed business conditions

and plentiful labor Judge Gary, on December 19, 1912, and again on December 17, 1913 issued the following instructions to the presidents of the subsidiary companies:

"It is a question simply as to whether or not when you consider the success of your corporation and the merits of the workman who does so much to make its business successful, you are giving him a reasonable division or share of the profits which are realized. I do not care whether the question is considered from the standard of good morals or not, ... I believe from the standpoint of what is for the best interests of your companies . . . it is wise to deal with your workmen not only fairly but liberally. . . . It is a pleasure to be connected with the business when you consider that, departing from the general rules which have obtained between employer and employee throughout the world, you have by your treatment of these questions established the relations which now exist between you and your employees."

"Now you will have some occasion perhaps during the immediate future to consider further some of these matters and they may involve considerable cost. If so, I should consider the money well expended. It is even possible that there may be some distress among some of your employees . . . I hope you will make an effort to keep posted." (After detailed and specific instruction as to what is to be done in the way of remitting rent, keeping men working even at a loss, etc., etc., the statement concludes,) . . . "You may expect to meet considerable loss during the coming winter but if in so doing you have added to the relief, benefit and comfort of employees, who in the nature of things are more or less dependent upon you, it should be a pleasure." (S. H., Part I, Excerpts, pages 237 to 238).

As has already been pointed out the Corporation operated at considerable loss during this period and stockholders' dividends were reduced to 3% then to 1¼% but wages were not reduced but were kept up by these reduced dividends and out of surplus funds. Moreover during this same period of 1912–1915, $24,502,699 was spent outright in improving working and living conditions of the employees.

At the annual meeting of stockholders April 16, 1917— just a year before the unionization drive began and two years before the strike, Judge Gary said,

"From time to time efforts have been made by outsiders to create dissension, to instill a feeling of animosity on the part of our men against

our corporation but these efforts have failed. I say we are proud of this
condition. . . . We have tried to treat our men justly and liberally and
as one man ought to treat another man but not simply because of our high
regard for them, . . . but also because we realize as a business proposition it is for *our* interest to do so. . . . We sometimes receive letters
from stockholders complaining because we pay too large wages . . . and
that we had better give to the stockholders in dividends a part of the
money which we are paying the employees. I have one answer only to
make to those stockholders . . . it is decidedly to the advantage of the
stockholder to have an organization that can retain in its employ
(when there was great labor shortage and the country was full of labor-
agitation) hundreds of thousands of men who are satisfied with their
condition and who consequently are doing everything possible to
protect and benefit the corporation'' (Senate Hearings, Excerpts,
pages 238 and 239).

There can be no question then as to the definite interest
of the Steel Corporation in the welfare of its men and as to
its deliberate policy of seeking to improve their working and
living conditions in order to make them more satisfied and
so more loyal and efficient employees. There remains, of
course, the question of the result of this interest and effort.

When the United States Steel Corporation was formed,
it was notoriously the largest corporation in industrial
history and both its size and other conditions gave rise to
certain serious questions as to its ultimate success. Both
the amounts of capital involved and these other conditions
demanded that its management should be of the highest
ability, and certainly Andrew Carnegie and the elder
Morgan were men who could judge and command such
ability. The original capital stock of the Corporation was
some $800,000,000 and it was widely considered that the
actual material assets of the company were less than that
sum. In eighteen years the management of the Corporation has not merely made a complete success of the original
venture but without any increase of capital has raised the material assets of the company to two and a half billion dollars.

When management of this type of proven ability appro-
priates $80,000,000 to improve the working and living

conditions of its employees with the express purpose both by such improvements and through removing any cause of grievance, of obtaining their good will and loyalty, and spends this money over a period of years during which it can carefully watch results and vary the details of its policy accordingly, surely the presumption of common sense is that such money is not being spent in larger and larger quantities year after year unless it shows results.

Moreover while in the coal industry which employs much of the same class of labor as in the steel industry, strikes and other labor troubles are so constant that the average worker throughout the industry loses, according to the U. S. Department of Labor figures, 30 days a year from strikes; and while repeated strikes and labor trouble have been one of the most conspicuous phenomena of labor conditions in many other prominent industries, the Steel Corporation under its policy of thus taking the initiative and the expense of cultivating the good will of its men went for 18 years up to 1919 with only one very ordinary size strike (in 1909) which lasted only a few weeks in a few mills.

This remarkable freedom of the steel industry from labor trouble in the past is of such common knowledge and was so conspicuously featured at the time of the strike that both the strike leaders and the Interchurch Report were compelled to attempt to reconcile it with their allegations of the general discontent of the steel workers. One of the grounds on which they both attempted to do this was by claiming that the steel worker had been so suppressed and intimidated that he did not dare express his grievance. A reading of the Senate testimony, in which an ordinary workman who was one of the steel company's own witnesses flatly contradicted Judge Gary to his face about a minor matter and in which another worker contradicted Judge Lindabury, and in which common laborers expressed themselves with much volubility and often profanity to senators, certainly fails to give any impression that the steel workers were in any sense suppressed or intimidated.

As a second argument to try to offset the well-known fact that the steel companies in the past had had practically no labor trouble, the Interchurch Report makes the ingenuous point that while there may have been no mass strikes in the past, the individual steel workers were constantly going on "individual strikes." On page 148 the Interchurch Report, in attempting to emphasize such so-called "individual strikes," which it claims show the steel workers' "rebellious frame of mind," points to what it calls the "high labor turnover in steel plants," using as its trump card in this argument the alleged fact that the labor turnover in the Homestead steel works for 1919 was 59%.

The General Electric Company is generally regarded as a model employer. It uses a very large per cent of labor of high special skill. Its Schenectady plant is in a town where large numbers of other jobs are not readily available and so men have a special incentive for keeping their jobs. The plant is unionized and has elaborate systems of collective bargaining. The company makes every effort to, and unquestionably succeeds in, keeping its men better than the great bulk of employers throughout the country. Yet in the Schenectady plant of the General Electric Company in 1919, their labor turnover was 68%, nine points higher than the Interchurch Report's figure for the Homestead plant.

In 1918 *Collier's Weekly* made a special study of the subject of labor turnover in a wide variety of industries and published (April 13, 1918) figures which showed that the "usual" labor turnover at this time was 120 to 180% or 2½ to 3½ times what the Interchurch alleges for the Steel Corporation and that at least during this particular period of labor unrest a "turnover" of 1300% was "by no means unparalleled."

Again the U. S. Bureau of Labor Statistics Monthly Review gives a number of detailed figures as to labor turnover during this period, the March, 1919, issue, page 36, showing the following facts for Cincinnati and the September, 1919, issue page 45 for Chicago.

Per Cent of Turnover	Per Cent of Plants	
	Cincinnati	Chicago
Under 50% turnover............	7%	None
50 to 100% "	15%	20%
100 to 150% "	21%	24%
150 to 200% "	21%	16%
200 to 250% "	7%	8%
250 to 300% "	18%	20%
300 to 350% " ....,	None	12%
350 to 400% "	7%	None
400 to 500% "	4%	None

The average labor turnover in both these great and diversified industrial centers was thus obviously at this same time some 150%, yet the Interchurch Report argues that this 59% labor turnover which it alleges against the steel industry proves the "rebellious frame of mind" of the steel worker. In view of the actual percentages of labor turnover in industry as a whole at this time a 59% turnover would certainly seem to show a very satisfied frame of mind.

Moreover the notorious fact that, at least during 1916–17–18 when the demand for labor in all industry was so great that rival employers and a host of employment agencies were combing the older industries to get employees for the new war industries, the Steel Corporation did not lose its workers but increased them by over 50% is the best possible evidence that the steel worker stuck by his job because he was satisfied with it and not because he was intimidated and oppressed into hopeless acceptance of it.

It is in connection with its elaborate and extensive "welfare work," which the Interchurch Report so carefully refrains from discussing, that the Steel Corporation has built up a most extensive organization which the Interchurch Report says it does not possess,[1] through which it keeps in

---

[1] "The conditions of labor were fixed by the Corporation without collective bargaining or *any functioning means of conference* also *without any aboveboard means of learning how decreed conditions effected the worker.*"

". . . Machinery of control gave but negligible information of working and living conditions," etc., etc. (Interchurch Report, pages 11–15).

direct and constant touch with the feelings and conditions of the workers, not only in their work but in their homes.

In the operation of its $80,000,000 worth of welfare equipment, the Corporation has an organization of 35,574 workers, chosen from every department and from every class of workers, who have in the past served on various welfare committees—as members of safety committees, as officers of employee clubs, as committees on the various activities of the workers, athletics and other forms of recreation, etc. As members of such committees these men worked in close touch with officers of the company, and having established this close touch, officers of the company, as a matter of policy, maintain this relationship as a point of contact with the feelings and points of view of all the great body of workers.

There is also at all times a similar group of current active committees composed of 7258 workers selected from all departments and classes of workers—a most considerable proportion, as is shown by their names, from among the foreign employees—who are in constant active touch with both the management and the men.

This system which has been established and functioning for years, which consists of an organization of 40 odd thousands, almost entirely of the workers themselves, may not constitute a "functioning means of conference" according to the Interchurch Report's definition, but it certainly is, despite the Interchurch Report's statement to the contrary, an "above-board means" of getting *more* than "negligible information of working and living conditions."[1]

---

[1] The special chapter on "Welfare Work" in the second volume of the Interchurch Report emphasized—partly in italics on page 257: "It is noteworthy that in this successful portion of the Corporation's labor policy *it has consciously enlisted the coöperation of its employees as a group.* Committees of workmen have been appointed *to advise* in the development of safety work and *help in carrying it out.* The committees are not elected but at least some attempt has been made to *tap the resources of practical knowledge and power in the forces of labor.* Over five thousand (7258) employees are serving on safety committees and about

Moreover the fact that under this system, information as to working and living conditions and the attitude of the men in regard to them comes to the steel official through members of the working force itself instead of through outside professional labor leaders, appointed by and responsible only to outside professional labor officials, does not necessarily make such information less valuable or accurate.

After stating that the Steel Corporation's machinery of control gave but "negligible information of working and living conditions," and that the Steel Corporation was "without aboveboard means of learning how decreed conditions affected the workers," the Interchurch Report states positively and repeatedly that it was impossible for steel workers to get their grievances considered by officers in power, and that in practice:

"Grievances which drive workers out of the steel industry are effectively stopped from getting higher than the first representative of the company reachable by the worker, the foreman" (page 26) ". . . he can't change his foreman and he *cannot get above the foreman,*" (page 136), etc., etc.

All the evidence, not only in the Senate Hearings, including the evidence given by the strikers' own witnesses, but the evidence on the subject presented by the Interchurch Report itself is definitely and positively to the contrary.

The Senate Investigation Committee went into considerable detail in regard to what opportunity the workers had to get their grievances reviewed. Many workers, foremen, and superintendents, who were company witnesses testified repeatedly that any steel worker could drop his

---

eighteen thousand have been trained in first-aid and rescue work." 35,574 more are ex-members of safety committees, etc. Yet in spite of the fact that it thus acknowledges that this number of representative employees are in necessarily continual touch with the management the Interchurch Report insists that the management has no "aboveboard means of learning how the decreed conditions affected the workers" or of getting more than "negligible information as to living and working conditions."

tools and walk right into the Superintendent's or even the General Superintendent's office at any time he felt he had a grievance. They testified as to various instances when this had happened. For instance, Mr. T. J. Davies, a tin mill roller from the Newcastle plant who for 14 years had been a union man, who was a delegate to the 1902 convention of the Amalgamated Association, and a deputy Vice President of that union, and who had served 15 months in France, testified as follows (Senate Hearings, Part I, page 447):

"*Mr. Davies:* Why, the humblest man in the mill, foreign or American, does not have to accept finally anything from them (foremen). Any grievance he may want to make, he can make it to the foreman and if the foreman won't take it up, he can just simply open the door of the main office and walk right in to the Superintendent. That condition obtains to the best of my knowledge and belief—to my knowledge (he had been 34 years with the company and had worked from day laborer up) all through the operations of the company. If grievances are felt the humblest man in the mill can walk past the foreman right to the general superintendent and get things remedied very quickly.

"*Senator Phipps:* Do you know of any instances where committees have been appointed to present these grievances to the Superintendent?

"*Mr. Davies:* I have never known of the necessity. Each man—all of us can go off-handedly if we like, to the Superintendent. . . . We can take it to the manager. Things that they want remedied. For instance we had a complaint which was a big one and it was taken to the assistant Superintendent. It was a rougher's question. . . . The roughers were asked to do something. They were asked to lift bars and put them in a place that was supposed to be of advantage to the company and the foreman said, 'You have got to lift them.' Some of the boys told him it was not necessary and they took their complaint to the manager. . . . That was a pretty good size committee. I suppose there were about 25 or 30 and that is a good size committee. They went in there to the manager and took their case up and they didn't have to do the extra lifting. . . . It was only a matter of about 18 inches of lift which they saved by making the complaint to the Superintendent but it was listened to and attended to."

But undoubtedly even more convincing evidence on this point is that which is given by witnesses brought by the strike leaders themselves for the express purpose of condemning the steel company's system of handling complaints. (See Senate Hearings, Part II, pages 676, 711, 712, 730.)

Of these perhaps the star witness for the strike leaders, because he was one of the few Americans who testified for them, was Matt O'Reilly of Donora, Pennsylvania. After a page of discussion about a petty quarrel with a foreman, the concluding testimony was as follows (page 677, line 8):

"*Senator Stirling:* You went back and since that time you never had any trouble with the foreman?

"*Mr. O'Reilly:* I went back and since that time I never had any trouble with the foreman but I had to go to the Superintendent.

"*Senator Stirling:* And in all of your years of work that is the only trouble you had?

"*Mr. O'Reilly:* That is the only trouble I had.

"*Senator Stirling:* And in this case you had—you did get a hearing from the Superintendent, didn't you?

"*Mr. O'Reilly:* I got a hearing from the Superintendent. I made it my business to get a hearing."

George Colson, another star witness for the strike leaders, because he was an American, and a most disgruntled witness, nevertheless, speaks on page 730 repeatedly and casually of taking up his grievance with the Superintendent as a matter of course.

From the point of view, however, of the Interchurch Report statement that "grievances are effectively stopped from getting higher than the foreman," the Interchurch Report's own evidence is undoubtedly the most significant of all because it definitely proves that statement untrue. On pages 213–218 of the Interchurch Report appear ten affidavits or statements—presumably of the "500 rock bottom affidavits"—in regard to specific grievances. *Six of these ten show a common workman taking up his grievance with an officer higher than a foreman.* The other four do not show that the worker made any effort to take his case higher than the foreman.

For instance it is plainly stated (Interchurch Report, page 213) in regard to Joseph Yart, obviously a foreigner, that his whole controversy was not with his foreman but with the superintendent of the mill. Again it is stated plainly (page 214) that Charles Bacha, also obviously a foreigner, took his case from the foreman to the Superintendent, Dunk May, and from the Superintendent to the General Superintendent, Mr. Lumpkin, and was moreover allowed the privilege of taking up his same case four times. And again, John Kubarda, also obviously a foreigner, was told by his foreman, "Go down to the general office and fix it up with them" (Interchurch Report, page 217).

Again on page 67 the Interchurch Report itself says:—

"It was surprising . . . to find *so large a number of strikers* complaining about hazards . . . concerning which they had complained to foremen *and superintendents month in and month out.* . . ."

and there are many other plain though inadvertent admissions in the Interchurch Report itself that all steel workers went over their foreman's head to Superintendent or Manager constantly as a matter of course.

All of the plain facts in regard to the relation of the Steel Corporation and its men show that the Steel Corporation deliberately decided years ago as a matter of fundamental policy to attempt to depart from the ordinary basis of relationship between capital and labor and win the loyalty and support of its men by treating them not only fairly but generously,—by voluntarily raising wages and keeping wages as high as possible, by paying special attention to and spending immense sums of money on their employees' working and living conditions—and by otherwise making a particular effort to keep its men specially loyal by keeping them especially satisfied.

Through at least ten years of hard times as well as good, the Corporation has consistently followed this policy.

It has for years maintained a policy of industrial democracy under which, on the testimony of hostile Interchurch and strike leaders' witnesses, any ordinary workman, including the least skilled foreigner, can and does individually take his grievance to his Superintendent or General Superintendent as casually and repeatedly as men in other industries go to their foreman.

In addition to this simple direct method of receiving and handling individual complaints, the Corporation maintains special contact with its men through committees consisting of over 40,000 of the men themselves through whom it is in constant touch with the general feelings and points of view of its men, which information it uses in taking the initiative in giving them every advantage that it reasonably can.

Such a system is not the proposed labor leader system emphasized by the Interchurch Report of trade union collective bargaining under which professional labor leaders become irresponsible partners in managing many of the most vital functions in business. It is a system in which men responsible for the results of management insist on doing the managing. But it is a system under which the management has maintained a production efficiency which over a period of years has given steady employment and higher wages to more workers than any other basic industry under any other type of management has ever done in modern industrial history. Moreover, under it, undoubtedly more men have worked longer without any serious labor trouble or agitation than in any other industry under any other system in modern times.

It is perhaps easy to understand why, not merely the difference of this system but particularly its success should prove a veritable red rag to the professional labor leader and the professional radical and make them particularly eager to attack the steel industry and particularly venomous in that attack.[1]

[1] The American Federation of Labor at its Thirty-ninth Annual Convention at Atlantic City, June, 1919, passed the following Resolution:

"WHEREAS, many steel corporations and other industrial institutions have instituted in their plants systems of collective bargaining. . . ."

"RESOLVED, That we disapprove and condemn all such company unions and advise our membership to have nothing to do with them; and, be it further

It is not so plain, however, why the Interchurch Report should ignore the existence of this system and insist so volubly in its "Conclusions" in the front of the book that steel officials, under the existing system, were not and could not get in touch with their men, and that the men, under existing conditions, could not take their grievances higher than the foreman, when it has, and itself plainly publishes in the back of the book, voluminous and detailed evidence that this is not true.

"RESOLVED, That we demand the right to bargain collectively through *the only kind of organization fitted for this purpose*, the trade union. . . ."

SPECIAL NOTE

The ten statements and affidavits referred to in the preceding chapter constitute the only groups of the 500 "rock bottom" statements and affidavits, on which the Interchurch Report itself states that it is chiefly based, which appear in the main Report.

The last two of these documents specifically state that the signer had been employed by the U. S. Steel Corporation. One of them, which four times specifies that the signer was discharged not by his foreman but by the Superintendent, is dated without comment August 15th, nearly 2 months before the Interchurch investigation.

The first eight of these documents on the other hand are prefaced with the statement (page 213) that they are part of 200 "signed statements and sworn affidavits" "obtained in *two days*" by "*an investigator* in November, 1919." Two of these—No. 7 and No. 8—are " sworn affidavits." But the notary's date on No. 7 is February 22, 1919, and on No. 8, February 24, 1919. To No. 7, the Notary has also added: "*Paper not drafted by Notary.*" As to the other, unsworn statements, the following is to be noted. All recite facts alleged to have occurred from 8 to 12 months before November, 1919. All are also very exact about dates and other details—including exact quotations of alleged conversations. Again the language throughout is so grammatical, direct and otherwise such that it seems hardly possible that the documents could have been composed by the signers. It seems inconceivable for instance, that Nick Poppovich who could not sign his own name should himself have said, "The foregoing occurred the forenoon of February 22d," "I believe I have a right to join a labor organization for my protection," etc., or that John Kubanda should have said, "I verily believe that it was through union affiliations that I was discharged," etc. Other of the documents are very formally expressed throughout in the third person, etc. etc.

The Interchurch Report, Volume II, page 178, in presenting another group of its "rock bottom" statements and affidavits, admits that "the language used in many of these documents is 'interpreters' English,'" the documents themselves being merely "a brief statement, summary or affidavit" composed by a third party. The documents here considered show on their face that they also are thus composed by some other person than the signer.

In considering who such third person or persons in this case were the question at once arises: is it reasonably possible that the one investigator stated to have "obtained" these documents in November, 1919, could have examined, often through an interpreter, 100 witnesses a day, and in addition have composed, with the frequent necessity of translating back again and correcting, 100 statements a day, with sufficient thoroughness and accuracy to warrant the specificness and exactness with which the facts are alleged throughout these documents? Again, is it possible that any men, and particularly such men as signed these statements, could have recalled 8 to 10 months after the event, dates, quotations and other details with such exactness as these statements give them? There is moreover the fact that two of these documents, specifically stated to have been "obtained" by this investigator in these two days, show by notaries' dates that they were composed ten months before they were thus "obtained."

Immediately following these ten "rock bottom" documents the Interchurch Report (top of page 219) says: "These are examples. The range of the commission's data is given in a sub-report." The one sub-report published containing a group of "rock bottom" affidavits admits frankly (Volume II, page 176) that part of these documents were obtained "from President Maurer of the State Federation," i.e. Pennsylvania State Federation of Labor. As is shown in detail in Chapter XXIII and page 419 of the present analysis actually all the affidavits and most of the statements there presented, were "obtained" from this notorious radical who signed himself in now published correspondence with the Moscow Soviet as "representing 300 radical groups in 42 States." These sections also show in detail that the documents themselves consist largely of utterly false or misleading statements skilfully composed for propaganda purposes. Because of the nature of the subject matter of the ten documents under present discussion, there is no available means of checking the truth or falsity of the basic allegations upon which they are built. There can be no reasonable doubt however, that like most of the other "rock bottom" affidavits as published, they were composed long before the Interchurch investigation was thought of and were merely borrowed by the Interchurch investigators from the strike leaders.

SECTION B

Issues in the Steel Strike and arguments of the Interchurch Report which involve facts as to the opinions of large numbers of men—facts as to motives and facts as to complex circumstances, conclusions as to which can only be reached by a determination of the weight of evidence.

CHAPTER XIV

THE effort to unionize the steel industry was made and the strike was called on the express grounds, as has already been emphasized, that the steel workers had certain grievances against the steel companies which it had been impossible for them to remedy under existing circumstances and for which the promise of remedy lay in trade union collective bargaining which the unionization effort and the strike specifically aimed to establish.

These alleged grievances, as stated by the Interchurch Report and the strike leaders, were principally and specifically unfairly low wages and unfairly long hours, and the lack on the part of the men of any voice in the management of their conditions of employment, which was not only a grievance in itself, but which was the alleged cause of many minor grievances.

The alleged grievance of unfairly low wages has already been argued on the basis of definite and known facts and it has been shown as a matter of fact that wages in the steel industry were not unfairly low but on the contrary were conspicuously high as compared with other industries.

The alleged grievance of the hardship and hazard of steel work, which is emphasized far more by the Interchurch Report than by the strikers themselves, has been shown to be without merit in fact.

It has been shown as a matter of fact that the steel companies themselves have taken the greatest interest in the welfare of the steel worker—that they have taken the initiative and spent immense sums of money in improving working and living conditions. It has been shown not only from general evidence but specifically from evidence which both the Interchurch Report and the strike leaders presented in regard to certain other points, that the men, under present conditions, have the simplest and easiest facilities for presenting any grievance they may feel.

The issue as to working hours in the steel industry centers chiefly around the 12-hour day. In so far as this issue involves matters of fact—as to the number of 12-hour workers, the nature of 12-hour work, the tendency as to working hours in the industry, and the relative length of working hours in the steel industry and in American industry as a whole—the Interchurch argument and conclusions have already been analyzed in detail and shown to be not only in general contrary to the plain facts but in 2 of its 3 main conclusions to be based on clever manipulations and falsifications or on flagrant misquotation of official statistics.

The steel companies have constantly maintained, and state this as a leading reason for the continuance of the 12-hour day, that the majority of the 12-hour workers themselves prefer these working hours because of the larger earnings they make possible. Mr. Clayton L. Patterson on page 68 of his pamphlet, "The Steel Strike of 1919," states that, "according to the best information available," "half of the 12-hour workers prefer these hours because of the larger pay"; about one fourth "are indifferent or have not expressed themselves on the subject" while the remaining quarter "are willing to sacrifice the larger earnings for the shorter working day."

On page 99, paragraph 2, in discussing "one of the real reasons why the 12-hour day has persisted in the steel industry," the Interchurch Report states that for "30% of steel workers," particularly the "simple foreign worker," "these possibilities of overtime . . . constitute the bait" and that "from this 30% the steel companies recruit their 12-hour gang in considerable part."

This paragraph admits this fact not in extenuation but in further condemnation of the 12-hour day. Nevertheless, in thus plainly stating that "30% of steel workers" do prefer the higher earnings of the 12-hour day, and that "from this 30% the steel companies recruit their 12-hour gang," which "gang" as a matter of fact does not constitute much if any over 30% of all workers even in primary production departments—the Interchurch Report has gone even higher than the steel companies themselves in its estimate of the percentage of 12-hour workers who prefer these hours.·

By this plain admission as to the large proportion of 12-hour workers themselves who prefer the 12-hour day—no matter how mistakenly—the Interchurch Report would seem plainly to eliminate the 12-hour day as one of the workers' grievances and make it necessary to argue the 12-hour question entirely on the basis of social expediency, irrespective of the wishes of the workers themselves. This particular paragraph however, and these particular admissions of the Interchurch Report, are only another example of its strange inconsistencies and self-contradictions, for throughout the rest of the Report, the 12-hour day is constantly featured as the major grievance of the steel workers and the major reason why it was claimed the steel workers wanted Trade Union Collective Bargaining.

Whether or not the majority of 12-hour workers themselves do desire the 12-hour day because of its higher earnings, or, on the contrary regard it as a grievance, of course involves the opinion of something over one hundred thousand such men, which, barring its possible ascertainment by a fair and free vote on this specific question, which has not and perhaps cannot be taken, must be determined on the weight of all such evidence as is available.

In the same way, the question as to whether or not other working conditions were felt generally by the steel workers themselves to constitute undue grievances obviously involves the opinion of nearly five hundred thousand such workers which opinion, except on the basis of a specific and fair vote, again can only be determined by the weight of all evidence available.

Finally, whether or not the proposed remedy for these alleged grievances—Trade Union Collective Bargaining— was regarded by the majority of the steel workers themselves as an adequate and desirable remedy also involves the opinion of some 500,000 men. Barring the possibility of its expression through a specific and fair vote, these opinions again can only be determined by the weight of all the evidence available.

The drive to unionize the steel industry was made expressly on the basis that the steel workers themselves did feel the alleged grievances to be real and desired trade union collective bargaining as a means of rectifying such grievances. The strike leaders stated in advance that the strike itself would constitute a vote by the workers themselves as to their attitude toward their alleged grievances and the proposed remedy.

There can be no question that if other conditions had been equal—if the response to the unionization drive and the strike order were not unduly complicated by other influences and considerations—the measure of that response constituted the strongest possible *prima facie* evidence as to whether or not the men themselves, at least at the time of the strike, regarded the alleged grievances as real and the proposed remedy as desirable.

But it was a question very much in dispute at the time as to how big a proportion of the workers did obey the strike order. Moreover it is strongly urged by the steel companies that as regards the strike being an expression of a feeling of grievance, even on the part of the majority of those who struck, other things were not equal—that on the contrary the strike, even to the extent it was effective, was brought about by outside professional labor leaders who, uninvited and undesired by any considerable proportion of the steel workers, began a campaign of agitation, including radical agitation, chiefly among the unskilled foreign workers, and by appealing to their ignorance and class prejudices, formed a strike nucleus, and then by skilful manipulation of mass psychology, coupled with intimidation, succeeded in getting only a minority of the workers to stop work and that even this minority rapidly dwindled as soon as protection against intimidation was assured.

Nevertheless the response of the steel workers to the unionization drive and the strike order—irrespective of the fact that it may have been far from a free expression of opinion on the specific questions involved and must be qualified accordingly—is certainly the most conspicuous evidence, and also the most definite comprehensive evidence available as to the feeling of the steel workers themselves in regard to the alleged grievances and the proposed remedy.

The question as to whether or not, and to what extent, the unionization drive and the strike represented such a free expression of opinion will be considered in the two following chapters, "Origin of the Strike Movement" and "Radicalism in the Steel Strike." The succeeding chapter, "Response of the Men to the Unionization Drive and the Strike Appeal" will discuss, with any reservations which may then be established, what the unionization drive and the strike actually showed to be the attitude of the steel workers themselves as to their alleged grievances and as to Trade Union Collective Bargaining as a remedy.

CHAPTER XV

In regard to the origin of the strike movement the Interchurch Report (page 144, line 27) says merely that:

"The labor movement initiated the organizing campaign, invited by the steel workers according to the labor leaders, invading where it was not wanted according to the employers. Both statements are correct and neither lays emphasis on the principle fact . . . these steel workers are more important than their leaders, etc."

The whole Interchurch argument and its conclusions as to the reasons for the strike and the relation of the steel workers to the strike are based on two assumptions both contrary to fact and the arguments from which are correspondingly fallacious. It is necessary therefore, although the Interchurch Report thus evades this point, to establish as part of the evidence of those fallacies the actual facts as to who originated the strike movement and why.

Up to the time of the steel strike in 1919 and the unionization drive which preceded it, there had been no strikes and no apparent agitation or unrest among the steel workers since 1910. Except for a small abortive agitation and strike which lasted only a few weeks and in a few plants at that time there had been no strikes or visible agitation and unrest since 1903. In other words before the 1919 strike, for this remarkably long period,—considering the average American conditions of labor unrest,—of sixteen years, the steel industry had enjoyed apparently peaceful and mutually satisfactory relations between employer and workers.

During the years 1916–17–18 general labor unrest and strikes throughout the country had multiplied till they had permeated every other basic industry and reached in the year of our entry into the war the unparalleled figure of 4,324.[1] Yet during these years of particular and acute general labor unrest, the steel industry, which had voluntarily raised wages eight different times during this period, had been conspicuously free from labor unrest. No suggestions of labor trouble or a strike had, according to the testimony of the steel leaders, been discerned by the watchful interests of the steel companies themselves and certainly no suggestion of labor trouble in the steel industry had come to public attention until the fall of 1918.

For a great many years Mr. William Z. Foster had been a prominent I. W. W. official and organizer. He was secretary of the Syndicalist League of North America and one of the American delegates to their international convention at Buda Pesth in 1911 (Senate Hearings, Part 1, page 421— last paragraph, page 422, line 47, etc., etc.).

In 1914, however, Mr. Foster announced his decision:

"that the only way for the I. W. W. to have the workers adopt and practice the principles of revolutionary unionism is to give up the attempt to create a new labor movement . . . get into the organized labor movement and . . . revolutionize these unions" (Senate Hearings, page 418).

Two years after the announcement of this conviction, Mr. Foster appears as an international organizer of the Brotherhood of Railroad Carmen, a regular trade union organization. The next year he presented an entirely novel plan to the American Federation of Labor for the unionization of the workers of the Chicago stockyards and in cooperation with the A. F. of L. was one of the leaders in the strike that succeeded in unionizing those workers.

It was at this time that Mr. Foster originated the idea

[1] U. S. Bureau of Labor Statistics Monthly Review, June, 1920, page 204–1510.

and the plan of unionizing the steel industry, which idea and plan he himself describes in his own book, *The Great Steel Strike*, beginning page 17, line 3, as follows:

". . . as the War wore on and the United States joined the general slaughter, the situation changed rapidly in favor of the unions. The demand for soldiers and munitions had made labor scarce; . . . the steel industry was the master clock of the whole war program and had to be kept in operation at all costs . . . it was an opportunity to organize the industry such as might never again occur. . . .

"The writer was one of those who perceived the unparalleled opportunity. But being at that time secretary-treasurer of the committee organizing the packing industry, I was unable to do anything substantial in the steel situation. . . . Immediately thereafter (at the end of the packers' strike) I presented a resolution to the Chicago Federation of Labor requesting the executive officers of the American Federation of Labor to call a general labor conference, and to inaugurate thereat a national campaign to organize the steel workers.

"It was intended," continues Mr. Foster (*Great Steel Strike*, page 21, lines 7–12) "that after the Chicago conference a dozen or more general organizers should be dispatched immediately *to the most important steel centers to bring to the steel workers the first word of the big drive being made in their behalf.*"

Mr. Foster states incidentally that his resolution was "endorsed by twelve local unions in the steel industry," but what these unions were, how many members or what part of the industry they represented, he does not state.

Moreover it must be borne in mind that the strike leaders themselves later claimed repeatedly that such local unions as existed in the steel industry were traitors to the workers' cause because they were against the strike and Mr. Foster himself says (*Great Steel Strike*, page 106, line 29):

"Much harm was done the morale of the strikers by local unions . . . refusing to recognize the national committee's strike call."

He also says (page 45, line 24):

"Company unions are invariably contemptible."

Mr. Fitzpatrick in his testimony (Senate Hearings, Part I, page 81) also bitterly condemns company unions as opposing the strike.

The American Federation of Labor passed a special Resolution at its 1919 Convention specifically condemning local steel unions and one of the twelve official demands made by the strike leaders on which the strike was called was that all local unions should be abolished.

Finally these twelve unnamed unions could not have been very important or representative or it would not have been necessary after the Chicago conference to send immediately men to the "*important steel centers to bring the first word . . . of the big drive being made in their behalf.*"

On June 10th to 20th, 1918, ten weeks after Mr. Foster presented his plan, Resolution 29, authorizing the carrying out of Mr. Foster's plan, was "adopted by unanimous vote" at the convention of the A. F. of L. at St. Paul.

After referring to Resolution 29 as "merely the shell," Mr. Foster goes on to describe his actual plan as follows: (Great Steel Strike, page 20):

"Its breath of life was in its strategy; in the way the organization work was to be prosecuted . . . The idea was to make a hurricane drive simultaneously in all the steel centers that would catch the workers' imagination and sweep them into the unions *en masse* . . . coöperating international unions were to recruit numbers of organizers and to send them to join the forces already being developed everywhere by the general organizers . . . at least $250,000 (was) to be provided for the work."

This sum refers only to the initiation of the whirlwind campaign. As a matter of fact $1,005,007.72 was actually provided (Finance statement, Great Steel Strike, page 231).

Moreover Mr. Foster says (page 236, line 6):

"The figures cited in the previous chapter as covering the general expenses, $1,005,007, is unusually low. . . . The United Mine Workers are authoritatively stated to have spent about $5,000,000 . . . about $400 per man involved . . . in the next campaign (next steel strike) all that must be different. The Unions will have to put some real money in the fight. Then they may win it."

Mr. Foster originated the plan of the steel strike. He was secretary-treasurer, one of the two most important officers, of the special committee that managed the strike, and the above account of how the steel strike was originated and carried out was deliberately given in a generally circulated volume which appeared six months after the end of the strike.

Moreover Mr. John Fitzpatrick, President of the special committee that organized and managed the steel strike gives, though in less detail, an exactly parallel account of the plan and the motives that were back of the attempted unionization of the steel industry. Mr. Fitzpatrick was the first witness before the Senate Committee. His statement was carefully prepared and committed to memory as is obvious from the fact that when interrupted he began again to repeat word for word what he had previously been saying. He says (Senate Hearings, Part I, page 8, line 6):

"The labor organizations, realizing what tremendous influence the steel industry has on all other industries, made up its mind that it would have to organize the steel industry, no matter at what cost."

As to the origin of the Steel Strike Movement, Mr. Fitzpatrick again testified on the following page:

"*Senator Jones:* Mr. Fitzpatrick, let me ask you, had the employees of the Steel Corporation made application to the American Federation of Labor for their organization or was the movement initiated by the organization?

"*Mr. Fitzpatrick: The A. F. of L. instituted the movement.*"

Mr. Fitzpatrick does say, and later, realizing the meaning of the insistence of this question as to who initiated the movement, Mr. Gompers emphasizes, but only in a very vague general way, what he had previously said in his letter to Judge Gary that "upon the request of a *number of men*" in the employ of the U. S. Steel Corporation the American Federation of Labor had instituted the unionization movement. There is no possible question, however, as to the whole impression Mr. Fitzpatrick had and gave as to the initiation of the steel strike. In the part of his speech

obviously committed to memory he states plainly and un-
qualifiedly that the American Federation of Labor "initiated" the unionization drive in the steel industry and he
constantly comes back to the fact that it was:

"absolutely imperative that the steel mills be organized, because it
held the balance of the labor movement back" (Senate Hearings, page
10, line 2).

"Our position was to protect ourselves. We had to save our organization, etc., etc." (Senate Hearings, page 27, line 26).

Mr. Tighe, President of the Amalgamated Iron, Steel and
Tin Workers Union, which is the big union of the metal
trades, stated definitely that one of the causes of the 1910
strike, and he plainly indicated that it was a reason that still
persisted, was that many other metal workers in his union
"had dropped out of the organization by reason of the fact
that we were not taking an aggressive initiative attitude
toward the (Steel) Corporation."

In addition to these plain definite statements of the highest officials among the strike leaders, that organized labor
and not the steel workers initiated the unionization drive in
the steel industry, is the strong circumstantial evidence of
the type of strategy used in the unionization drive.

All the facts of the elaborate plans and preparations made
to unionize the steel industry—the number of organizers
required—the big sums of money—indicate of course that
the drive expected opposition and had to be prepared to
overcome that opposition.   There are obviously but two
possible sources of such opposition—the hostility or indifference of the steel workers themselves or the hostility
of the companies.   It is equally obvious that in proportion
as the organizers expected the opposition to be the indifference of the men, one type of organization strategy would be
employed, and in proportion as they expected the chief opposition to come from the steel companies another type of
strategy would be employed.

Now it is entirely obvious that the steel companies could

186 ANALYSIS OF THE INTERCHURCH

only fight the unionization movement in two ways, by hindering or persecuting the union organizers or by discharging the men who joined the unions. If the union organizers expected to be received and welcomed by the men and only this type of company opposition was to be overcome, it is plain that the best way to conduct such an organization campaign would be to hide their plans as much as possible from the steel companies, to keep their workers and work as inconspicuous as possible—to meet the men in small groups in their homes or otherwise and work from man to man. This would of course require large numbers of organizers and considerable money and time but the organization committee had money and a year's time.

It is equally obvious that if this big opposition, which was being so elaborately prepared against, was to come from the hostility or indifference of the men themselves, that the best strategy to overcome such hostility or indifference was to play on collective mass psychology and mass enthusiasm to get the movement started and rush the men off their feet.

"The idea," says Mr. Foster, "was to make a hurricane drive simultaneously in all the steel centers that would catch the workers' imaginations and sweep them into the unions *en masse*. . . . Great mass meetings built up by extensive advertising would be held everywhere at the same time throughout the steel industry . . . the heavy stream of men pouring into the unions would be turned into a decisive flood by the election of committees to formulate the grievances of the men and present these to the employers, etc., etc." (*Great Steel Strike*, page 21).

Again there is another group of facts which, by establishing clearly a strong motive, also constitutes at least strong circumstantial evidence as to who was responsible for the attempted unionization of the steel industry. These are the definite unquestioned facts as to the extent to which the labor organizations and the professional "organizers" would profit from the successful unionization of the steel industry.

Out of the $1,005,007.72 put into the steel strike—a large part of this put in by the labor leaders themselves out of the treasuries of other workers they "represented"—some

$348,509.42 was put into the commissariat to supply food to "the small impoverished minority of the workers" who did not have enough money saved up to support themselves and their families the three months they did not work. This leaves a balance of over a half a million dollars which was spent in two ways, the chief of which was in paying salaries to the principal, and a host of lesser, professional labor leaders, who were engaged in persuading the steel workers to accept them as "representatives."

In the next strike into which "real money must be put"— Mr. Foster mentions a minimum of $5,000,000—there will be some four or four and a half million dollars available— chiefly for paying salaries to a very much larger host of professional labor leaders.

But this applies only to the unionization or strike period. Governor Allen of Kansas in his speech before the Harvard Union in April, 1921, stated that less than 4,000,000 American workers, under the American Federation of Labor plan of trade union collective bargaining, are paying $50,000,000 a year into the hands of 150,000 professional labor leaders who "represent" these workers in their collective bargaining. If the steel strike had succeeded the 500,000 workers, at an average of 50c a week dues—these are the dues of the United Mine Workers and are exceptionally low—would be paying $12,000,000 a year to its "representatives," a small percentage of which would be added to a cumulative strike benefit fund, a certain percentage for other benefits, but at least $7,000,000 to $9,000,000 of which would go every year to pay the office rent and salaries of about 20,000 professional labor leaders to "represent" these steel workers in "collective bargaining" with the steel companies.

Moreover as Mr. Fitzpatrick particularly emphasized the unionization of the "key" steel industry would make it much easier to unionize other industries, which other industries would yield correspondingly similar profits.

As regards the origin of the campaign to "unionize" the steel workers then these points are plain as matters of fully established fact. The steel industry had for years enjoyed a conspicuous freedom from the labor troubles that had become more and more general. During a period in which the cost of living had gone up only about 80% steel wages had been voluntarily raised among the different classes of workers from 111% to 163%. Relations between the companies and the men were apparently entirely satisfactory. The plan to attempt to unionize the steel industry was originated among professional labor leaders entirely unconnected with the industry. It is alleged that after the plan had thus been independently developed Mr. Foster submitted it to certain individuals or minor organizations in the industry but no evidence is presented or suggested as to who these were and Mr. Foster does not pretend that this changes the fact, and Mr. Fitzpatrick definitely states it to be a fact, that the initiation of the steel unionization drive was entirely with the A. F. of L. Moreover the whole scope of the plan of unionization as described by Mr. Foster, its author—the emphasis that was placed on its particular type of strategy—show plainly that those who originated it and were prepared to carry it through expected to meet the greatest indifference on the part of the workers themselves. Finally the immense profits in jobs and income and influence which the successful unionization of such a great industry would bring to the professional labor leaders who unionized it, establishes an entirely adequate motive to explain why such an effort should be made to seek to overcome this anticipated indifference on the part of the men themselves.

CHAPTER XVI

RADICALISM IN THE STEEL STRIKE

THE daily press at the time particularly emphasized the influence of radicalism in the steel strike. It characterized Foster as the "radical leader of the strike." Many of the witnesses for the steel companies before the Senate Investigating committee and witnesses and evidence presented by the government emphasized the radical influence in the strike. Large quantities of radical literature were announced as having been found in various strike centers and the U. S. Department of Justice arrested a number of men for radical agitation. Because of these facts and because of the widespread feeling as to the development of radicalism after the war, there is no question but that the public thought radicalism a large factor in the steel strike.

The Interchurch Report, however, flatly denies that this was true. It says in its conclusions:

"13. Charges of Bolshevism or of industrial radicalism in the conduct of the strike were without foundation." (Interchurch Report, page 15, line 24).

"Evidence on this interpretation of the strike as a Bolshevist plot failed entirely to substantiate it. On the contrary it tended to show that this conception was without foundation in fact" (page 20, line 17).

The Interchurch Report questions Mr. Gary's sincerity in charging radicalism in the steel strike (page 35, line 10).

The Interchurch Report states the allegations in regard to radicalism in the strike which it thus concludes are without foundations in fact, as follows:

". . . the allegation that the strike was plotted and led by Reds or syndicalists or Bolshevists, that it was supported mainly or entirely by alien radicals and that its real objects were the overthrow of established leaders and established institutions of organized labor and perhaps the overthrow of the established government of the country" (page 21, line 18).

This is undoubtedly not a fair or accurate statement of the charges made or the feelings held in regard to radicalism in the strike. These did not insist that the radicals involved were "alien" except in their point of view. The most conspicuous leaders accused of radicalism were in fact known to be American citizens. Moreover it was probably never seriously felt, that the "direct objects" of the strike were the overthrow of established organized labor or of the established government of the country. All that was felt or seriously alleged was that the strike was conducted by men who had that general object and who meant to use the strike as far as possible as a step in that direction.

This statement by the Interchurch Report of the allegations of radicalism are so precise and definite, however, that it offers perhaps the most simple outline on which to analyze the question of radicalism in the strike.

The first allegation as stated and denied by the Interchurch Report is:

"The strike was plotted and led by Reds or syndicalists or Bolshevists."

The idea and the plan and the strategy of the steel strike were originated by Mr. William Z. Foster personally.

Mr. Foster states this fact specifically and with details as to steps of procedure, in his book *The Great Steel Strike*, page 27, which has already been quoted extensively. This fact was also alleged frequently during the strike and was never publicly officially denied by labor leaders and as far as is known never denied at all. The Interchurch Report itself states (page 157, line 1):

"He (Foster) saw the stockyards unorganized, the steel industry unorganized. Instead of merely trying to sting the A. F. of L. into

moving . . . he thought out a plan of action . . . He took the plan to Mr.
Fitzpatrick who saw its possibilities, the A. F. of L. indorsed it, etc."

Moreover the Interchurch Report constantly features
Foster as the conspicuous moving spirit of the steel strike.
There is no question that Mr. Foster had been a pronounced and extreme radical. He had been secretary of the
Syndicalist League of North America—had been a conspicuous leader of the I. W. W.—had been the official delegate
from these organizations to the world famous radical convention in Buda Pesth. Through a period of years he had
not only written a widely circulated book on radicalism but
had been a constant contributor to ultra radical magazines.
In these various writings he had said:

"The wages system is the most brazen and gigantic robbery ever
perpetrated . . . the thieves at present in control of the industries
must be stripped of their booty . . . this social reorganization will be
a revolution. . . . For years progressive workers have realized the
necessity for this revolution. They have also realized that it must
be brought about by . . . themselves . . . the Syndicalist . . . con-
siders the state a meddling capitalist institution. . . . He is a radical
opponent of 'law and order' as he knows that for his unions to be legal
in their tactics would be for them to become impotent. . . . With him
the end justifies the means. Whether his tactics be legal and moral or
not does not concern him so long as they are effective. . . . He proposes to develop, regardless of capitalist's conceptions of legality, fairness, right, etc., a greater power than his capitalist enemies have . . .
He proposes to bring about the revolution by the general strike. . . .
Besides its program of incessant skirmishes (ordinary strikes) the trade
union is engaged in the work of integral emancipation . . . Its fundamental task is to take possession of the social wealth now in the hands
of the bourgeois class and to reorganize society on a communist basis.
. . . Every great strike is accompanied by violence . . . but the prospect of bloodshed does not frighten the syndicalist worker . . . he has
no sentimental regard for what may happen to his enemies during the
general strike." Excerpts Senate Hearings, page 387, 394, 392, 417, 418.

These writings were all shown by the Senate Investigating Committee to Mr. Foster and were acknowledged by
him as his own.

Such was the man who conceived and planned the Steel

Strike. Moreover Mr. Foster was one of the two principal officers of the committee who organized the strike. His name was one of the five signed to the letter asking the conference with Judge Gary which conference was to put the steel industry on a trade union collective bargaining basis with Mr. Foster as one of the official bargainers. These are all matters of printed record.

Moreover, Mr. Foster not only personally conceived and developed the plan of the steel strike and was one of the two highest official leaders in organizing and conducting the strike but there can be no doubt that his ability and personality made him the dominant factor on the labor side.

Of the labor leaders who appeared before the Senate Committee one was obviously a strong, sincere, stubborn fighter but with a mind palpably slow and awkward. When he got away from his set speech or from questions that could be answered by stock phraseology, he floundered, made ridiculous statements and contradicted himself to an extent that was only saved from being humorous by his obvious sincerity. Some of the other labor leaders that appeared before the Senate Committee showed skill in parrying and thrusting with verbal phrases, appeared adroit, experienced manipulators and negotiators but were patently opportunists and fundamentally "soft."

Mr. Foster stood out. He was a dynamic force. He showed quick, keen insight and sure power of mind and tongue. No one can read the whole of the Senate testimony and particularly Mr. Foster's testimony, which for over an hour constituted a battle of wits between Mr. Foster and the five experienced cross-examiners who made up the Senate Committee, and not realize that with his particular ability and his official position, Mr. Foster must inevitably have been the dominant factor among the strike leaders.

The men at the head of the steel companies and the men at the head of our public press are presumably familiar with the general workings of committee management—including the disproportionate influence of any dominant personality in that management,—and also at least average judges of human nature. Both the steel men and the newspaper men undoubtedly knew well before the strike the notorious history of Mr. Foster including his beliefs and points of view. They knew that he originated and planned the unionization drive of the steel industry and of course knew his official position on the managing committee and the committee that sought to make itself the instrument of collective bargaining in the steel industry. They undoubtedly also knew, what the Interchurch Report admits, that radicals were actively agitating among the steel workers. They undoubtedly knew also, what the Interchurch and Mr. Foster freely admit—that the unionization work was being most conspicuously carried on among the foreigners who were most inclined and most susceptible to radicalism.

On the basis of these outstanding facts, all known before the strike, there can be no question, not only that the steel officials who were asked to turn over a considerable part of the management of their industry to a collective bargaining arrangement with such a committee, but the leaders of the press, were justified in believing and charging that the "strike was plotted and led by reds and syndicalists or bolshevists." Moreover that they were entirely right about this was freely admitted by Mr. Foster as soon as the steel strike was over, and is also admitted (as will be emphasized later) in the later and more obscure sections of the Interchurch Report.

All this evidence as to the extreme radicalism of the man who was one of the two most officially prominent, and who in the public mind was the most conspicuous of the strike leaders, was so widely published at the time and radicalism became such a prominent factor in the strike situation that the strike leaders made a special effort, particularly before the Senate Committee, to offset this impression. This effort was made along two lines: first, to show that Mr. Foster had given up his radicalism; and

13

second, to show that Mr. Foster was not really an important factor in the strike management.

In the Senate Hearings, Part I, page 77, Mr. Fitzpatrick testified in regard to Mr. Foster and his radical views:

" They are things that are past and gone . . . they have not got any-thing on Foster except something that has been dead and buried so long that it has no more use . . . absolutely they are not his present views. . . . (He is) absolutely confining himself to the activities and scope of the American Federation of Labor."

In regard to Mr. Foster's alleged change of attitude Mr. Gompers testified as follows: .

" *Chairman:* You say then, do you, Mr. Gompers, that his (Foster's) views expressed by him in his book on Syndicalism and his views ex-pressed at the time you speak of have changed?

" *Mr. Gompers:* I have no doubt and I have no hesitancy in saying so, sir."[1]   (Senate Hearings, Part I, page 112, line 26.)

Mr. Foster himself was cross-examined at great length by the Senate Committee as to whether or not he still held his old syndicalist views. His first line of defense was to assert that his personal views were not material as he was working with the American Federation of Labor. This point of view the Senators refused to accept and they presented to him extensive excerpts from a volume and pamphlets and letters which he was alleged to have previously written, each of which Mr. Foster acknowl-edged as his own writing and his own views at the time they were written. In each of these cases he was particularly

---

[1] " Foster is just back from Russia where he was in touch with Lenin and Trotzky. Judging from his own statements no man visiting the Soviet was ever treated better. . . . Immediately upon his return to the United States he proceeds to organize the Trade Union Educational League. Presumably Foster is the educator . . . Back of that resolu-tion (Foster's) is the propaganda of radical revolution to overthrow the Constitution of the United States . . . and William Z. Foster wants to become an autocrat of America."

SAMUEL GOMPERS,
April 30, 1922.

pressed to state whether or not he held the same opinions at the time of the strike. Mr. Foster evaded direct answer to such questions with great cleverness by giving such answers as "Well, I have my own ideas about the functions of government of course:" "That does not seem to be a very startling proposition nowadays:" "No. I would not state it that way now." "I do not think I would state it in exactly the same terms but I believe the men in the industries as far as possible should be given a right to operate those industries." "I wouldn't go that far probably," and otherwise skillfully evaded being cornered into saying specifically that his convictions had changed from his former extreme radicalism to any material degree.

Thus the much heralded "repudiation" of Mr. Foster's past radical views consisted merely of a repudiation of them for him by his fellow leaders in organized labor.

The *Liberator*, the leading organ of the Syndicalist Party said at this time (issue of Dec., 1919) of Mr. Foster:

"The intellectual honesty which distinguishes his type prevented him when on the stand at Washington from even pretending to disavow his motives. And though his present tactics enjoin a discreet silence about those motives, they are an open secret. He is in the A. F. of L. to assist that organization in its *transformation* into a modern labor organization."

The second argument by which the strike leaders sought to overcome the charge of radicalism in the steel strike on account of Mr. Foster's radical views, was by emphasizing Mr. Foster's unimportance in the unionizing and strike management.

Mr. Fitzpatrick dwelt at length in his testimony on the fact that the strike was called and was entirely managed by twenty-four International Unions and avoided any mention of Mr. Foster's connection with the strike until specifically asked, and then insisted that Foster was absolutely confining himself to the "activities and scope of the American Federation of Labor."

Mr. Gompers after carefully describing the strike as an

effort of twenty-four International Unions went out of his way to insist:

"Mr. Foster is not an executive officer; he is not a member of that body. He has been chosen by them as secretary to perform the secretarial work." (Senate Hearings, Part I, page 112, line 34.)

In view of the fact that Mr. Foster had just previously planned and successfully led the stockyards' strike—one of the greatest victories organized labor had achieved in a good many years—that he had originated and set in motion the whole steel organization plan, and that the carrying out of that whole plan had been deferred till he was personally free to put his energy into it—that in all labor's own official documents in connection with the strike Mr. Foster is referred to, and deferred to, far more frequently than any other labor leader—and particularly in view of the comparative quality of mental strength and energy which all the evidence shows Mr. Foster to possess, this statement of Mr. Gompers, volunteered under the circumstances, can hardly evoke more than a smile.

The Interchurch Report while it states the same conclusion as that of the strike leaders, namely that radicalism was not a factor in the strike, reaches this conclusion by quite another course of reasoning, to which particular attention is called.

Instead of denying Mr. Foster's importance in the strike the Interchurch Report insists (page 35, line 7) Mr. Foster was a "causative factor in the strike." It speaks of the whole organizing strike movement as "the Foster machine" (page 153, line 21). It calls him the "large scale promoter" of the unionizing movement (page 157, line 14); as "In active charge of the organization drive" (page 169, line 32), and toward the end of the book, devotes ten continuous pages chiefly to Mr. Foster's importance in the steel strike and otherwise frankly recognizes him as the dominant factor on the labor side.

Moreover the Interchurch Report carefully avoids not

only any admission but any direct discussion of Mr. Foster's alleged "repudiation of radicalism" by attacking this question offensively instead of defensively. It accuses the steel companies of having "dug up" Mr. Foster's syndicalist book and his voluminous writings on radicalism and of having borne the expense of reprinting these documents and supplying them to the newspapers. In other words instead of arguing the question on its merits as to whether Mr. Foster, who the Interchurch Report itself features as the "large scale promoter" of the strike, was an ultra radical, an I. W. W. and a syndicalist or not, it attempts to evade and cover up these questions with a counter charge which it concludes merely with the counter question:

". . . the question was Mr. Foster really sincere in recanting syndicalism inevitably raises the other question, was Mr. Gary really sincere in charging Bolshevism? It seemed best to leave such analysis to speculative psychologists."

After thus side-stepping the first point at issue as to radicalism in the steel strike, the Interchurch Report seeks to justify its conclusion that radicalism was not a factor in the strike by the other argument used by the strike leaders themselves, namely: that Mr. Foster, irrespective of his personal views, was, as far as the steel strike was concerned, working entirely along standard trade union lines.

Whatever weight, however, might otherwise be given to this argument, which both the strike leaders and the Interchurch Report strive so hard to maintain, is entirely overbalanced by two further groups of evidence, the first consisting of Mr. Foster's own account of the history and aims of the steel strike as stated in his book the *Great Steel Strike* and second, the last two chapters of the Interchurch Report itself in which, in a lengthy technical discussion of the relation of the steel strike to the labor movement, the Interchurch Report entirely contradicts its conclusions in the front of the book and entirely bears out Mr. Foster's own evidence that the steel strike was not only plotted by an alien-minded radical, but, at least as far as Foster's faction in the leadership was concerned, was a deliberate attempt on an immense scale to further substantially the same type of rádical aims as those Foster had expressed in his book on syndicalism and which aims, the Interchurch Report states, the whole American Federation of Labor were "in 1919 forced automatically into considering."

Rousseau pointed out over a century ago that the minority laboring class, if it were organized as a unit, could, without any positive action, but merely by stopping work and doing nothing, exert a more powerful pressure on all society than could be exerted by all the rest of society in spite of its numerical superiority or any superior ability or leadership. Concretely, if it could be organized and persuaded to do so, coal labor or railroad labor or steel labor or the labor of any other basic industry could, by merely slowing up work, decrease production and raise prices to the whole country— or by stopping work and shutting off the nation's supply of coal or steel or railroad service or some other vital national necessity, bring more pressure on modern society to enforce its own interests irrespective of general social interests than can be exerted in any other way by any other class or by all other classes. Moreover society is particularly helpless against any such united action on the part of all the workers of any industry for it can find no adequate substitute for the labor of a whole industry. Even if it sought to make such action by the labor of a whole industry unlawful, which it at present is not, it is futile to attempt to fine a largely propertyless class, and radical leaders have more than once dared a government to try to put all the workers of a great industry in jail.

These particular facts and conditions in modern industry have been seized on by radicalism as the basis of its organization because in them radicalism sees its one hope of realizing its aims.

The "general strike" which Mr. William Z. Foster continually refers to in passages already quoted and elsewhere, as the method by which syndicalism, I. W. W.ism, etc., proposed to bring about the seizure of industry, is necessarily based on the organization of *all the workers in an industry* and *their control as a unit.*

Mr. George Soule says in his "New Unionism," page 191:

"An analysis of the strategy of the (new) unionism will discover in it two fundamental objectives to which all other policies are subordinated. The first is to organize *all* the workers in the industry; the second is to develop them . . . into a class-conscious army able and ready to assume control of industry."

This radical plan of labor organization is called "radical unionism," "revolutionary unionism" or "industrial unionism," all meaning the same thing and is also spoken of as the One Big Union Idea. This is the form of labor organization on which the Amalgamated Clothing Workers, the I. W. W. and the W. I. I. U. are all built, and on which syndicalism, Bolshevism and all other kinds of radicalism insist.

The ordinary form of trade union is organized craft by craft instead of industry by industry because the craft union contributes best to the purposes of ordinary trade unionism. The industrial union on the other hand, and every step toward industrial unionism is distinctly a step toward radicalism because the industrial form of organization is incompatible with the objects of ordinary trade unionism and inherently works toward radical ends.

As a result therefore, there has been for years a constant conflict between the advocates of craft unionism and of industrial unionism.

When Mr. William Z. Foster left the I. W. W. and joined the A. F. of L. under whose auspices he conducted the steel strike, he definitely stated in his letter of October 4, 1914, to his fellow radicals his purposes in doing so. He said:

"I am satisfied from my observation that the only way for the I. W. W. to have the workers adopt and practice the principles of revolutionary (industrial) unionism is to give up the attempt to create a new labor movement . . . get into the organized labor movement and by building up better fighting machines within the old unions, . . . revolutionize these unions.

"Yours for revolution,
"WILLIAM Z. FOSTER."

As soon as he became a member of the A. F. of L. Mr. Foster at once began putting "a more effective fighting machine" into operation with conspicuous success in the stockyards strike and at least with great energy and determination in the steel strike. These two facts as well as his announcement that he intended to build up in the A. F. of L. a radical fighting machine, make it particularly pertinent to examine the type of machine which Mr. Foster tried to build up, and to a certain extent did build up, in the steel strike.

In regard to Mr. Foster's plan and organization in the steel strike the Interchurch Report says (page 157, line 1):

"He saw the stockyards unorganized, the steel industry unorganized. . . . He thought out a plan of action which was to get all the unions having 'claims' on stockyard trades, to *unite* in one onslaught . . . and they led the *united unions* triumphantly through the stockyards. Then they turned to steel."

In the next paragraph, the Interchurch Report speaks of the proposition of consolidating the efforts of a score of unions to control a whole industry as "a prospectus of *trust magnitude*" of which Mr. Foster was the "large scale promoter," which prospectus of trust magnitude was managed as a unit by a single small strike committee of which Mr. Foster was the prominent member and which committee the Interchurch Report speaks of as at least a "specious *industrial* effort."

Moreover that the existence and functioning of this committee definitely worked toward industrial unionism is later specifically stated by the Interchurch Report when it says on page 176, line 11:

"The committee attempted to carry the temporary and artificial unity of the 24 Internationals into permanent organization in two directions. One was in setting up District Steel Councils, designed to maintain united or *quasi-industrial* action in dealing with separate plants. . . . The other Committee effort specifically authorized by the May 25 congress was towards setting up a national council or Iron and Steel Department within the A. F. of L."

Thus the whole plan of the unionization of the steel industry involved a unionizing effort which was contrary to all former trade union practises and conspicuously suspicious of industrial unionism. That the whole tendency of the movement was suspiciously in that direction was emphasized by Mr. Gompers' warning that his "Endorsement (of the plan) in no way meant any personal leaning toward the One Big Union idea."

Moreover, in regard to the operation of the plan in certain particulars, Mr. Foster says,

"This *splendid* solidarity and *rapid modification of trade union tactics and institutions* to meet an emergency is probably without a parallel in American labor annals." (*Great Steel Strike*, page 214, line 17.)

and he otherwise emphasizes the revolutionary significance of the steel campaign in trade union practise, the revolutionary significance being all in the direction of revolutionary industrial unionism.

In other words, the unionization drive in the steel industry while it did not nominally and perhaps not technically attempt to organize industrial unionism in that industry in that it recognized the rights and turned over a certain percentage of the members secured to craft unions, did contemplate and largely achieve such a coördination of present unions with a single small organization in charge of unionizing and strike work, that it was in its operation and effect equivalent to the radical One Big Union plan. Finally and most important of all it had the same effect as the One Big Union idea in that it attempted to tie up a whole industry irrespective of whether large classes of the workers had grievances or not.

Again the strike leaders' report in regard to the number of steel workers "organized" and the way they were apportioned to the different craft unions is very significant in this connection. This report which is reproduced in both the Interchurch Report and the Great Steel Strike show that according to the strike leaders' own figures, 40% of all the steel workers enrolled were not thus turned over to the craft unions. How this 40% which were not turned over to craft unions would have been organized if the steel strike had succeeded and the union organization had become permanent can only be surmised, but the 40% which were not turned over to craft unions would certainly have made a very effective nucleus for an industrial union in the steel industry.

Finally the Interchurch Report specifically admits (page 160, paragraph 2) that:

"In many plants the instinct of the immigrant recruit was to associate with his shopmates of different crafts rather than with his craft mates from other shops. He fell more easily into a shop or plant union which however would have been an *industrial union*. Some local leaders so organized him. Thus an internal conflict arose . . . the artificial harmony of the 24 International Unions conflicted with the inexperienced immigrant drift (?) *toward real industrial unionism*."

If, in view of this array of facts, Mr. Foster who had come into the A. F. of L. for the express purpose of working to turn it into a radical or industrial union organization, had been able successfully to carry out his plan by winning the steel strike, it seems impossible to doubt that such a success following such a success as the stockyards unionization would have been regarded as so great a strategic triumph for the radical influences within the A. F. of L. that it would have constituted a most important advance for all radical influence in American industry. That, irrespective of its defeat, Mr. Foster himself regarded the steel strike as a marked victory for radical unionism, is not only clearly indicated by a careful reading of his whole book, the *Great*

Steel Strike but is specially emphasized in the last chapter which is devoted to showing that the steel strike marked a great advance in trade union methods and practises which advance he describes as follows:

"For many years radicals in this country have . . . maintained that the trade unions are fundamentally non-revolutionary. . . . If they were to look sharply they would see that the trade union movement is traveling faster than any other body toward the end they wish to reach. . . . Like various other social movements (trade unions) have more or less instinctively surrounded themselves with a sort of *camouflage* or protective colouring designed to disguise the movement and thus to pacify and disarm the opposition. This is the function of such expressions as 'a fair day's pay for a fair day's work'— 'the interests of capital and labor are identical,' etc. *In actual practice little or no attention is paid to them.* They are for foreign (public) consumption. . . . It is an indisputable fact that the trade unions always act upon the policy of taking all they can get. . . . They are as insatiable as the veriest so-called revolutionary unions. . . . In every country they are constantly . . . solidifying their ranks, building ever more gigantic and militant combinations . . . and they are going incomparably faster towards this goal than any of the much advertised so-called revolutionary unions" (Excerpts, *Great Steel Strike*, pages 255–265).

In spite of the Interchurch Report's insistence in its "Conclusions" in Chapter I and in its discussion of radicalism in the steel strike in Chapter II, that the strike was not "plotted and led by reds or syndicalists or Bolshevists and that "its real objects were not the overthrow of established leaders and established institutions of organized labor," parts of Chapters VI and VII at the end of the book not only show plainly and in detail that the authors of the Interchurch Report knew Foster's radical views—knew that he had come into the A. F. of L. merely to use it as a vehicle to radical ends but these chapters constitute through page after page only a thinly veiled glorification of Foster and his aims.   The Interchurch Report says:

"Mr. Foster's business might be described as making the labor movement move. . . . When he took up making the labor movement move, he tried it first as a very intense syndicalist, an I. W. W. outside the trade unions. Little motion resulting, he 'repudiated' syndicalist methods and joined the Railroad Carmen's union in order to 'bore from within' the A. F. of L. In *the steel campaign he was most intensely boring from within* and the labor movement knew it and let him bore. It was considered that his boring might be through the unions but was certainly against the anti-union employers. That is, he decided the labor movement was the A. F. of L. and not the I. W. W. and that his job was making the A. F. of L. move. . . .'

"It ('boring from within') did not mean a campaign among the steel workers at the end of which they voted the I. W. W. ticket. . . . *It does mean putting inside the trade unions radical minded men* who will make more trade unionists. It does involve the possibility *that . . . these radically minded organizers may convert the trade unions if they can.* . . . The *real problem which confronts the A. F. of L.* . . . is *industrial unionism* and the larger side of it is not borers but economic conditions . . . which latterly have exposed weaknesses in craft unions and have driven them to essay *amalgamations and other approximations of industrial organization.* When a craft union on strike sees brother unions in the same industry sticking to work . . . that craft union begins to do a lot more thinking about industrial unionism. . . . *When craft unions promulgate ambitions as did the A. F. of L. in 1919 (date of the steel strike)* . . . *they are forced automatically to considering industrial union problems*" (Interchurch Report Excerpts, pages 156–159).[1]

This whole quotation—in fact most of the entire section from which it was taken continually resorts to the "under-

[1] It will be better appreciated after reading Chapter XXIV of the present analysis that the Interchurch Report constantly faces this dilemma: Its basic policy puts it under the necessity of white-washing the whole strike movement to the general public and at the same time urging upon the working classes the desirability of *industrial* as contrasted with craft unionism. As part of that argument it constantly points out in this section how the A. F. of L. in the steel strike was forced to "various specious *industrial* efforts," or to "quasi-*industrial* action," or to "leaning towards the One Big Union Idea," all leading up to the present definitely stated point of view, which Foster and Debs and "Big Bill" Heywood and all ultra-radicals insist on, namely that industrial conditions are making *industrial* (radical) unionism necessary and inevitable and therefore the workers should repudiate craft unionism and adopt industrial unionism. (See also pages 343 to 345 of the present analysis.)

cover" phraseology of technical radical terms which are carefully calculated to convey much more meaning to those who are familiar with these terms than to outsiders.

The Third International, in its convention July, 1921 at Moscow, is on record as officially recognizing three different radical programs in America:—that of the I. W. W. which is seeking to radicalize the American worker; Big Bill Heywood represents this group which has just been awarded 3 of the 16 American votes in the supreme world radical council;—that of the "independents" like Foster who are "boring from within" the A. F. of L. and who have just been awarded 2 of America's 16 votes; and that of the "New unions" (described by Mr. Soule in his book, the *New Unionism*), chief among which is the Amalgamated Clothing Workers, who are organizing chiefly the foreign workers into industrial unions and whose power has just been greatly increased by being awarded 11 of America's 16 votes in the Third International.

To any one who is familiar with these facts and the phraseology used and its real meaning, the above quotations from the Interchurch Report, taken in connection with the voluminous intervening context, plainly show without any regard to any other information about the individuals who wrote them, that those individuals intimately sympathize with the "industrial unionism" for which Mr. Foster stands, but regard "boring from within" the A. F. of L. as too indirect and subject to too much antagonism to be an effective way of advancing "industrial unionism." They obviously believe and glory in the fact that the A. F. of L. is rapidly progressing toward "industrial unionism" but they believe this progress is less because of the influence of such men as Foster than because it is being forced, by the class-conscious ambitions of certain types of labor and by its own chauvinistic ambitions, to see that craft union principles continually handicap it and that the only real scope for those ambitions is along the line of industrial unionism. Even without the eulogy of the Amalgamated Clothing

Workers, the open approval or disapproval of each other form of labor organization in proportion as its theories and practises do or do not coincide with those of the A. C. W., makes it entirely obvious that the authors of the Interchurch Report are in intimate sympathy with this latest third type of revolutionary unionism,—the so-called "New Unionism"—and look at the whole labor problem accordingly.

The Amalgamated Clothing Workers, whose radical aims are specifically stated in the preamble to its constitution,—which Mr. Heywood, the escaped I. W. W. leader, especially referred to in his speech before the Moscow Radical convention as "one of the few favorable influences in America" and which is the chief exponent of the "New Unionism," is defended by Mr. George Soule in the June 8th, 1921 issue of the Nation as not actually being radical on the grounds that its members have not "marched in with red flags and taken possession of the factories" or "thrown bombs into the City Hall."

Following the same line of argument, the Interchurch Report concludes that because the "steel strike did not mean a campaign among the workers at the end of which they voted the I. W. W. ticket," that therefore the whole strike was not radical but on the contrary "extremely old-fashioned." Such a course of reasoning, however, will undoubtedly seem to the average American to show, not that the steel strike was less radical, but that the authors of the Interchurch Report are more so.

Not only, however, is it a matter of the plainest fact that the steel strike was planned and as far as its most prominent leader was concerned, "led by alien-minded radicals"—whose object was to go as far as possible in "overthrowing the established principles of organized labor"; not only is it plainly admitted by Mr. Foster and the Interchurch Report that the whole organization movement verged so close to "industrial" union as to be "without parallel in American labor annals" but there is ample evidence that radicalism in the steel strike permeated the rank and file of the strikers themselves.

This was repeatedly alleged by the managers and better class of workers who were called as witnesses by the steel companies and also was conspicuously evident in the testimony of strikers that the Senate Investigating Committee picked at random on the streets of the steel towns. The fact that these men testified in practically the same words of broken English that they were striking for "eight hour day—no boss—dollar an hour—government run mills—get on street car—no pay nickel—government run street cars, etc.," speaks for itself.

In regard to all such evidence of radicalism among the rank and file of the strikers the Interchurch Report *in its second chapter* insists that all great strikes are always taken advantage of by independent radical proselyters and that this must have been particularly the case in a strike involving so many illiterate foreigners as the steel strike, but that such a fact cannot be held against the strike leadership. Moreover the Interchurch Report further insists *in its second chapter* that in this strike, of the large number of radicals arrested in many districts, few if any were tried and convicted.[1] It states that certain radicals who attempted to go among the men or circulate radical literature were pre-

---

[1] The Interchurch Report tries to give the impression that the fact that men arrested as radicals were not convicted indicated that there was little or no evidence of their radicalism. Pages 911 through 951 of the Senate Hearings are devoted to detailed and specific evidence of radicalism in the steel strike and of prominent strike leaders who were radicals, including the president of the strikers' organization at Gary, also their attorney, Paul Glaser, an I. W. W. worker who admitted to government officials, "you bet I am a Bolshevik" and dared the officials to try and do something about it (page 925). The reason why these men were not convicted was not lack of evidence but as Senator McKellar remarked (page 945) because "we have a very liberal provision in our Constitution about the freedom of the press and freedom of speech." Yet the Interchurch Report devotes pages to discussing the infringement of the right of free speech in the steel strike.

vented by the labor leaders. It emphasizes that local steel officials offered insufficient proof for their allegation of radicalism in the strike; and it particularly emphasizes that in certain instances I. W. W. leaders and Mr. Eugene V. Debs "severely criticized the whole plan in public speeches. *It was necessary to send a committee to Debs before he could be induced to drop the subject*" (Interchurch Report, page 36, line 15). Incidentally it would be interesting to know what this committee said to Debs that he thus so quickly changed his point of view as to the steel strike.

Again, however, all these arguments in Chapter II of the Interchurch Report entirely lose whatever weight they might otherwise have in face of the fact that the Interchurch Report itself in Chapter VI entirely repudiates them and devotes page after page to showing that radical points of view on the part of the strikers were primary causative factors in the strike. In describing what it calls the "psychological causes" of the strike the Interchurch Report, beginning page 148, line 12, says:

"Whetting this state of discontent were two other psychological factors . . . together they were far more important than Mr. Gompers, or Mr. Foster or anybody, possibly except Mr. Gary. . . .

"The data before the Commission show that at the beginning of the steel strike workers *in great numbers* had the liveliest expectation of governmental assistance . . . some believed Mr. Wilson will run the mills.

"The second psychological factor . . . sprang from events in Europe. The news of two years' happenings there deeply influenced all labor but the evidence indicates peculiar influence on steel workers," these foreign influences being, "news of the probability or possibility of a labor government of the British Empire . . . (and) the 'Russian idea' embedded in the mind of the *great majority of immigrant workers* . . . that the Russian government is a laboring man's government."

In view of the fact which will be emphasized later in detail, that the unionization drive and the strike at no time had the active support of more than 20% of the steel workers and that these were almost entirely from the "mass of low-skilled foreigners" these statements by the Interchurch

Report that "Steel workers *in great numbers* had the liveliest expectation of governmental assistance—that some believed "Mr. Wilson will run the mills"—that the "fact that the Russian government is a laboring man's government (was) embedded in the minds of the *great majority of the immigrant workers*" and that these "were psychological factors" of major importance in causing the strike can hardly mean anything else to the average American than a strong bias towards radicalism on the part of such "great majority of immigrant workers." The fact that the Interchurch Report does not seem to regard such a point of view as radical again may merely indicate not that the steel strike was less radical but that the authors of the Interchurch Report are more so.

14

CHAPTER XVII

RESPONSE OF THE STEEL WORKERS

As a general proposition leadership is of primary importance in any movement but this is not necessarily nor universally true. There are conspicuous instances of events or movements which have originated spontaneously and, though perhaps coördinated by leadership, have developed and moved independently and irrespective of that leadership.

In spite of the fact, therefore, that the whole idea and plan of the steel unionization movement which culminated in the strike, was plainly originated outside the steel industry by men who had no connection with the steel industry and at least some of whom had ulterior motives, it is still possible that when that plan was once put into operation, the steel workers themselves might have been so conscious of their grievance and so eager for any favorable opportunity for seeking a remedy, that their own impetus and influence in the organization effort and the drive made all leadership, and so all facts as to the origin of the plan itself and as to the radical or other motives of the strike leaders, entirely secondary.

This is precisely the point of view toward the whole strike movement which the Interchurch Report takes. It says in its "Conclusions," page 15:

"12. No interpretation of the movement as a plot or conspiracy fits the facts; that is, *it was a mass movement in which leadership became of secondary importance.*"

In Chapter VI (page 153, line 21), irrespective of the long eulogies of Foster and his organizing ability and his scheme already quoted which occur in almost succeeding pages, the Interchurch Report says:

"To the very end the Foster machine was a poor thing as *a system of control;* the strike moved on its own legs; it was a walkout of rank and file."

In spite of the lengthy emphasis which it later puts on the brilliancy and strategy of Foster's plan and of what Mr. Fitzpatrick and the A. F. of L. thought of its possibilities and of how it won triumphantly in the stockyards campaign, in the argument in connection with its featured "Conclusions," the Interchurch Report passes this all over with the statement (page 144, line 27 and 147, line 17):

"The labor movement initiated the organizing campaign, invited by the steel workers, according to the labor leaders, invading where it was not wanted according to the employers. Both statements are correct and neither lays emphasis on the principal fact . . . these steel workers are more important than their leaders. . . ."

"It cannot be too strongly emphasized that a strike does not consist of a plan and a call for a walkout. There has been many a call with no resultant walkout; there has been many a strike with no preceding plan or call at all. Strike conditions are conditions of mind. . . ."

"What made 300,000 steel workers leave the mills on September 22 and stay away in greater or fewer numbers for a period up to three and a half months?"

But did 300,000 steel workers leave the mills on September 22d or did any important proportion of 300,000 stay away from the mills anything like three and a half months? The Interchurch Report offers no evidence that they did, and there is every evidence that they did not.

It is true that at the time of the strike the strike leaders issued flaming statements that over 300,000 men were out, just as it is true that before the Presidential election a year later, the Democratic political leaders issued flaming statements announcing in statistical detail the rising flood of Democratic sentiment which was sweeping the country to overwhelm the Republicans; and just as it is true that in any great movement dealing with average psychology, leaders invariably talk in big figures of sure victory to keep up the enthusiasm of the rank and file.

These figures of the strike leaders were specifically contradicted at the time by the steel companies. Although of course the steel companies had an equal motive for putting out small figures as the strike leaders had for putting out large figures, the strong denial by the companies that anything like 300,000 men were out at least indicates that these figures are open to question.[1] But the Interchurch Report not only accepts the strike leaders' figures but does not suggest there is the slightest ground for questioning them. It simply assumes as a basic hypothesis, disregarding all the evidence, of which there is much, about the soundness of that hypothesis, that the steel strike actually consisted of an open revolt against unbearable working conditions on the part of over 60% of the whole industry, or, considering only the manufacturing departments which were actually involved, a bona fide revolt of over 75% of the whole industry. On this and one other pure assumption the Interchurch Report bases its whole argument as to the causes of the strike and reaches its conclusions that it was a "walkout of rank and file . . . in which leadership was secondary."

The method of reasoning of the Interchurch Report as to the cause of the steel strike is simple and obvious. Entirely disregarding the fact that a strike has become a very ordinary thing and a very casual thing to many workers and that this had become particularly true in the period under discussion in which the country had been having from

---

[1] Mr. George Soule, who had charge of field investigators which were sent by the Commissioners of Inquiry into the Pittsburg district, has stated that in view of the utterly contradictory claims of steel officials and of strike leaders in regard to the number of men on strike and in view of all the circumstances surrounding the strike situation, he found it impossible to gain accurate data as to the number of men striking or working.

three to four thousand strikes a year—many of them for such objects as sympathy for the Irish Republic or as a protest against Poland's fighting Russia or as a political move in some Brindell's ambition to get rich quick and a host of similar causes—the Interchurch Report thinks of a strike only as a great desperate last resort of men in a desperate last resort frame of mind. This assumption that a strike is necessarily a great desperate last resort step on the part of men in a desperate last resort frame of mind plus the assumption that an overwhelming proportion of the steel workers so revolted is the basis of the Interchurch Report's whole argument as to the grievances of the steel workers and of its conclusion that these grievances were actual.

Moreover the line of reasoning of the Interchurch Report based on this hypothesis is not only correspondingly subject to fallacy but becomes more and more fallacious the farther it goes until it finds itself accusing the Federal Administration and Attorney General Palmer and General Pershing and the Senate Committee (pages 148–149)—and what has more truth—the success of the Russian revolution of being major contributing causes of the steel strike.

It has already been emphasized in the introduction to this section of the analysis that in regard to the question of working hours, working conditions and similar alleged grievances of the men, the fact as to whether or not they were grievances depended on whether or not the majority of the steel workers regarded them as grievances and that the best available evidence on this point, other things being equal, consisted of the degree to which the workers themselves actually responded to the unionization drive and strike order, which at least to a certain extent was supposed to constitute a "vote" on these very points.

Again for the same reason, the best available evidence as to whether or not the men themselves wanted the proposed Trade Union Collective Bargaining as a remedy for the alleged grievances and therefore whether or not Judge Gary was justified in refusing to institute such Trade Union Collective Bargaining is to be found in the actual response of the men to the unionization drive and the strike order.

Finally it is the plain statement of the Interchurch Report that its "rock bottom evidence" was the "affidavits of 500 strikers" and it is most obvious that its chief method of reasoning and presenting evidence consists of finding out and showing the attitude of a few strikers and then predicating the same attitude to the whole industry on the assumption that the whole industry struck.

For all these reasons, therefore, the actual facts as to how the workers did respond to the unionization drive and of how big a percentage of workers really responded to the strike call is perhaps the most important single group of facts in the steel controversy.

In spite of the fact that the Interchurch Report does not even mention its existence, there is a very considerable amount of very definite evidence as to the actual response by the workers to the strike order. This evidence is available chiefly from three sources: first, the evidence of the Senate Hearings; second, evidence from the financial statements and wage budgets of the Steel Corporation which the Interchurch Report accepts as authoritative in other connections; third, evidence from the circumstances and development of the whole situation.

On September 25th John Fitzpatrick, Chairman of the Special Strike Committee, testified (Senate Hearings, Part I, pages 25 and 26) that *over* 300,000 men had joined the unions and that all of them were on strike.

The official statement signed by the National Committee of organization of steel workers circulated generally at the time and reproduced in full in Senate Hearings, Part II, page 498, says:

"On September 22 . . . the following is the number of men on strike at the various places:

Homestead..........................	9,000
Braddock..........................	5,000

Rankin.............................   3,000
Clairton...........................   4,000
Duquesne and McKeesport............   12,000,
etc."

Mr. Foster in his book, *The Great Steel Strike* (page 100) says:

"On Tuesday the 23rd (September) 304,000 had quit their posts in the mills and furnaces. All week their ranks were augmented till by September 30th, 365,000 were on strike. . . . The number of strikers were as follows:

Homestead........................   9,000
Braddock.........................   10,000
Rankin...........................   5,000
Clairton.........................   4,000
Duquesne and McKeesport..........   12,000,
etc., etc."

In regard to the number of men on strike in two cases, Donora and Wheeling, the evidence before the Senate Investigation tends to show that the strike leaders' figures were substantially correct. In every other case, however, where the subject was investigated, the Senate Investigation showed conclusively that the official figures of the strike leaders were not merely inaccurate but ridiculously untrue.

The strike leaders' figures show 9,000 men on strike at Homestead. The Senate Committee personally visited and went through the Homestead Mills on October 10th. Out of a normal working force of 11,500, 9044 were actually at work and only 2455, of whom none were Americans, were away from work for any reason. Moreover at the Senate Committee's request, Mr. Oursler, the Superintendent, furnished an exact tabulation of the number of men working and the number of men away from work for each day the strike had been in force. On no day had there been more than 4358, or a little less than one half the number the strike leaders claimed, absent from the mills for any reason. (Senate Hearings, page 481.)

The strike leaders' statement claimed that 4000 workers—the entire working force—were on strike at Clairton. The Senate Committee found by personal visit that 2600 men were working and only 1400 men were away from the plant for any reason.

The strike leaders' statement claims 12,000 men actually on strike at Duquesne and McKeesport. The Senate Committee personally visited the Duquesne works. Out of a normal working force of 5700, 5370 were actually at work and only 330 men away from work for any cause. Again at the request of the committee, Mr. Diehl, the manager, furnished the committee a statement as to the number of men working or absent each day since the strike began. This statement again showed that instead of the 100% claimed by the strike leaders to be on strike, on only the first two days of the strike had there been as many as 25% of the men absent from the mills for any cause. The balance of the 12,000 total working force of the Duquesne, McKeesport district, which the strike leaders claimed were all on strike, consisted of the employees of the National Tube Company at McKeesport. Of the normal working force of 7000, the Senate Committee found by personal visit to this plant that 6500 were at work and only 500 absent for any reason. For this district therefore instead of a total of 12,000 men on strike, as the strike leaders stated, only 830 men were absent from the mills for any cause.

In other words in these four important districts in which the strike leaders claimed in detailed public statements that 25,000 men were striking the Senators found by personal visit that at the beginning of the third week of the strike only 3696 men, or only 16% of the number claimed by the strike leaders, were away from their jobs for any cause.

Because of motor trouble the Senate Committee could not make a personal visit to Braddock and Rankin but there is ample evidence to indicate that instead of all the men being on strike, as the strike leaders claimed, at these plants, these plants were practically in full operation.

Judge Gary stated before the Senate Committee[1] that the Steel Corporation was keeping the closest possible record of the number of men away from the mills during the strike and that at no time were there more than 28% of all steel workers, or more than 40% of the men in the plants actually involved in the strike, absent from the mills for any cause, which included those sick, intimidated, or playing safe by taking a vacation, as well as those striking, and that the high mark of absenteeism was reduced rapidly after the first few days of the strike when measures were taken to protect the workers from strike violence.

In other words Judge Gary stated that the number of workers absent from the mills for all causes and in all plants was, when at its height, less than half the number claimed by the strike leaders and that that percentage reduced itself rapidly from day to day as soon as protection was furnished.   Ten days later the Senate Committee by personal investigation at a number of the mills found that the number of workers absent for all causes averaged only 16% of the number the strike leaders claimed to be on strike and even less than 16% of the total number of employees. Considering the fact that the strike leaders' statements were entirely untrue in the case of the mills visited by the Senate Committee and the fact that the Senate Committee's personal investigation, as far as it went, entirely substantiated Judge Gary's statements in regard to the whole industry, it is correspondingly probable that the strike leaders' statements were equally false in regard to most other plants and that at the end of the first two weeks of the strike the percentage of strikers everywhere dropped to some 20% of the workers even in the plants actually involved.

That the number of strikers throughout the industry had dropped to approximately 20% by that time and dropped even lower during the succeeding period is also clearly indicated by the second group of evidence which

[1] Senate Hearings, page 154.

specifically includes all the plants of the Steel Corporation.

The eighteenth annual report of the U. S. Steel Corporation is the official statement of the directors of the company to their stockholders in regard to its operation during 1919. This report was made on March 23, 1920, more than two months after the steel strike had ended in victory for the steel companies and had ceased to be an issue. This report consisted chiefly of a financial statement as to the company's condition which was audited by Price Waterhouse and Company and which was accepted by the United States Treasury Department as the basis on which 466 millions of dollars taxes was levied and paid. It is inconceivable that any attempt should have been made under such circumstances to manipulate this statement because of a strike that had ended victoriously for the company months previously.

On page 29 of this report is a table showing in detail for 1918 and for 1919 the number of steel employees and the wage budgets. Both the total number of employees and the wage budgets, as shown in these figures, the Interchurch Report accepts and uses without question in its chapter on wages, and, as has already been stated, they are an important part of the general financial statement by the corporation which was certified to by Price Waterhouse and Co. These figures show that the average number of employees per month in 1919 was 6.18% less than in 1918.

Now in 1918 the war was at its height. 1919 was a year of at least some let-down and it is inevitable that, without considering the strike, there should have been some decrease in employment all through the year. But even if it is assumed that there was no decrease in employment whatever as compared with 1918 up to the time of the strike, and that this whole decrease was concentrated into the strike months, from September 22nd on—one quarter of the year —this would only be a decrease of 24% for these months.

But it is a known fact that[1] there were less men employed from January to September, 1919, than during the height of the war period so that the average number of men on strike must have been correspondingly less.

This same table also states specifically that during the month in 1919 in which the average number of employees was least—October, the peak of the strike period—the payrolls show an average of 213,081 men working. This is just 39,025 less than the average for the year therefore is 15% of all employees. Assuming that these absentees were all from the manufacturing plants which were affected by the strike, they show only 20.5% of such workers away from their work for any reason during the month the strike was at its height.

Both the Interchurch Report, and Mr. Foster in his book, the *Great Steel Strike*, repeatedly assert that the steel strike involved chiefly the low-skilled foreign workers.

The Senate Committee, through personal visits to leading steel plants, established as a fact that on October 10th, some two weeks after the strike started, that *at least in those plants*, an average of not more than 16% of the steel workers who the strike leaders claimed were striking, were actually away from the mills for any cause.

The official payroll and wage budget figures of the U. S. Steel Corporation state specifically that in only one month during the year—October, the peak of the strike period— did the number of men actually working drop as low as 15% under normal for the entire Corporation or as low as 20% under normal for the manufacturing plants and the same figures show clearly that for the rest of the strike period less than 20% of the normal working force in the manufacturing plants were away from their jobs for any cause.

The whole steel strike itself, therefore, far from being an

[1] U. S. Bureau of Labor Statistics Monthly Review for June, 1920, page 152 says: "Maximum (steel employment) is reached in the month of January, 1919. From that point there is a general tendency to decline."

open revolt of three-fourths of all steel workers was very plainly a movement involving half, and probably less than half of merely the low-skilled foreign workers of the industry.

The question remains as to whether, even in regard to this half of the low-skilled foreigners which constituted only a fifth of the steel workers, the movement was actually a "walkout of rank and file" as the Interchurch Report states, "in which leadership became secondary," or whether it was merely the result, as the steel companies stated, of clever and persistent agitation which achieved such success as it did entirely through an appeal to the ignorance and prejudice of these unskilled foreign workers.

The whole unionizing attempt was begun, as has been shown, by Foster's original plan to send into the steel centers "crews of organizers with large sums of money" to "hold great mass meetings built up by extensive advertising everywhere" and to make a "hurricane drive that would catch the workers' imaginations and sweep them into the unions en masse." This whole plan was obviously based on strong leadership and the clever manipulation of mass psychology by that leadership.

At the psychological moment the movement was to be turned into a "decisive flood" by the "formation of committees to formulate grievances." Then these grievances were to be presented to the employer on threat of strike. The basis of this second step—the decision as to when the psychological moment had arrived and the manipulation of events accordingly were preëminently matters of wise and able leadership.

The instigation of the unionization drive was heralded immediately and stentoriously to steel workers throughout the country not only by the labor leaders but everywhere in the public press. Yet not only did the steel workers themselves fail to show any signs of starting any "mass movement which made leadership secondary" but their primary response was so negligible that it necessitated an entire change of tactics on the part of the leaders. This initial failure

Foster specifically admits and blames specifically and repeatedly on the lack of enough leadership and enough money to "lead" properly.

In regard to the decisive nature of leadership or lack of leadership at this stage of the movement, the Interchurch Report itself says:

". . . great drops in active membership had occurred . . . after the 'flu ban' in the Chicago district had caused the National Organizers to be withdrawn" (page 154, line 14).

The unionizing effort failing in its original aim of unionizing the steel workers by assault, "by catching their imaginations and sweeping them into the unions en masse," the union leaders entirely changed their tactics and for their previous plan of unionization by assault, substituted the plan of unionization by siege and accretion. More organizers were called in, more money was raised and a prolonged campaign begun to bring home to the workers a realization of their grievances and to educate them as to the need of Trade Union Collective Bargaining as a remedy for those grievances. In other words more leadership was applied.

The basis of this campaign of siege was the constant plea to the workers of: "Organize and all these things shall be added unto you" (Interchurch report, Page 160, line 1). As to what "all these things" were that were to be "added unto" the steel worker it is clear from the Interchurch Report's own statements that they consisted of almost any promise which the individual organizer thought could get the individual foreign worker's name or mark on the union card.

Foster refers repeatedly to the effectiveness in this part of the campaign of many clever devices of leadership, in regard to one of which, a red, white and blue membership card, he says, "more than one man joined merely on that account" (*Great Steel Strike*, page 35, line 33), and in regard to the general effect of this leadership he says on page 38:

"Organization . . . depends almost entirely upon the honesty, intelligence, power and persistence of the organizing forces."

And again on page 105:

"It is noteworthy that the strike followed strictly the lines of *organization*. In hardly a single instance did the unorganized go out spontaneously."

But again far from arousing any mass revolt that took matters out of the leaders' hands and made leadership secondary, this second line of tactics obviously succeeded little or no better than the first.

The skilled and the American worker were practically not being influenced at all. Even Mr. Foster says in regard to the American worker:

"It has been charged that the unions neglected the American Steel workers . . . If anything the reverse is true. . . . the Americans and the skilled workers generally proved indifferent union men in the steel campaign . . . when compared with the foreigners they made a poor showing. . . . They organized slowly; then they struck reluctantly and scatteringly. . . . the foreign unskilled workers (however) covered themselves with glory. . . . They proved themselves altogether worthy of the best American labor traditions" (Excerpts, *Great Steel Strike*, pages 196, 200).

Even in the case of the unskilled foreign worker, however, whose ignorance and prejudices could be so much more easily played upon by skilled agitators, the unionizing effort so failed in general to educate them as to their grievances, just as it had failed to "sweep them off their feet en masse," that even by August, 1919, a year after the drive started, the strike leaders themselves did not claim a union membership of more than 100,000—20% of all steel workers, or ½ even the unskilled foreigners.

As to this fact there is no question. In making his report to the A. F. of L. on the steel campaign, in July, 1919, Mr. Fitzpatrick only claimed the union membership to be 100,-000 and he testified later (Senate Hearings, Part I, page 15):

"*Senator Wolcott:* What was the total number of members in the steel mills in your organization at the time this vote was taken?"

"*Mr. Fitzpatrick:* At the time the vote was taken (August) I should say about 100,000."

"*Senator Wolcott:* And the total number of men in the industry available for entrance into the organization, if they saw fit, was how many?"

"*Mr. Fitzpatrick:* There was probably about 500,000. We had *one-fifth.*"

Moreover this conspicuous failure on tne part of the great mass of steel workers to show any interest in the unionizing drive after a whole year of such intensive and expensive effort was not the only problem that confronted the strike leaders. By the summer of 1919 even their one-fifth began alternately to show signs of getting out of hand and of disintegrating.

Foster said:

"The foreigner wants more money. . . . His idealism stretches about as far as his shortest working day. . . . He comes in (to the union) quite readily but if you don't get him the results, he drops away quite readily also" (Interchurch Report, page 162).

The Interchurch Report itself states on page 154:

"*Herd psychology* was far more powerful than . . . doctrines . . . the leaders' greatest difficulty beginning in the spring . . . was in withstanding *the mass feeling they had fostered* . . . the movement before getting to the hundred thousand mark reached a point where by the working of the very idea that built it, it threatened to break out in sporadic strikelets or break down altogether."

It was obviously these conditions—the meager success of their year long agitation and the immediate threat of losing even what they had achieved, which in the summer of 1919 forced the strike leaders back to their only alternative strategy—that of risking everything in a second "sweeping the workers off their feet" campaign.

The election of committees to "formulate grievances and present these to the employers" under threat of strike was, according to the original plan, to have been the climax of the first "hurricane drive" a year before. But this drive, as has been stated, had not achieved sufficient results to warrant risking such a step. The situation was such in August, 1919, however, that as the last trump card it had to be risked.

"The leaders had to let it (the whole movement) go on to a strike as the next means of success or let it go all to pieces" (Interchurch Report, page 155).

Accordingly the "grievances were formulated" consisting of 12 demands and although Judge Gary was the head of only one of the many employing companies, a sensational appeal was made to him under circumstances of the utmost publicity. The strike vote was widely advertised and taken at the same time this appeal was being made. Announcements were sent widespread that 50,000 men a week were now joining the unions. The President of the United States was appealed to through the newspapers as well as directly, and in general every possible method of arousing and manipulating mass psychology was used with all the ability and force the Labor Movement could command.

At the time of the strike itself, whether or not the threats, intimidation and violence played as big a part as was claimed, there is no question but that every psychological device was adopted to make the strike *seem* a mass movement—an "overwhelming revolt of rank and file." The widely published statement that 300,000 and then 365,000 workers were actually on strike was obviously one such device. Yet at the very time such claims were being advertised, the Senate Committee found *in the plants it visited* an average of over 84% of all workers at work as usual and during the first and admittedly most successful month of the strike, an average of over 80% of *all* workers of the Steel Corporation even in the plants directly affected by the strike, worked as usual.

In so far then, as the unionization drive and the strike constituted a vote—as the strike leaders insisted in advance that it would—as to the attitude of the steel workers themselves towards their alleged grievances and towards trade union collective bargaining, both the unionization drive and the strike showed that 80% of the steel workers did not regard the alleged grievances as real, and did not desire trade union collective bargaining in the steel industry.

Moreover, even in regard to the 20% of steel workers, who, through their action in the unionization drive and the strike, "voted" that they did believe the alleged grievances to be real, and did desire trade union collective bargaining as a remedy, these further facts must be taken into consideration.

This 20% consisted almost entirely of illiterate, unskilled foreigners. It represented only about one-half even of such unskilled foreigners in the industry. Such unskilled foreigners obviously were most susceptible to skilled agitation cleverly calculated to take advantage of their ignorance and prejudices, so that their "vote" did not necessarily represent their own unbiased judgment.

When therefore, after a year of intensive and expensive but largely unsuccessful effort—and under the additional incentive of the fact that even such organization as they had was showing signs of going to pieces—the strike leaders took the bold step of publicly demanding that Judge Gary should meet them in a conference which was to institute trade union collective bargaining, and thus officially give them the recognition which the steel workers themselves had consistently refused to give them, Judge Gary in refusing to meet the strike leaders in such conference, undoubtedly represented, as he stated he did, the opinion and desires of the steel industry itself, including the great mass of steel workers as well as of the management.

.   .   .   .

There can be no question, however, that as a matter of fact, and more and more as a matter of general recognition, industrial controversies and particularly controversies that

15

affect great basic industries or have to do with the working and living conditions of great masses of people, involve the interests of three parties—not only of the employers and employees that constitute the industry, but of the public as well.

Even if it must be granted then that the steel industry itself, by an immense majority vote of all parties in the industry, refused to recognize the 12-hour day and other conditions existing in the industry as grievances, and refused to accept trade union collective bargaining for the industry, nevertheless the question still remains as to whether or not these, and perhaps certain other issues raised during the strike, have such a social significance as to warrant an independent and perhaps a different decision as to their desirability in the steel industry from the point of view of public interest.

The Interchurch Report lays great stress on the general social aspect of collective bargaining as a means of controlling working conditions.   It makes a particular point of the social aspect of the 12-hour day.   It raises and strongly emphasizes other social questions in connection with the steel strike.   Moreover it advances points of view and expresses conclusions in regard to these questions which it specifically seeks to apply to industry as a whole, and especially recommends to public attention as a basis of public opinion and action.   The social aspects of such issues in the steel strike therefore deserve special attention.

PART ONE

SECTION C

Issues in the Steel Strike and arguments of the Interchurch Report which largely involve social issues or questions of public police and therefore personal opinion or point of view.

No attempt is here made to present a full, adequate argument on such subjects. What is chiefly attempted is to analyze the argument and conclusions of the Interchurch Report as to such subjects and to present briefly facts whose consideration is necessary to any sound conclusion but which the Interchurch Report has failed to consider.

CHAPTER XVIII

SOCIAL ASPECTS OF THE TWELVE HOUR DAY

THE grounds upon which the Interchurch Report most bitterly and frequently denounces the 12 hour day are those of its alleged social effects.

It characterizes the 12 hour day as a "barbarism that penalizes the country." It claims that workers are being

"Un-Americanized by the 12 hour day" and that "Americanization . . . cannot take place while the 12 hour day persists" (page 84)

and recommends (page 250) that the

"Government provide by law against working days that bring over-fatigue and deprive the individual, his home and his community of that minimum of time which gives him an opportunity to discharge all his obligations as a social being in a democratic society."

The Interchurch Report however entirely fails to make any adequate argument or present any adequate evidence as to the unsocial effects of the 12 hour day. Its whole evidence consists of:

First: A page of testimony of A. Pido, an immigrant striker who was a witness of the strike leaders before the Senate Committee and who stated he could not go to night school because of his long hours:

Second: The testimony before the same committee of Father Kazinci, a Slovak priest, who, in contrast to practically all other priests and ministers in the strike district, who Mr. Foster complains were unanimously against the strike, became a prominent strike leader and who stated that working hours and conditions were disgusting the foreign worker with America and tending to make him go back to the old country:

Third: A table showing that over a certain period, whether of months or years is not mentioned, 169 workers "dropped out" of night English classes in South Chicago public schools "for reasons connected with hours"; and

Fourth: Miscellaneous references to strikers' statement that the 12 hour day left no time for family life.

The Interchurch Report, moreover, does not even suggest that anything may be said in favor of the individual or social value of long hard work and otherwise treats the whole subject of the social aspect of the 12 hour day as though the mere statement of one of its smaller aspects carried its own conclusion as to the whole problem.

This type of argument, which seeks to show through quoting isolated instances that the 12 hour day makes education impossible, can of course be met by a host of isolated instances of men who have worked 12 hours or more a day and still educated themselves and advanced rapidly in the world. Charles M. Schwab, Farrell, Buffington, Frick, Carnegie, Carnegie's famous group of 29 partners, and most of the other outstanding steel leaders all came up from day labor in the steel industry and every one of them worked the 12 hour shift. Abraham Lincoln, James A. Garfield, Thomas Edison, are merely conspicuous examples of a great class of Americans whose success has been our special national pride because it was built up in spite of the fact— or perhaps, as many of these men themselves have claimed, because of the fact—that they have had to get their own education while working 12 hours or more a day at harder work than the steel employee with his modern automatic machinery, is perhaps ever called upon to do. There is no doubt that the well-known type of modern sentimental writer could have become most pessimistically eloquent over

the probable fate of a young Lincoln splitting rails 14 hours
a day with a 16 pound maul and then walking 20 miles to
borrow a single book which he had to read before an open
fire for the lack of money to buy candles.

Any argument on this basis, however, merely resolves
itself into the question of the personal point of view of the
arguer. The man who has achieved, or is capable of achieving, under such circumstances is temperamentally prone to
glorify hard work and to think of its results chiefly in terms
of Lincolns and Schwabs and Edisons. The man who himself has not, and probably could not, achieve under such
conditions inherently shrinks from the rigors of such a system and is temperamentally impelled to be most impressed
with its failures.

But the merits or demerits of the question of long hours of
work from the social point of view, cannot be satisfactorily
argued on an individual basis, which inevitably consists
of sentimentalizing over isolated instances either of men
who have stayed down under its strenuous demands or of men
who have found in strenuous necessity a specially valuable
schooling for marked accomplishment. From the social
point of view, it is the average results and the general effect
on the whole social body which are most important. These
the Interchurch Report does not discuss or mention.

In discussing any such broad question it is of course
necessary to begin with a clear understanding of just what
the discussion does and does not involve.

The seven day week is *not* being here discussed.

Practically all farming is necessarily on a seven day a
week basis. The public demands that drug and many other
retail stores stay open, that milk be delivered and police
and fire protection be afforded seven days a week. Moreover in such cases it is hardly possible to employ special
help for Sunday so that seven day operation means seven
day work by the individual worker. The public demands
that trains and street cars be run seven days a week. Physical laws necessitate that blast furnace departments be

operated continuously. In both these cases however, it is possible to employ special "swing crews" so that seven day operation can be maintained with a six day working schedule for the individual worker. It is hardly possible to condemn seven day work in stronger language than the officials of the U. S. Steel Corporation have condemned it and they state categorically that with the exception of the war period their employees have all been for years on a six or less than six day schedule. All the detailed government statistics on the subject from 1913 on, substantiate this statement. To the extent that seven day work exists in the rest of the industry, no matter how small the actual number of workers involved, and irrespective of the attitude of the worker himself, the fact that the seven day schedule is both inherently unnecessary and unsocial leaves it without defense.

Long hours which unduly exhaust or impair the health of the worker are *not* being here discussed.

A 12-hour working day is not in itself unduly exhausting or detrimental to health. Our 10,000,000 farmers who consistently work these or longer hours are notoriously about the healthiest class in the population. All Americans, in fact all the world, up to a generation ago worked such hours. Eight hours at many kinds of work are more exhausting and detrimental to health than 12 hours at many others. The really hard work in the steel industry has for years been on an eight-hour schedule and five days a week; and it is generally considered in the industry that such jobs at eight hours are harder than the 12-hour jobs both in themselves and because the 12-hour workers are seldom actually working more than half of the hours on duty. Government agencies have been active for years, and very properly so, in regulating hours or other working conditions which are detrimental to the health or longevity of workers. They have reduced the hours in copper mines to 6 a day; they have regulated work in brass foundries; in industries using sulphur and in many other special industries. Various government studies of working conditions in the steel industry have already been discussed in the present analysis. Their detailed reports have been quoted to show that steel workers are only subject to extreme heat for a few minutes at a time—generally about 1 minute to 7 minutes—intermittently, and generally for a total time of only some 20 minutes to 2 hours out of the 12 hours. These government reports show by detailed time studies that the 12-hour worker only actually works some 5 to 7 hours out of the 12. Steel work in the 12-hour departments is particularly emphasized as "necessarily of rather leisurely character."

The Interchurch Report throughout insists on making a distinction between the high skilled American steel worker and the low skilled immigrant worker. It says (page 11):

"Rates of pay and *other principal conditions* were based on what was accepted by common labor; the unskilled and semi-skilled force was *largely immigrant labor.*"

"The amounts earned by the low skilled (the bulk of the labor) are determined chiefly by the extraordinarily long hours" (page 90), etc., etc.

Moreover the fact that it insists (page 13) that:

"Skilled steel labor was paid wages disproportionate to the earnings of the other two thirds, *thus* binding the skilled class to the companies"

and

"The twelve hour day made any attempt at 'Americanization' or other civic or individual development for one half all *immigrant* steel workers arithmetically impossible" (page 12) and

"Americanization of the steel workers cannot take place while the 12-hour day persists" (page 84).

—all make it plain that the Interchurch Report is not discussing the 12-hour day and the American worker but the 12-hour day and the Americanization of the immigrant worker.

What *is* here discussed then, is whether or not 12 hours on duty—which of course brings 12-hour pay—necessarily means that "Americanization of the steel worker cannot take place" or whether as a matter of fact higher pay may not be one very practical road to the Americanization of the worker and his family.

America is a nation of immigrants and we have had much experience with immigrants and their Americanization. Our immigrant forefathers created out of a wilderness the America and Americanism of today, including American education, ideals, social system and all. How did they do it, by working hard and long for bigger returns or through leisure? To the America of today have come, particularly in the last generation, hosts of other immigrants. They have come largely from different races than our forefathers and their Americanization has involved different problems—those of adopting and absorbing Americanism rather than of creating it. Large proportions of such immigrants, and particularly their children, have become the best kind of Americans—in education, in ideals, in every social sense. How, *not* as a matter of theory and sentimentalism, but as a matter of *practical fact*, have they chiefly or most effectively done this—through long, hard work or through leisure?

It has already been pointed out that American standards of living are distinctly an achievement. It is equally true, and cannot be over emphasized, that all advanced social standards are achievements. Many such advanced social standards have been so largely achieved in America today that it is easy to take them for granted as things that have always existed and will go on existing irrespectively. The war, however, and many events in connection with it, plainly showed that even such "always-taken-for-granted" standards of modern social advancements as enough food to sustain life, the most ordinary liberty of individual action, the very principles of individual freedom and right, far from being inherent, have required a world struggle to reëstablish.

The shorter working day is in no sense inherent or to be merely taken for granted as something that exists irrespective of other circumstances.   It is distinctly an achievement and one of the most recent and advanced achievements of modern social life, and its possible existence absolutely depends on the prior establishment of other facts and circumstances.

One of the chief characteristics on which Americans have always prided themselves, has been their national energy which at least for all the earlier years of national history meant a willingness and habit on the part of the whole people to work hard and long.

When Alexander Hamilton first advocated governmental encouragement of American industry in order that Americans might enjoy more and cheaper manufactured commodities, and when Washington signed the first American protective tariff to encourage American industry, one of the stated reasons was to make American women and children more economically productive.[1]

Howe invented the sewing machine after a 12 hour day's work in a machine shop in Cambridge.   Peter Cooper did the research work that laid the foundations of American railroading after 12 hours in a glue factory, and Fulton and Morse and McCormack made other basic mechanical inventions on which modern industrial and social life is built, under similar conditions.

In other words, American energy in other generations meant not only a universal 12 hour or longer working day for men, women and children but it meant that much of the inventive and other special progress was achieved through hours of work beyond these.

Through inventions and improvements in machinery and through better methods of combining individual skill with that machinery, the average American today produces about three times as much as the average individual could produce in 1850 which immense extra margin of production

---

[1] This fact which is repugnant to our social standards of today is worth particular notice as evidence of how far from inherent and merely to be taken for granted our modern American standards actually are.

has been used in eliminating child labor and the hardest part of women's labor, in improving standards of living and finally in shortening the working day. But these modern standards of living and working hours and other standards generally referred to as American, have plainly been possible only because former generations of Americans built up, by long hard working hours and foresight and sacrifice, the margin of production which could be used as capital to create more and better machinery and the better methods which have brought about the greater productivity which has made the modern American standards of living and leisure possible.

Moreover, though of course there are many isolated exceptions, the average American individual and family have progressed exactly as the nation has progressed. Either through hard work and sacrifice and foresight, a margin of capital is built up, the use of which in farming or trade is added to personal energy, or by special education or in some other way, some type of extra ability or efficiency is acquired and added to personal energy to command the living standards and the leisure which the average individual American enjoys.

But for generations now this normal American development has been complicated by the fact that increasing numbers of immigrants have come into our national, industrial and social life. These immigrants have seldom had either the heredity or education for measuring up to American standards of individual productivity which are necessary to command American standards of living and leisure and they have seldom had any reserves of capital to use to increase their individual productivity ability.

In earlier years the great bulk of such immigrants went directly to the land and there in general through exactly the same methods of long hard work with which Americans of earlier generations accomplished the same results, they built up the margins of capital, consisting of land and tools and money in the bank, which made it possible for them, in their later years, to enjoy at least higher standards of living and leisure than they had ever known or could have achieved in the countries from which they came; and which made it possible for them to give their children, thru that capital and the special educational advantages it made possible, every chance for full American standards of living and leisure.

In later years the great mass of immigrants have been going, not to the land but into commercial and industrial centers. No American who has ever paid the least attention to the type of names across the store fronts along the main as well as the side streets of almost any American city can fail to realize that the immigrant has had his full share of American *commercial* success. As a matter of fact in a number of prominent lines of retailing, in the tremendous business of public entertainment and in certain lines of manufacturing, the more recent American dominates the entire business, and he has become an important factor in almost every commercial field.

Moreover there are probably few Americans who have not had the opportunity to observe personally the means by which such immigrants succeed,—how, beginning with a vegetable wagon or a corner stand or in some other small way, they build their success bigger and bigger through inordinately long hours of work and through accepting standards of living which makes possible a maximum saving to be combined as further capital with their hard work to make that work still more productive.

Both on the farm and in commerce then, great classes of immigrants, initially lacking either the capital or special personal efficiency to individually produce an American standard of living in an American standard of hours, have compensated for their inherent handicap by initially accepting less than the American standard of living and working more than the American standard of hours and by this means have built up a margin of capital and acquired a special ability which have later made themselves and particularly their children full productive, and later social, factors according to full American standards.

The great majority of immigrants who have gone into industrial work, however, have had a very different and in general much less favorable experience. There are doubtless a number of reasons for this. The older established industries are operated on a large scale with large capitalization. There is far less chance therefore to begin with a few dollars and the energy of the worker's own family and perhaps a few friends as has been possible in retail and commercial lines and in the clothing industry.

But no careful analysis can fail to reveal one very significant fact in connection with the immigrant worker in industry as compared with the immigrant worker in farming or commerce and that is the fact that under the fixed working conditions of a large part of industry, the immigrant is denied the opportunity to overcome his special inherent handicaps—lack of special individual productive ability— by a maximum employment of his single biggest asset—his willingness to work hard and long and sacrifice for his future.

For when the immigrant worker goes into the average American industry, he is automatically barred by fixed standards of working hours, based upon supposed standards of individual productive ability of the American workers, from compensating for his own less individual productive ability by harder work. Moreover he is at once introduced into an atmosphere in which any ambition to achieve American standards of productivity, and consequently to achieve by his own efforts American standards of living, is subject to organized discouragement and organized propagation of a theory that shorter hours of work are primary and production secondary.

Considered then not on sentimentality or mere isolated instances but on the real facts and merits of the case the whole question of the Americanization of immigrant labor resolves itself into these propositions:—

Given the undisputed fact that the immigrant worker generally lacks American standards of industrial efficiency which handicap him in competing on the same level with American labor for general American standards of living and leisure, can the immigrant worker advance more rapidly and surely to full American standards through an initial economic advancement. irrespective of American standards of hours, or by being artificially limited to American standards of hours in the hope that he will use his leisure to achieve in some other way other American standards?

The first proposition that economic advancement is a definite and direct step toward other forms of social advancement, is supported not only by all the conspicuous facts and experience available as to the methods by which American immigrant workers actually do advance, but by all general human experience as to the invariable method of all human advancement.

The cultural supremacy of Athens came only after its acquisition of the Delian treasure and the Laurium silver mines had given it the commercial supremacy of the ancient world. The Renaissance was the foundation of modern cultural advance of all western civilization, but the Renaissance came only after the great economic advances due to the development of East Indian trade and South American gold mines. The great era of popular education in western Europe and America came only in the countries and only after the tremendous economic advancement of the modern era of industrial machinery. Throughout the world national standards of education and living conditions are invariably in proportion to per capita wealth.

As regards the second proposition that leisure is the foundation stone to social advancement this may be said. Socialists and all other radicals can appeal to the individual or mass much more succesfully in proportion as the individual or mass is still economically unsuccessful. The immigrant who is both ignorant in regard to American institutions and principles and at the bottom of the economic ladder offers the most promising material for education along radical lines. All radical leaders therefore may hope to derive maximum advantage out of a situation in which immigrant workers are prevented by arbitrarily restricted hours from using their chief asset to economic advancement and because of these restricted hours have ample leisure to receive the kind of education to which they are most susceptible under those conditions. Radical leaders therefore always seek to emphasize the "Leisure for education and Americanization." But this proposition is invariably supported by mere sentimentalities and as far as is known cannot be supported on any other basis.[1]

Certainly the Interchurch Report does not advance one scintilla of evidence to show that in the many industries where the immigrant's hours are limited to 8, he does as a matter of fact use his extra leisure for self-education or any other effort to acquire American standards. Nor does it even advance any theory to show why he may be expected to do this. Instead it quite characteristically bases its whole conclusion on the mere assumption that the immigrant worker would do this. Moreover the Interchurch Report does not seem to have the faintest suspicion that all the facts and experiences as to how human progress is, and

[1] It is interesting to note in this connection that the affiliated radical organizations, of which the Amalgamated Clothing Worker is the chief unit, and which has recently been given, by the "Third International," the leadership in the American radical movement—taking that place from the I. W. W.—particularly features its educational efforts among the workers. The head of this "Educational Committee" is Mr. David Saposs, named by the Interchurch Report as one of its special investigators and as the author of part of the Second Interchurch Report. Mr. George Soule, another such special Interchurch investigator and joint author of the second Interchurch Report, has been connected with this general organization and his wife is a member of this "Educational Committee." Mr. William Z. Foster is featured as one of the special lecturers of this "Educational Committee." To what extent such "educational" efforts have succeeded is unknown, and whether or not they contribute towards Americanization of course depends on the definition given Americanism.

always has been, actually achieved plainly refute its assumption.

The 12 hour day in the steel industry represents the most conspicuous opportunity in industry for the immigrant worker to better his economic standing by making up for his inherent handicaps through a maximum use of his greatest asset. Because of the 12 hour day the immigrant steel worker could earn $34.19 a week which, according to United States Bureau of Labor statistics already frequently quoted, was about the average wages at the time of carpenters, cement workers, electric wiremen, sheet metal workers, linotype operators, railroad machinists, boiler makers and other great classes of American *skilled* labor. In other words by working 12 hours a day in the steel industry the *unskilled* immigrant worker was on practically the same economic plane as the average *skilled* American worker in other industries, which meant that except in the matter of personal leisure he had available the same standards of living for himself and his family as a large percentage of American skilled workers.

The average immigrant worker, however, coming from a country where wheat is too much of a luxury to be consumed even by the man who raises it, and where the staple article of national food is black rye bread—where not only the whole family but often various domestic animals live in a single room, naturally and generally sees less need for trying to maintain American standards of living than he does for saving up a margin of capital which will help carry himself and his family still further on the road to economic and ultimately general advancement.

The tendency of the great proportion of the immigrant steel workers to save money was repeatedly emphasized in the Senate Hearings. Mr. Foster in his book *The Great Steel Strike*, on page 117, says:

"When they tried to foreclose on the Church mortgage, he (Father Kazinci) promptly laid the matter before his heterogeneous congrega-

16

tion of (Slavic) strikers who raised the necessary $1200 before leaving the building and next day brought in several hundred dollars more."

Again the fact that some 50,000 strikers, mostly unskilled foreigners, could support themselves and their families for three months "on their own resources" indicates considerable prior saving. Finally the plain fact that the very class of workers (immigrants) who have so conspicuously shown a tendency to go into fields of work where they could work long hours in order to save margins of capital, have gone in far greater numbers into the 12 hour steel than into any other industry, and stayed in it in spite of the temptation of ample wages for much shorter hours which was held out to them during the war by other industries, raises the strong presumption that this was in general deliberately done for the purpose of making and saving this extra money.

It is, of course, not possible to trace directly the social result of the extra money made and saved by immigrant workers in the steel industry as it is possible to trace directly the social result of money saved by the immigrant who works from 7 in the morning till 10 at night building up his corner fruit stand into a leading fruit and confectionary and ice cream parlor; or as it is to trace the social result of the savings which the immigrant worker puts into a vegetable patch, which by long hard work he develops into one of the profitable truck farms which dot the outskirts of our great cities. It is obvious on every side, however, that foreign born citizens are multiplying every type of small business venture, all of which require capital which the immigrant does not possess when he comes to the country. The fact that the 12 hour day in the steel industry has long offered perhaps the most conspicuous opportunity in the whole country for the immigrant without any asset but his willingness to work to earn and save most quickly the few hundred dollars with which such workers are able to start in some little business of their own, makes it reasonable to presume that the steel industry has contributed more than its share to the capital which has started tens of thousands of our immigrants on the road of steady economic advancement which according to all experience is the most direct and sure road to full Americanization.

Moreover, it must be borne in mind that years before the present Americanization movement, as such, had ever come to public notice the steel companies were spending tens of millions of dollars in an Americanization movement of their own among their immigrant workers. This movement offers the worker himself easy and special educational advantages, far beyond those the 12 hour working earlier American ever had available. But it has also made an even more direct and intensive effort to reach the children of such workers who, according to all sociological authorities, offer the most fertile field for Americanization not only as it will affect the next generation but for its reaction on the immigrant parents themselves.

There are of course certain types of people who are temperamentally impelled to judge the social results of an industry or of any other system chiefly by its effect on the "small impoverished," or otherwise disaffected minority of which few human institutions, irrespective of other conditions, are free.

There may be many other Americans who have the same faith as the Interchurch investigators that if the immigrant worker was arbitrarily handicapped in the steel industry, as he is in many other industries, from taking the same road to Americanization that practically all immigrants have taken,—through first achieving their own economic advancement,—and if American standards of leisure were made compulsory; that such a free gift of what the American people themselves have had to earn through generations of hard work and sacrifice and foresight, would inspire such immigrants to acquire more rapidly full American standards of efficiency and responsibility.

Various other points of view are possible and different shades of view inevitable, for the problem of the Americanization of the immigrant worker is undoubtedly broad and complicated and many of its phases necessarily involve matters of opinion.

Nevertheless, the fact cannot be disputed that long hard work which brought correspondingly big returns, was fundamentally the basis on which all modern American standards of living were built and through which alone they were made possible. It cannot be disputed that the 12 hour day in the steel industry offers exactly the same opportunity today which earlier Americans all used to make possible modern American ideals and which the immigrant worker had consistently used in other fields to make possible his enjoyment of full American standards. The 12 hour day is not a "barbarism without valid excuse" which is inconsistent with "the Americanization of the steel worker." On the contrary it offers one type of special opportunity, and is being widely used as an opportunity, towards Americanization.

Whether or not a different opportunity or method might be better may be open to question. But there is little doubt that that question cannot be answered merely on the opinion of an Interchurch Report which entirely fails to grasp its real merits. Nor can that question be turned over for answer to Foster, the radical and his I. W. W. partisans or to Fitzpatrick or other members of the A. F. of L. who are definitely committed by self-interest to one side and who under no circumstances would have to, or would be willing to, bear the responsibility of their decision.

Judge Gary took the initiative before the Senate investigation committee of personally suggesting that the best method of solving the great social problems that are inherent in industry would be to put at least the great basic industries under the supervision of a governmental body similar to the Inter-State Commerce Commission which could go into such subjects impartially and make decisions which were intelligent and based on real public policy. (Senate Hearings, Part I, page 216.)

In March, 1921, when the chief interest of the steel worker was in keeping his job and there was no question of any labor troubles, Judge Gary again took the initiative in suggesting in an official public statement, that the Steel Corporation would welcome the assistance of a properly constituted governmental commission as a means of solving the social problems of the steel industry on a basis of real public policy.

If public opinion feels, or shall come to feel, that the 12 hour day constitutes a social problem, surely such a means of solution promises more truly social results than a blind yielding to organized agitation and propaganda which will put the solution in the hands of irresponsible, self-interested professional labor leaders.

CHAPTER XIX

TRADE UNION COLLECTIVE BARGAINING

ON page 15 and again on page 144 the Interchurch Report says,

"The organizing campaign . . . and the strike were for the purpose of forcing a conference in an industry where no means of conference existed; this specific conference *to set up trade union collective bargaining.*"

It says on page 15,

"15. Causes of defeat (of the strike) . . . lay in the organization and leadership not so much of the strike itself as of the American labor movement."

"16. The immigrant steel worker was led to expect more from the 24 International Unions of the American Federation of Labor conducting the strike than they, through indifference, selfishness or narrow habit were willing to give."

It insists on page 35:

"That the control of the movement to organize the steel industry, vested in 24 A. F. of L. trade unions, was such that Mr. Foster's acts were perforce in harmony with old line unionism."

On page 158 in discussing Foster's activities and known "boring from within" tactics in the strike, it says:

"It (boring from within) does mean putting inside the trade unions radically minded men who will make more trade unionists. It does involve the possibility that after all the unorganized are gathered into

246

the old line trade unions, these radical minded organizers may convert the trade unions, if they can.   That is the trade unions' lookout."

It doubtless has already been made sufficiently clear that in the attempt to "organize" the steel industry which led up to the 1919 steel strike, the difficulties to be encountered were so clearly recognized by the strike leaders, yet the prize of victory would have been so great, that the Labor Movement decided to put its united strength—of both old line unions and radical organizations—into the effort.   In apportioning the leadership accordingly, and for obvious strategic reasons, general control was vested in the hands of "24 old line trade unions" and the active management put in the hands of the radical, Foster, with each side constantly working for its partisan advantage as well as for general victory.   Moreover, in spite of its insistence in its "Conclusions" in the beginning of the book that the movement was entirely in the control of "old fashioned trade unionism"—that as a matter of fact "the whole strike seemed extraordinarily old fashioned"—that Foster was working along old fashioned trade union lines—there is no question, in view of the quotations above and all the general evidence through the last two chapters of the book, that the Interchurch Report clearly recognized this dual nature of the control and aims, and distinctly sympathized with the tactics, leadership, and aims of the radical faction.

Thus when the Interchurch Report—except for some of the generalizations in the entirely separate and afterwards added "Findings" and "Recommendations"[1] argues

[1] On page 17 at the end of its Introduction, there is incorporated among a great many other Recommendations two very brief sections which recommend that the government should: "Devise with both sides and establish an adequate plan of permanent free conference to regulate the conduct of the industry in the future" and "continue and make nationwide *this* (the Interchurch Report) inquiry into basic conditions in the industry." In view of the fact that the government just had, through the Senate Committee, made a far more lengthy and detailed and specific examination into the steel strike than the Interchurch Report, which arrived at opposite conclusions, which investigation and

throughout for trade union collective bargaining, standard trade union collective bargaining is plainly at least the minimum for which it is arguing.

Quite characteristically, however, the Interchurch Report does not argue the subject of trade union collective bargaining on its merits at all. Except that it frequently insists that in European countries trade union collective bargaining is regarded as a matter of course and the lack of it as being "industrially extraordinarily old fashioned," it entirely assumes and takes for granted the one-sidedness of what was recognized by common consent as the chief issue in the whole steel strike.

The fact that Bishop McConnell, Chairman of the Interchurch Commission of Inquiry, in one of his recently published works which will be referred to later and other men connected with the Interchurch investigation in other published works have so much to say about English trade union collective bargaining and the fact that Foster as the

---

conclusions the Interchurch Report condemns, this recommendation seems rather puzzling on its face. The strategy of such a recommendation is discussed in greater detail later but it should be indicated at this point that strike leaders' strategy is frequently first to appeal to the government to give them just what they want but which they doubtless know in advance the government will not give them, after which they loudly proclaim that so long as the government refuses to do what they want for them, they have to do it for themselves. The Interchurch Report follows this strategy precisely. At the beginning of Volume I it asks in effect that the government repudiate its own investigation and asks specifically that the government act on the Interchurch investigation and recommendations. In its second volume a year later on pages 327 to 330 the Interchurch Report emphasizes that this unstressed 7th sub-section of its 19th recommendation was the principal recommendation of the entire Report, and as the government did not repudiate its own investigation and act on this recommendation of the Interchurch Report, the Interchurch Report here emphasizes and repeats that:

"The government as much as the Steel Corporation is to blame and again the Corporation and the government have seen fit to leave the field of reform to the Trade Unions."

climax of his *Great Steel Strike* sets up the English labor unions as the model for American radicalism, makes this frequent reference of the Interchurch Report to English trade union collective bargaining as a reason for American trade union collective bargaining extremely interesting.

This argument is advanced by the Interchurch Report in several places but is most definitely stated on page 41 by a quotation from the London *Times* that—

"They (American employers) have been apt to compare with some complacency their own relations with labor to those existing in this country (England) and to attribute their comparative immunity from labor troubles to the superior atmosphere of the United States or to their own superior management. It is really due to the simple fact *that the Labor Movement in the United States is historically a good many years behind our own.* But it will infallibly tread the same broad course . . . and *to resist the inevitable is a great mistake.*"

That there are two sides to the argument in regard to the advantages and disadvantages of trade union collective bargaining and trade unionism may be admitted. But that these particular arguments—that America has less labor trouble because we haven't yet got much of "Labor Movement," and that the Labor Movement is inevitable and it is a "great mistake to resist the inevitable"—constitute valid and sufficient reasons why American industry and American public opinion should unquestioningly embrace the "Labor Movement" and its "trade union collective bargaining," is a proposition that at least a great many Americans very definitely refuse to accept.

The expressed reason advanced by Judge Gary for opposing trade union collective bargaining in the steel industry was that the steel industry and its workers themselves preferred the Open Shop.

Herbert Hoover says,[1]

"The principle of individual freedom requires the Open Shop."

[1] (Open Shop Encyclopedia, page 278).

Cardinal Gibbons says, (*ibid.*, page 276)

"The right of a non-union laborer to make his own contract freely, and perform it without hindrance, is so essential to civil liberty that it must be defended by the whole power of the government."

Bishop McCabe (Methodist) says, (*ibid.*, page 276)

"I want to state the attitude of the church and this statement is official. We are opposed to having a small percentage of laboring men run the entire laboring class in a high handed and authoritative manner . . . it is an imposition for a few men to say, 'Join our union or you cannot work. . . . *As now constituted labor unions cannot long stand.*'"

Archbishop Ireland says, (*ibid.*, page 276)

"Labor unions . . . cannot be tolerated if they interfere with the general liberty of non-union men who have a right to work in or outside of unions as they please . . . it is wrong in the labor unions to limit the output of work on the part of its members. The members themselves are injured. They are reduced to a dead level of inferiority."

President Eliot of Harvard is quoted by the Citizens Alliance of Minneapolis as follows:

"Nothing in the way of good industrial relations is to be expected from organized labor as represented by the American Federation of Labor and the four (railroad) brotherhoods. The only peace which can come out of those organizations is the peace of an absolute domination, not only of the American industries but of the government itself."

Woodrow Wilson, as an economist and historian, in his last Baccalaureate sermon at Princeton, said,

"You know what the usual standard of the (union) employee is in our day. *It is to give as little as he may for his wages.* Labor is standardized by the trades unions . . . no one is suffered to do more than the average workman can do; and in some trades and handicrafts no one is suffered to do more than the least skillful of his fellows can do . . . I need not point out how *economically disastrous such a regulation of labor is* . . . the labor of America is rapidly becoming unprofitable under its present regulation by those who are determined to reduce it to a minimum." (Senate Hearings, page 98).

President Hadley in his last Baccalaureate sermon at Yale (1921) condemned the class conscious theories of organized labor as one of the most serious menaces to Americanism.

President Harding in his message of August 18, 1922, to Congress in connection with the coal strike said:

"These conditions cannot remain in free America. If free men cannot toil according to their own lawful choosing, all our constitutional guarantees born of democracy are surrendered to mobocracy and the freedom of a hundred million is surrendered to the small minority which would have no law."

Senator Beveridge has said in regard to labor forcing over the "Adamson" law on threat of tying up the railroads during the war:—

"When (labor) organizations by threat to strangle the nation can dictate laws for their own advantage at the expense of all the people, then regular government by all for the good of all is annihilated."

—and Chief Justice Taft, Vice President Coolidge, Lyman Abbott, Theodore Roosevelt and a host of our most able and public-minded citizens have all pointed out the anti-social effects of many of the principles and practises of the Labor Movement in terms equally definite and specific.

Again Los Angeles, San Francisco and Chicago are the three great American communities in which the modern labor movement has been perhaps longest and most strongly established, and where, therefore, there has been the best opportunity for the results of modern organized labor's theories and practises to have been thoroughly demonstrated. In all these three conspicuous cases—as well as in many other communities throughout the country—not merely the employer but the whole public have become so utterly disgusted with the inefficient un-American results of organized labor theories and practises—not only as they have affected the employers and the public but as they have affected the workers themselves—that Los Angeles has, and Chicago and San Francisco as well as St. Louis, Boston and many other American communities are at present conspicuously engaged in, literally running the "Labor Movement" out of town.

In view of the fact therefore that the four last Presidents of the United States—the Presidents of our three great universities and of many other similar institutions—the leading bishops of the two largest religious bodies in the country—and perhaps the majority of other unbiased, informed public leaders, and many of the great American communities in which the modern labor movement's theories and principles have been most thoroughly tried out, thus sweepingly condemn the whole "Labor Movement" as at present constituted or at least many of its notorious theories and practices, it seems little short of ridiculous for any body of investigators merely to assume that the question of trade union collective bargaining has only one side and, irrespective of what it thinks of conditions in the steel industry, merely assume that trade union collective bargaining would better those conditions.

As trade union collective bargaining does not exist in the steel industry and the question of whether or not it would improve conditions in the steel industry cannot therefore be determined on the basis of the results in the industry itself, it is necessary to judge this question on the basis of how trade union collective bargaining has affected other industries, and then to determine whether or not there are any particular reasons why it should operate any differently in the steel industry.

Certain of the chief complaints against the theories and practises of the modern labor movement are emphasized in the foregoing quotations. They are;

First, that the modern labor movement systematically and deliberately attempts to decrease production which not only puts an immense tax on the public but reduces the worker himself to "a dead level of inferiority."

Second, that the modern labor movement seeks to dominate absolutely, for its own group interest, all conditions of employment, irrespective of the interest or rights of the individual worker, and often of a majority of the workers or of the industry itself or of the public.

Third, that the modern labor movement insists on operating entirely outside the laws which govern all other human relations, and that, through its lawless disregard of contracts, its lawless factional feuds, and its lawless and arbitrary insistence on enforcing its own will, wherever possible, irrespective of right or justice, it constitutes not only a menace to all orderly operation of industry, but a menace to all orderly government.

FIRST, *Decrease of production*:

It is a basic economic axiom that the more of all kinds of goods there are produced, the more there will be for the whole country to have and use and enjoy, and therefore the greater will be general prosperity and the general demand for more goods and consequently the greater employment of labor. All American industrial advancement has been based on and has demonstrated this principle. Yet organized labor insists on acting entirely on the opposite principle. From Mr. Gompers down, its leaders with perhaps a very few notable exceptions have blindly insisted that the less work each individual does the more work there will be to go round, and "Organized Labor" has consistently applied this principle of lessening production in every industry on which it has obtained a sufficient hold to put it into effect.

In printing newspapers it is necessary in order to save time to have an advertisement set into type in advance from which type matrixes or "Mats" are made and furnished to different papers all over the country. The unions, which almost completely dominate the printing field, allow the use of "mats" in order to save time but they arbitrarily insist that after using the "mat" and printing the paper from it that each such advertisement shall be set up in type all over again and then immediately unset.

Throughout the country some 16,000 printers are said to be thus employed in merely setting up type that is never used and is immediately "knocked down."

In the Lincoln Motor Company, 400 of certain automobile parts were polished per man per day and a good man could polish 600 such parts. The unions, however, in the shops they control arbitrarily stipulate that no man shall polish more than 80 such parts per day in a day of the same number of hours.

An average molder can easily set 75 to 80 "snapflasks" a day. Under union control the men are arbitrarily limited to setting 30 a day.

After the complete union domination of the building trades in Cleveland, because of labor shortage during the war, a Cleveland grand jury Investigation reported that carpenters, paper hangers, painters, brick layers and practically all other such classes of workers, in spite of the fact that their pay had been doubled, actually did only about half as much work per man per day.

These are some of the union rules which, entirely in addition to the encouraged inefficiency of the union worker, add to the cost and delay of building jobs.

Plumbers and steam fitters union rules provide that all pipe up to 2½ inches must be hand cut on the job instead of being machine cut at a great saving of time and effort, in the shop.

Ornamental plaster work used to be made in molds in the shop. Union rules now say it must be hand done on the job.

Spraying machines are much more cheap and efficient for painting large flat surfaces. Union rules do not allow their use and will not allow the use of a brush more than 4½ inches wide.

Bath tubs, radiators and heavy plumbing can not be swung up to the proper floor by derrick to save time and labor. Union rules provide that skilled plumbers must be paid for their time to take it up by hand.

Such union rules needlessly decreasing efficiency and piling up costs could be recited literally by the hundreds.

These cases are in no sense exceptional. On the contrary they are typical of the universal experience throughout all industry wherever the modern Labor Movement obtains sufficient control to put its fundamental principles into practice. That all such consistent decreasing of efficiency and piling up of costs have raised prices tremendously to the whole country cannot be doubted.

But the "Modern Labor Movement" has not only consistently lowered current standards of efficiency in production, but has fought advanced standards or methods of production.

It is an obvious fact of all industrial history that the introduction of new or better machinery not only cheapens prices to the public but consequently results in far more employment of labor. It is a matter of the commonest knowledge, for instance, that in the present age of machinery, every trade employs thousands of workers to every one worker the same trade employed before the age of machinery.

Yet in 1900 unions condemned, and union workers struck against, the introduction of the turret lathe which has since made the modern automobile industry possible. If the unions had been strong enough to win this fight, the whole automobile industry on its present scale would have been impossible.

Today machinery exists which could materially increase the production of coal. Yet the powerful United Mine Workers Union is able to and does prohibit its introduction in the coal industry. It costs $2000 for every day the average ocean-going vessel is loading in American ports. Machinery exists which could greatly facilitate loading operations. The President of the longshoremen's union personally approves the introduction of such machinery but the "Labor Movement" prohibits its introduction and handicaps all shipping accordingly.

Again such instances in which the use of labor-saving machinery to increase production is absolutely prohibited by the "Labor Movement" wherever it has had the power to do this, could be multiplied indefinitely.

As indicative of how such theories and practices actually work out, "The Constructor" (June, 1922) publishes a study covering Wages, Savings Bank Deposits, Building Activity, Rents, and Employment, doubtless the chief factors indicative of local prosperity and particularly labor's prosperity, in a large group of "union" cities as compared with "open-shop" cities. The conclusions are in part as follows:

"Comparisons between cities where building is on an open shop basis and on a closed shop basis reveals 56% more building, 34% higher money wages and 18% greater average savings deposits in the open shop towns, . . . with 126% more *un*employment and rent increases 30 times as great in the closed shop cities."

SECOND, *The modern labor movement seeks to dominate absolutely for its own group interest all conditions of employment, irrespective of the interest or rights of the individual worker or often a majority of the workers, or of the industry itself or of the public.*

That it is the fundamental principle of the modern "Labor Movement," and its consistent practice in every industry where it has gained sufficient control to enforce its principles, to force all workers, irrespective of their desires, into the union and to insist that non-union men shall be refused employment, is so consistently admitted by the leaders of organized labor themselves as to require no further proof. Also these admissions are so widely known that they do not require repetition.

But the modern labor movement today goes far beyond this.

New York City is what is called a "union town" just as Chicago, San Francisco and St. Louis have been until recently "union towns." There is at present writing a Joint Committee of the New York Legislature to investigate housing conditions (Lockwood Committee) investigating certain union conditions in New York City. This legislative committee has already discovered and published a host of such organized labor practices as the following:

Certain carpenters were expelled from Carpenters' Union Local 1456 for criticizing Brindell, the New York labor leader who is now in state prison for extortion. Being expelled from the New York union they could not join the union in any other town or get work in any "union town" in America. And as this particular union is very powerful this meant most of the country.

Although there are from 12,000 to 15,000 electric workers living in New York City, the Electrical Workers' Union has arbitrarily limited its membership to 3800 and will not admit any of these other New York electrical workers into its union or allow them to work in New York except, under "permits" to work from week to week at its pleasure on the payment of $2.50 a week to the union.

In October, 1920, the Plumber's Union "closed its books" admitting no new members except the son or brother of men who were members on that date. Not only has it been impossible, therefore, for two years, for any plumber to come from outside communities into New York, even though they were union members in these outside communities, and work at their trade, but the Committee brought out that New York Plumbers' apprentices who had spent four and five years working up in their trade were prevented from joining the union at the end of their apprenticeship and so from following their trade in their own town.

The fact that the same or worse conditions were discovered by the courts or legislative or citizens' committees to have existed in Chicago, San Francisco, and St. Louis and many other communities, was among the chief reasons why the labor movement has been forcibly ejected from power in these cities. That they exist to a greater or less degree throughout the country where organized labor is in the saddle is known, though in the absence of specific public

17

investigation it is of course not possible to state to just what degree they exist.

There is another widespread group of arbitrary labor union practises which operate in the opposite direction to handicap a large part of the workers and raise prices and otherwise tax the public. There are about 500,000 workers in the bituminous coal industry. This is about 100 to 150 thousand more workers than the efficient operation of the industry requires. This has been stated by former Fuel Commissioner Garfield and by many other competent authorities. Because of this excess of workers, the average coal miner can only get work some 150 to 200 days a year and the union leaders say that he only averages about 6 hours' work even for these days. If this 100 to 150 thousand men were distributed among the many other industries where under normal conditions there is a shortage of labor, the remaining coal miners could work a normal amount of time and earn a very good wage at a much lower wage rate. But except for the workers in West Virginia and a few isolated sections, all these men belong to the United Mine Workers' Union and pay dues—between $11,000,000 and $20,000,000 a year dues—into the Union Treasury. Therefore this union, which has for years dominated the coal industry, insists on keeping all these men in the industry and forces the payment of such a high wage scale that these men can earn ordinary wages by thus working about half the time. There are, of course, other factors which contribute to the excessive price of coal but there is little question that the chief cause is the fact that all the consumers of soft coal—and so ultimately the public—must pay this tax to the unions of one and a half men's wages for one man's work on every ton of coal they buy.

THIRD, *the modern "Labor Movement" insists on operating outside the law.*

That men and organizations shall keep their word and their contract and otherwise be responsible for their acts, is the only basis on which orderly human relations are possible. Every other class in American society takes this for granted and if it does not do so is forced by law to live up to these fundamental business and social obligations.

That modern labor organizations as a matter of fact frequently do not keep their contracts and frequently try to avoid responsibility for their acts is of course generally known. But that the modern "Labor Movement" insist, *as a matter of principle* and *right*, that it shall not be subject to the laws on which all organized society and all modern civilization are based, has been frequently hinted at and has recently been frankly and officially admitted by Mr. Samuel Gompers.

In his already famous, and what will doubtless prove historic cross examination before the Lockwood Committee, April 21 and 22, 1922 (pages 6714 to 6889 of the Record), Mr. Gompers testified as to organized labor's own point of view as to its relations with its members, with employers and with the public. It must be particularly remembered throughout this testimony that New York is a "union town" in which no man in the trades discussed can get work unless he is a member of the union, and no employer can get workers to do his work except through the unions and on the union terms.

After discussing many labor union practices which result in injury and often extreme injury to the workers themselves, and which practises Mr. Gompers had to admit were wrong in themselves, Mr. Untermeyer, Counsel for the Lockwood Committee, asked:

"*Mr. Untermeyer:* Where they (the unions) do confessedly a wrong thing, an oppressive thing, a vicious thing to their own people, don't you think the law should step in and give redress?

"*Mr. Gompers:* No sir.

"*Mr. Untermeyer:* Suppose it appeared, as it does in the record here, that practically every Labor Union in this state connected with the building trades, and certainly in this City, having a constitution and by-laws, have provisions for expulsion of members without any power of review; don't you think that the State should regulate that so that the courts would have the right of review over the expulsion of members?

"*Mr. Gompers:* No sir.

"*Mr. Untermeyer:* You think that the Labor Unions should be permitted to exercise this autocratic and despotic power of capital punishment without any say-so by the courts?

"*Mr. Gompers:* God save Labor from the courts.

"*Mr. Untermeyer:* You would not allow the right of review to a man who wanted to get into a Union and who was refused admittance on the pretext that he was not qualified, if he could show, overwhelmingly, that he was the best qualified man in the Union, you would not allow the right of review in the courts in such a case, would you?

"*Mr. Gompers:* I would not.

"*Mr. Untermeyer:* You also heard did you not, those two young men, one of whom had been a plumbers' apprentice four years and a half and the other for five and a half years, tell of their efforts to become journeymen plumbers, did you?

"*Mr. Gompers:* Yes Sir.

"*Mr. Untermeyer:* And you would disapprove, would you not, of any relief for them except through the Union?

"*Mr. Gompers:* Yes sir. That is not through the courts.

"*Mr. Untermeyer:* Then as I understand you, you would prefer to see them go without any redress until they can get redress from the Union?

"*Mr. Gompers:* Yes sir.

"*Mr. Untermeyer:* Would it be true no matter to what extent the abuse might go?"

"*Mr. Gompers:* Yes sir.

"*Mr. Untermeyer:* It appears here that some of these Unions keep no books, no accounts of receipts; that their officers take in dues in cash, dispose of them, and that there is no accounting. There is no relief from that unless the Union chooses otherwise, is there?

"*Mr. Gompers:* Until the Labor movement——

"*Mr. Untermeyer:* I mean there is no relief now. We are not talking about the dim future and the Labor movement we are talking about existing conditions.

"*Mr. Gompers:* Yes.

"*Mr. Untermeyer:* Take a case in which the officers steal the funds of the Union, and there are no books to show and no way of proving that they steal, don't you think the Legislature should regulate those associations to the extent of requiring that they should keep books of accounts of their receipts and expenditures in the interest of common honesty.

"*Mr. Gompers:* I think the Legislature should not interfere in the matter at all, regrettable and bad as the condition may be.

"*Mr. Untermeyer:* If all the trade unions in New York, engaged in the Building Trades agree with all the employers engaged in the building trades that the rate of wages for a plasterer for the year should be nine dollars, it would be a gross breach of contract for the employers, because of a depression in business, to try to get them to work for eight dollars, wouldn't it."

" *Mr. Gompers:* Yes sir.

" *Mr. Untermeyer:* Wouldn't it be an equal breach of contract on the part of the union and its members to take advantage of an activity to try to get ten or twelve dollars in the face of its contract to work for nine dollars?

" *Mr. Gompers:* No.

" *Mr. Untermeyer:* Then what is the good of a contract if it cannot be enforced?

" *Mr. Gompers:* Because time develops self-discipline.

" *Mr. Untermeyer:* They (the members of a union) ought to be able to flaunt the contract and disregard it just as they please?

" *Mr. Gompers:* I did not say that.

" *Mr. Untermeyer:* Is not that a flaunting of the contract, if they simply stop in the middle of a job and demand a 30% increase?

" *Mr. Gompers:* Well, flaunting is disregarding the contract.

" *Mr. Untermeyer:* And you say that there ought to be no remedy?

" *Mr. Gompers:* Not by law.

" *Mr. Untermeyer:* Where are you going to get the remedy?

" *Mr. Gompers:* By the organized labor movement.

" *Mr. Untermeyer:* But there is no such remedy now, is there?

" *Mr. Gompers:* But there is constantly growing improvement.

" *Mr. Untermeyer:* But there is no such remedy now. Never mind what is growing. There is no such remedy now is there?

" *Mr. Gompers:* There is no remedy now."

The jurisdictional dispute between the plumbers and the steamfitters upon a $30,000,000 power house at Hell Gate being built by the city was drawn to Mr. Gompers' attention. He said that the President of the International of which both local unions were members had rendered decision in the matter, but acknowledged that the President had nothing to do with the enforcing of his decision and that the American Federation of Labor was without power to enforce it. The testimony continued:

" *Mr. Untermeyer:* There being this jurisdictional dispute between the two unions, and there being no authority within the unions or within organized labor that can function so as to enforce a settlement of that dispute, do you want us to understand that you would not approve of any interference by the courts to protect that contractor against the consequences of that jurisdictional dispute between the Unions?

"*Mr. Gompers:* I hold that the courts could not compel these men to work.

"*Mr. Untermeyer:* Won't you answer my question? Do you think there should be no right of redress to the courts?

"*Mr. Gompers:* I say that there is no——

"*Mr. Untermeyer:* Won't you answer me?

"*Mr. Gompers:* I think that the courts should not be given that power.

"*Mr. Untermeyer:* Do you think then that in such a case that man should be entirely without redress?

"*Mr. Gompers:* The man——

"*Mr. Untermeyer:* Won't you answer me?

"*Mr. Gompers:* That is not the alternative.

"*Mr. Untermeyer:* Has he any redress?

"*Mr. Gompers:* I do not know.

"*Mr. Untermeyer:* If he has no redress, you think he should be without redress?

"*Mr. Gompers:* From the courts?

"*Mr. Untermeyer:* Without any redress—if he has none, do you think he should remain without redress? It is a plain question. You can answer it yes or no.

"*Mr. Gompers:* That is one of the risks of the industry. . . . I do not see where he can have any redress.

"*Mr. Untermeyer:* Do you think he should remain without redress?

"*Mr. Gompers:* Yes sir, rather than——

"*Mr. Untermeyer:* I am going to ask you the next question. Don't you think that in such a case the courts should have the right to give him redress?

"*Mr. Gompers:* The courts cannot give him any redress.

"*Mr. Untermeyer:* Don't you think they ought to have the right to make the try?

"*Mr. Gompers:* No sir.

"*Mr. Untermeyer:* Did you know that in the Plasterers' Union where their own men did an inferior job of work against the protest of the employer, that they would send for the employer and fine the employer for that work and make him pay for doing it over again and not fine the men who did the work; did you know that?

"*Mr. Gompers:* No.

"*Mr. Untermeyer:* That was proven here before this Committee by the men themselves; you would not approve of that would you?

"*Mr. Gompers:* No."

Counsel drew attention to the fact that in the erection of the Ambassador Hotel in New York, the owner had mantels made of Keene's cement which enables the affixing of the mantel to the building at less cost than by other methods. The plasterers compelled the builder to destroy these mantels and substitute others to be attached by a more costly method. The testimony continued:

"*Mr. Untermeyer:* Don't you think that if such a practice is indulged in under resolution of the Union, that the employer who suffered that loss should have a remedy in damages against the union for the one hundred and odd mantels that he lost in that way?
"*Mr. Gompers:* No.
"*Mr. Untermeyer:* You think he should have no remedy whatever?
"*Mr. Gompers:* Not by a recourse to any new law.
"*Mr. Untermeyer:* Where should the remedy be, what remedy should he have?
"*Mr. Gompers:* He has none. That is the risk of the industry."

Counsel referring to the record advised the witness that the Executive Committee of the Plasterers' Union had compelled the owner of the Ambassador Hotel to tear down part of a wall because the delegate, a plasterer by trade, did not approve the color and style in the imitation of Travatine marble from an artistic point of view, although it was entirely satisfactory to the owner and the architect. The testimony reads (page 6861):

"*Mr. Untermeyer:* But what would you do about it? The owner has had to tear down the walls and he has had to do the thing in a different style to meet the view of that gentleman, Mr. Pearl, I think his name is. Don't you think there ought to be some right lodged somewhere to that owner to get damages for the action of the Executive Committee?
"*Mr. Gompers:* I think not.
"*Mr. Untermeyer:* I know but why shouldn't you be in favor as a just man, of giving a remedy to the man who has suffered damages by that act? That is what I mean to ask you . . . don't you think we can bring you to the point, Mr. Gompers, at which you will agree with us that there should be a legal remedy for such a wanton act?
"*Mr. Gompers:* I think not."

Mr. Gompers went on to explain that labor is:

"An organization of a mass—masses of men and are likely to make mistakes, likely to err. They have the right to err. They have the right to make mistakes in their struggle for their protection and improvement."

"*Mr. Untermeyer:* If they do err and make mistakes that injure the public and injure innocent third parties with whom they deal, is it your idea that there should be no relief for that?

"*Mr. Gompers:* Not by law.

"*Mr. Untermeyer:* Where should the remedy lie?

"*Mr. Gompers:* The law should not provide a remedy.

"*Mr. Untermeyer:* Where should the remedy lie?

"*Mr. Gompers:* By their own experience and sense of justice.

"*Mr. Untermeyer:* That means you would support no regulation whatever except by the unions that are committing the abuses?

"*Mr. Gompers:* No.

"*Mr. Untermeyer:* Where would there be any redress for these abuses except through their correction by the unions by which the abuses are being perpetrated?

"*Mr. Gompers:* By the general labor movement.

"*Mr. Untermeyer:* But you say none of these general labor movements have any compulsory power over a local?

"*Mr. Gompers:* And I would not.

"*Mr. Untermeyer:* You would not give them any, would you?

"*Mr. Gompers:* I would not.

"*Mr. Untermeyer:* Then why do you say that the general labor movement could do anything toward correcting these admitted abuses for which you will allow no other form of correction?

"*Mr. Gompers:* The influence of the American labor movement has been great in eliminating many of the abuses which have existed; it has not succeeded entirely.

"*Mr. Untermeyer:* Are you not aware, Mr. Gompers, as a historical fact, that as the labor unions have grown in power the abuses have accumulated and increased?

"*Mr. Gompers:* In some instances, yes.

"*Mr. Untermeyer:* But don't you know that that is the rule, a natural thing, that where the power gets stronger and stronger the abuses grow greater and greater?

"*Mr. Gompers:* In some instances, yes.

"*Mr. Untermeyer:* In the last five years is there a single reform in all the constitutions and by-laws of these different unions, in some of which there are as many as fifty abuses in a single union?

"*Mr. Gompers:* Probably.

"*Mr. Untermeyer:* Has one been reformed?

"*Mr. Gompers:* Not those to which you refer.

"*Mr. Untermeyer:* Any others, can you refer to one that has been reformed in five years in any union in Greater New York?

"*Mr. Gompers:* I cannot say that I can."

Of course the country has been long familiar with a host of such arbitrary, utterly lawless acts on the part of individual unions or union officials. The public has been apt, however, to regard these as merely isolated and exceptional incidents. But Mr. Gompers' plain statement made categorically and in detail that the "Labor Movement" demands the right of practising the widest variety of the gravest injustices to labor itself, to the employer and to the public "no matter to what extent the abuse might go," without any responsibility before the law or any other authority than their own will, has established the fact that lawlessness is not a mere incident in its practices but is claimed as an inherent right of the modern "Labor Movement." That is why our unbiased public leaders who are really informed have long insisted just as has Senator Beveridge that:—

"When (labor) organizations by threat to strangle the nation can dictate laws for their own advantage at the expense of all the people then regular government by all for the good of all is annihilated."

—and as does Bishop McCabe that:

"As now constituted labor unions cannot long stand. Either they must reform themselves or they will cease to exist."

There is one further important fact in regard to "Organized Labor" which also explains the attitude of informed public leaders in regard to it but will doubtless come as a surprise to the average American who has obtained his ideas of the "Labor Movement" chiefly from "Organized Labor" propaganda.

Organized labor itself has always made every effort to spread the fiction that it represents American labor as a whole. The Interchurch Report speaks of the fight of the Steel Corporation for the Open Shop against the Labor Movement. As a matter of fact, however, the opposite is true and this whole situation is the result of an attack on labor and labor conditions as a whole by the surprisingly small percentage of all labor which is under the domination of the "Labor Movement."

Dr. Leo Wollmann, who is himself entirely favorable to and is at present working for one of the great factions of the modern "Labor Movement," in an article entitled, "The Extent of Trade Unionism," prepared on the basis of the last official figures in 1917, states that of all American labor only 7.7% are members of unions and that even considering the limited classes of labor among which the labor unions have made their greatest success, only 18.4% were members of unions. In Mr. Gompers' own trade, for instance, the cigar makers, less than 25% belong to the union.

There is, of course, another side to the whole trade union question. Undoubtedly organizations of workers, not only for mutual protection but for the discussion of questions of mutual interest and united decision and action on legitimate programs for mutual advancement, would often be to the best interests not only of the workers but often of their industry. Many sincere and intelligent men who recognize all the evils of modern trade unionism still feel that it performs a valuable service at least to the extent that it serves as a constant threat to the short-sighted employer who otherwise might not only take advantage of his own men but establish a standard which more decent employers might believe they had to meet in order to meet his competition.

Large numbers of people who hold such views—some of them inside as well as outside of modern trade unions—believe that industry can be best served by a reformed trade unionism.

Moreover, there are unquestionably a certain percentage of individual unions in the modern Labor Movement which, because of the high type of their individual membership or leadership or both, adequately represent the best spirit and ideals of American Labor and have proved a valuable constructive force for both their members and their industry.

The fact, however, that 80% of the steel workers themselves—tens of thousands of whom were former union members—definitely refused to accept the kind of trade union collective bargaining that was proposed for the steel industry, together with all the facts which have already been considered in connection with that proposed unionization, and the leadership under which it was agitated, raise a strong presumption that it did not promise to be more democratic or otherwise very different from the ordinary modern trade unionism which 90% of all American workers have refused to accept because of its working and results in industry in general.

Nevertheless, the proposition of the unionization of the steel industry has been so particularly stressed by both the first and second volumes of the Interchurch Report and the interest of the great basic steel industry so vitally affects the public interest that the probable particular results which would follow the unionization of that particular industry warrant specific discussion.

CHAPTER XX

TRADE UNION COLLECTIVE BARGAINING AS PARTICULARLY
APPLIED TO THE STEEL INDUSTRY

It was frankly admitted by the strike leaders themselves that they planned the steel unionization drive without even the knowledge of the great majority of the workers, and that otherwise the whole idea of trade union collective bargaining in the steel industry was originated, and all the organization arrangements for attempting to carry it out were put into operation, by professional labor leaders.

Judge Gary stated, and the results of the unionization drive and the strike showed, that the great majority of the steel workers themselves were either indifferent to or did not want trade union collective bargaining in the steel industry.

These facts in themselves indicate that unless the contrary can be shown it must be taken for granted that the particular trade union collective bargaining proposed for the steel industry was the stereotyped professional labor leader kind which involved the adoption in the steel industry, as rapidly as should prove practicable or possible, of the fundamental principles and practices of the "Labor Movement" which have already been described. The only apparent probability that trade union collective bargaining would have worked any differently in the steel industry than it has in most other industries was the possible extent to which Mr. Foster and his faction might have been able to modify it toward radicalism.

After the failure of the unionization drive to interest more than a fifth of the workers, after the first week of the strike when at least the National leaders probably already knew that the strike was a failure, and particularly after Judge Gary had especially attacked, both in public statements and in his Senate testimony, the proposition of the closed shop in the industry, the strike leaders attempted in their testimony before the Senate Committee to insist that they were not demanding the closed shop in the steel industry.

The closed shop is a fundamental policy and practice of the Labor Movement in general and particularly of the 24 International Unions involved in the steel strike. It is a matter of common knowledge that the closed shop has been insisted on and exists in every industry in which organized labor is strong enough to make its policies effective, and that in each new industry where the Labor Movement obtains a hold it enforces the closed shop just as rapidly as it can acquire the power to do so.

Moreover, even while they were insisting that they were not then demanding the closed shop in the industry, Mr. Fitzpatrick and Mr. Gompers were forced under cross-examination by the Senate Committee to admit that their unionization plans and policy led directly and inevitably to the closed shop and Mr. Tighe, President of the Amalgamated Association, in answer to Senator Walsh's question as to whether or not the strike leaders "had it in their hearts," or in any way proposed to bring about the closed shop in the steel industry, merely answered that that question had not, as far as he knew, been definitely discussed by the strike leaders.

Mr. Gompers testified (Senate Hearings, Part I, page 95):

"*Senator Phipps:* What is the attitude . . . as regards employing non-union men in shops where you have organized the employees?

"*Mr. Gompers:* The national trade unions' effort has been to try to organize the workers.

"*Senator Phipps:* And to exclude the employment of non-union men wherever possible?

"*Mr. Gompers:* To organize the workers, to try to have the workers organized in a plant 100%."

In regard to the same point Mr. Fitzpatrick also after much cross-examining finally testified (Senate Hearings, Part I, page 53):

"*Senator Stirling:* And you object in a union shop to the taking in of non-union men, do you not?

"*Mr. Fitzpatrick:* No.

"*Senator Stirling:* Do you not try to prevent the employment of non-union men in the union shop?

"*Mr. Fitzpatrick:* In the union shop the employer and the employees have agreed that the union men will be employed. Then . . . in case of inability of the union to furnish union men or of the employer to secure union men, that in that situation, then the employer can employ non-union men. . . .

"*Senator Stirling:* That is only however in case he is not able to secure union men that he is permitted to employ non-union men?

"*Mr. Fitzpatrick:* Yes."

Moreover, number 9 of the 12 demands which the strike leaders made of the steel companies shows plainly, as will be developed later, that it was the express intention of the strike leaders to enforce the closed shop in the steel industry or otherwise demand number 9 would be meaningless.

Considering then the fundamental principles and practices of the present Labor Movement, and that the 24 International unions which instigated the steel strike held to exactly these same principles and practices and often carried them to extremes, and considering the fact that their trade union collective bargaining in the steel industry was to have worked directly towards the closed shop under which as a matter of fact and practice every worker would have had to come under direct and secret union control or lose his job, there is obviously every reason to believe that trade union collective bargaining in the steel industry would also have meant the decreased production, the interference with the introduction of new machinery and other technical improvements, and the subjection of the whole industry to the constant labor agitation fostered by the selfish ambitions of rival labor leaders or rival unions, which have marked conditions in most other industries which have come under the control of the Labor Movement.

Entirely in addition to this, however, there were many specific factors in connection with the proposed unionization of the steel industry which would have exaggerated these ordinarily unfavorable results.

These special factors were:

First, the particular professional labor leaders who were to have instituted and who would undoubtedly have continued to have a large voice in carrying out of trade union collective bargaining in the steel industry.

Second, the fact that there were 24, and the particular rivalries and other relations of these 24, International unions which would have controlled the majority of the steel workers and whose many various individual and often hostile interests and policies would necessarily infinitely complicate the labor policy of the steel industry; and

Third, certain of the special 12 demands which the strike leaders made on the companies as a basis for collective bargaining in the steel industry.

Mr. Foster was one of the chief leaders who was to have instituted trade union collective bargaining in the steel industry.   On his own plain definite admission and that of the Interchurch Report, Mr. Foster's whole interest in trade union collective bargaining in the steel industry or in any other industry was to make every possible use of it as a means to carrying out certain aims of his own, which aims he described several years before the strikes as being to seize industry and set up a syndicalist soviet government and which aims he described after the strike merely by the words "radical" and "revolutionary."

It is accordingly clear that as far as Mr. Foster's leadership in it was concerned, the particular proposed trade union collective bargaining would not be for the best interests of the steel industry or the country.[1]

The second most important individual among the steel leaders and also on the committee which was to inaugurate the proposed trade union collective bargaining in the steel industry was John Fitzpatrick.

Mr. Fitzpatrick testified:

Some of them (steel workers) get $20 and $40, as I understand it as high as $60, a day but . . . it is not anything like what he ought to have, no matter what he gets," (Senate Hearings, Part I, page 61, line 29);

also,

"A group of steel emplyees . . . passed resolutions stating that the conditions in the steel mills were very satisfactory; that the wages were all that could be hoped for, and that there was absolutely no complaint on which to justify any kind of grievance and therefore that they were absolutely content with the conditions that existed. *Then they . . . went in to their slave holes in the steel mills*" (Senate Hearings, Part I, page 81, line 22);

and again

"*Mr. Fitzpatrick:* If we undertook to postpone the strike or wait until October 6th (as President Wilson requested) . . . then we would have been shot to pieces. There would not have been anybody here to make any report.

"*Senator Smith.* You said if you had delayed the strike you would have been shot to pieces; your organization would have been shot to pieces.

---

[1] "Foster is just back from Russia where he was in touch with Lenin and Trotzky. Judging from his own statements no man visiting the Soviet was ever treated better. . . . Immediately upon his return to the United States he proceeds to organize the Trade Union Educational League. Presumably Foster is the educator. . . . Back of that resolution (Foster's) is the propaganda of radical revolution to overthrow the Constitution of the United States . . . and William Z. Foster wants to become an autocrat of America."

SAMUEL GOMPERS,
April 30, 1922.

"*Mr. Fitzpatrick:* And with the shooting of our organization to pieces our members would have been shot in cold blood . . . "(Senate Hearings, Part I, page 20).

Mr. Fitzpatrick's whole Senate testimony indicates his sincerity. But the point of view which believed that, in view of the relation between wages and prices, workers ought to receive $18,000 a year and "more if they can get it," and which scathingly condemned any workers who stated that they did not feel the grievances which his self-interested prejudice thought they ought to feel, and which argued volubly and in perfect seriousness that the strike leaders didn't dare postpone the strike two weeks, as President Wilson requested, for fear that all their members would have been "shot down in cold blood," so that "no one would have been left to report," hardly represents a point of view which the public can afford to have given a dominant voice in the management of the steel industry. Moreover the quality of Mr. Fitzpatrick's executive ability is further indicated by the fact that in the Chicago district where he had for years been President of the local American Federation of Labor grand juries have recently uncovered more labor graft, blackmail and intimidation and general preying on the public than has ever been known to exist in any other city in the country.[1]

The continuation of collective bargaining, if it had been established in the steel industry, would have been carried out as it effected about 60% of the men, by the 24 International unions who claimed jurisdiction over the steel industry and to whose organizations (according to Mr. Foster's records) 60% of the unionized steel workers had

[1] As a climax to organized labor conditions in Chicago which have been growing worse and more notorious for years, on May 10, 1922, the Chicago headquarters of the various unions were raided by the police, material for bombs found and seized and 200 labor leaders arrested, who were characterized by the Chicago Chief of Police as "hoodlums and ex-convicts," who "no more represent honest labor than the Haymarket anarchists did."

18

been variously assigned. In other words, all such questions as "control of the job," "promotion," "working hours"—which the Interchurch Report particularly mentions—and in general all questions having to do with labor, including rate of production and pay, would all have been determined under the proposed trade union collective bargaining by representatives of the company and representatives of each of these 24 International unions.

Mr. Gompers' testimony before the Lockwood Committee plainly indicates that the large proportion of all strikes and other labor agitation and trouble which notoriously and constantly disrupts the country's building operations, is caused, not by any question between employer and employee affecting the interests of the men, but because of the rivalries and jealousies of the different unions involved. That the same conditions applies to a more or less degree wherever the Labor Movement is in control, generally in proportion to the number of unions which claim jurisdiction in the particular industry is well known.

The very fact then that there were 24 rival International unions involved in the proposed trade union collective bargaining in the steel industry of itself was particularly calculated to make such trade union collective bargaining particularly hectic.

Moreover the fact that these 24 International unions could not even wait until they had established such trade union collective bargaining to demonstrate how hectic and generally disruptive that bargaining would be is repeatedly admitted and emphasized by both Mr. Foster and the Interchurch Report.

The Interchurch Report states

"The third cause (of the failure of the strike) was the disunity of labor" (p. 179). "The Stationary Engineers and the Switchmen, two of the 24 Internationals, did not call their members out of the steel plants and yards but a number of Switchmen's locals did. The Amalgamated Association of Iron, Steel and Tin Workers after a month began ordering its men back into independent plants" (175). "In the Calumet district, the Switchmen refused to pull out their men because the organizer said 'Trade control was at stake.' The Switchmen were rivals of the Trainmen for the men in the plant yards and if they'd have struck, the Trainmen would have stuck, filled up the places, broke the strike and the Switchmen could never have got back" (p. 181) "Electrical International officers say their people did not want steel organized because electrical workers, during slack times in union shops like to be free to get steel jobs which they couldn't if steel was organized" (p. 181). "Among the 24 unions, besides the fights over segregating recruits, there came up in devastating form the unsolved problem of the sacredness of contracts . . . the Amalgamated was acrimoniously charged (by rival unions) with choosing between its contracts with employers and its contracts with fellow unions. Its choice was called treason. . . . Moreover there was no unity . . . as between the steel unions and the American Federation of Labor," p. (179).

Mr. Foster goes into even greater detail to show how utterly impossible it was for these 24 unions to forget their jealousies and rivalries and work together even for a few months in order to achieve a common advantage that admittedly they could not achieve save by the strongest possible unity of action.

But under trade union collective bargaining, these 24 unions would have to work month in and month out, not only with each other but with what they at least secretly regard as their inherent class enemies—the steel companies—as well. Working agreements would have constantly to be formulated and maintained not merely in regard to a few simple policies but on a host of practical details, on many of which every separate union might have a different point of view and interest.

For the interests and policies of each of these 24 unions is inevitably determined not by conditions or necessities in the steel industry, where most of them would only have a minority of their members, but by conditions or necessities in other industries where most of them would have their majority memberships. This condition would also inevitably involve many further complicating probabilities. The unions embracing the low-skilled foreign workers would have a constant tendency toward radicalism. The personal ambitions of some Skinny Madden or some Brindell would be 24 times as likely as ordinary to further agitate the labor political waters or muddy them with graft and corruption. In view of these perfectly plain and admitted facts, there can be no doubt that any attempt to establish such a hydra-headed type of trade union collective bargaining in the steel industry would constitute the deliberate establishment of a condition which, according to all available labor experience and all general experience, would merely promise a state of industrial chaos of which the building trades offer a most conspicuous example.

The third particular factor in the steel situation which promised to exaggerate the normal tendency of trade union collective bargaining towards decreased production and a general condition where the worker must give his loyalty to his union instead of his job, and depend on the union instead of on personal efficiency and ambition for advancement, consisted of certain of the particular 12 demands which the strike leaders made upon the steel companies as the basis of the proposed trade union collective bargaining in the steel industry.

Of these official 12 demands, number 3 and number 6 called for the 8 hour day throughout the industry and an "increase of wages sufficient to guarantee an American standard of living." The merits of these demands and the results of their possible acceptance have already been sufficiently discussed.

Demand number 10 insisted that "Principles of seniority apply in maintaining, reducing or increasing working forces"—this demand meant that all incentive among the workers to be efficient in their jobs in order to achieve more rapid advancement was to have been taken away. The most able worker was to be always kept below even the most inefficient worker who had merely been employed longer than he had. In any reduction of the working force the newer employees, no matter how efficient or brilliant, had to be let go and slightly older employees, no matter how inefficient, retained. Under such a system workers like Schwab, and Buffington and Farrell and all of Carnegie's 29 partners would still be, merely because of age and number of years worked, just getting out of the semi-skilled into the skilled worker's class or else they would have had to seek the outlet for their ambitions in labor politics or in some other industry.

Demand number 12 called for "abolition of physical examination." The steel industry to a particular degree involves the handling of molten metal and very heavy machinery, both of which involve possible danger to many workers. The companies in their regard for the safety of the men and the machinery have always insisted on a careful physical examination as to the eyesight, hearing, mental and muscular reactions, and other physical qualifications of the workmen to whom such responsibilities were entrusted. It was one of the basic demands of the unions that such examinations be abolished, the object of course being to take away the company's last vestige of control over its employees.

Demands numbers 11 and 9 insisted on "the abolition of company unions" and "check-off system of collecting union dues and assessments." The first of these, providing that no steel worker could continue to belong to the local steel unions to which many of them had belonged for years before the strike, was of course only a step towards providing that he must belong to one of the unions which instigated the strike. The "check-off system" provided that the unions, instead of having to collect their regular dues and special assessments from the men themselves, should collect all dues in a lump sum from the steel companies, the companies in turn to take such sums out of the wages of the men. The whole purpose and effect of the "check-off system," which is so obviously pernicious that only a few of the most powerful and radical unions dare resort to it, is to make it automatically impossible for any workman to stay out of the union or to leave it while he keeps his job. Moreover it gives the National union, through its local business agent who collects all revenues directly from the companies, a secure, arbitrary power and leaves the local members correspondingly powerless in union affairs. The "check-off system" is so generally recognized as pernicious that when it was brought up in the Senate Hearings, certain of the strike leaders attempted to explain that they only meant to apply it to a part of the industry. But it was one of the plain, unqualified general demands upon which the strike was called and there can be little question that if the strike had been won and the strike leaders had had power to do so, they would have enforced it to the letter.

Mr. Tighe, who incidentally was not a member of the National Committee of Strike Management, may not have, as he said in the Senate Hearings he had not, heard any definite discussion of the closed shop in the steel industry but discussion was not necessary in the face of demands numbers 9 and 11 whose direct effect would have been, and obviously whose only purpose was, to establish a very tightly "closed shop" in the steel industry.

Agriculture, coal, the railroads and steel are the four cornerstones of modern industrial existence and progress. Railroads and the coal industry are highly unionized. Agriculture and steel are not. During the special exigencies of the war, the railroads and the coal industry conspicuously failed to measure up to the national needs. This was of course due to other factors also, but it is notorious that when the government took over the railroads during the war, the Labor Movement "held up the government," to quote President Garretson of the Railroad Conductors Union, not only for wage increases which except for government support would have bankrupted the railroads, but for a system of lessened efficiency which required that nearly 200,000 extra workers be added to run the railroads at this time when the maximum use and efficiency of all labor was of paramount national importance; and the coal industry held on to the 150,000 men it didn't need but which the rest of industry did need, just as it has held on to them (by demanding full time earnings for half time work) both before and since.

Because of the peculiar importance of steel, the war undoubtedly made heavier comparative demands on the steel industry than on either the railroads or the coal industry. Yet not only did the non-union steel industry never show the least sign of breaking down or requiring special artificial assistance, but under the spur of this crisis, the non-union steel workers turned out steel faster than the railroads could furnish facilities to transport it or manufacturing equipment could be multiplied to use it. And there can be no question that this fact was due primarily to consistent, able management, including labor management, which in turn included the unhampered ability to control promotion and working conditions against which the Interchurch Report argues so strongly and for which it would substitute the kind of trade union collective bargaining which holds in the coal industry and the railroads.

Since the war both the railroads and the coal industry have again become notorious national problems, largely because of conditions which have been created by the power of the unions to enforce trade union collective bargaining and the kind of bargains they have used that power to enforce. But no one except the defeated and disgruntled strike leaders and the Interchurch Report have ever even suggested, either before or since the war, that the steel industry constituted or threatened to constitute such a national problem as our other two great basic industries conspicuously constitute.

But all the circumstances surrounding the unionization drive including its leadership, the diversity and rivalries of the different unions claiming jurisdiction, and the official demands on which it was to be based, all indicate that if the proposed trade union collective bargaining had been established in the steel industry, the steel industry might very rapidly have become, not merely a national problem, but the kind of national scandal that the building trades, with their many-rival-union control, have so notoriously become.

But this kind of trade union collective bargaining did not get its hold on the steel industry because, contrary to the statements and impression of the whole Interchurch Report, the men themselves did not want it.

On August 1, 1920, two days after the Interchurch Report was released for distribution, the books of the U. S. Steel Corporation showed *90,952* owners of its common stock. On November 1, 1920, *53,000 employees* of the U. S. Steel Corporation were actual stockholders and *26,000 more employees* were paying for stock. (Figures furnished by the U. S. Steel Corporation.)

These steel workers which the Interchurch Report describes as being in "a state of latent war" and "waiting only for the next strike" thus constitute by far the largest number of their company's stockholders. This fact and the whole relation between the men and the company which it typifies, constitutes a far more promising industrial and social prospect for the workers, the industry and the whole country, than any trade union collective bargaining arrangement with the men tied hand and foot by union regulations, union politics and the "check-off" system and with Foster, Fitzpatrick *et al* as their official bargainers.

CHAPTER XXI

"SOCIAL CONSEQUENCES" OF THE ATTITUDE OF THE PUBLIC TOWARDS THE STEEL STRIKE

THERE can be no question that all the social forces in closest touch with the strike situation—press, pulpit, citizens organizations, and public opinion in general—were overwhelmingly against the steel agitation and the steel strike, just as were the great majority of the workers themselves. Foster complains of this continually and most bitterly and the Interchurch Report admits it freely.

Foster speaks in his book, *The Great Steel Strike* (page 2), of the

"Crawling, subservient and lying press, which spewed forth its poison propaganda in their (the steel companies') behalf . . . selfish and indifferent local church movements which had long since lost their Christian principle . . . hordes of unscrupulous municipal, county, state and federal officials whose eagerness to wear the steel collar was equalled only by their forgetfulness of their oath of office . . . with the notable exception of a few honorable and courageous individuals here and there among these hostile elements, *it was an alignment of the steel companies, the state, the courts, the local churches and the press against the steel workers.*"

Also, according to Mr. Foster:

"the lackey-like mayors and burgesses" in steel towns (page 30), "the organized bodies of war veterans" and . . . "the petty parasites who prey upon the steel workers—the professional and small business men" (page 97) . . "the local unions" who refused "to recognize the national committee's strike call" (page 106) . . . "the rowdy element of the American Legion" (page 110) . . . "the infamous (Attorney General) Palmer" (page 111) . . . 'the plug-ugly state constabulary' (page 119) . . . "pliable city authorities and business men from the steel towns" (page 145) . . . "the slip-shod haphazard" Senate committee (page 157) . . . "the whole news gathering and distributing system" (which he calls) "a gigantic mental prostitution" (page 165) . . . General Wood who used the steel strike merely as "a political stunt to give General Wood publicity?" (page 172) . . . Mobs "led by W. R· Lump, Secretary of the Y. M. C. A. and H. L. Tredennick, President of the Chamber of Commerce" (page 189) . . .

all, he says, opposed the steel strike and the whole strike movement.

Except then for Father Kazinci and the few other "honorable and courageous individuals here and there" who are not mentioned by name, and the Interchurch Investigation which "impressed (Mr. Foster) by the scientific methods and apparent desire to get at the truth" (page 157), every general social organization or group which came into close touch with the steel strike, from the Senate Committee to local American Legions, Y. M. C. A.'s, Chamber of Commerce, Churches and Merchants and Citizens in general, were, according to Mr. Foster's specific statement, openly opposed to the methods and aims of the strike leaders, just as were 80% of the workers themselves.

The Interchurch Report is not so vituperative as Mr. Foster in regard to the forces which were against the unionization and the strike movement. In general it takes the attitude toward such forces of pity rather than censure and in effect assures them that they know not what they do. But the Interchurch Report is equally specific with Mr. Foster in stating that in general all the agencies of government and of public opinion which had first-hand information about the unionization movement and the strike opposed it.

After saying the same thing over again and again on the preceding pages, the Interchurch Report says in summary on pages 238 and 239, that "great numbers of workers came to believe

—"that local mayors, magistrates and police officials try to break strikes";

—"that state and Federal officials, particularly the Federal Department of Justice, help to break strikes, and that armed forces are used for this purpose";

—"that most newspapers actively and promptly exert a strike breaking influence; most churches passively."

". . . The Steel Strike made tens of thousands of citizens believe that our American institutions are not democratic or not democratically administered."

The Interchurch Report then proceeds through a number of pages to "hastily summarize" the evidence which it states is at "the basis of such beliefs."

It states that Sheriff Haddock of Allegheny County had a brother who was a superintendent of an American Sheet, Iron and Tin Plate plant; that Mayor Crawford of Duquesne was the brother of the President of the McKeesport Tin Plate Company, and that three other local public officials were connected with the steel company.

That out of the scores of plants in which the strike was agitated, and that out of the thousands of public officials in these communities, these five were thus themselves connected, or had some relative connected, with the steel industry is the first reason which the Interchurch Report advances as to why the strikers had a

" deep-seated suspiciousness of everything and everybody connected with public executives, courts, Federal agents, army officers, reporters, or clergy" (page 239).

The Interchurch Report then spends a paragraph in alleging that strikers were fined "from ten to fifty or sixty dollars" and imprisoned for terms which "ran up to months" for causes which the Report alleges were insufficient.   Therefore, concludes the Interchurch Report:

"local mayors, magistrates and police officials try to break strikes."

On page 240, it condemns the Department of Justice for coöperating with private detectives and condemns Attorney General Palmer for his activities and statements about 'reds' in the steel strike. This is its basis for the allegation that

"Federal officials, particularly the Federal Department of Justice, try to break strikes."

Next the Interchurch Report condemns the Senate Committee's investigation as having

"filled the strikers with a bitterness only to be understood by detailed comparison of the Committee's report and the facts." (Page 240)

The Interchurch Report next condemns the use of armed forces in the strike area and particularly the use of the United States army under General Leonard Wood. In order to show that the use of armed forces was entirely unnecessary and that the strikers were the victims rather than the cause of such violence as there was, the Interchurch Report states (page 241):

"The strikers made frequent complaints of violent raids carried out by bands of citizens calling themselves Loyal American Leaguers, who were charged with clubbing groups of strikers on street corners at nights. A crowd of strikers leaving a mass meeting tried to pull a negro strike breaker off a street car; the negro was slightly injured and a number of strikers were clubbed. On this case of 'mob violence' . . . Indiana state guards were sent in, parades were forbidden." . . . Ten thousand strikers held a parade . . . in disregard of the guardsmen. "On this second case of mob violence, known as the Outlaw Parade, the United States regulars occupied Gary with General Wood in personal charge, proclaiming martial law. The regulars were equipped with bayonets and steel helmets and the force included many trucks mounting machine guns and bringing field artillery.

"General Wood declared that the army would be neutral. He established rules in regard to picketing." When these rules were broken, "strikers would be arrested. Delays and difficulties would attend the release of these men from jail or bull pen." The feelings of the steel workers then was "that local and national government not only was not their government, i.e. in their behalf, but was government in behalf of interests opposing theirs."

The Interchurch Report (page 242) next accuses the

"Press in most communities," because it "suppressed or colored its records, printed advertisements and editorials urging the strikers to go back, denounced the strikers, and incessantly misrepresented the facts. . . . Foreign language papers largely followed the lead of the English papers."

In regard to the "pulpit," however, the Interchurch Report plainly hedges; it states (page 243)

"Research among clergymen revealed a large minority deeply suspicious of the newspaper version of the strike, but ineffective for organizing concerted action even for purposes of self-information." It however follows Foster at least to the point of stating that "where some clergyman preached or wrote against the strike or where another gift to a local church by a steel company became public . . . the workers' attitude to the church followed these few individuals, deeming the church another strike breaker," after which series of carefully calculated insinuations is added the phrase, "after the strike, workers generally were making no effort to make the church *their* church."

Now it would seem, as a matter of plain common sense, that these very facts—that the local press and the local churches which obviously receive their support in far greater proportion from steel workers than from steel officials—that the great body of local merchants whose customers were obviously in far greater proportion among the steel workers than among steel officials—that local American legions and Y. M. C. A.'s who are certainly made up of a far greater proportion of workers than capitalists—that foreign language papers who receive their entire support from the lowest ranks of the workers, were admittedly all thus opposed to the unionization drive and the strike, should in itself raise a strong presumption that all these other forces of society in close touch with the situation and disinterested or naturally sympathetic to the worker, were probably right, and the strike leaders and their minority following probably wrong. Such an obviously logical presumption from the facts, however, never seem to have occurred to either Mr. Foster or to the Interchurch Report.

As regards Mr. Foster's point of view he saw in such facts, merely another argument to radical labor that all society was against them and must be fought accordingly. His conclusions from these facts are merely that

"In the next steel strike," all labor must unite, and fight the rest of society "with such a combination of allied steel, mine and railroad workers . . . (that there will be) small likelihood that the steel companies *or the public at large* would consider the question of the steel workers' right to organize of sufficient importance to fight about." (*Great Steel Strike*, page 239.)

But Mr. Foster, of course, is frankly a radical and, on his own admission, against all the rest of society and against all modern social institutions and on his own admission was organizing labor to fight the rest of society and overthrow modern social institutions. Foster's conclusion, therefore, that when all the rest of society opposed him and his plans, all the rest of society was of course wrong, is at least natural and understandable.

The Interchurch Report agrees with Mr. Foster that when all the rest of society opposed his steel strike plans, all the rest of society was wrong. But instead of following Mr. Foster in openly threatening all the rest of society with the power of organized labor it seeks rather to point out to and warn all the rest of society of the cost of defending its interests and of how much trouble could be escaped by merely yielding gracefully to Mr. Foster and his program. It sprinkles such warnings throughout the book, and uses all of Chapter VII, which it calls "Social Consequences," in emphasising and summarizing these warnings.

These "social consequences"—including the "degradation, persisted in and approved by public opinion, of civil liberties"—which the whole public has brought upon itself because the steel companies and public opinion were not willing to turn the steel industry over to the collective bargaining of Mr. Foster and his fellow strike leaders, the Interchurch states on page 197 to be as follows:

". . . for the employers:
"1. 'Discharging workmen for unionism,'" i.e. for agitation during the unionization drive.
"2. 'Black lists'"; that is keeping a list of radicals, agitators and other undesirables and exchanging such lists with each other.
"3. 'Espionage and the hiring of labor detective agencies' operatives."

The use of detectives, the Interchurch Report regards as a particularly awful "social consequence." It practically always refers to detectives by the sinister sounding titles of "under-cover men" or "under-cover spies" just as it refers to the police as "cossacks." It spends pages in proving that both the steel companies and the United States Department of Justice used detectives in the Steel Strike and that they sometimes coöperated with each other and as its climax of this frightful accusation, states on page 221 in italics, that

"These company spy systems carry right through into the United States Government. Federal immigration authorities testified to the Commission that raids and arrests for "radicalism" were made . . . on the denunciations and secret reports of steel company 'under cover' men and the prisoners turned over to the Department of Justice."

The last emphasized dire "social consequence" to the employer was—

4. The necessity for hiring "strike breakers, principally negroes."

These, however, are only the social consequences to the employer. Entirely in addition to them, are the "social consequences" which the whole country must suffer because of the blind unwillingness of the steel companies and public opinion, to give Mr. Foster and the other strike leaders their way in the steel industry. These "social consequences" the Interchurch Report goes right on to solemnly warn the whole country, are: (Page 197)

"1. The abrogation of the right of assembly, the suppression of free speech, and the violation of personal rights.

"2. The use of state police, state troops and of the United States army and "the expenditure of public money."

"3. Such activities on the part of constituted authorities and of the Press and the pulpit as to make the workers believe that these forces opposed labor."

As regards this whole general argument as to the dire "Social Consequences" to employers and all the rest of the country because employers and all other interested social forces refused to give Mr. Foster and his fellow strike leaders a free hand in the steel industry, the most striking thing is its remarkable similarity to the well-known argument of Wilhelm II that the rest of the world brought all the consequences of the war on itself by not quietly and peaceably permitting him to do anything he pleased.

Certain particular arguments on this subject, however, because of the way they are advanced and repeated and emphasized, and because they presume to involve a discussion of fundamental American rights deserve special attention. These are the so-called "Abrogation of the Right of Free Speech," "Police Brutalities" and "Judicial Discrimination."

CHAPTER XXII

" ABROGATION OF THE RIGHT OF FREE SPEECH AND ASSEMBLY"

THE argument of the Interchurch Report in regard to the alleged unwarranted abrogation of the right of free speech and assembly by local authorities during the steel strike merits detailed consideration not only because of the emphasis which the Interchurch Report places on it, but because the whole argument touches upon one of the most fundamental questions in modern democracy.

Beyond this it merits particular consideration because of the fact that there has been developed in recent years a system of organized propaganda which has been persistently and widely disseminated for specific ulterior purposes which propaganda entirely misrepresents the plain law and the facts in regard to this whole subject.

Freedom of speech and the right of assembly are unquestionably fundamental American rights, constituting one of the most important guarantees of American liberty. Moreover there are perhaps no rights which Americans have insisted more tenaciously on exercising or would fight more vigorously to protect, if they were actually threatened.

But this does not mean that these rights are without limit. On the contrary they are, as are all other individual and group rights, strictly limited by the superior rights of the public as a whole. And when the rights of free speech and assembly, just as in the case of any other individual or group rights, come, for any reason, into conflict with the superior right of the public as a whole, it is not only a basic principle of our law but is a basic principle of democracy itself that this individual or group right must be subordinated to the public right. For any theory or practice which puts individual or group rights above the public rights of course leads directly to despotism or anarchy.

The practical exemplification of many of the ways in which the rights of free speech and assembly are thus limited is a matter of commonest knowledge. The regulation that the soap-box orator may not indiscriminately collect a crowd in the middle of a main thoroughfare and block traffic is of course a limitation on the right of free speech on the part of the orator and his listeners, in favor of the greater right of the public to pass uninterruptedly up and down its own thoroughfare. There are many similar limitations of the rights of free speech and assembly, established and enforced in proportion as the exercise of the individual right in the given circumstances would endanger the free enjoyment of the greater rights of the public. Such limitations therefore vary with circumstances. Limitations are enforced as to main thoroughfares which are not enforced as to side streets; in large communities which would be unnecessary in small communities; special limitations are frequently set in time of fire, flood, riot or other exigencies, so that what may be done or said under ordinary circumstances may not be done or said under those exigencies. Under many circumstances a man might have the right to call out the word "fire" but to call out "fire" in a crowded theatre when there was no fire, would constitute an obvious crime. A man may freely express criticism of the government's policy under ordinary circumstances which if expressed in time of war, might, by giving aid to the public enemy, constitute a crime against the public welfare. No man of course may carry his individual right of free speech to the extent of counselling or urging crime.

Perhaps the most frequent occasion in which the individual right of free speech may come into conflict with the superior rights of the public is under circumstances in which the unlimited exercise of this right would subvert or endanger the public peace. As a matter of fact from the beginning of our history and back into the earlier history of the common law, the conflict between the right of free speech and the public right to peace and order, has been so recurrent and the law in such cases is so firmly established that the very legal definitions of the right of free speech have almost invariably included the statement of this particular limitation.

Justice Story, one of the greatest of all our constitutional authorities years ago defined this fundamental but not unlimited right of free speech to mean that:

"Every man shall have a right to speak, write or print his opinions upon any subject whatever, without any prior restraint, so always that he does not injure any other person in his rights, person, property or reputation; *and so always that he does not thereby disturb the public peace* or attempt to subvert the government." (Story, *Commentaries on the Constitution*, Sect. 1874.)

Moreover it is plain fundamental law as well as plain justice and common sense that where there is a question as to whether or not the exercise of the individual right of free speech does, under a given condition, endanger the public peace or otherwise conflict with the superior rights of the public, the right to decide that question shall rest with the public and not with the individual or individuals in the case. If the rule were otherwise, and each soap box orator for instance, or the group which at the time were interested in listening to him, had the authority to decide whether or not the exercise of their individual right of assembly under the circumstances was in conflict with the right of the public to use the streets freely, there would of course be no limitations whatever to the exercise of such individual rights and the public right would be made subordinate instead of superior; which of course is incompatible with the whole theory of democracy.

But on the other hand it is equally against our theory of democracy that any majority, no matter how great, merely because it is a majority and has the power, shall be permitted to construe its rights as greater than they actually are, or otherwise to limit individual rights where they do not, as a matter of fact, conflict with the public rights. Therefore the courts will always carefully review the actual facts in any case of alleged conflict between the rights of individuals and the right of the public, and if it finds, as a matter of fact that they do not actually conflict, it will uphold the individual in his rights and enjoin the public, through its duly elected public officials or otherwise, from any unwarranted infringement of individual rights.

In the question of the fundamental rights of free speech and assembly and their alleged abrogation during the steel strike two other basic principles of law are involved and must be considered.

Since 1842, the courts without the aid of any legislative enactments have recognized the "right to withhold labor," i.e., the right to strike, as a legitimate economic weapon. A strike in its essence, is an agreement among a number of individuals to withhold their labor. It is generally the specific purpose of this agreement to injure the employer as a means of forcing him to accede to the demands of the workers. An agreement to act in concert to cause injury to a third party is generally regarded as a conspiracy and *ipso facto* illegal. Therefore in recognizing the right to strike the courts have modified the law of conspiracy in favor of labor. Labor itself has widely and loudly criticized the courts for what it calls their assumption of legislative function. It is, therefore, interesting to note that perhaps never in any other connection have the courts more clearly "made law" or made law involving more fundamental and sweeping changes than in this case of the recognition of the right to strike,—a change wholly in favor of labor.

During the rapid rise of industrialism in the first part of the last century, in the same period when the use of the strike as an economic weapon was being developed and recognized by law, there arose in Europe a strong movement, led by the Russian anarchists Bakounin and Nechayeff, that insisted that the strike should not be used merely as an economic weapon of competition with the employer for a fair share in the proceeds of industry, but should be used as a weapon to overthrow the employer and seize the control of industry. This movement insisted that violence constituted a part of the strike weapon and was necessary to make it really effective.

For a generation this movement fought for, and for considerable periods held control of at least the European continental labor movement. To it later was added the influence of the Syndicalists who had the same views as to violence and from time to time the I. W. W. and other forms of radicalism. Partly as a result of the constant agitation of such doctrines and partly as a result of the tendency of human nature to use the most effective means possible to its ends, there is no question that labor's theory of the strike has been permeated with the notion that the right to strike involves the right to indulge in at least the minor forms of intimidation or violence.

The law, however, under no circumstances recognizes any right to commit violence great or small. The man who commits or threatens murder is of course more severely punished by the law than the man who commits or threatens mild bodily injury. But the law does not recognize the *right* to commit mild violence any more than it recognizes the right to commit murder. Thus, when exercising their entirely legal right to strike, workers have no more right to commit the mildest forms of intimidation or violence than they have to commit the most serious violence. When therefore the law condemns and punishes or enjoins the committing of any form of violence during a strike that does not mean that the law is denying the right to strike any more than the fact that the law would punish a man for breaking windows as he passed down the street, would mean that the law was denying him his right to walk down the street.

The rules of law involved then are plain and simple:

1. All Americans have the fundamental rights of free speech and assembly so long as the way or the conditions under which they exercise those rights do not infringe the greater rights of the public;

2. The public has the right to judge, through its duly constituted officials, whether or not in a given case the exercise of those individual rights would conflict with the public right;

3. But the law at the same time very plainly guards against majority or official tyranny and will carefully review the facts in any given case and if the facts do not show that the authorities were warranted in believing that the exercise of the individual rights would jeopardize public rights, it will protect the individuals in the exercise of these rights;

4. The courts clearly recognize the right to strike;

5. They do not recognize the right of strikers, any more than any other persons to commit or threaten violence, and they refuse to admit, in the case of strikers as in all other cases, that anyone can have the right to commit a crime merely on the grounds that it is a small crime;

—which basic law will doubtless appear to average Americans as also the plainest common justice and common sense.

During the steel strike the authorities in various communities involved placed certain limitations on the rights of the strikers to hold meetings. These limitations varied. In some cases merely open air meetings were prohibited. In others it was specifically required that all speeches be in English. In some cases all strikers' meetings were finally prohibited. In each case these various limitations were established on the specific grounds that violence had occurred or was threatened and the public peace was thereby endangered. The Interchurch Report contends, as the strike leaders contended at the time, that these limitations infringed the strikers' rights of free speech and assembly. They further contended that such regulations were unwarranted by the conditions—that the real reason for their being enforced was not because of fear of violence but because of an alleged relation between the public officials and the steel companies. This last contention, however, which the Interchurch Report makes very strongly, it fails to reconcile with its other equally strong contention, already referred to in detail, that Church, Press, Business associations and all other forces of society in the strike areas were equally against the strike and that therefore the officials at least represented overwhelming public opinion.

Moreover the strike leaders at once took the case to the courts, advancing substantially the same arguments the Interchurch Report advances. But in every case, the courts held that the local officials, because of the special circumstances in each case, were entirely within their rights. The labor leaders carried one of these cases—doubtless the one they considered strongest—to the Supreme Court of Pennsylvania, which court held (City of Duquesne *vs.* Fincke; 112 Atl. 130 Pa.) that:

"A strike was on which divided even the working men into opposing factions and thus gave to those agitators who are the enemies of all government the opportunity, which they eagerly seized, to stir up strife and disorder by distributing anonymous and seditious pamphlets throughout the city; and hence, as the Mayor was responsible for the maintenance of peace and good order, he was justified, if he believed the public good required it, as he says he did, to refuse an open air meeting at this particular time. . . . *The liberty of speech does not require that the clear legal rights of the whole community shall be violated.*"

As a matter of fact in its second volume the Interchurch Report admits (page 164) that:

"A well-known attorney has stated that there is no legal escape from either of these restrictions (*i.e.* refusing or revoking permits for meetings), since the city ordinances regulating meetings have been tested and found constitutional, and the Sheriffs' proclamation can be attacked only on the ground that the situation did not warrant it. With the local officials of the same mind as the Sheriff, as they were in this case, it would be practically impossible to prove in court that the sheriff's action was unwarranted."

As a matter of plain logic then, the Interchurch Report can only argue to its conclusion, that the meetings should not have been thus limited, on one of three grounds:

1. That the rights of free speech and assembly should be absolute irrespective of the fact that it may endanger the public peace, or—which amounts to the same thing;

2. That the power of deciding whether or not such meetings endangered the peace of the public should be taken out of the hands of the duly elected officials of the community and turned over to the individuals who wanted to hold such meetings, who in most cases were not even citizens of the community; or

3. That the courts decisions in these cases were, either through error or bias on the part of the court, against the actual facts.

The Interchurch Report assumes to condemn the limitations of strikers' meetings on this third ground, that such limitations were not warranted by the facts, but actually throughout this argument it obviously tries to argue to its conclusions on all three grounds.

Before analyzing the specific Interchurch argument, however, which is based on only part of the facts, and on a very special interpretation and explanation of each of those facts, consideration should be given to certain phases of the general situation which the Interchurch Report does not consider, and certain facts should be stated which the Interchurch Report does not state, but all of which doubtless had a determining influence on the decisions reached by local public opinion, local officials and the courts, which decisions the Interchurch Report is condemning.

New York witnessed a milk strike, in the Fall of 1921 in which every milk driver who remained on his job, carried his life in his hands, in which women were followed and intimidated merely for buying milk for their children, and in which 40 strikers were arrested for violence in a single day.

Chicago, at about the same time, witnessed a packers' strike in which the strikers seized housetops from which to fire into the crowds of workers and went to other similar extremes of violence. The whole country knows of the "war in Mingo" in which thousands of union men armed with rifles and machine guns, marched into West Virginia seizing train and private automobiles and private supplies of all kinds, and otherwise depleting the country like an enemy army on their march. In other words the whole country has long been forced to recognize that great strikes and violence frequently if not usually go hand in hand.

In the industrial districts of western Pennsylvania a great strike is likely to involve a far greater proportion of the population than in New York or Chicago and is therefore a matter of far greater public concern.

Foster, in his book, *The Great Steel Strike*, speaks on page 11 of the great Homestead steel strike of 1892 as characterized by "extreme bitterness and violence." He emphasizes the bitterness with which the steel strike of 1909 was fought. The Interchurch Report on page 4 speaks of the Homestead strike as being "with guns and flames." The Homestead strike was spoken of in the Senate investigation as running red with blood.

Particularly in the old steel towns, therefore, responsible citizens and officials could hardly be expected to forget the blood and guns and flames of former steel strikes.

In 1919 they knew that the conspicuous leader of the new strike was Foster who had widely published his opinions that "whether his tactics be legal and moral or not does not concern him so long as they are effective"—that "he allows no consideration of legality, religion, patriotism, honour, duty, to stand in the way of his adoption of effective tactics," etc., etc. They knew that the nominal leader of the strikers was John Fitzpatrick, local head of the labor unions in Chicago where labor corruption and violence has perhaps reached its high water mark. Mother Jones whose trail of violence and bloodshed through past labor conflicts was common knowledge appeared early on the scene. They knew from frequent past experience how crowds of ignorant foreigners are susceptible of having their mass psychology whipped to a frenzy by clever agitators. These very definite facts and experiences were the basis on which many local citizens and public officials, who themselves would have to meet the situation and whose own cities would have to pay the price if violence did occur, were led to conclude that strike meetings under these circumstances would probably endanger the public peace.

If therefore, local public opinion and local officials in many cases in the steel strike did, and local public opinion and local officials in general often do, believe that the very existence or prospect of a great strike raises a presumption of violence; and if, acting on this presumption such officials and local public opinion believe it is necessary to limit the holding of strikers' meetings during such times; and if organized labor and the Interchurch Report believe that labor's interests are thereby prejudiced, they have only labor itself, and its present as well as its past record to blame.

But local officials in many cases in the steel strike, did not have to base their decision as to the likelihood of violence in the steel strike on merely past experience.

It will be remembered that agitation had been going on among the steel workers for nearly a year before the strike and that during August and September it was cleverly brought to a climax by means that have already been described.

The Senate Hearings, page 888 and succeeding pages, presents a number of affidavits from the Mayor and leading citizens of McKeesport, Pennsylvania,—where the limitation of meetings is specifically condemned by the Interchurch Report—stating that on September 2nd, three weeks before the strike, a crowd consisting of 4000 foreigners had marched to the local police station and threatened to destroy it, and had made other threats as it marched from point to point in the city.

On page 885 and succeeding pages of the Senate Hearings appear affidavits and petitions signed by large numbers of ministers, doctors, merchants, lawyers, business men and men of all walks of life, of Donora, Pa., stating that mobs, in one instance of 3000 foreigners, largely armed, were marching through the city and that already there had been "several clashes between the authorities and these foreigners." These petitions particularly requested the help of the state constabulary.

That inflammatory propaganda was being widely disseminated at this time is specifically declared by the Supreme Court of Pennsylvania in the quotation appearing above. The exact nature of much of such propaganda that was openly radical is shown by reproductions of voluminous quotations from it in the Senate Hearings pages 912 and succeeding pages, 948 and succeeding pages, etc.

Such inflammatory propaganda, however, counselling extreme violence, was not limited to the radicals. Following are excerpts from a "Manifesto" by a prominent member of the A. F. of L. widely circulated some three weeks before the strike (see Senate Hearings page 670 to 672).

"HOW TO WIN A STRIKE"

(By Bob Edwards of Martins Ferry, member Amalgamated Association.)

" Now that the steel workers of the United States are on the verge of a tremendous struggle, a strike that will decide for the coming years whether the steel workers are to remain wage slaves or freemen, it behooves every worker who has the welfare of his class at heart to devote the entire powers of his mind and intellect to study and devise a means, a strategic plan, by which the forces of labor can win the conquest with the consequent defeat and demoralization and, we hope, the utter destruction of the enemies' powers of resistance. A strike of workers in this period is an actual declaration of war between the proletariate (the workers) and the capitalist; between a system of coöperation and a system of exploitation; between right and wrong; between humanity and brutality in short, between all that is noble and elevating and that which is debasing and low. *A strike is war, because all the horrors of the battlefield are repeated in a strike*—men killed, homes disrupted, noble and conscientious workers put on the list of tramps and undesirable citizens. . . .

A strike then is war, and war recognizes one end—the imposition of the will of the conqueror upon that of the vanquished. To do this properly we must so manipulate and direct our forces that the offensive must immediately be taken, so that the struggle will be short but strenuous. . . .

Second plan is to change the ownership of the means of producing the stock of wealth of the capitalist. This plan is the most reasonable and logical that can be adopted and will do away with and eliminate the hardships, brutalities, and killing that is incident and inevitable in all strikes and particularly so in the coming struggle.

If the representatives of the United States government do not see fit to take over the steel industry and control and use it for the benefit of the people, then let them keep hands off in the coming struggle and be an impartial observer of the conflict. . . .

When a community is in a state of anarchy, the individual man must take the law into his own hands, and defend his life and his rights with violence, if need be.

When armed thugs and strike breakers are imported into a community, that community is in a state of anarchy and every individual is fully empowered to take up arms and defend his life and rights."

Affidavits through pages 902 to 906 of the Senate Hearings recite instances of attacks on police officers with bottles, clubs, and pepper, by mobs, or individual men *or women* from mobs of strikers.

Senate Hearings pages 806 to 809 also by specific quotation of official proclamations and other records, show the methods by which such very obvious threats or actual breaches of the public peace were met by the officials and united public action.

Quite characteristically however, the Interchurch Report does not mention any of this Senate evidence or refer to the facts which it brings out. In several instances, it makes a strong point of the fact that orders prohibiting strikers' meetings were issued before the strike began. In view of the fact that threatening and violence was begun long before the date of the strike, this argument is obviously a mere quibble.

It will doubtless be remembered that the Interchurch Report particularly insists in its introduction on page 4 that the 1919 steel strike was "without violence" and though as a matter of fact, it mentions violence frequently—the "gun riot" at Wheeling (page 181), the "mob violence" at Gary (page 241) and frequently "slight riots," or "almost riots" or "riots with no serious consequences," it nevertheless insists in general throughout this argument that there was no violence or at least not sufficient violence to warrant suppression of strikers' meetings, and it insists particularly that where there was violence, it was not because of strikers' meetings and where there were strikers' meetings, there was no violence.

Disregarding the fact that the Interchurch Report makes no mention of the voluminous Senate evidence in regard to threats, intimidation and actual violence, and considering merely the evidence and argument which it itself advances to support its contention that where there was violence it was not because of strikers meetings and where there were strikers' meetings there was no violence—taking that argument paragraph by paragraph and merely discounting certain tricks of phraseology and quibbles the essential facts, as there stated, show (Interchurch Report, Vol. II, page 165 and succeeding pages):

At Braddock, meetings were allowed till a crowd of strikers gathered at a mill gate and precipitated a street fight.

At Duquesne there were no meetings and no serious violence.

At McKeesport, permits to hold ordinary meetings were granted but denied for one particular meeting because of particular circumstances and immediately there was a riot.

At Homestead there were meetings and there was violence.

In each of these cases then, the simple facts are directly to the contrary of the Interchurch Report's argument. In each case however the Interchurch Report has some particular explanation—the "riot had no serious consequences," a number of men had merely been beaten up but no one was actually killed, the violence did not occur *at the meeting* or as a *direct result* of the meeting, etc., etc.

In other words, in each case, where there were meetings the Interchurch Report admits the violence but insists upon substituting itself, just as the strike leaders insisted on substituting themselves, in place of the responsible public officials and the courts as the judge of whether or not the violence was sufficient to endanger the public peace.

In the next chapter it will appear by quotation from numerous of the Interchurch Report's "500 rock bottom affidavits" that when duly elected public officials or police officials, in searching houses for arms "disregarded the presence of mother and child. They entered the house to search. They tore down the curtains, and broke the flowerpots and overturned the chairs . . . because of the terrorization the children didn't sleep that night"—because officers similarly searching for arms used a hatchet in opening a trunk and scattered the clothes around—because an officer, obviously refused admission by a woman swung her roughly against the door—because various men were fined $5 or $10 for things they themselves said they didn't do—because a man who was arrested didn't get his dinner on time—because Trachn Yechenke was arrested in connection with the shooting of Peter Luke even after he himself had told the officers he didn't do it; the Interchurch Report features such "police brutalities" in special affidavits as "a degradation, persistent and approved by public opinion, of civil liberties."

It is correspondingly interesting therefore, to speculate in connection with this present Interchurch argument as to just how large a *strikers'* riot would have to be, or just how many people would have to be "actually killed" by the *strikers* to constitute what the Interchurch Report would regard as a breach of, or even a serious threat, to the public peace.

The Interchurch Report continues its argument (page 166 and 167) by mentioning three localities where meetings were allowed and where it alleges no violence occurred, "*at the meeting*" or "*during the assemblies.*" These were Johnstown, Pa., Farrell, Pa., and Wheeling, W. Va. The specific degree of violence that occurred at or away from the meetings at these particular places, does not seem to be a matter of public record. But it is to be noted that the Interchurch Report itself speaks incidentally (page 181) of the "gun riot" at Wheeling, and two statements, one made by a local ex-Senator appearing in the Senate Hearings (page 884 and 885) refer indirectly to the attempt at violence in Farrell.

The Interchurch Report then makes the same statement in regard to Steubensville, Youngstown and Cleveland, localities whose record for violence during the strike, is a matter of public record.

At the bottom of page 167, Part II, the Interchurch Report says·

"In Steubensville, O., . . . three or four meetings were held every week. *No disturbance of any sort ever occurred in this town . . . perfect peace was maintained throughout this district* both at the public meetings and on the picket lines."

The Senate Investigation (pages 472 and 473), however, emphasized conspicuously and in detail and published copies of the public records of the action that it was necessary for the governors of West Virginia and Ohio to take to prevent 5000 of these same Steubensville strikers from carrying out a resolution which they *passed at one of these strike meetings* to march over en masse into West Virginia and attack 1000 workers at Weirton who had refused to strike. It seems strange that the Interchurch Report which quotes so freely Senate evidence that may be interpreted in favor of the strikers should have so completely overlooked all the evidence in regard to such a conspicuous case of the direct relation between the holding of a strikers' meeting and violence or is it depending on the quibble that the prompt action of the governors of two states prevented the program of violence which was specifically adopted at the meeting from being actually carried out?

In the next paragraph on page 168, the Interchurch Report states that at Youngstown, Ohio,

"On an average, nine mass meetings a week were held. *At none of these meetings* was there ever any necessity for police intervention and at no time was there any disturbance *at a meeting.*"

The Senate Investigation on the other hand on pages 309 to 316 lays special emphasis on the amount of intimidation and threatening and stoning of American workers by foreign strikers at Youngstown and particularly emphasizes that the only attempt to interfere with a meeting in Youngstown was when the strikers themselves stoned a meeting of Americans who remained at work.

In the next paragraph, the Interchurch Report states:

"In Cleveland, O. . . . . from 3 to 6 meetings were held daily from the beginning of the strike . . . *no trouble of any nature developed.*"

Ex-Governor Joseph F. Brown of Georgia has made a special study of violence in the 1919 steel strike from original public records, affidavits, and other specific data available to any responsible investigator and much of which was widely published at the time. His study has also been published in a pamphlet entitled, "The Threatened Strike in the Steel Plants." This record for violence in Cleveland include such attacks on non-striking workers as follows:

C. Brailey attacked evening of September 23rd by four men—laid up for about 3 weeks;

J. Galganski attacked evening of September 23rd on way to work—jaw broken—laid up for several weeks;

4 colored employees attacked September 24th by crowd of strikers—escaped to street car but were followed and pulled off—one sustained broken arm, two cuts and bruises;

Henry Arps, 65 years old, knocked down and beaten by striking wire drawer November 13th while on way home from work;
and 17 other Cleveland steel workers who did not strike similarly beaten or stabbed or shot in Cleveland during this short period.

Either the Interchurch Report regards this as "*no trouble of any nature*" or else it is basing its whole argument that the strikers' meetings which were held did not result in violence and therefore public officials elsewhere were not justified in prohibiting or stopping strikers' meetings on the mere quibble that the violence did not occur in the meeting itself.

The Interchurch Report in its main volume mentions only one strikers' meeting. On pages 240 and 241 it says:

"At Gary . . . agreements . . . were reached with the city authorities concerning picket line rules. Huge mass meetings were held in the open air . . . a crowd of strikers leaving a mass meeting tried to pull a negro strike breaker off a street car: the negro was slightly injured. . . . On this case of violence, the only one alleged, Indiana state guards were sent in. Parades were forbidden." The meetings were also forbidden.

It is interesting to note that in this only mention of a strikers' meeting in the main Interchurch Report, violence in direct connection with the meeting is admitted. The Interchurch Report tries to emphasize the point, however, that the strike-breaker was only injured "slightly" which is untrue. It entirely fails to state, as plainly brought out in the Senate evidence that 4 or 5 other workers were attacked by strikers in the official picket line and only saved by the police; that another negro was shot in the outskirts of Gary and that it was only because of these and many other circumstances which are detailed at great length in pages 906 to 952 of the Senate Hearings, that the city authorities revoked the permission for meetings and parades which they had previously freely granted.   In addition to hiding or distorting the plain evidence in this case, the Interchurch Report further resorts to insinuations for which it gives no

20

shred of evidence that all the trouble was started by police or citizens and not by the strikers. It says:

"The strikers *made frequent complaint* of violent raids carried out by bands of citizens calling themselves 'loyal American leaguers' *who were charged with clubbing groups of strikers* on street corners at nights."

In describing the attack of the "crowd of strikers leaving a mass meeting" on the negro, it passes lightly over the injuries of the victim but stresses the fact that "a number of the (attacking) strikers were clubbed," and otherwise shows the highest degree of bias as well as inaccuracy.

Passing from specific instances which the Interchurch Report itself brings up to general conditions as to violence Governor Brown's records show such further facts in regard to the quantity and degree of violence in the steel strike as follows:

At South Chicago and Joliet, the "union organizations and strikers had several automobiles circulating the districts inhabited by steel mill workers from which attacks were made on workers, stones thrown at them or their homes," etc., etc. On October 24th one of these automobile squads was caught threatening Mrs. John Schorey by a group of deputy sheriffs and in escaping arrest one of the strikers was shot.

W. R. McGowan and Harry F. Stock swear that on October 12, 1919, on going home from work they were accosted by 4 men of foreign appearance who after charging them with working for the Illinois Steel Company assaulted them, beating and kicking them and then disappeared on a passing train;

53 similar affidavits are on record from the employees of the Illinois Steel Company or members of their families:

On October 23rd John Johns, an employee of the American Sheet and Tin Plate Company of Elwood, Indiana, who refused to continue in the steel strike was stopped by a crowd of strikers. Dave Rogers, a former fellow-worker, held him while the crowd clubbed him almost to death;

At New Kensington, Pennsylvania, T. B. Pollard, a tin mill doubler was shot on his way to work on October 20th;

On November 2nd the homes of Pollard, Charles Spencer, August Adams and Peter Smith were dynamited, etc., etc.

At Bridgesport and Martins Ferry, Ohio, strikers were stationed on the hillside above the plant with high powered rifles to fire at workers in the plant. A special watchman was wounded. Later Harry Lemon was killed;

The homes of David Jones and Don Cecil were dynamited and two other non-striking employees were killed;

Howard Green was shot point blank by a striker while stepping off a street car and subsequently died—the striker, Jake Ulrich, was tried for the shooting and convicted;

53 of the non-striking employees of the American Steel and Wire Company were shot, stoned, stabbed or otherwise assaulted during the strike, one of them so badly that he was disabled from October 24, 1919, to April 6, 1920, and another one died."

These are typical of hundreds of affidavits of cases in regard to which detailed evidence exists, in many cases supported by court records. To the average American with his sense of fair play it will also be interesting to note that in only two cases were these victims attacked by as few as two assailants—in most cases the worker was attacked by from 5 to 20 strikers whom the affidavits or other records often mentioned as wearing union badges or being parties from the union picket lines.

The Senate Investigation abounds not only in detailed evidence such as already quoted in regard to intimidation and violence in the steel agitation and strike, but also in evidence that further and greater violence was in many cases only prevented by the prompt action of local authorities and local public opinion in taking steps to prevent it. (See particularly Senate Hearings, pages 883–892.)

This Senate evidence in regard to violence of strikers was taken and largely made public before the Interchurch investigation began and was published in full months before the first Interchurch Report appeared. The same thing is true of much other evidence in regard to violence on the part of the strikers. The Interchurch Report makes no attempt either by analyzing such evidence, by making fuller investigation of the specific facts it brings out or otherwise to refute it. It merely ignores it and insists on the fiction that the "1919 steel strike was without violence," at least on the part of the strikers. It is on this pure fiction which it attempts to support by the suppression or distortion of facts or clever quibbles as to facts that the Interchurch Report builds up its whole direct[1] case as to the alleged "abrogation of the right of Free Speech" and makes its sensational appeal to the national government and national public opinion against the judicially approved exercise of the rights of local self-government in Pennsylvania.

[1] The Interchurch Report is constantly actually arguing through this section for a fundamental change in our laws which would place the right of the individual agitator above the right of the public. This will be still more clearly appreciated after consideration of the facts brought out on pages 354 to 359 of the present analysis.

CHAPTER XXIII

"POLICE BRUTALITY" AND "DENIAL OF JUSTICE"

Including an analysis of one group of the "500 rock-bottom
affidavits" on which the Interchurch Report
itself states it is based

ALTHOUGH strongly denying violence on the part of the
strikers themselves, the Interchurch Report makes the
strongest and most sweeping allegations as to violence in the
steel strike on the part of local public officials and police
officers and local citizens whom it spends pages in accusing
of systematically practising every form of brutality on the
entirely peaceful and non-resisting strikers.

In its main volume, on pages 238 and 240, the Interchurch
Report makes categorically the sweeping general allegation
that:

"During the strike violations of personal rights and personal liberty
were wholesale; men were arrested without warrants, imprisoned without charges; their homes invaded without legal process, *magistrates'
verdicts were rendered frankly on the basis of whether the striker would go
back to work or not* . . . the charges of beatings, clubbings, often substantiated by doctors' and eye witnesses' affidavits, were endless and
monotonous."

Volume II which is supposed to present the evidence on
which Volume I makes its categorical and unqualified
statements, says on page 177.

"The charges brought against the state constabulary, deputy sheriffs
and company police deal with *the murder of men and women*—one as he

309

was in his own yard—and *the wounding of hundreds of others;* the *clubbing of hundreds;* the assaulting of men while lawfully and peacefully pursuing errands on the streets and of prisoners while they were locked up in their cells . . . the excessive punishment meted out to these strikers by the different justices of the peace, burgesses and police courts, and the *frank discrimination in the courts between those who were at work and those who were out on strike. . . .*"

These charges of "murdering men and women, wounding hundreds, clubbing hundreds," of false arrest, false imprisonment and judicial discrimination against inoffensive strikers, are made on the basis of 41 statements and affidavits which the Interchurch Report publishes and which it states are representative of hundreds of others which it has. As the only evidence offered for a most sweeping attack on the whole basis of our organized social system, and particularly as this is the only considerable group it anywhere publishes of the "500 rock-bottom affidavits and statements" on which the Interchurch Report itself says all its findings are chiefly based, these documents deserve the most careful attention.

The first thing to be noted is that, with two or three possible exceptions, all these documents are signed by names that are distinctly foreign and that the affidavits signed by such names as Harry Barstow, H. J. Phillips, Henry McNeely make no such accusations as those signed by the obvious foreigners. It is noticeable also that many of these affidavits are signed by marks indicating that the foreigner could not read or write even his own name.

The Senate investigation took the testimony of many ignorant foreign steel workers. Its verbatim stenographic records of the testimony show that these witnesses have an inevitable tendency to talk very vaguely and ramblingly, to repeat themselves over and over again and frequently to unconsciously contradict themselves and to leave out important connective parts of their statements, which contradictions and omissions were only straightened out by cross-examination.

It is to be particularly noted on the other hand, that the

affidavits presented by the Interchurch Report usually tell a clean, concise story, go directly to a point and make that point clearly and even cleverly and even frequently show the utmost cleverness in the use of exclamations and vivid descriptions to create strong impressions without actually alleging anything.

The Interchurch Report, Volume II, page 178, frankly states that:

"The language used in many of these documents is 'interpreters' English' . . . . Generally after a lengthy examination of the witness, a brief statement, summary or affidavit would be written out in English, translated back to the witness by the interpreter and after final correction signed by the witness."

But the whole value of affidavits so arrived at of course depend on the clear understanding and scrupulous impartiality of the one who formulated the affidavits and of the interpreter. It is extremely material, therefore, to consider whether the men who played such an important part in determining the nature of these affidavits were competent or scrupulously impartial.

The Interchurch Report itself states that part of these statements and affidavits were taken by the Interchurch investigators and part of them by Mr. J. H. Maurer who is mentioned or quoted repeatedly in connection with them.

Mr. Maurer was at this time president of the Pennsylvania Federation of Labor. He and Scott Nearing signed the famous cablegram to Russia of March 3, 1918 stating that they represented "300 radical groups in 42 states" and urging the Soviet authorities to stand by peace terms substantially the opposite of those to which America and the allies were committed.[1]

The question of the competence and impartiality of the Interchurch Investigators who prepared such affidavits as were not prepared by Mr. Maurer, is discussed in Part II of the present analysis.

[1] For full text of this document see New York State Investigation of Radicalism, Vol. I, page 1076.

The Interchurch Report, Volume II, page 176 specifically says:

> "*Most* of these affidavits were obtained by joining strikers' groups casually in the different communities. Other affidavits which were sent to Governor Sproul by President Maurer of the State Federation and were presented to the U. S. Senate Committee are included in the Report, but only after re-examination of them in conference with Mr. Maurer's investigator. Not more than one day was spent in any of the towns by the investigators and on several occasions two or three nearby towns were covered in the same day.
>
> "In most instances a line of men and women ready to testify and swear to their accusations had formed and had to be broken up when the investigators left."

But in spite of this seeming superfluity of original evidence thus described by the Interchurch Report as offered to its own investigators, an examination of these affidavits themselves—as far as they are published—immediately reveals the fact that 20 of the 41 show dates of or before October 3rd—that is before the Interchurch investigation of the steel strike had even been proposed. Thirty of them show dates before the Interchurch Commission of investigation was even appointed and several more of them before any of the investigators, as such, could have reached the strike area. As far as these published affidavits are concerned then, it is plain that practically all, if not all of them, are those collected by Mr. Maurer, President of the Pennsylvania State Federation of Labor who officially signed himself in his correspondence with the Soviet authorities as "representing 300 radical groups in 42 states."

When these affidavits are examined in detail a number of very interesting and on the surface puzzling facts appear. A large number of what seem to be allegations prove on examination to be merely exclamations or pieces of vivid description cleverly bound together and sworn to. Although these affidavits are signed by a wide variety of people who live in widely different places, and though the details vary the substance of the allegations, the main points emphasized and the way they are emphasized appear strangely similar. The victim is regularly described as entirely peaceful—frequently performing an errand of mercy at the time—trying to save some little children or trying to persuade an officer not to beat a helpless victim —the assaulting police seemed drunk or crazy—they suddenly charged without cause, "firing as they came" when the victim is prostrate they continue to beat him—the woman victim almost invariably has a child in her arms or is in a "delicate condition," etc., etc.   To this strange similarity must be added the fact of frequent lack of plausibility.   For instance one or two blows on the head with the heavy type of police club known to be used would seem almost sure to render a man unconscious.   The allegation therefore, that a mounted officer continued to beat a man over the head for "about a block" does not on its face seem plausible.

A great deal of light, moreover, can be thrown on these affidavits as a whole by analyzing them with reference to certain well-established and pertinent outside facts and it is only through an understanding of these outside facts that the strange inconsistencies and consistencies—including the general uniformity of date—of these affidavits can be understood.

It is a well-known fact that the moment any great strike is started its leaders immediately begin to circulate "atrocity stories" for the obvious purpose of inflaming the workers and stirring them to greater determination and resistance. At the very beginning of the strike, before any incidents which could be interpreted as atrocities have had time to occur, such stories are often brought in from outside and connected in some vague way with the current strike. But as the current strike proceeds, every possible little incident that can be so turned to account is at once seized on by the strike leaders and cleverly colored or distorted to build up a larger and larger supply of atrocity stories to continue and strengthen such propaganda.

Exactly this method of procedure was instituted at the very beginning of the steel strike. Before it was possible to get "atrocity" stories in connection with that strike itself a story was imported in regard to the death of a Mrs. Fanny Sellins which had occurred in connection with a previous small local coal strike. This story was vividly colored. Gruesome photographs of Mrs. Sellins as she lay dead were prepared and widely circulated. Foster in his book *The Great Steel Strike*, pages 147 and 148 goes into this story in gory detail. It was introduced into the first day's hearings before the Senate Committee and although a thorough investigation had been made, the Coroner's Findings fully published and these findings reviewed by a grand jury—which facts were brought out at the first day's Senate Hearings—nevertheless, ten days later at a psychological moment, Mr. Rubin, the strikers' attorney tried to introduce before the Senate Committee some bloody clothes said to have been worn by Mrs. Sellins when she was killed in this entirely different strike, and the strike leaders otherwise again and again brought up this story, circulating it always with more and more gruesome details in connection with the steel strike as though it were part of the steel strike.

The Coroner's Verdict, specially reviewed by a grand jury had stated that Mrs. Sellins came to her death from a gun shot wound in the left temple caused "during attack on the sheriff's deputies." The Coroner's jury also particularly condemned the use made of this incident by "foreign agitators" who "instil anarchy into the minds of un-Americans and uneducated aliens."

An understanding of just how this story was exaggerated and colored for propaganda presentation in a form that was provably at least 95% false is extremely significant because of the parallel between this known stock propaganda story and a large share of the Interchurch affidavits. The story of Mrs. Sellins' death, as widely circulated by strike leaders and as published specifically by Foster in his "Great Steel Strike," pages 147 and 148 accompanied by one of the grue-

some photographs, which in view of the coroner's verdict was
entirely faked, alleged:

1. "All was going peacefully."
2. "When a dozen *drunken* deputy sheriffs . . . suddenly rushed
the pickets, *shooting as they came.*"
3. Mrs. Snellins "rushed first to get some children out of danger."
4. "Then she came back to *plead with the deputies* who were *still
clubbing* the prostrate Strzelecki."
5. She was not on company ground but just outside the fence of a
friend.
6. Then a mine official brutally snatched a club and felled the woman
to the ground.
7. As she was *trying to get away* they shot her three times, "each
taking effect."
8. As she lay prostrate they shot her again. Then they brutally
dragged her by the heels.
9. Then another police officer "took a cudgel and crushed in her skull
before the eyes of the *throng of men, women and children who stood in
powerless silence before the armed men.*"
10. Then "Deputy——picked up the woman's hat, placed it on his
head, danced a step and said ' I'm Mrs. Snellins now.' "
11. "She was 49 years old, a grandmother and mother of a boy killed
in France fighting to make the world safe for democracy."

This story, which as a matter of the most careful court
records is known to be—at least as here published—almost
purely inflammatory propaganda, brought in from outside
and used in the steel strike merely for that purpose, obviously
consists of the most clever arrangement of phraseology and
ideas to have a maximum inflammatory effect on credulous
hearers. Yet when the Interchurch rock bottom affidavits
as published are analysed, it appears that these documents
admittedly composed not by the men who signed them but
either by Maurer or the Interchurch investigators, are many
of them to a greater or less extent, carefully arranged and
phrased to bring out the same kind of ideas and to get the
same kind, though not always the same degree of effect.
This parallel will be remarked on more specifically as the
Interchurch affidavits are individually referred to.

The first widely circulated atrocity propaganda based on

incidents occurring in connection with the steel strike itself —and which the Interchurch Report strongly features— consist of two statements by the Reverend Father Kazinci of Braddock which appear in slightly different form in letters to Governor Sproul, in the Senate Hearings and in a letter to William Z. Foster in which latter form they were widely published for propaganda purposes. As published on page 122 of the *Great Steel Strike*, Father Kazinci's atrocity charge made through clever insinuation by description and exclamation which obviously does not actually allege any atrocity at all, is as follows:

"Tuesday afternoon the little babies of Number 1 were going to the school. They loitered for the school bell to summon them. And here come the Kozaks (Cossacks). They see the little innocents standing on the steps of the school house, their parents on the opposite side of the street. What a splendid occasion to start the 'Hunkies' ire. Let us charge their babies. That will fetch them to an attack upon us. They did, but the Hunky even at the supreme test of his coolheadedness refused to flash his knife to save his babies from the onrush of the cruel horses' hoofs."

Also—

"Oh, it was great; it was magnificent. They, these husky, muscle-bound Titans of raw force walked home . . . only thinking, thinking hard."

Although it was of course recognized that this clever insinuation which actually states nothing at all was pure inflammatory propaganda, this statement was so widely published by the strike leaders that Governor Sproul made a special investigation and it was found to be based on the trivial incident that some school children gathered out of curiosity around the horses of Corporal Nelson Smith and Private John Tomek while the horses were tied near a school building—that the officers warned the children away for fear the horses might hurt them and later rode off in another direction (Senate Hearings, page 881).

The Senate Committee also cross examined Father Kazinci on this statement (Senate Hearings, page 543):

"*Senator Stirling:* Were any of the children hurt?

"*Father Kazinci:* By some miracle, I do not know how, they were not hurt.

"*The Chairman:* How could they have 'jumped the horses in among those children' and not any of them hurt?

"*Father Kazinci:* I suppose they acted the same as you and I act. When I see the horses coming I run.

"*Chairman:* Did you see that yourself?

"*Father Kazinci:* I had it from the sisters.

"*Mr. Rubin* (strikers' attorney): Do you know the sisters and do you know where they are?

"*Father Kazinci:* They are all willing to testify to what they have seen.

"*Mr. Rubin:* Will you bring one of the sisters here this afternoon?

"*Father Kazinci:* They are under the jurisdiction of the authorities and not allowed to leave their convent without their permission or I would do it.

"*Mr. Rubin:* Will you try to have permission for one of the sisters to come here?

"*Father Kazinci:* Yes sir."

No witness to this widely published atrocity of "Charging the children" was ever produced.

The Senate Committee at the same time went into the second allegation by insinuation of Father Kazinci's which the strike leaders had widely circulated as part of their "atrocity propaganda" (Senate Hearings, page 543):

"*Father Kazinci:* On the 21st *I personally* walked out in the middle of the street leaving the church *to stop these men* (state police) and ask them what did they mean by *clubbing peaceful worshippers leaving the church.*"

On cross examination, however, the following was brought out:

"*Senator McKellar:* Have you seen any persons clubbed by the state constabulary?

"*Father Kazinci:* No, sir, I have not.

"*Mr. Rubin* (striker's attorney): Have you seen them after they have been clubbed?

"Father Kazinci: I have seen one.

"Mr. Rubin: Did you see any wounds? Describe the wounds.

"Father Kazinci: He did not show me any of the wounds but he told me about the *incident.* "

Yet as the first evidence presented under its heading "Assaults and Police Brutality" the Interchurch Report written months later and fully familiar with all this Senate testimony says (Volume II page 175):

"At the very beginning of the strike charges of *brutal assaults and attacks* were made by the strikers and their leaders against the State Constabulary, the deputy sheriffs and the company guards. The first audible protest against these *violations* from an outside person came from the Reverend (Father) A. Kazinci of Braddock when he wrote to Governor William C. Sproul and *described in detail* the *assault* of state troopers upon his people as they were coming out of church; and *the driving of horses by the same State Police upon little children* as they were assembled in the school yard. Numerous charges of assaults and attacks were also brought out before the U. S. Senate Committee. "

The Interchurch Report does not mention or suggest the fact that Governor Sproul thoroughly investigated these charges and proved them false or that Father Kazinci himself under oath and cross-examination had entirely repudiated all the essential part of these charges.

It will be noted that Father Kazinci's "atrocity" charges, as they were originally published, and as they are published by Foster and in part by the Interchurch Report, even after their repudiation before the Senate Committee, parallel the standard atrocity propaganda allegations as built to order around the incident of Mrs. Snellins' death in that—

1. Alleged victims were entirely peaceful.

2. The "act of mercy" idea is supplied by "peaceful worshippers coming out of church"—"little children going to the schools."

3. The attack is brutal, wanton and reckless though craziness and drunkenness are not here charged.

4. The "powerless silence before the armed men" of the Snellins story is paralleled by the "coolheadedness" of the

"muscle bound Titans of labor who were only thinking—thinking hard."

5. The charge of diabolical heartlessness, as shown by the alleged taking of the dead woman's hat, donning it and the ribald dance over her dead body is at least approximated by the charge of deliberately attempting to ride down little children.

Another early incident connected with the steel strike itself, which the strike leaders immediately seized on, highly colored and published widely in most inflammatory form, grew out of the breaking up a strikers' meeting in North Clairton, Sunday afternoon September 21st, the day before the strike. The question of whether or not this meeting should have been allowed was in dispute but this point was entirely overshadowed by the atrocity allegations which grew out of the affair.

As six state troopers were dispersing the crowd one of them evidently accidentally knocked down an American flag which is variously stated to have been on the platform and carried by one of the strikers. The flag was picked up by Mr. Brogan, or picked up and handed to Mr. Brogan, a Secretary of the A. F. of L., one of the speakers at the meeting and one of those arrested. While the crowd was being dispersed, some of the strikers threw only "ashes. There is no brickbats there" (Senate Hearings, page 549). The police then evidently fired over the heads of the crowd. No one was hit or otherwise hurt in this connection although in the same afternoon, a woman on her way to the store who got into the crush along the road was knocked down by a mounted trooper and her hand stepped on so that she had to carry it in a sling for a week.

Around these incidents the strike leaders immediately built the most vivid atrocity stories. Twenty-two special affidavits, according to the Interchurch Report, were obtained obviously by Mr. Maurer—of which the Interchurch Report itself publishes two—one by Mr. Terzich exclaiming but making no statements whatever (page 185) that—

"But when the state troopers rushed to the platform and tore down our flag that the men became incensed and some ex-soldiers, seeing our flag being insulted and defiled, rushed at said troopers in defense of our flag and started the excitement and almost caused a riot. . . . That there was no provocation for said interference and riding over women and children."

The other Interchurch affidavit concerning this circumstance surrounding the breaking up of this meeting is signed P. H. *G* rogan. This man, however, when he appeared before the Senate Committee gave his name as *B* rogan. He is also referred to by his associate W. Z. Foster in his book *The Great Steel Strike* (page 59) as P. H. *B* rogan. Before the Senate Committee he, moreover, stated that he was Secretary of the A. F. of L., which fact the Interchurch Report fails to mention in his Interchurch "affidavit." No. 38. Mr. Brogan like Mr. Terzich gets his entire atrocity effect by vivid insinuation and description instead of by direct statement, as follows (page 184):

"State policeman . . . acted like he was 'either crazy or drunk.' He started to shoot and the people were scrambling as fast as they could get away. He emptied the gun more than once—I could not tell how many shots. . . . He got to shooting the people for trying to get up the hill and get away . . . (then he) started to shoot in the other direction. Horses were standing up on their hind feet. . . . There were lots of women and children—many children in baby carriages." He then states that he and another man tried to pick up the flag and then he was arrested.

When these "affidavits" are compared with the standard propaganda agitation document built up around the death of Mrs. Sellins, it is again seen that the incidents are grouped and colored and carefully focused to build up almost exactly the same points:

1. That the people were entirely peaceful.

2. The police acted like they were either crazy or drunk.

3. The impression is built up that the attack was wanton and unnecessary and the troopers fired as they came.

4. The "act of mercy" in this case was rescuing the flag; according to one affidavit Mr. Brogan and another man picked it up and were arrested; according to the other, the people started to run away but "some ex-soldiers, seeing our flag being insulted and defiled, rushed to rescue our flag and almost caused a riot."

5. "Firing volley after volley into a fleeing crowd"; "shooting"—not shooting at or over the heads of but "shooting the people for trying to get up the hill and get away"; "riding over women and children"—particularly in connection with the strikers' general claims and the Interchurch Report's context about "men and women being murdered and hundreds being wounded"—all seek to build up the same kind of picture of utter brutality as the allegations that the police fired repeatedly into Mrs. Snellins' dead body, dragged it about by the heels, etc.

The Senate Committee went very particularly into this widely alleged atrocity also. The strikers brought two witnesses. The first, a Mr. Lurgu Sidella, testified about the "trampling and defiling of the flag," under oath as follows (Senate Hearings, page 569):

"*Mr. Sidella:* . . . and the first thing he done he got hold of the club and he knocked the flag down. The horse he walked a little bit and came over on top of the flag.

"*Mr. Rubins* (strikers' attorney): Do you mean the horse trampled the flag?

"*Mr. Sidella:* The horse he came over the flag. . . . I said 'don't knock no flag down.' He said 'we never knock any flag down.'

"*Senator Stirling:* Do you think he struck at the flag deliberately for the purpose of knocking down the flag, or did the flag get knocked down, he striking at it accidently?

"*Mr. Sidella:* I could not say that. I know I say here he went and strike the flag down, he went and struck the flag down and grabbed Mr. Brogan and he says, 'watch I am going to get that flag' and Mr. Brogan grabbed the flag off of the ground and he had it in his hand.

"*Senator Stirling:* But you would hardly say that he deliberately knocked the flag down—intended to knock the flag down?

"*Mr. Sidella:* I could not say."

21

The second witness the strike leaders brought to testify as to the North Clairton atrocities was Mr. P. H. Brogan himself, local secretary of the A. F. of L., one of the speakers at the meeting and the man who picked up the flag—and the man whose lengthy affidavit the Interchurch Report publishes over the signature of P. H. Grogan.

In his testimony before the Senate Committee Mr. Brogan obviously attempted to build up the same atrocity picture by vivid description of how the troopers fired into the crowds, etc. Under cross-examination he for a time tried to avoid admitting that the firing was done only over the heads of the people and that no one was hurt but the final testimony on this point was as follows (Senate Hearings, page 549):

"*The Chairman:* And he didn't hit anybody?

"*Mr. Brogan:* Well, he was shooting mostly at those who were on the side of the railroad company's right of way. There were a couple of thousand people at the meeting.

"*The Chairman:* Was he shooting *at the people?*

"*Mr. Brogan:* Yes. Those that were piling up trying to get away from him on the bank of the railroad.

"*Senator McKellar:* He was not a very good shot then, was he?

"*Mr. Brogan:* He was a good distance away, you know. He was too far away for them to throw any brickbats.

"*Senator McKellar:* Do you think he was shooting to frighten them?

"*Mr. Brogan:* I could not tell.

"*Senator Stirling:* Nobody was hit?

"*Mr. Brogan:* Nobody was hit that I know of."[1]

Mr. Brogan tried also before the Senate Committee to give the same impression about women and children being trampled (Senate Hearings, page 549):

"*Mr. Brogan:* Yes, sir, then they (state police) got *in on the ground* and they knocked down *some* women.

"*Senator Phipps:* Are those women here?

---

[1] It need hardly be pointed out that in handling a sullen crowd of 2000 to 3000 who were throwing ashes and might momentarily break out into worse violence 6 less experienced and disciplined men than these state troopers might quite possibly have lost their heads and precipitated some real tragedy.

"*Mr. Brogan:* Yes, sir. One lady had a little baby in her arms and he trampled on her wrist. The baby rolled down over the bank.

"*Senator Phipps:* Did you see that?

"*Mr. Brogan:* I did not see it but I have got the lady here . . . this gentleman (indicating) *was standing alongside the lady. This gentleman had a flag that was torn down.*"

The Senate Committee then called this woman—Mary Wickowicz, who said through an interpreter that she *had not been at the meeting at all but was on her way to the store* (Senate Hearings, page 568).

"*The Interpreter:* She says she went down to the store . . . she was not right in the crowd but along the road some place . . . she says the state police came up on a horse and walked over her and the baby rolled off her arms and then finally she rolled over and got up and picked up the baby and looked up to see what happened and she saw this state trooper hit one of the men over the head.

"*The Chairman:* Did any policeman hit her?

"*The Interpreter:* No, just the horse. The policeman did not touch her; just the horse; walked over her hand."

Yet in spite of the fact that Mr. Brogan himself swears that nobody was hit as far as he knew and his testimony to this effect appears in the Senate Hearings, the Interchurch Report months afterwards published his original "affidavit" about "drunk or crazy troopers" firing into the crowd and about "riding over women and children" as evidence of its charges that "men and women were murdered," hundreds wounded, etc., not only without mentioning the fact of Mr. Brogan's sworn repudiation, but publishing his "affidavit" without his title, with half of the name of the locality omitted and with the first letter of his name changed so that through neither the index of the Interchurch Report or the Senate Hearings can the fact that he repudiated the whole substance of the Interchurch affidavit be discovered.

The Interchurch Report in repeating the charge about the "murdering of men and women . . . one on the steps of his own home" on page 190, Volume II, says:

"The policy of the Farrell authorities, it may fairly be inferred, was to shoot to kill. Thus in Farrell two persons were killed outright, one while on the steps of his own house; several persons were wounded badly among them a mother of 6 children."

Immediately after this charge of deliberate killing the Interchurch Report publishes three affidavits. One of these only alleges that one man, standing on a street corner in the trouble area, but who it is emphasized was "not provoking any disorder whatever," heard firing, turned to see what it was about and was hit by a stray bullet fired "from up street." The other affidavit only alleges that a woman was struck by a stray bullet fired "from up the street." Neither of these affidavits even insinuates anything beyond an accident from a stray bullet from distant firing. Yet they are thus closely tied up and given as evidence of the deliberate policy of the police to shoot to kill, and also are directly tied up with the third affidavit which does plainly insinuate but does not directly charge deliberate shooting.

This third affidavit, if it could be considered entirely alone, makes a very serious charge in a plausible manner. But no matter how favorably its evidence may be regarded it cannot be regarded as conclusive, nor can it be regarded alone. First, it is obvious that there was a coroner's inquest at which facts were of course more fully brought out than in any single statement by one man. Yet neither the coroner's inquest nor other evidence that must have been available in regard to so serious an affair is mentioned. Again the date of this "murder" affidavit—September 23d —indicates plainly that it belongs to the Maurer group. The fact that this affidavit is also signed by a foreigner who could not even write his own name, and the whole nature of the document shows plainly that it was composed and its phraseology and arrangement entirely determined by the Maurer investigators. Finally a close examination of it shows that it also contains all the earmarks of the other affidavits which are provably standard atrocity propaganda, for it alleges that:

1. Two brothers were in their own yard entirely peaceful.
2. The state troopers came out from the gates of the wire mills "firing shots in all directions."
3. He was playing with his little four year old child at the time and was shot as he was trying to take her into the house.
4. His brother was first wounded, then shot and killed as he was *trying to get away* into the door of the house.
5. Before he was taken to the hospital his house was searched and the police would not allow him to attend his dead brother.
6. His wife was in a "delicate condition."

On its face then the credibility of this Interchurch "affidavit" is open to serious question. Moreover in a different connection in Vol. II, page 126, the Interchurch Report itself, quoting from a local newspaper, publishes an entirely different statement of this case. This statement briefly is as follows:

The house of Nick Gratichini, known commonly as Nick Grato, overlooked the mill gate. Men going to work and guards at the gate were being systematically fired upon from this neighborhood. Finally the firing was located as coming from Nick Grato's house and four State police armed with Springfield rifles were sent to arrest the inmates. While one inmate was resisting arrest on the porch, the officers were fired upon from within the house. When therefore Nick Grato was seen to come out of the house and sneak around the corner towards one of the officers, he was immediately fired at by another officer, and his brother, who ran into the yard at the same time was shot in the leg.

In other words, the Interchurch Report is on notice that the facts of this case as locally stated and believed at the time are substantially the opposite of those alleged in its "affidavit." Yet without making the least reference to police court records or coroners' findings which of necessity examined and recorded the evidence in such a case in great detail, or furnishing one shred of outside evidence to support this entirely different version, it publishes this "affidavit" composed and phrased by a notorious radical labor leader and merely signed by the mark of the accused in the case, as the only evidence on which it makes its sensational statements about "the murder of men and women."

The above affidavits are all that can be related to the Interchurch Report's sweeping general allegations about the "murder of men and women," and all that can be related to the alleged "wounding of hundreds, the clubbing of hundreds" in so far as that alleged wounding or clubbing involved other than single individuals.

There remain two other groups of affidavits, those relating to alleged brutalities to single individuals and those relating to alleged false arrest and imprisonment and a general discrimination by both police and courts against strikers merely on the ground that they were strikers.

It is almost impossible, in the very nature of the case, to express any final conclusion in regard to a certain proportion of the large number of Interchurch affidavits which allege individual brutal acts, in regard to which the man or woman claiming to be the victim of the act makes the affidavits, and where there is no other evidence with which to check the affidavit.

Paul Yagodisch swears (Interchurch Report, page 206) that he was standing in the street doing nothing and that:

". . . As he was standing watching, two deputies came over and placed him under arrest. As they grabbed him to take him to the police station he refused to go, claiming that they had no right to arrest him as he had done nothing. He was then kicked and thrown on the ground while a third deputy who came over, hit him first across the shoulders with a piece of iron pipe and later *took a knife out and deliberately cut his head open.*"

But a large proportion of the Interchurch affidavits are of this kind—mere allegations of an individual that he was beaten over the head without any reason or grabbed like a dog and arrested without reason, etc—none of them supported in any adequate way, none of them cross-examined and in many cases, though the Interchurch Report calls them affidavits there is no evidence in the form or otherwise that they were sworn to.

Aside from the points already emphasized—that this is all evidence of highly excited and incensed men reciting their own grievances, and that the affidavits were collected and to a large extent formulated not by impartial investigators but except for a few cases by one highly interested individual or his representatives—there are two outside sources of information against which these affidavits can at least in general be checked.

As has been stated some hundred of these "atrocity" affidavits were sent to Governor Sproul. He had some of the worst of them carefully investigated and found the allegations to be utterly without foundation or highly colored exaggerations of trivial incidents. The facts brought out by Governor Sproul's investigations of these affidavits were supplied to the Senate Committee and are published with the detailed statements of many witnesses in the Senate Hearings, pages 879 to 906. It does not appear from the records that Governor Sproul went on to make a detailed examination of every such individual allegation. The Interchurch Report affidavits here considered are with one exception among those in regard to which there is no other record except in the archives of the local police or court.

The only basis on which such affidavits can be judged then is to consider their source, the man or men who actually composed at least most of them together with his motive and the use to which he originally put them, the fact that many other affidavits of the same nature and from this same group proved under careful examination by Governor Sproul or the Senate Committee to be without any substantial basis in fact; that many of them cleverly insinuate as facts what they will not thus state under oath as facts, and finally that the Interchurch Report publishes such affidavits as valid evidence after they have been repudiated under oath by their maker.

In this particular connection this fact cannot be overlooked. In the charges of "hundreds wounded, hundreds clubbed" the Interchurch Report often and particularly features Braddock as one of the storm centers. Father Kazinci was one of the most conspicuous strike leaders in addition to his relation with his people as their priest. It seems incredible that any of them should have been clubbed without his knowing it. Yet in repudiating the statement by insinuation of the clubbing of his congregation he says he never saw any one clubbed and only knew of one person being clubbed and that seems not to have been at all serious.

There are a surprising number of the Interchurch affidavits, however, which far from even alleging any actual brutality consist chiefly of petty complaints of obviously trivial happenings which only the context gives any particular significance to. Men make affidavits to the fact that when they were arrested they didn't get dinner for seven hours. On page 187 the Interchurch Report spends one whole affidavit of its 41 brutality documents alleging that George Koshel was arrested in a perfectly ordinary way and fined $10 for refusing to move on when ordered to by the police. This might of course happen under any conditions in any city in the country.

The Interchurch Report spends two full affidavits and four attestations confirming the first affidavit which is in full as follows (Vol. II., page 187):

"Ella Syrko of 633 Third Street at about 7.15 A.M. told trooper to go to bed and not bother around her house. Trooper swung her against the door, breaking it in. This woman was in a delicate condition."

The strike leaders brought a group of the makers of such affidavits to the Senate Hearings. The record shows pages of their excited and obvious exaggerations of such trivialities, many of which are amusingly contradictory. Finally (Senate Hearings, page 786) Senator Stirling, turning to Mr. Rubin, the strikers' attorney asked:

"*Senator Stirling:* Mr. Rubin, don't you think this is a little far fetched to bring a man on the stand, as precious as our time is at present, to testify that somebody shot through his house?"

But Mr. Rubin did not withdraw his witness and the. testimony continued.

"*Senator Stirling:* Where did you find that bullet?
"*Mr. Supinen:* Inside of the stove . . . it went through the wall and went through the stove and stopped inside of the stove.
"*Senator Stirling:* Now how did it enter the stove?
"*Mr. Supinen:* It went through the stove and stopped inside of the stove.
"*Senator Stirling:* It is a cast-iron stove is it?
"*Mr. Supinen:* A cast-iron stove.
"*Senator Stirling:* Would not you have supposed that it would have battered that bullet if it went through the house and the stove? The bullet is smooth."

Finally two pages later the testimony ended in about the way it had continued, as follows:

"*Senator Walsh:* Is there anybody else here who has seen the hole in the house—in the wall?
"*Mr. Supinen:* Yes, sir.
"*Senator Walsh:* You are the only one here who saw it?
"*Mr. Supinen:* Yes, sir."

After Mr. Rubin had put a Mr. Colson on the stand to testify as to what kind of a bullet he thought the one found by a striker in his house was, he produced Mary Kropeck, whose affidavit the Interchurch Report publishes (page 186), doubly attested. The Interchurch Report makes no reference to the fact that the important Father Kazinci evidence was cross-examined under oath before the Senate Committee. It does not mention the fact, and sufficiently changes the spelling of his name to make the fact difficult to discover, that its sensational Brogan evidence was cross-examined under oath before the Senate Committee. But it calls special attention to the fact that its Kropeck affidavit was also part of the Senate Hearings. In view of this fact it is interesting to note that the trivial subject matter of this affidavit appears so increasingly more trivial through three pages of cross-examination that Mr. Rubin himself finally shuts it off.

All such circumstances—that a man finds a bullet in his parlor stove, or that a woman is fined $10—are of course unfortunate. But under the strained conditions of a great strike with sullen mobs gathering to the number of 4000 and attacking a public building; frequently gathering by hundreds to threaten workmen at the mill gates; throwing bricks from alleyways, and ashes and pepper into the faces of the police; parading with arms and issuing threats;—all of which violence or threats of violence is only a small part of that brought out by the Senate Committee and to which specific reference is made herein—the chief wonder is that the Interchurch Report finds so few really serious cases that it spends pages detailing how a man didn't get his dinner for seven hours, that some flower pots were broken and chairs overturned and that children didn't sleep one night; that a woman was pushed roughly against a door or that a man was fined $10 for something he said he didn't do.

The foregoing "rock bottom affidavits" deal chiefly with, or have been analyzed in connection with their allegations of "police brutality." Most of these "affidavits" however, which complain of arrest also complain of the injustice or discrimination of the courts.

In its general summary of the charges as to "Denial of Civil Rights" the Interchurch Report, Volume II, page 177, repeating in substance the same charge in Volume I, particularly emphasizes:

"the excessive punishment meted out to these strikers by the different Justices of the Peace, Burgesses, and Police courts and the *frank discrimination in the courts between those who were at work and those who were out on strike.*"

In addition to these generalizations, the Interchurch Report cites the following specific charge (Volume II, page 216) that in Pittsburgh:—

"'Attorneys for the strikers testified before the Senate Committee that they were not permitted to consult with their clients; that they were refused transcripts of the proceedings; that magistrates discharged men who promised to go to work and fined others who insisted on remaining on strike.'"

The facts as to any fine or imprisonment including the reason for such fine or imprisonment are of course matters of police court record. The Interchurch Report investigators could have examined those records. They could have talked with the judge in the case concerning those records. Instead of this, however, they merely print affidavit after affidavit from the prisoner in which the prisoner affirms he is innocent and complains that his sentence of $10 or $15 fine or 5 or 10 days in jail was unjust and excessive. Does the Interchurch Report think that the average prisoner ever admits his guilt or is unbiased enough to discuss his case fairly or that a piling up of protestations of prisoners that they were not guilty proves that they were not guilty?

The Senate Committee, however, did go into this widely repeated charge of the strike leaders that police and judges "frankly discriminated against strikers," going in detail into the one specific case which the Interchurch Report brings up, that quoted above in regard to Pittsburgh. The Interchurch Report, features that "Attorneys for the strikers testified before the Senate Committee" as to such discrimination as though the mere fact that they *testified* proved the case. It is strangely silent, however, on what that testimony showed under cross-examination and in regard to the other evidence.

The "Attorneys for the strikers" were Mr. McNair and Mr. C. W. Sypniewski. The former's testimony is contained on pages 575 to 581 and the latter's on pages 587 to 596. They allege about what the Interchurch Report alleges, namely that:

1. They were "not permitted to consult with . . . clients."

2. They "were refused transcripts of the proceedings."

3. "The magistrates discharged men who promised to go to work and fined others who insisted on remaining on strike."

The Senate Committee called the Pittsburgh Police Commissioner Peter P. Walsh and cross-examined him under oath (Senate Hearings, pages 681–687) in regard to, among other things, these three complaints of Attorney Sypniewski that—

1. *"Strikers' lawyers were not permitted to consult with their clients."*

"*Senator McKellar:* It has been testified at this hearing that even when a person charged with being a suspicious person had lawyers to represent him, that the judge of the court would not permit the lawyer to examine him. . . .

"*Mr. Walsh:* Well, in the last three weeks there have been three different attorneys here. Perhaps I could enlighten you if I knew which one said he was refused. That man Sypniewski? Was that the man?

"*Senator Phipps:* Yes.

"*Mr. Walsh:* I can state about him.

"*Senator Phipps:* Go ahead.

"*Mr. Walsh:* He came over there in the morning and he said, 'I am to represent some of these men, Judge.' He said, 'Who?' He said, 'I do not know. I want to go into the cell room.' I said, 'How do you know who you represent if you have not got his name?' 'Well,' he said, 'he was arrested.' I said, 'Give me his name. There are 7 men back there; give me the name, and whatever man you are representing I will bring him out.' He could not tell. I said, 'Wait until the hearing begins, and if you can recognize him and he asks you to be his counsel point him out and you can defend him.'

"*The Chairman:* Did not you know that he was employed by the American Federation of Labor to represent its men who had been arrested there?

"*Mr. Walsh:* No, sir, he did not make that known. The hearing began and there was one man that came up—*there were four men who were arrested and charged with being suspicious persons. They were arrested in an alleyway up near 30th Street, around 5 o'clock where there had been several complaints of men being attacked going to work.* Those four men came down, and I asked him, 'Is any one of these four men the man you represent.' He pointed out a man and I said, 'All right.' The Judge asked this man 'Are you a citizen?' This man said he could not speak English. Mr. Sypniewski said, 'He cannot speak English.' The Judge says, 'He knows what I am talking about.' Mr. Sypniewski then said, 'If you was in France you would not be able to understand French.' He (the Judge) said, 'I was in France,' and Sypniewski yelled out, 'You are a liar; you never were in France.'"

After this it seems that this strikers' attorney hurriedly left the court room.

After Attorney Sypniewski had thus left court Mr. McNair according to his own testimony (page 576) was sent to take Mr. Sypniewski's place.

"Mr. McNair: The attorney before me had been expelled from the court and refused—*they had refused him permission to defend a man,* and I was taking his place."

He thus obviously got into court late when it seems but three persons remained. In regard to his complaints about not being allowed to represent strikers, Mr. Walsh testified as follows (page 687):

"Mr. Walsh: I believe they had a man here this morning that complained; . . . by the name of McNair. This man came here, and he said he came to represent some person but he didn't know who; and three men came out charged with being drunk and he stepped up to defend those men and he did not know the men and he didn't know who he was to defend. They were discharged by the magistrate."

A third attorney, Mr. Brennan, testified that they (the Courts) "always treated me right over here."

2. *Strikers' Attorneys were refused transcripts of the proceedings.*

After Attorney Sypniewski had left court as already described, it seems he came back.

"Mr. Walsh: He went out and later on he says, 'I want some transcripts.' I said, 'Leave 75 cents for all you want and you can get them. You as an attorney know you have five days to take an appeal.'
"Senator McKellar: Was 75 cents the only cost for the transcripts?
"Mr. Walsh: For each one.
"Senator McKellar: Was there any reason why any lawyer could not take an appeal upon paying 75 cents?
"Mr. Walsh: Not at all."

Moreover in spite of the fact that Attorney Sypniewski had specifically alleged that he couldn't get transcripts he later testified (page 592, Senate Hearings):

"This is one of the men I represented and *here is the whole transcript*."
"Lieutenant McAfee sworn: Arrested defendant at 1.45 in front of
2520 Carson Street for stopping men on the street. Had much trouble
on the street with this man last week. Ordered him away several times.
Officer Connors sworn: Defendant has been stopping men going to
work . . . warned him several times. Officer McCullough sworn: Have
had complaints of this man, etc., etc."

Attorney Sypniewski brought up this transcript to allege
that it was inaccurate in that according to him the true
testimony was that:

"This man came out of a pool room and there was complaints by the
pool room keeper against threatening other people in that house and
they arrested this man as he came out."

Whatever else Attorney Sypniewski showed by this point
he at least showed he could and did get his transcripts.

3. Judges and magistrates *"frankly discriminated
against strikers."*

Senator McKellar in cross-examining Mr. Walsh summarized strikers' Attorney McNair's charge of discrimination against strikers with special reference to certain particular cases and questioned Mr. Walsh as follows (Senate
Hearings, page 685):

"*Senator McKellar:* There has been a charge made here that there is
a custom of arresting those who look like strikers on a charge of (being)
suspicious persons . . . (when) brought up before this particular
magistrate he asked them whether they were citizens or whether they
were foreigners and whether they were at work. . . . If they said they
were at work they were discharged but if they said they were not at
work, well, they were put in jail and fined and put in jail and kept in
jail. Is that correct?
"*Mr. Walsh:* No, sir.
"*Senator McKellar:* Explain that, please.
"*Mr. Walsh:* Well, they have been arrested at 5 o'clock in the morning or half past 5 or 6 o'clock, four or five men who were standing in alley-
ways and doorways near the street car stands. . . . They interfered with
the men going to work and wherever they may be going. In a great
many cases we found bricks in their pockets. These men were charged

with being suspicious persons and were arrested at 5.30 o'clock and they had a hearing on the charge at 8 o'clock. The judge would ask them if they were at work. He said, 'No.' Then the Judge would say to him—he would ask, 'What were you doing out on the street at 5 o'clock in the morning with a brick in your pocket?' They would say, 'I don't know.' Then the Judge would say, 'Are you on a strike?' They would say, 'I don't know.' Then the Judge would ask, 'Are you a citizen?' 'No.'

"He would then get a man to interpret and speak to this man, and the judge would ask the question, 'What were you doing on the street or in the alleyway with a brick in your pocket at 5 o'clock in the morning,' and they would not answer the question.

"*Senator Stirling:* The officer had previously testified that that was the condition in which he found the men?

"*Mr. Walsh:* Yes, sir, and he would show the brick to the magistrate. Before the magistrate would question the person he would take the testimony of the officer.

"*Senator Stirling:* Is that lawyer (strikers' attorney McNair) here?

"*Mr. Rubin:* No.

"*Senator Walsh:* That man omitted any reference to the brick."

CHAPTER XXIV

THE ACTUAL PURPOSE AND EFFECT OF THE INTERCHURCH REPORT

THE object of the publication of the Interchurch Report on the Steel Strike six months after the end of the strike itself was, according to the statement of the Report itself (pages 3 and 4), to call public attention:

(1)—to what the Interchurch Report states were the real facts at issue in the steel strike which it states were "uncomprehended by the nation," and also the "engulfing circumstances" which also persist, both of which it seems to think are "in general characteristic of American industrial developments."

(2)—to the alleged fact that "the main issues were not settled by the strike."

(3)—to the alleged fact that the steel industry therefore continues "in a state of latent war" in which employers and employees are both "merely waiting for the next strike."

(4)—and finally to the alleged fact that "if the steel industry is to find a peaceful way out of its present state (of latent war) it must do so on the basis of a general understanding (by the public) of such facts as are here (in the report) set forth."

In other words the Interchurch Report, signed by prominent religious leaders of the country and countersigned by the Interchurch World Movement, and certain of whose signers have publicly stated that it represents the official opinion of American Protestantism, definitely states that it embodies the results of a careful impartial study of one of America's greatest basic industries and constitutes an impartial report to the American people of conditions in that industry on which it is recommended that they judge that industry.

As a matter of fact, however, a careful analysis of the Report itself clearly shows that the Interchurch Report is in no sense a careful or impartial study of conditions in the steel industry. For entirely in addition to its mere assumptions, its unwarranted and sweeping generalizations and other faulty methods of argument which constantly lead it into palpable self-contradictions and other logical absurdities, the Report itself admits at the outset that it bases its conclusions chiefly on "500 affidavits" largely of low-skilled foreigners—it deliberately leaves out practically all the important facts that in any way favor the steel companies, and constantly resorts to a studied expurgation of testimony and other evidence, to misleading insinuations and statements and to the clever manipulation of statistics and tables in an effort to make plausible entirely false and obviously preconceived hypotheses and conclusions.[1]

The question remains, and is very pertinent, as to just what these obviously pre-conceived hypotheses and conclusions are. In other words, what is the actual purpose of the Interchurch Report as far as that purpose can be determined by an analysis of the Report itself, and where do the fallacious arguments, which it goes to such lengths to bolster up, actually lead?

[1] "It (the Interchurch Report) has quite obviously been prepared from the standpoint of some mind convinced beforehand that the United States Steel Corporation is an insincere, oppressive and iniquitous organization . . . the Interchurch protested impartiality and those who saw the inquiry begin certainly expected something like a judicial rendering of opinion—not a brief for the prosecution."
The Continent (Presbyterian),
Editorial, Nov. 4, 1920.

From the first appearance of the Report—as a matter of fact, during the investigation that preceded the Report, it has been widely alleged that the Investigation was largely conducted by radicals and that the Report itself was largely merely radical propaganda. Such allegations, however, were in general based on entirely insufficient evidence and contained many obvious misstatements of fact. Moreover, most such allegations dealt chiefly in personalities and paid only a minimum of attention to the principal fact, i. e.—the merits of the Report itself.

The New York State Legislative Investigation of Radicalism, the most thorough and competent official study yet undertaken on this subject, states on pages 1137 and 1138:

"The most recent proof of the invasion of the churches by subversive influences is the Report on the Steel Strike by a committee appointed by the Interchurch World Movement. . . . It is not generally known that the direction of this inquiry was not in the hands of unbiased investigators. The principal 'experts' are David J. Saposs and George Soule (Heber Blankenhorn joined the investigators later)—whose radical viewpoints may be gathered from their association with Mr. Evans Clark acting under the direction of Ludwig C. A. K. Martens, head of the Soviet Bureau in the United States, their connection also with the Rand School of Social Science, and certain revolutionary labor organizations."

Again in many cases in the present analysis, arguments and points of view in the Interchurch Report have been pointed out as being exactly parallel to arguments and points of view advanced by radicals and in certain instances it had been pointed out that arguments presented by the Interchurch Report undoubtedly show a distinct sympathy with radicalism.

The term radicalism, however, is in general so loosely used to mean anything, depending on the user, from merely an intelligent questioning of modern economic values to pure Bolshevism that it is correspondingly important that in an analysis of the Interchurch Report in regard to its possible radicalism, the term "radicalism" should be specifically defined and used merely within these limits.

In so far as it is significant to the present consideration, radicalism consists of the advocacy of—

First: a revolutionary, as distinct from an evolutionary, change in our modern social and industrial system—the basic fulcrum of that change being the ownership and operation of industry by the workers themselves, and

Second: the bringing about of such revolutionary change by other means than those of the orderly processes of government by majority action.

In other words a consideration of radicalism involves a consideration not only of the radical theories themselves, but also of the means advocated for carrying out those radical theories. For it must be clearly recognized even by the most bitter opponents of radicalism that throughout history the various social and industrial systems which in the heighths of their acceptance were the basis and bulwark of conservatism, were generally, at the time of their inception, regarded as radical. While therefore much that is called radicalism may be combatted—and is combatted by the great majority of Americans—as unsound and undesirable, nevertheless the men who advocate such theories and seek to extend them, are entirely within their rights as American citizens, *so long as they only seek to extend such theories by persuading a majority of their fellow citizens of their desirability and seek only to bring about such changes by orderly processes of majority self-government.* [1]

---

[1] It is necessary to make a distinction though that distinction is generally somewhat vague and often imaginary—between radical theories and some of the individuals who hold those theories. An individual may hold theories which are themselves revolutionary, which actually could only be realized through revolutionary action, and whose main body of adherents and their official leaders recognize as revolutionary and necessitating revolutionary measures, yet such an individual may protest that he is trying to realize those aims only through peaceful evolutionary means. Undoubtedly in some cases such protestations are sincere; in many others they are a mere cloak behind which the individual radical believes he can work most effectively.

One such individual for instance in a private conversation with the

Modern radicalism does *not* seek to advance its theories through orderly processes of government by means of majority action. On the contrary it definitely and admittedly seeks to bring about its revolutionary changes through deception and a strategic application of force against, or irrespective of, the will of the majority. August Claessens, socialist member of the New York State Legislature, said in a speech at the Park View Palace November 7, 1919:

"If we thought for a minute it (socialism) was merely . . . a great political controversy, until we have a majority of men elected, and then by merely that majority declare the revolution, if any of you smoke that pipe dream; if that is the quality of opium you are puffing now, give it up, give it up."

The American Socialist Left Wing Manifesto of June, 1919, says:

"The conquest of the power of the state is an extra-parliamentary act. It is accomplished not by legislative representatives of the proletariat, but by . . . the political mass strike. . . . The power of the proletariat lies fundamentally in its control of the industrial process."

---

author and another person, expressed the hope that his theories about the ownership of industry by the workers could be realized peaceably. He stated however that they would be realized by revolution if necessary and stated particularly that if the government should attempt certain action which President Harding specifically recommended in his last message, the revolution would come within five years. Because of this and other expressions of very radical opinion, the writer asked him why he did not have the mental honesty and moral courage to express such views openly instead of posing publicly as a mere "liberal." He replied that it was because he believed he could" serve the cause better outside of jail than in."

The term "radical" therefore as used in the present analysis, when applied to a theory or movement, means a theory or movement that aims at revolutionary changes which its official advocates propose or seek to carry out by revolutionary measures. When applied to an individual it means one who advocates or is working to advance such theories or movements irrespective of what he may individually think or admit about the way they should be carried out.

Moreover that all schools of modern radicalism advocate the accomplishment of their ends, not through legitimate majority legislative action but through getting control of the production of all the peoples' necessities of life by organizing and controlling the workers, and then using that control to force the acceptance of its further theories, is stated as a fundamental principle of all radicalism by Eden and Cedar Paul in their "Creative Revolution"—in the constitution of the Socialist Party—in the constitution of the I. W. W.—in manifestos of the Communist party—in printed literature of the Amalgamated Clothing Workers— by Mr. Foster and his group of radicals working within the A. F. of L.—and by all other known radical groups.

Radicalism, as thus defined, consists of many schools whose theories and objects and methods differ in detail. All of them, however, irrespective of whether their ultimate aim may be the enforced revolution of society to an anarchistic, socialistic, syndicalist, or other state, are seeking to bring about that revolution by certain definite methods. These are:

First: the control of industry through an organization of the workers;

Second: this organization of the workers to be along *industrial* union lines, as opposed to *craft* union lines, with a view of bringing all the workers in any given industry under united control in order to make possible the "general strike";

Third: agitation and propaganda among all workers to the effect that under the present system they are invariably and inevitably exploited by their employers, through the employer's alleged control of the government, the courts, the police power, the army and all present forces of law and order, and that therefore all these forces must be fought by the workers;

Fourth: it is generally possible of course for radicals to keep secret or cover up their unlawful conspiracies and often their acts. Agitation and propaganda, however, which are necessary to influence and organize the workers, cannot be thus hid. All radicals therefore insist that "the right of free speech" be made absolute under all circumstances. They demand constantly and loudly that neither the courts or police or local officials or local public opinion as a whole shall be permitted to prevent their *saying* or *writing* anything they please including the counciling and urging of criminal acts.

Fifth: in addition to the organization of the workers into industrial unions, under a single control, as a means of controlling and owning industry, all radicals seek to facilitate and hasten the ownership and control of their industry through the practice of every possible device which will make the ownership and control of industry unprofitable or otherwise undesirable to present ownership and management. Radicalism's principal and most emphasized such device is that of forcing up wages so disproportionately to production that the business cannot be run at a profit and therefore cannot maintain or obtain operating capital to continue.

Sixth: with the same object of making industry unprofitable to its present owners, radicalism admittedly openly preaches and encourages sabotage;

Seventh: in order to give its workers free scope in practising sabotage and carrying out other practices to the detriment of their industry and as a means of getting control of their industry more and more in the hands of the workers, radicalism continually insists on the adoption of every type of device that will take the possibility of disciplining or controlling the workers out of the hands of the employers, even to the extent of openly denying the employer the right to hire or discharge the workers.

Because radicalism's whole object is the dictatorship over the majority by a minority class which it can only hope to achieve by strategy, and because its aims and methods are in general so unlawful that many of its leaders have gone to jail for a too open acknowledgment of them, radicals today are particularly careful to state those aims specifically only where necessary and to state only as much of them as is necessary under the circumstances. Doubtless largely for the same reason, radicals have also adopted an elaborate technical phraseology, whose meaning is entirely clear to all fellow radicals and can easily be made clear by word of mouth to those for whom it is intended, but is not sufficiently explicit to make its full import entirely clear to the average non-radical reader. It is almost invariably necessary therefore in order to get the full meaning of almost any radical document to build up the true meaning through a comparison with many other utterances that are known to be radical.

The Interchurch Report of course assumes to be something very different from radical propaganda. In the nature of the case, therefore, if it is radical propaganda, as has been so frequently alleged, its chief hope of effectiveness as such propaganda would consist chiefly of keeping that fact from being apparent.

A careful comparison, however, of the main and most featured arguments and conclusions of the Interchurch Report, with the seven main principles and aims of radicalism as above stated, together with a careful comparison of statements in regard to those principles and aims made by leading known radicals with the arguments and conclusions and phraseology of the Interchurch Report on the same subjects clearly brings out a number of facts that are entirely unapparent in a casual reading of the Report.

The seven main principles and objects of modern radicalism have been stated as:

FIRST, *the control of industry through an organization of the workers.*

The Interchurch Report insists throughout on the necessity of the organization of the steel workers. It is of course true that the necessity of the organization of the workers is also insisted on by many entirely non-radical trade unionists and is advocated by many thinkers who have no connection with either radicals or the workers themselves. But while non-radical trade unionism insists on organization of the workers by *crafts*, all radicalism denounces craft unionism which, as such, works against radicalism, and insists on—

SECOND, *the organization of the workers along industrial lines with One Big Union under one control in each entire industry.*

Eugene V. Debs says:

"The *trade union* is outgrown and its survival is an unmitigated evil to the working class. *Craft* unionism is not only impotent but a crime against the workers."

The preamble to the constitution of the Amalgamated Textile Workers, an ultra-radical union associated with the Amalgamated Clothing Workers, states in terms that are typical of similar statements in the constitutions of other radical unions, that:

"The working class must accept the principles of industrial unionism or it is doomed to impotence."

The New International (an official radical propaganda organ) in February, 1918, states what all radicals were particularly emphasizing at the time, that—

"We are convinced that the technical development of the capitalist world makes conditions ripe (for industrial unionism) . . . at this very moment." . . .

The Interchurch Report continually condemns craft unions and definitely presents the exact argument of Debs and other radicals that craft unionism is inimical and industrial unionism favorable to the interests of the workers and that economic conditions are making industrial unionism inevitable.

It tells the steel workers (on page 15) that the "indifference, selfishness or narrow habit" of the A. F. of L. (craft unions) was one of the chief reasons for the defeat of the strike.

It speaks on page 157 of the officers of the A. F. of L. (craft unions) tending to be "job holders rather than apostles" and more expert "in figuring out scales of dues for their own organizations than in figuring out what is due to laborers."

It says on page 179 that many of the workers felt "they had been let down by the Labor Movement" (craft unions) and in general—though usually indirectly by the addition of "it is alleged" or "the workers thought"—the whole Report continually undermines craft unionism.

In regard to industrial unionism, it says on page 159:

"economic conditions . . . have exposed weaknesses in craft unions . . . when craft unions promulgate ambitions . . . they are forced automatically to considering industrial union problems,"

and again on page 158:

"The real problem which confronts A. F. of L. trade unions . . . is industrial unionism, and the larger side of it is . . . economic conditions."[1]

THIRD, *radical agitation and propaganda always emphasizes to the workers that they are, under the present system invariably and inevitably exploited by their employers through the employers' alleged control of the government, the courts, the police power, the army, and all present forces of law and order, and that therefore all these forces must be fought by the workers.*
Even the most casual reader of the Interchurch Report cannot fail to note its constant condemnations—often qualified, but generally more effective for the qualifications —of courts, magistrates, the Attorney General of the United States, public officials, the police; and its constant insistence to the workers that all these were used against them and in favor of the steel trust and that this was one of the chief causes why they lost the strike. As a matter of fact, not only the attitude of the Interchurch Report itself towards all the forces of law and order in the country, but the peculiar grounds on which it condemns them and the peculiar phraseology it uses in this connection cannot fail to be noted.
To any one familiar with average radical propaganda literature, these sections of the Interchurch Report are self-explanatory. A comparison of these sections with any typical radical propaganda document cannot but make this

[1] The way in which the Interchurch Report carefully leads up, through numerous tentative qualified statements, to these definite statements has been pointed out in Chapter XVI and specifically emphasized in the footnote on page 204.

plain even to those most unfamiliar with radical aims and methods.

Just about the time of the steel strike, the New York branch of the Communist party—undoubtedly the most radical organization in America—issued a manifesto to the longshoremen who were then engaged in an "outlaw" strike. This manifesto is a typically radical document, in the propaganda it seeks to advance, in the forces of present government it attacks, and in technical, radical phraseology which means much more to the radical than it does to the average American reader.

This official Communist Manifesto says:

"1. Workers . . . you have repudiated your *scab form* of A. F. of L. unionism. You must . . . unite with all those who are employed in the transportation industry for One Big *Industrial* Transport Workers' Union."

On this specific point the Interchurch Report on page 159 says:

"When a craft union on strike sees brother unions in the same industry *sticking to work or even filling the strikers' jobs* (i. e. *scabbing*) that craft union begins to do a lot more thinking about *industrial unionism.*"

The Communist Manifesto says:

"The bosses hired their strike breakers *from strike-breaking agencies.*"

One of the most featured charges which the Interchurch Report brings against the steel companies in Chapter VII is that they hired "strike breakers" and it spends pages in emphasizing that they sometimes hired them from "strike-breaking agencies."

The Manifesto continues:

"Now they use the army itself as a *strike-breaking agency.*"

The Interchurch Report on pages 238, 241 and 242, emphasizes: "the use of the Federal army to break the strike"

Again, the Communist Manifesto says:

"The Government (Federal) Wage adjustment Board, . . . did it decide in your favor?"

The Interchurch Report says on page 238:

"Federal officials, particularly the Federal Department of Justice, help to break strikes."

The Communist Manifesto says:

"The police, whose heads are they going to crack, when you go on the picket line?"

The Interchurch Report on page 238 says:

" . . . police officials try to break strikes," and on page 240 it says: "the charge of beatings and clubbings (of strikers by the police) were endless and monotonous."

The Communist Manifesto says:

"The Press! whose side are the newspapers taking, yours or the bosses?"

The Interchurch Report on page 238 says:

"Most newspapers actively and promptly exert a strike-breaking influence" and repeats the same statement on page 242 and elsewhere.

The Communist Manifesto says:

"Don't you see that the bosses own and control the whole governmental machinery?"

The Interchurch Report on page 242 says:

" . . . that local and national government not only was not their government [i.e. in their behalf], but was government in behalf of interests opposing theirs; that in strike times, governmental activities tend to break strikes."

In other words each ridiculous attack which this ultra radical Communist Manifesto makes on each force of law and order in language that is calculated to arouse most the prejudice and hostility of the workers, is, in argument and phraseology, almost exactly paralleled in the Interchurch Report.

This further point is to be noted. The term "scab" or "strike breaker" (meaning the same things) is the most arousing and damning term, from the point of view of the radical workers, that can be used against any individual or group of individuals. Foster's *Syndicalism* says on page 14:

> "A large portion of the syndicalists' success in their strikes is due to their energetic treatment of the strike breaker. . . . He becomes so much vermin to be ruthlessly exterminated."

The Communist Manifesto, it will be noted, only calls certain of the forces of law and order by this ultimate epithet "strike breaker." The Interchurch Report, on the other hand is carefully worded to call each separate force of law and order by this, from the radical point of view, worst possible epithet—"strike breaker."

Now it will be noted that in its argument for industrial (radical) unionism, in its attack on the U. S. Department of Justice and in all similar attacks, as these have already been emphasized and otherwise, the Interchurch Report builds up an elaborate case by a mixture of unsupported statements, alleged evidence, insinuation, etc., which exactly parallels standard radical propaganda, and then states in almost standard radical phraseology the standard radical conclusion—but generally qualifying it with the phrase "the workers believed," or "this made the workers believe," etc. By the use of such qualifying phrases the Interchurch Report, of course, technically shifts the responsibility for the conclusions to which its whole argument plainly leads and with which it obviously agrees from its own shoulders to that of the workers, thus creating a loophole through which the author or authors of the Interchurch Report may attempt to escape actual responsibility for the logical and psychological effects of their whole argument. But the very method by which it seeks to do this is standard radical propaganda practise.

Mr. Heber Blankenhorn, together with Messrs. William Z. Foster, Scott Nearing, Carl Sandburg, Representative of the Finnish Red government, Paul Hanna, publicity agent of the I. W. W., and other well-known radicals are now openly and officially working as correspondents of the Federated Press which supplies news service to the *New York Call*, *The New Solidarity*, the *Chicago News Majority*, the *Daily Free Russia*, the *Chicago Socialist*, the *One Big Union Monthly* and other official radical publications.

Mr. Blankenhorn's other and previous sub rosa radical activities will be discussed later but at present he is openly and officially engaged in writing the kind of feature articles on industrial subjects which are used by the editors of official radical publications for official radical propaganda or as the basis for such radical propaganda. Mr. Blankenhorn is also engaged in agitation propaganda to the general public. But to the public of course the whole effect of his radical arguments would be lost if they were openly and admittedly radical. So Mr. Blankenhorn in his propaganda to the public resorts to exactly the same methods used in the Interchurch Report, including the qualification of the conclusions which he carefully builds up to, by the same phrases, "The workers believed," "this made the workers believe," etc., etc.

An agitation propaganda article of this sort to the general public and signed by Mr. Blankenhorn appeared in the September 14, 1921 issue of *The Nation*. This article is in defense of the union miners who recently marched into West Virginia to force the non-union miners to unionize at the point of the rifle and machine gun. By quoting somebody's comparison of this attack to John Brown's rebellion at

Harper's Ferry and then reiterating this comparison by clever insinuation and sarcasm, by unsupported accusations against the courts and the state constabulary, by accusing the local government of all sorts of discrimination against union leaders including the suppression of meetings, in other words, by precisely the same type of argument so generally employed in the Interchurch Report—this whole article which seeks to justify the miners' taking the law into their own hands ends with this statement:

"Thus 10,000 mountaineer miners *have come to believe* that certain persons have been taking the law pretty completely into their own hands. They retaliate in kind. It is hard to interest them in senatorial investigations. They *may come to believe* that the Federal as well as the State Government cloaks operators who take the law into their own hands. Then they will talk even more of John Brown and Harper's Ferry."

This interesting parallel is even more significant in view of the fact, which will be established later, that Mr. Blankenhorn who was officially secretary of the Interchurch Commission was the actual author of the Interchurch Report on the Steel Strike.

Such remarkable parallels in what is argued for and against, in the arguments used, in the way the argument is presented, in the conclusions and particularly in the very extraordinary phraseology used, between the Interchurch Report and the arguments of Debs and other well-known radicals, and of various official communist and socialist propaganda documents is so striking, so point by point even to detail, so repeated that it is obviously impossible to lay it to coincidence. As a matter of fact, the non-radical simply does not know and could not use such technical radical terms and phraseology—even radical slang—with the fluency and subtle effects with which they are consistently used in many parts of the Interchurch Report.

Moreover such parallels are not only found in the numerous instances and in connection with the subjects already pointed out but extend to the subjects of methods of cost accounting, of labor management, of bonuses and could be multiplied almost indefinitely. Certain of these will be touched on in other connections later.

There is however one other particular parallel between this sweeping Interchurch attack on the forces of law and order and standard radical propaganda that deserves special attention.

Anyone who is familiar with the history of radical activities and points of view or with radical literature, whether in Europe or America, knows that while the socialists and the followers of Proudhon disagree with Bakounists and Syndicalists and Bolshevists as to whether their chief enemy is the capitalist or merely capitalism—that while the same groups differ even more widely as to whether the "bourgeoisie" or middle class is to be won over or treated with contempt and ignored, the one group in all organized society against which all radical schools in all countries and from Nechayeff to the present are united in bitter hatred and implacable enmity is the police.

In 1870 Bakounin himself in one of his most vindictive diatribes against certain of his enemies, after calling them "doctrinaire, insolent, loathsome, stupid," works up to the climax "*police blood flows in their veins—they should be called policemen and attorney generals in embryo.*"

Even as early as the time of Stellmacker, Austrian radicals began the custom of holding special meetings of honor for those who murdered officers of the police.

One of the earliest meetings of French radicals was held to decide what conspicuous public building—whether the Bank of France, the Palais d'Elysée or the Ministry of the Intérieur—should be blown up in order to strike most terror to the government and the people. But the hatred against the police was so strong that they decided on the home of the Prefect.

The first great radical outrage in America was the throwing of dynamite bombs among a crowd of police officers in Haymarket Square, Chicago.

Johann Most's statement, "Murder is the killing of a human being and I have never heard that a policeman was a human being" has become a radical proverb.

That the radical individuals and schools which openly preach and seek to practise violence should have this inherent hatred of all police powers seems perhaps natural but as a matter of fact the very radicals which have been the loudest in publicly disclaiming the use of violence seem to be often most bitter and vituperative in their attacks on all police agencies.

Even so mild a socialist as Mr. Robert Hunter in his book *Violence and the Labor Movement*, dedicated to Eugene V. Debs, and which is written to express the author's personal disbelief in the efficacy of violence, devotes his longest and next to the last chapter to a most bitter and sweeping denunciation of the police.

Mr. Hunter, though writing in 1916, goes back to 1869 in American labor history and to 1832 in European and combs the field for alleged police atrocities. The latest police "atrocities" he actually attempts to allege were in connection with strikes of 1886 to 1892, a period during which nation-wide anarchistic bomb outrages led to certain, not always mild, police counter activity, which has long since however died down or been stopped by public opinion. Yet Mr. Hunter not only wrote in 1916 as though these were current police practise but in his anti-police frenzy he entirely changes the comparatively restrained style of his other chapters and launches into a most unrestrained, sweeping and often self-contradictory charge of "police brutality" which can only be compared with the Interchurch charges of "men and women murdered," "hundreds wounded," "hundreds clubbed" based on affidavits or statements about "drunk or crazy" police firing volley after volley into fleeing crowds, "riding down women and children," "clubbing peaceful worshippers leaving church," which "affidavits" and "statements" are on their face largely mere exclamations or descriptions and not statements at all and which under oath and cross-examination were publicly repudiated by their own authors.

Again "The Socialist Party Platform" 1920 says:
"Industrial"
"1. Congress should enact effective laws . . . to abolish *detective and strike-breaking agencies*" . . .

and all radical groups argue, in season and out, against "detectives" or "spies" or "under-cover men," beginning with "strike-breaking detective agencies," against which certain arguments can be reasonably advanced, but always carrying this argument on to an insistence that *all* "detective activities" should be abolished. The motive of such arguments in such cases is of course apparent.

There is little question that the very idea of the use of detectives or "spies" to get information by misrepresentation or deceit is distasteful to the average person. No right minded person approves the use of such means except where necessary or will fail to condemn the misuse of such agencies.

Unfortunately, however, as long as criminal cupidity and passion threaten life and property; or criminal fanaticism plots Haymarket or Wall Street bomb outrages; or equally criminal but more cowardly fanaticism furnishes the propaganda or "justification" which incites the more ignorant or daring of their fellows to thus take the law into their own hands, detective activity is at least a necessary evil.

That the Interchurch Report continually attacks "under-cover men" and "spy" activities from those of the "Federal Department of Justice" down, has already been emphasized. It builds its attack on the fact that one "Sherman Agency" representative was indicted—but not convicted—of "conspiracies of riot, insurrection and murder." It tries by insinuation to tie this case up with the steel strike but does not directly allege any such connection.

Beyond this one incident the Interchurch Report builds its case against "under-cover men" almost entirely on information which it specifically states was freely given it by

23

the steel companies themselves. This evidence so fails to prove anything in connection with the steel strike that the Interchurch Report itself admits in connection with it (Volume II, page 4):

> "It is impossible then to criticize the present Report on under-cover men in the steel strike as 'an exceptional instance'; instead it is a typical spadeful out of the subsoil of 'business enterprise.'"

Yet through page after page to a total of over 100 pages it mulls this evidence over, weaving it through with insinuations and otherwise trying chiefly through mere volume of words to make plausible the conclusion which anyone familiar with this type of argument knows is coming; namely, that *all* detective activities should be abolished. This conclusion in this case is featured as the climax of the Introduction in the second volume and it is frankly signed by Mr. Heber Blankenhorn's initials. It says:

> "The questioning sweeps wider. Must our social organization, our civilization, be shot through with spies? . . . Can we live without spies? The question is raised by the facts: hence the importance of this study.
>
> H. B."

FOURTH. *It is generally possible of course for the radicals to keep secret or cover up many of their unlawful conspiracies and acts. Agitation and propaganda however, which are necessary to influence and organize its followers cannot be hid. All radicals therefore, insist that the "right of free speech" be made absolute under all circumstances. They demand continually and loudly that neither the courts or police or local officials or local public opinion as a whole shall be permitted to prevent their saying or writing anything they please.*

"The Socialist Party Platform," 1920 says:

"POLITICAL"

"1. The constitutional freedom of speech, press and assembly should be restored." . . .

The fact that the Interchurch Report makes a major argument out of this subject of "free speech" and that its argument and conclusions in regard to "free speech," the "right of assemblage" and so-called "Civil liberties" are built up by hiding the true facts as to violence and threat of violence and by resorting to either the deception or the quibble that there was no violence merely because there was no violence at strikers' meetings has already been emphasized. A careful comparison between the Interchurch arguments on this much radically agitated subject and the arguments that are advanced by official radical propaganda on the subject, is correspondingly interesting.

Mr. Roger Baldwin was, at the time of the preparation of the Interchurch Report, the conspicuous radical head of a radical organization known as the National Civil Liberties Bureau, devoted during the war to propaganda against preparedness and the draft—for attempting to carry out whose theories Mr. Baldwin served a year in prison—and known since the war as the "American Civil Liberties Union" of which Mr. William Z. Foster is a director and whose theories and activities Mr. Baldwin has himself described as follows: (New York Legislative Investigation of Radicalism, page 1979, and succeeding pages).

"The American Civil Liberties Union was organized on January 12, 1920, being a reorganization of the National Civil Liberties' Bureau . . . a change in name to indicate that the character of the organization had changed from a bureau of legal service to a propaganda organization. . . . Expression of opinion, as we define it, includes any language unaccompanied by any overt act— . . . language unaccompanied by such an act even if the logical consequences of it lead others to the commission of the act, is legitimately within our conception of free speech. For instance *the advocacy of murder, unaccompanied by any act, is within the legitimate scope of free speech.* . . . The view I have set forth, however, is I believe the view of those who believe in free speech, without reservations, as do the great majority of our Committee. . . . I would say on behalf of the entire committee that all of them disbelieve the legal theory of constructive intent, and that all of them believe in the right of persons *to advocate 'the overthrow of government by force and violence,'* while all the members of the Committee totally disbelieve in any such doctrine themselves. . . . Because of the nature of the attacks on the assumed rights of individuals and organizations, the work is organized chiefly in coöperation with labor unions and radical political groups."

In connection with the war activities of this organization and particularly in the organization of the "Peoples' Council" which was "to imitate in this country the Workingmen's and Soldiers' Councils of Russia," Mr. Baldwin wrote Mr. Louis D. Lochner:

"We want to also look like patriots in everything we do. We want to get a lot of good flags, talk a good deal about the Constitution," etc.

Perhaps no better example need be cited of a point already emphasized—that in regard to the "undercover" nature of radical activities, and the difference between the individual's protestations about *what he believes* and the actual effect of his acts. Mr. Baldwin states that he personally doesn't believe in "the overthrow of the government by force and violence" nevertheless he is directing his whole activities "chiefly in coöperation with labor unions and *radical political groups*" in trying to obtain for these radical political groups the right to "advocate the overthrow of the government by force and violence" and he specifically includes in this the right to "advocate murder," posing all the time "like patriots in everything we do" with a "lot of good flags" and "talk about the Constitution" and "our forefathers."

The officially signed propaganda pamphlets of Mr. Baldwin's and Mr. Foster's organization state:

"The hysteria aroused by the war . . . is now directed against the advocates of industrial freedom . . . in the passage of laws against 'criminal syndicalism,' 'criminal anarchy' and 'sedition.' . . .

"We are attempting to meet the present crisis—

"(1) By sending free speech organizers and speakers into areas of conflict to dramatize the issue of civil liberty . . . (and) . . . by securing nation-wide publicity on all important civil liberty issues."

The Interchurch Report devotes many passages throughout and a large part of Chapter VII in thus "dramatizing and securing nation-wide publicity" for precisely the same so-called "issues of Civil Liberty" which Mr. Baldwin and his "Liberties Union" specifically emphasize and advocate; and the supplementary Interchurch Report, Volume II, spends 60 pages, signed by Mr. George Soule, quotations from whose other published works appear herein, which he devotes to arguing why the rights of local self-government should be taken away from the people of Western Pennsylvania, basing his arguments on a series of 41 affidavits which are at least more "dramatic" than they are anything else.

Mr. Baldwin's organization in its official pamphlets specifically names and condemns certain social forces as being thus "directed against the advocates of industrial freedom" and as seeking to infringe the "Civil liberties" of those who are standing upon their "American rights of free speech" in preaching "Syndicalism, Anarchy and sedition." These social forces are according to Mr. Baldwin "patrioteering societies," "vigilantes," "citizens' committees," "strike breaking state constabularies," "the hired gun-men of private corporations," "the Attorney General (Palmer)" and "zealous local prosecutors" . . . "by whom meetings are prohibited or broken up" and "speakers are mobbed and prosecuted."

It has already been emphasized in specific detail how each one of these same "social forces" which are thus accused by Mr. Baldwin of "infringing the civil liberties" of those preaching "industrial freedom," "anarchy" and "syndicalism," are also specifically named and accused by the Interchurch Report of "infringing civil liberties." These include "bands of citizens," "Loyal American Leaguers" (doubtless "Patrioteers"), the officials of Gary accused of stopping strikers' meetings and parades merely because they resulted in pulling negroes off street cars and "injuring them slightly" —the Attorney General of the United States who becomes second only to Judge Gary as the "bête noire" of the Interchurch Report because of his "infringing of Civil Liberties," and a blanket accusation brought (page 235) against "local legislative bodies, police authorities, judges, state police troops, Federal government departments, and the United States Army" as having "affected civil liberties in whole communities."

Returning to Mr. Baldwin's official Civil Liberties Pamphlet the following then appears:—

"FREE SPEECH—

"There should be no prosecutions for the mere expression of opinion on matters of public concern, however radical, however violent. . . .

"No *discretion should be given to police* to prohibit parades or processions,"—and *that such parades should be allowed to display red flags or other political emblems.*

Except for the fact that it does not mention "red flags" this is specifically the argument—as already shown in detail—which the Interchurch spends its whole "Free Speech" section in both volumes in "dramatizing" and giving "nation-wide publicity."

In connection with a consideration of the arguments and conclusions of the Interchurch Report and the vociferous present campaign of the "American Civil Liberties Union and of all radicals to be allowed the unlimited "right of free speech" in order to be unhindered in carrying on their radical propaganda, there is another fact that deserves note.

The New York state legislative investigation of radicalism, on page 1991, describes the organization by Mr. Louis B. Lochner, Scott Nearing, Roger Baldwin and other well-known radicals of:

"An International labor news service, which has for its purpose the spreading of news relating to the *revolutionary progress* in foreign countries and in general of a *propaganda* nature."

In December, 1919, in the midst of the steel strike, this organization reorganized, changed its name to the *Federated Press* and added to the list of its officers and correspondents a large number of additional notorious radicals. Its own published list of those so officially connected with

the Federated Press includes the name of Mr. Heber
Blankenhorn, and later that of Mr. William Z. Foster.
On page 243 of the Interchurch Report appears a very
significant little advertisement of this radical propaganda
organization, as follows:

". . . workers in many sections of the nation, in steel towns and
out, redoubled efforts to set up their own press and *inaugurated their
own federated news service.*"

And again in Volume II, page 89:

"Immediately after the steel and coal strikes there was quickly established the first national news service owned by the labor unions, the
Federated Press."

In other words in view of the fact that the man who wrote
the Interchurch Report has since been openly working for an
off-shoot of the American Civil Liberties Union, which the
Interchurch Report thus advertises adds to the significance
of this parallel between the argument as to "free speech"
which the Civil Liberties Union seeks to "dramatize" and
the argument which the Interchurch Report goes to such
lengths to "dramatize."

FIFTH: *in addition to the organization of the workers into
industrial unions under single control as a means of controlling
and owning the industry, for which purpose all radicals demand the unlimited right of free speech, all radicals seek to
facilitate and hasten the ownership and control of their industry
by themselves, through the use of every possible device which will
make the ownership and control of the industry unprofitable or
otherwise undesirable to present ownership and management.
The means to this end which radicalism most emphasizes are
those of forcing up wages so disproportionately to production
that the business cannot be run at a profit and therefore cannot
maintain or obtain sufficient operating capital to continue.*

All leaders of labor and all labor, including the most
conservative, are of course always interested in increasing
wages and are in general making a constant effort in this

direction. Many non-radical labor leaders are also seeking blindly to limit production per worker on the theory that more workers will thus be employed. Such interests and efforts in regard to wages and production however, are essentially different from the expressed interest and effort of radicalism which is to increase wages and lower production, not primarily for the sake of the immediate benefit to the worker, but primarily for the harm to the industry.

In the "Revolutionary I. W. W." Grover W. Perry says:

"The preamble of the I. W. W. constitution says in part, 'By organizing *industrially,* we are forming the structure of the new society within the shell of the old' . . . *we will demand more and more wages from our employers. We will demand and enforce shorter and shorter hours. As we gain these demands we are diminishing the profits of the bosses. We are taking away his power. We are gaining that power for ourselves.*"

Mr. George Soule (joint-author, Vol. II, Interchurch Report and member staff of field investigators) in his book "The New (revolutionary) Unionism" on page 274 says:

". . . real wages can rise only by diverting a larger share of the earnings to the workers; but under the present economic régime, this process cannot go beyond a certain point without driving the employers out of business by making it impossible for them to secure further capital,"

and again on page 172—

". . . business consideration is to the new unionist only secondary . . . immediate gains (higher wages and shorter hours) are, both to the members and the leaders, a by-product derived in process of work on the main task—the preparation of the workers for actual control of production."

One of the most surprising and mystifying sections of the Interchurch Report, on first analysis, is the lengthy and elaborate arguments in regard to steel wages.

The hourly steel wage rate and weekly wage rates were

not only widely known but are published, as taken from government statistics, in the Interchurch Report's own appendix. At the time of, and for years before the strike, not only every opportunity but every inducement was given the steel workers to work full time and more than full time. All these official government figures and figures compiled by all other authorities showed plainly that all steel workers received class by class the highest wages in American industry. Even the president of the strikers' committee admitted that "of course the steel companies came up with the wages." Yet the Interchurch Report entirely fails to mention or consider all these plain, incontrovertible facts and spends page after page in arguing through false analogy, through leaving out of consideration important facts of the commonest knowledge, and through statistics that are manipulated and falsified, to the ridiculous conclusion that steel wages were not sufficient for a "minimum subsistence" and that they are "the lowest for all trades for which there are separate statistics for common labor," etc.

Only in the light of radicalism's expressed policy of constantly agitating for "more and more wages," irrespective of any possible justice in their demands as a deliberate attack on the financial solvency of the industry involved, is this whole wage argument even rational.

Again, one of the most obvious and widely criticized misleading statements in the Interchurch Report is that in regard to surpluses. A reasonable surplus, to be used as liquid capital and to stabilize business operations and wages in times of depression, is regarded by business men in general, by economists, and by all intelligent leaders of labor, not only as highly desirable, but the friends of labor in recent years have argued that it is morally incumbent on business to build up such surpluses as opportunity offers to protect the public and the workers from the necessity of too sudden readjustments in times of business depression.

In 18 years, the Steel Corporation had built up a surplus equal to about 20% of its assets, or at the rate of slightly over 1% a year. This surplus savings per year represented about 2% of total business per year. These figures show the entire reasonableness both of the size and of the rate of accumulation of this surplus. Moreover in times of past depression, when wages throughout the country were being reduced the Steel Corporation although it cut its dividends used this surplus to maintain wages and employment.

Yet without in any way even suggesting any of these facts, the Interchurch Report attempts, by utterly misleading language, to create the entirely false impression already described in detail in regard to this surplus, and to argue by insinuation that this surplus was illegitimately accumulated at the expense of the workers and ought to be wiped out by being turned over to the workers.

The whole effect of the Interchurch argument on this point is to prejudice the workers and the public, by misrepresentation, against a highly desirable policy of sound financing which, if it could be broken down, would, to just that extent, result in the accomplishment of radicalism's express purpose, of undermining the solvency of the industry.

In this connection it is to be especially noted that on page 177 the Interchurch Report, in its discussion of the causes of the failure of the steel strike, lists second: "*It* (the U. S. Steel Corp.) *had too large a cash surplus.*" Ergo, if this surplus could in some way be broken down it would be just that much easier to win "the next strike."

Again, on page 77, the Interchurch Report quotes a lengthy argument from a W. N. Polakov to the effect that when steel demand is below normal, steel prices should not include overhead on entire equipment—which of course the company has to pay—but only on that part of the equipment actually used in the sub-normal production. Again, if such a theory should be accepted by the public and government agencies, and enforced it would be most effective—to quote Mr. Soule—"in driving the employers out of business by making it impossible for them to secure further capital."

SIXTH : *With the same object of making industry unprofitable to its present owners, radicalism admittedly openly practises and encourages sabotage.*

"Sabotage," says Mr. Robert Hunter in his book which is entitled, "Violence and the Labor Movement," (page 236) is:

> "If a strike is lost and the workers return only to break the machines, spoil the products, and generally disorganize a factory, they are Saboteurs. The idea of Sabotage is that any dissatisfied workman shall undertake to break the machine in order to render the conduct of the industry unprofitable, if not actually impossible."

Sabotage, however, does not necessarily consist of violence, and the fact that public opinion and the enforcement of the laws have become much more strict against property wrecking through mere spite or grievance, has resulted in the development and propagation, by radicalism, of another type of sabotage, less sensational, but in the long run even more effective. At the Indianapolis convention of the Socialist Party Delegate Slaydon said:

> "Sabotage as it prevails today means interfering with the machinery of production without going on strike. It means to strike but stay on the payroll. It means that instead of leaving the machine, the workers will stay at the machine and turn out poor work, slow down their work, and in every other way that may be practicable, interfere with the profits of the boss."

Sabotage generally constituting a crime, is of course, not openly preached. Moreover while it has always been secretly advocated and more or less indulged in by many radicals, the American Socialist Party, during the period in which it was trying to gain influence by legitimate, political means, and in order to free itself from the stigma of its past reputation, added in 1912 Article II, Section 6 to its constitution which specifically prohibited sabotage.

In recent years, however, when all radicals have given up their attempt of seeking their aims through legitimate, majority political action and have concentrated their efforts on enforcing their aims through getting control of industry, the theory and practice of sabotage has become a leading part of their policy. As part of this general movement, the Socialist Party in its National Convention in 1917 just after America entered the war officially revoked their constitutional edict against sabotage.

There is no question that as a part of its effort to make industry unprofitable to its present owners and managers, radicalism is today encouraging, and the members of radical unions are practising at least the minor forms of sabotage with the express aim of handicapping and slowing up production on a more widespread and thorough scale than ever before.[1]

The Interchurch Report, in many sections, condemns the alleged "speeding-up" of workers. The burden of its whole argument on the subject to workers and the public is that the workers should do less work. It frequently efers by way of condemnation to the "organization of the jobs for production" or the "running of the job for production" (pages 120–121, etc.)—that "the steel industry (is) being run for the making of profits" (page 77).[2]

The Interchurch Report, however, does not directly or indirectly touch on or advance any argument that could be interpreted to specifically encourage or point toward sabotage as such.

Moreover the Report in its "Findings," published at the

[1] It is only fair to state in this connection that the Amalgamated Clothing Workers, previously mentioned herein as a leading exponent of radical unionism, two years ago partly abandoned and have seemingly in the last year entirely abandoned previous practices which resulted in large decreases in production, and are maintaining production at an agreed rate. Whether this is merely being done as a matter of present expediency, along the lines of the recent Russian Soviet compromise with its principles to gain certain immediate ends, or represents a basic change of principles can doubtless only be determined by time.

[2] In this connection it is interesting also to note that the "Report of the Findings Committee" of the Interchurch Industrial Relations

end of the Report but written by a different group of men at a different time and in general only slightly related to the Report itself, does specifically condemn labor's theory of slowing-up production and specifically demands that labor unions change their methods to encourage production on the part of the individual workers.

SEVENTH: *In order to give its workers free scope in practising sabotage and carrying out other practices to the detriment of their industry and also as a means of getting the control of their industry more and more into the hands of the workers whom it controls, radicalism continually insists on the adoption of every type of device which will take the right of disciplining or controlling the workers out of the employers' hand even to the extent of openly denying the employer the right to hire or discharge the workers.*

The Interchurch Report constantly urges as a major grievance that "control of working conditions" was in the hands of the employer—that "promotion was at pleasure of company representatives" and otherwise continually argues to the workers and the public that the present power of controlling and disciplining the workers should be taken out of the hands of the employers and placed in the hands of the workers and their representatives.

It never suggests, however, directly or indirectly that "control of the job" be taken out of the hands of the management and put into the hands of the workers for the purpose of giving the workers special power or protection to facilitate any form of sabotage.

Moreover it must be borne in mind that the whole influ-

Department as published by the Interchurch World Movement, Document "No. 187, II. 10, Nov., 1919," states:—

"III.   The present industrial system is on trial."

"VIII.   Increasing numbers of intelligent and conscientious people believe that the conflict between the principles of Jesus and an industrial system based upon competition for private profit is sharply drawn."

ence of organized labor, including that part of it which is not radical, has for various reasons sought to get much of the power to control and discipline the workers out of the hands of the employer, not at all to encourage sabotage or further any other radical aim, but merely to increase its own power as compared with that of the employer. Therefore the constant insistence of the Interchurch Report that the power to control and discipline the workers be taken out of the hands of the employer does not necessarily have any relation to radicalism. Moreover there is the definite fact that the Interchurch Report in its "Findings" specifically condemns the practice on the part of workers of deliberately slowing-up production.

On the other hand, it cannot be overlooked that one of the chief reasons why it has been so easy for radical "borers from within" organized labor to get such a hold on organized labor that Foster definitely states, and many authorities and facts bear him out, that radicalism has a dominant hold on the A. F. of L., is because radicalism has seized on many such practices which, while not established for radical ends, are so susceptible of being radically used, that radicalism has been able to turn them most effectively to its own ends.

Whether, therefore, the authors of the main section of the Interchurch Report were actuated by the same motives as the different authors of the "Findings" which definitely condemn sabotage or were actuated by different motives, the fact remains that in their insistent advocacy of taking "promotion" and "control of the job" out of the hands of the responsible management, they are advocating a system which has almost invariably resulted in the minor forms of sabotage and which, once established, radicalism is able to use as a major weapon in its attacks on industry.[1]

[1] As has already been stated, radicals in general have long been, and have been particularly in the last number of years, advocates of sabotage, which advocacy has been strong enough and general enough to force the whole Socialist Party recently to officially revoke its disapproval of sabotage.

As a matter of fact, except for Section V of the separate "Findings" which chiefly condemns organized labor's tendency to deliberately decrease production, and for certain isolated recommendations as to government regulation of the steel industry, such careful study of the entire Interchurch Report as the present analysis has been able to make not only does not reveal one single argument or conclusion, directly or indirectly incompatible with the principles of radicalism, but it has not found one single argument or conclusion which is not in entire keeping with the principles and practices of radicalism, and entirely susceptible, of being quoted and used in favor of radicalism.

Throughout, the Interchurch Report constitutes a violent attack on the steel industry which is perhaps the only great basic industry on which modern organized labor theories, including radical theories, have gained no hold; and it goes to the greatest lengths in disregarding important evidence, expurgating and twisting evidence, and manipulat-

---

But in the meantime the whole world has witnessed the conspicuous inability, first of the Russian worker to operate the factories which he had taken possession of, and then of the Italian worker to operate the factories which he temporarily seized but was soon very glad to give back to capitalist management. As a result, very recently certain members of the so-called "intelligenza" among radicals have begun to talk a great deal about a theory which they call "the assumption of responsibility for production" by the workers. The way they interpret this newly discovered theory to the workers is that the workers must begin at once to educate themselves on industrial subjects as a preparation for the seizure and operation by them of industry. To the public, they have somewhat vaguely interpreted it to mean reform as to their former theories of reducing production. The fact that the Amalgamated Clothing Workers seem to have instituted very decided reforms along this line may be a case in point.

The Interchurch Report in at least two instances, accuses the craft unions of not being willing to "assume the responsibility for production." The use of this mere vague phrase without any further explanation or argument of course does not in itself commit the Interchurch Report one way or the other as to the generally accepted radical theory of sabotage to decrease production.

ing facts and figures in order to make that attack more violent and sweeping than the worst interpretation of the real facts could possibly warrant. Moreover as part of its attack on the steel industry, and frequently in generalizations in regard to industry as a whole, it constantly attacks fundamental principles and practices of our whole modern industrial system which it is the express aim of radicalism to attack and destroy.

Although in at least certain respects, the steel industry has been generally regarded as a leader in American industrial advancement; although the present industrial system has unquestionably been a chief factor in America's growth and material prosperity, on which our social advancement has been largely based; and although an overwhelming proportion of all Americans unquestionably believe in the modern industrial system, as at least the best that is presently practicable, the Interchurch Report, as far as can be discovered, does not advance one argument or conclusion in favor either of the steel companies or of our modern industrial system.

Although there are almost inevitably two sides to any industrial dispute, the Interchurch Report without reservation or qualification argues the case of the worker whom radicalism is trying to organize in its attack on modern industry. Moreover it particularly and strongly champions, even against the American workers, the foreign worker who is most susceptible to, and forms the bulwark of radicalism in America.

Although it is wholly in favor of labor the Interchurch Report frequently criticizes openly, and constantly criticizes, indirectly and by insinuation, the elements and principles in organized labor, particularly craft unions which, as such, are incompatible with radicalism, and frequently openly, and constantly indirectly and by insinuation, argues in favor of industrial unionism, which works inevitably and directly toward radicalism.

The Interchurch Report shows an intimate knowledge

of radical theories and technical, radical phraseology and frequently uses that knowledge in arguments which, though they may seem on their face innocuous, have a very pertinent meaning to those who understand their full import. Of all those connected with the strike the Report is most openly sympathetic with Foster, the radical leader.

Radicalism, in attempting to advance its theories, has seven principal lines of attack. As regards all seven of these it has been shown in detail that the Interchurch Report strongly attacks the particular enemies that radicalism attacks—and attacks them on exactly the same grounds, and generally in exactly the same phraseology which radicalism uses.

Radicalism has certain strategic conditions and practices and relationships which it is constantly seeking to establish in industry with the express purpose of using them to special radical ends. The Interchurch Report does not, of course, argue these ends—in one case the "Findings" repudiate the logical radical end—but otherwise it argues strongly in favor of each one of these strategic conditions and practices and relationships.

From its very nature, as assuming to be an impartial investigation of a modern industry, operating under the accepted industrial system, it is obvious that, irrespective of how extreme the radicalism of its authors may be, or how essentially radical its arguments, the Interchurch Report could not carry such arguments to any openly radical conclusion. For this would unquestionably, immediately and *ipso facto* have condemned the whole Report in the eyes of the great majority of the American people, and would undoubtedly have resulted in a refusal of the Interchurch World Movement as a whole to approve and underwrite it, which approval by the Interchurch World Movement, and unsuspecting acceptance by the public, constitute the essence of the Report's whole value.

Moreover, even from the ultra-radical point of view, it is

24

entirely unnecessary that the Report should go farther than it does. For to the ultra-radical agitator who is condemning the modern industrial system on the stereotyped grounds on which radicalism seeks particularly to condemn it; or who is attacking the courts and police and public officials and Press as mere tools of the capitalist; or who is arguing with labor to form "industrial" instead of "craft" unions, or who is otherwise preaching the fundamentals of radicalism, it is entirely sufficient that he can point to this supposedly high, impartial investigation of the very conditions he is attacking, as supporting his fundamental claims and arguments from a point of view and in phraseology that perfectly supports his argument.

It is the fact that the Interchurch Report is today being used by radicals everywhere in exactly this way that was the chief incentive of the present analysis.

CHAPTER XXV

Considering then merely the Interchurch Report itself without reference to any outside facts as to its origin or authorship, it is plain and conclusive that:

First: The Interchurch Report as a whole, and in general as to its separate and detailed conclusions is based on evidence that is plainly insufficient. The "rock-bottom evidence" of the whole Report is stated by the Report itself to consist of "500 affidavits" which are chiefly from "the mass of low-skilled foreigners." Irrespective of the value of these 500 affidavits themselves, it is hardly possible under any circumstances that 500 such affidavits could constitute adequate evidence of facts as to the point of view of 500,000 workers and as to the operation of a great basic industry.

Moreover, in specific and detailed argument throughout the Report, the evidence presented is equally inadequate, repeatedly consisting merely of some one or few isolated, dramatic incidents or allegations from which the Report immediately generalizes and draws sweeping conclusions.

Second: Chiefly because of its persistence in generalizing from insufficient evidence, the Interchurch Report is repeatedly and conspicuously self-contradictory in regard to major conclusions. For instance:

It frequently repeats the statement—as one of its main arguments for the need of "Collective Bargaining"—that the workers as a matter of practice cannot take their grievances any higher than the foreman. Yet in a majority of the evidence which the Report itself later presents, consisting of affidavits of low-skilled foreign workers in regard to specific grievances, these affidavits definitely state that these workers actually did take their grievances "from the foreman to the superintendent," or "to the main office," or "to the General Superintendent," or "to the general manager."

The Interchurch Report states, as a major conclusion, that common labor worked (1919) 74 hours a week—over 12 hours a day. It states as another major conclusion that the annual wage of steel common labor for 1919 was "under $1466 a year." As a matter of simple arithmetic, based on the known and admitted wage rate, if common labor averaged over twelve hours a day, their wages were not "under $1466 a year," but between $1700 and $1800 a year, or else common labor worked only 249 days a year which would entirely contradict the whole Interchurch argument that the industry was "speeded up in every direction"— that the workers only got a Sunday off once in 6 months, etc.

The Interchurch Report spends a major part of Chapter II arguing to the conclusion that the steel strike was not "plotted or led by reds or syndicalists or Bolshevists"— that it did not seek to "overthrow established leaders and established institutions of organized labor." Chapter VI, however, is devoted mainly to showing in detail that the whole unionization and strike movement was planned by, and its most important leader was, a man who has himself admitted in writing, both before and since the strike, that he was an ultra-radical working in general, and in the steel strike in particular, towards overthrowing what are at least the expressed present aims of organized labor, and he specifically refers to the steel strike as an example of the degree to which they are being overthrown. Moreover the authors of the Interchurch Report state plainly in this Chapter VI that they were entirely and in detail familiar with his point of view and his aims; in which chapter it is also stated that circumstances at the time of the steel strike and in general are forcing all organized labor from its present theories of "craft" unionism to the "industrial" or radical unionism for which they admit Mr. Foster is working. Moreover in this same later chapter the Interchurch Report specifically states that the two principal "psychological factors" which influenced the big majority of the "unskilled foreigners" in the strike—and it is plainly admitted that in general the unskilled foreigners were the backbone of the strike—were such radical motives as that the workers had got control of the Russian government; that they had or were about to get control of the British government; that they expected as a result of the strike that "Mr. Wilson was going to run the steel mills," etc.

On page 95 the Report states that the steel companies, in their efforts to force workers to over-exertion, made each wage raise just enough to meet the increased cost of living, yet, in a footnote on page 97, it states that earnings had gone up 150% during a period in which it is a matter of official record that the increased cost of living had gone up only half that much.

Other of the most important major conclusions and many minor conclusions throughout the Report are similarly irreconcilably contradictory.

Third: The Interchurch Report is openly and wholly an *ex parte* argument. The statement in the beginning of the Report that the scope of the inquiry was chiefly among the "mass of low-skilled foreigners," and that "the statements and affidavits of 500 (such) steel workers constituted the rock-bottom of the findings," and the repeated statements that the Interchurch Report investigators received little support or evidence from the Steel Companies constitute palpable admissions of the *ex parte* nature of the whole Report. Such admissions, however, are entirely superfluous. *The authors of the Interchurch Report had available all the evidence presented in the present analysis.* They obviously, however, not only made no effort to seek out evidence except on one side but they deliberately omitted to consider the most widely known and official facts—even facts which often form an integral part of the evidence the Report does use—whenever these facts are in any way favorable to the steel companies.

In its entire discussion of wages, the Interchurch Report attempts to prove the contrary without once mentioning the existence of the official government figures and other authoritative studies which show plainly and specifically that steel wages are by far the highest in industry, even though some of these figures are found buried away in the Appendix of the Report itself.

The whole weight of evidence in the Senate Investigation was against the strike, as both Foster and the Interchurch Report tacitly admit by their repeated condemnation of the Senate Investigation. The Interchurch Report quotes frequently and voluminously from the Senate Investigation. Yet not only does it not quote any Senate evidence whatever that is in the least favorable to the steel companies, but in the unfavorable evidence which it does quote, it carefully expurgates any statements or remarks that are favorable to the companies' side and quotes only that part which is favorable to the workers' side.

For instance in Chapter III the Interchurch Report quotes on page 67, in an expurgated form, the testimony of Mr. Colson before the Senate committee (for . complete Colson testimony see Report of Senate Hearings, Part II, pages 728 to 735). Mr. Colson's complaint was that while he had a good job before the war with the steel company at 17½c an hour, and while he got 44c an hour when he came back, he had to wait five months for his job and then only got a disagreeable and dangerous job. The Interchurch Report's expurgated quotation from this testimony entirely leaves out the fact which Mr. Colson inadvertently let slip and then was forced to explain completely under cross-examination that, as a matter of fact, Mr. Colson, though only a common laborer, was given a good, semi-skilled job on a crane immediately after he came back from the war, but was discharged because he deliberately refused to keep up steam and therefore had to go back to common labor work.

Again on page 143 the Interchurch Report quotes *almost all* the Senate testimony of striker Frank Smith, an un-naturalized Hungarian, who said he was not naturalized because "I have never stayed long enough in one place; stayed long enough to get my papers." Mr. Smith received $4.73 for a *ten hour day* which he said he could not live on because of his large family of seven. (For complete Smith testimony see Report of Senate Hearings, Part II, pages 526–527.) The Interchurch Report quotes all the part against the steel company, but carefully leaves out the following:

> *The Chairman:* "Are there any other causes that led you to strike except the lack of money?"
> *Mr. Smith:* "Well, my conditions are all right. I can say nothing about the conditions. My conditions are all right; and I would gladly do it; and I would gladly keep the work if I could make a living. The conditions I was satisfied with."

The Interchurch Report also carefully leaves out the fact that this man, who said that his wages were not enough to support his family of seven, testified that he had bought liberty bonds, contributed to the Red Cross and the Y. M. C. A. and appeared so well dressed that it caused one of the Senators to comment on the fact, and that he himself explained that he dressed well out of his savings. The Interchurch Report also carefully leaves out the following:

> *The Chairman:* "Do you work on Sundays?"
> *Mr. Smith:* "Well, not so much."

Fourth: The Interchurch Report continually resorts to insinuations and to misleading language to create impressions about facts which it fails to state openly or argue on their merits.

On page 14, line 1 and elsewhere the Interchurch Report makes, merely in passing, the ambiguous criticism that "increases in wages during the war in no case were at a sacrifice of stockholders' dividends." As a matter of fact, wages were increased more than dividends. (See page 68.)

On page 11, line 25 and repeatedly elsewhere the Interchurch Report makes the criticism that "Promotion was at pleasure of the company representatives" but it fails to state whether it would recommend that the men themselves elect their bosses, or vote for promotion on the basis of popularity, or put promotion on the basis of seniority without regard for efficiency, as the strike leaders demanded, or what substitute it would offer for a practice that is common and basic in all American industry.

Again in the midst of its discussion of steel wages and grievances (page 95), the Interchurch Report goes into a bitter denunciation of the speeding-up system which continually "shaves rates," paying less and less in order to make the men work harder and harder, creating the impression—though it is careful not to state it—that this is an evil of the steel industry. As a matter of fact all steel workers work on a fixed wage and only a small class of the highest paid are affected by bonuses which they get in addition to their regular wages, for extra efficiency. In the same way, the Report bitterly denounces, in such connection and language as to *seem* to condemn the steel industry certain other industrial practices which may or may not exist in other industries but which certainly do not exist in, and have no relation to, the steel industry.

Many other statements which create entirely false impressions have already been emphasized. Reference has also already been made to the repeated use of misleading phraseology. In referring to the class of steel workers who actually work 7 or 8 hours a day—40 to 48 hours a week—the Interchurch Report always refers to them as workers "who work *under 60 hours a week*." On page 198 it uses the magniloquent phrase "among the Atlantic industrial nations," obviously to give the impression of many nations when actually it refers only to Great Britain; etc., etc., etc. Misleading is the mildest term that can be used in regard to the phraseology of the Interchurch Report concerning surpluses; the phraseology used being particularly calculated to create an entirely false impression that the Steel Corporation had accumulated in each of several years a surplus which as a matter of fact took 18 years to accumulate.

Misleading is also the mildest term which can be applied to the Interchurch Report's complaint of the lack of statistics in regard to steel hazards—to its whole argument that strikers' meetings did not result in violence on the cleverly worded quibble that the violence did not occur in the meeting—and to many other of its arguments and statements throughout.

Fifth: In regard to its major conclusions, in so far as they are susceptible of being arrived at on a basis of definite fact —which includes those in regard to the most important subjects of wages, profits, hazards, the number of 12-hour workers, the nature of 12-hour work, the attitude of the companies toward the men, etc.—it has been shown specifically and in detail that the conclusions of the Interchurch Report are the opposite of the provable truth.

In regard to other major issues in the steel strike, such as the attitude of the steel workers towards their alleged grievances, toward trade union collective bargaining, in regard to the number of workers who actually struck, in regard to radicalism in the strike movement, etc., which issues, because they largely involve facts as to the opinions and points of view of large numbers of men and other complex facts or complicated circumstances, must be arrived at by a careful determination of the *weight of evidence*, it has been shown specifically and in detail that the strong weight of real evidence, which is seldom even considered by the Interchurch Report, clearly shows that the conclusions which the Interchurch Report assumes to reach are in general unwarranted and often definitely untrue.

As regards the broader general social aspects involved in the steel controversy, it has been shown specifically and in detail that the Interchurch Report in almost every case entirely begs the question by merely assuming one point of view and building on that assumption without discussing or even mentioning many vital facts on which the opposite point of view is based, or even considering the existence or legitimate possibility of other points of view, which as a matter of fact are widely and soundly held.

Sixth: It is obvious from the foregoing that the Interchurch Report is not, as it specifically assumes to be, and as the fact that it is signed by the Interchurch World Movement gives the impression that it should be, an impartial investigation or argument on the merits of the case, but that on the contrary it is a self-evidently inaccurate, self-contradictory and blatantly *ex parte* argument and as such not a safe textbook even for those who desire to agree with its conclusions.

Seventh: But the Interchurch Report cannot be regarded merely as an over-zealous *ex parte* argument for it reaches its conclusions, which it itself frequently admits are the opposite of those held by American public opinion in general, not only through the faulty arguments and questionable methods already emphasized but repeatedly through means that are utterly indefensible on any grounds.

A. The Interchurch Report advances, as has been pointed out, three arguments as to steel wages. The first of these self-evidently contradicts or is contradicted by its whole 12-hour argument. The second fails to consider one of the most important economic facts and one of the most commonly known facts in American industrial life. The third argument which assumes to compare hourly wage rates in different trades is built around a table on page 102 which assumes to compare common labor wage rates in coal mining and building trades with those in steel. This table is grossly manipulated and falsified:—(1) in that while its own quoted authorities plainly show 22 industries, trades or occupations for which there are separate statistics for common labor, this Interchurch table states that the three trades given are the only trades "for which there are separate statistics for laborers; (2) in that, while all of these trades show far lower weekly or daily earnings than steel, and 19 of them show also lower hourly earnings, yet ignoring these 19 and featuring only the special two, the Interchurch Report makes in italics the absolutely false statement that "steel common labor has the *lowest rate of pay* of the trades for which there are separate statistics for laborers." In order further to bolster up this absolutely false conclusion, the Interchurch Report further falsifies this table by (3) adding in semi-skilled labor in the building trades as common labor, and (4) adding in exactly the same semi-skilled labor twice and counting all other classifications of common labor only once (See pages 40 to 47, present analysis).

B. The entire 341 pages of Volume IV of Senate Document 110, to which the Interchurch Report frequently otherwise refers, is devoted to an elaborate statistical study of steel hazards. The Interchurch Report elsewhere refers to an obscure sentence on page 189 of the Senate Hearings, on the opposite facing page to which appears a conspicuous detailed table of insurance statistics in regard to steel hazards. The Interchurch Report refers to the U. S. Bureau of Labor Bulletin for October, 1919, more frequently than to any other document. The most conspicuous section of this document is devoted to an elaborate study of steel hazards. At least two other government studies of steel hazards are also available. All these government studies with all their conspicuous tables and charts plainly show and specifically state a conclusion in regard to steel hazards which is the opposite of the whole argument and conclusion of the Interchurch Report. In connection with one such study, however (October, 1919), there is one special table which plainly states that it represents only a special 37.8% of all industrial accidents and plainly states that it is used to show percentage of compensation, not of accidents. Yet, while specifically complaining about a lack of statistics, the Interchurch Report, ignoring all these elaborate government studies of steel hazards, including the one in connection with which its own table appears, takes this one table, expurgates all the figures in regard to the percentage of compensation, leaves out the plain statement as to what this table actually represents, and then so introduces and features this expurgated table as to make it seem to bolster up a conclusion which is the opposite of the truth (See pages 146 to 155, present analysis).

C. In its "12-hour" chapter, in discussing steel working hours, the Interchurch Report consistently refers to the great groups of 7, 8, and 9 hour workers with the entirely misleading phrase, workers who "can work under 60 hours a week." It uses as the basis of all its argument throughout the chapter, figures which it calls "for 1919" and "October, 1919" and otherwise represents as substantially normal, but which are plainly stated in their original source, and attention called to the fact that they are chiefly for December, 1918, and January, 1919, the first two months after the war. Beyond this the Interchurch Report bases its whole sensational case about the 7-day week chiefly on a somewhat lengthy quotation on page 72 from page 17 of the U. S. Bureau of Labor Bulletin 218 and states both before and after this quotation a conclusion which is the opposite of what the U. S. Bureau of Labor itself twice plainly states these figures actually to mean. Moreover, the Interchurch Report's quotation, though given as continuous, is plainly shown by reference to the original to be a handpicking of this Bureau of Labor evidence, paragraph by paragraph, from which the Interchurch Report publishes only the figures or statements which it can thus misinterpret and entirely leaves out the intervening figures or statements which are so plain that they cannot be thus misconstrued (See pages 84 to 85, present analysis).

D. To support its last and seemingly most damning arraignment of the 12-hour day, the Interchurch Report undertakes to show that steel hours have "tended to lengthen over a decade" and that the number of 12-hour workers is constantly increasing. This utterly false conclusion, it attempts to bolster up, partly by representing the December, 1918–January, 1919, figures as for the year 1919 and as for normal, and comparing these with other government figures for 1910 and 1914. Particularly on pages 54, 56, 71 and 72, the Interchurch Report quotes a variety of tables from U. S. Bureau of Labor records but in each case especially rearranges or rewords these tables and especially divides them up to compare 1910 and 1919, and 1914 and 1919 but never 1910 and 1914. It then carefully separates these manipulated comparisons by so many intervening pages or buries them under such complicated rewordings that their meaning which is entirely plain in their normal chronological sequence seems on casual reading of these carefully manipulated rearrangements to be the opposite, and then the Interchurch Report states and emphasizes that this manipulated rearrangement does show the opposite of the real facts which these tables in their normal order plainly show.

In this same connection the Interchurch Report prints certain figures which it specifically states are from U. S. Bureau of Labor, October, 1919, Monthly Review. One group of these figures show on their face they are false because they contradict each other. When the other group is compared with U. S. Bureau of Labor figures from which it is stated to be taken, it is found that the figures are utterly different from the original government figures—that they allege to show almost the opposite of what the original government figures plainly show—that they are so wholly different that no possible "weighting" or possible mathematical error, or error of copying or computing from the original, can reconcile them with the actual government figures—that as far as being what they are stated to be is concerned, they are made out of whole cloth to support an equally false argument—(see pages 93 to 107 present analysis).

Moreover, in each of these cases and others, the manipulation and falsification is so skilfully done as to just what is left out and just what is put in, as to just how the arrangement is made, the conclusions sought to be shown are so cleverly led up to or heightened by the context, and this manipulation and falsification is so repeated in regard to statistics in such widely different fields, that it is impossible to explain these or other similar cases on the grounds of coincidence or accident.

Eighth: The publication of its second volume, including one considerable group of its "500 rock-bottom affidavits" shows that this fundamental evidence on which the Interchurch Report itself states that it is based is, at least as far as there is any basis for judging or checking it, as manipulated and falsified as the foregoing "statistics."

The Interchurch Report begins the section in which it presents these "rock-bottom affidavits" by citing as evidence of "police brutalities" Father Kazinki's sensational statements, which were widely used as strike propaganda, alleging an "assault by state troopers upon his people as they were coming out of church" and "the charging by mounted troopers upon little children as they were assembled in the schoolyard" and does this without any explanation of or reference to the fact that Father Kazinki himself, under oath and cross-examination, had publicly repudiated all the material parts of these statements.

The Interchurch Report itself admits that these "rock-bottom affidavits" were not in general composed or phrased by the men who signed them with their names or marks. It states that they were largely composed and phrased by its own investigators or by James R. Maurer, President of the Pennsylvania Federation of Labor. Mr. Maurer is a conspicuous radical who signed himself in now-published correspondence with the Russian Soviet as "representing 300 radical groups in 42 states." Of the 41 "rock-bottom affidavits" published, over 30 show dates before the Interchurch investigation began and therefore must have been secured by Mr. Maurer.

Although from the very nature of the case, police court or other records of the facts alleged in many of these affidavits must necessarily have existed, the Interchurch Report makes no mention of having examined into any such other evidence, but publishes only these complaints of the alleged victims of police brutality or judicial discrimination unsupported, or in a few cases supported by other strikers or strike leaders.

Although at most these affidavits self-evidently tell only a small part and only one side of the story, many of them do not even make any direct allegation at all but consist solely of vivid description and exclamations, cleverly worded to give an impression of fact which obviously whoever is actually responsible for such affidavits was unwilling to swear to as facts. Throughout, these "affidavits" consist far more of vivid, emotional and plainly propaganda description than of specific allegation, their phraseology, the points they make and the way they make them being not only strikingly similar to each other but strikingly parallel to stock propaganda, for which purpose they are known to have been originally used by Mr. Maurer. The fact, therefore, that they were largely composed and written by Maurer or his assistants and merely signed by the name, or frequently the mark, of a man or woman who couldn't read or write English, is correspondingly significant.

Moreover Governor Sproul, to whom these Maurer "affidavits" were originally submitted, investigated the most striking allegations and found them to be utterly without foundation. Some of them were also gone into again by the Senate Committee. But except in one immaterial case, the Interchurch Report does not mention this. It does, however, publish one such "affidavit." It signs it P. F. Grogan. This "affidavit" goes into the most harrowing details about drunk or crazy troopers firing volley after volley into fleeing crowds of helpless strikers, their wives and babies. It follows a reiteration by the Interchurch Report itself of charges of "men and women murdered," "hundreds wounded." It is followed by another "affidavit" which ends with the exclamation: "There was no provocation for said riding over women and children." Before the Senate Committee this same P. F. *Grogan*, who there gave his name as *Brogan*[1] attempted to give the same description of the brutal and indiscriminate shooting and riding down of helpless men, women and children, but under cross-examination was forced to admit and reiterate that no one was hit as far as he knew, and except for one woman whose hand was hurt, no one was injured. Yet 8 months later, the Interchurch Report published as the chief of its "rock-bottom evidence" of "hundreds wounded" the original propaganda statement of Mr. Brogan—without mentioning the fact that he was a strike organizer and a Secretary of the American Federation of Labor, without mentioning the fact that under oath and cross-examination he had repudiated all the sensational and material part of this statement, and also leaving out the first half of the name of the town where the incident occurred, and changing the first letter of Mr. Brogan's name so that this repudiation cannot be referred to through the index of either the Interchurch Report or the Senate Hearings (See Chapter XXII, present analysis).

Ninth: The lengths to which the Interchurch Report thus constantly goes to support its *ex parte* argument naturally raises the question as to just where that *ex parte* argument leads.

That it is in favor of the workers,. and particularly the unskilled foreign workers, and their demands, is of course obvious, but it is also obvious that the Interchurch Report argument constantly goes much further than this and it is conspicuous that at least certain parts of the Report argue to certain theories and conclusions which are generally regarded as radical.

Following this lead, a careful comparison between the

[1] Foster also gives his name as Brogan; see Great Steel Strike, page 59.

seven chief aims to which the Socialist, Communist, Syndicalist and other radical groups are in common committed, with the principal arguments of the Interchurch Report, shows that—in the attacks and the kind of attacks it makes on certain specific forces of law and order,—in the type of labor organization it specifically favors—in both the quantity and quality of its argument on free speech—in the phraseology in which it words these attacks and advances these theories—and otherwise, the Interchurch Report exactly parallels official manifestos of the Communist Party and other official ultra-radical propaganda documents. Moreover with this fact established, an examination of the whole Report shows clearly that many of its arguments and conclusions are entirely incompatible with the operation of the whole modern industrial system, while, except for one conclusion in the separate "Findings," not only is no argument in the Report incompatible with radical theories and aims but all its principal arguments in regard to wages, surplus, control of industry, labor unions, social consequences are, at least as far as they go, exactly parallel to the fundamental arguments of radicalism, entirely and particularly susceptible of being quoted and used in favor of radicalism, and are as a matter of fact being so quoted and used by radicals in all parts of the country today.

* * * * * * *

If the Interchurch Report on the Steel Strike had been published by any ordinary author, or had been presented by any ordinary investigating committee the document itself would have had to stand or fall on its own merits. Even though it had used the original device, which the Interchurch Report uses, of stating its most important conclusions in the beginning of the book and arguing them later, still under ordinary conditions, those conclusions would have had little weight until the argument on which they were based had been carefully analyzed. In other words, under ordinary circumstances, the authorship of a report is

25

entirely secondary to the merits of the report itself, and under such circumstances, such an analysis as the present—if it had seemed necessary at all—could have stopped at the present point.

The Interchurch Report on the Steel Strike, however, was not presented by any ordinary author or any ordinary investigating committee. It is stated in its title to be the work of a great nation-wide Christian organization. It is specifically signed by eight men[1] and one woman of national standing in the Christian world. Moreover it states that it was "unanimously adopted" and approved by the Executive Committee of the Interchurch World Movement, a body largely made up of men whose great prominence in our national religious life has made their integrity and high-mindedness unquestioned.

These facts obviously make the question of the actual authorship of the Interchurch Report of paramount importance. For if such a document as the Interchurch Report under analysis clearly proves itself to be could have been actually prepared and presented with full knowledge of its contents to American Christians as an adequate treatise on a great economic problem by such prominent Christian leaders as the men whose names are specifically signed to it —if such a document could have been knowingly, "unanimously approved" by the Executive Committee of the Interchurch World Movement as an expression of the Protestant Church's official point of view toward modern economic problems, that fact is far more significant than the Report itself to the whole American public.

[1] Also by Mr. Heber Blankenhorn as Secretary to the Commission.

PART TWO

HISTORY OF THE INTERCHURCH REPORT ON THE STEEL
STRIKE

*Facts and circumstances which led up to the Interchurch
World Movement Investigation of the Steel Strike, including a
chronological statement as to the principal resolutions, author-
izations, and findings upon which committees were appointed
or acted; as to the personnel of committees and other bodies that
assisted toward or in the investigation; together with a brief
history of the investigation and the composition and authorization of the Report.*

CONTENTS OF PART TWO

INTRODUCTION TO PART TWO

THE Interchurch Report on the Steel Strike is a published document. Its conclusions and the alleged facts, figures and other evidence on which these conclusions are based are matters of definite record. As such they can be definitely analyzed and compared point by point in detail with other facts and figures and evidence and with the original sources from which they themselves were taken.

Conclusions as to the merits of the Interchurch Report, therefore, in no way depend on any facts as to its origin. Whatever circumstances led up to its preparation and whoever were its authors cannot change the facts already presented as to the Report itself. These facts as to the merits of the Report, on the other hand, are themselves so conclusive as to the quality of its authorship that they inevitably raise the question as to whether it is possible that the conspicuous Christian leaders who signed the Interchurch Report could have been its actual authors.

The question of the actual authorship of the Interchurch Report has been frequently raised. The New York Legislative Investigation of Radicalism states definitely that the inquiry on which the Interchurch Report is based was under the direction of certain well-known radicals. But it does not go beyond this mere statement.

Part II of the present analysis, therefore, is devoted to an effort to present as clearly and definitely as possible all the facts available as to the origin, preparation and actual authorship of this Report.

The facts surrounding the preparation of the Interchurch Report are chiefly *not* matter of printed or even written record. Many of them can only be gathered from statements of men, often with different points of view. These men were all officially connected with the Interchurch Movement and had personal knowledge of the facts they state. But detailed recollection and interpretation of facts two years after their occurrence, while often the best evidence available is obviously not infallible. Certain conclusions must be qualified accordingly.

In addition to certain documentary evidence, the facts and information presented in Part II have, except as otherwise stated, been acquired through personal interviews with the gentlemen who are given as authority for each particular fact or statement when it is presented. Written memoranda of the substance of each conversation were made by the author immediately after such interviews. What is herein stated on the authority of such individuals has with the two exceptions noted, in each case been submitted in its present form to such individual for correction, and includes any such corrections as have been made.

CHAPTER I

ORGANIZATION AND PERSONNEL OF THE DEPARTMENT OF
INDUSTRIAL RELATIONS WHICH ORIGINATED THE
STEEL STRIKE INVESTIGATION

THE year 1919, during which the Interchurch World Movement was organized, was a period in which more new big questions—political, social, economic, and religious—were being agitated and pressed than at perhaps any other time in our own, if not in world, history.

The League of Nations, Women's Suffrage, Prohibition, the Plumb Plan for government ownership of the railroads, were merely typical of a great number of plans and theories and ideas which were being urged upon a nation which, with many of its former ideals and systems uprooted by the war, was honestly questioning whether or not there might be better ideals and systems before it decided to return to its old ones.

Again in the consideration of economic or political or religious or any other broadly human problems, it is inevitable that there should be widely divergent opinions as to the ends to be sought, the means to those ends, and the methods by which those means should be pursued—in short, that in such fields of thought or endeavor there should be radicals and liberals, progressives and conservatives.

Moreover in any period of such general questions and questionings as that which immediately followed the war, it is inevitable that a disproportionately large number of men's minds should be influenced by the spirit of the times to a tendency to a more extreme point of view than they would normally hold.

Finally it must be borne in mind that whereas the man of conservative or moderate views is generally interested and occupied chiefly along some line of normal work, it is characteristic of the man with extreme or radical views that he is most actively interested and engaged in furthering his views.

All these particular facts must be taken into account in any attempt to analyze any of the activities of the Interchurch World Movement which was itself a great new effort, typical of the period, to find new ways to accelerate the spiritual and idealistic progress of the whole world.

From the beginning of the Interchurch World sessions a certain faction had strongly and consistently urged, as one means of broadening the churches' influence, a much more definite and concrete appeal to the laboring classes as such. Part of this group also strongly urged that the churches should seek to make their influence felt in the great industrial problems of the day.

In July, 1919, a certain organization within the Catholic Church made a general public announcement of a policy which undoubtedly materially influenced the formation by the (Protestant) Interchurch World Movement of its Industrial Relations Department[1] whose principal activity was the investigation of the Steel Strike.

Mr. Tyler Dennett, Chief of Publicity of the Interchurch World Movement—and through his long business relationship with Mr. G. Earl Taylor, General Secretary of the or-

[1] "This is inaccurate, the first step towards an Industrial Relations Department was taken at a general committee meeting in Cleveland May 2nd, 1919. Formation of the department came as a matter of course, and it was partly in existence before the Catholic Report became public."   J. E. C.

"Craig's note is correct. Nevertheless there is no doubt that the Catholic manifesto served as a great stimulus to the I. W. M.'s industrial activities."   S. W.

ganization, as well as because of his own position, in intimate touch with its activities—in his book, *A Better World* (page 75, lines 18–32), in referring to the influence of this announcement of the Catholic Church, says:

"Nor can we overlook the fact that the Roman Catholic Church in the United States, through the National Catholic War Council, has gone on record for *a form of social ownership of the means of production which is far* more explicit and *more in line with the democratic movement of the age in industry* than many a Protestant denomination can claim,"

and he specifically quotes—

"Nevertheless the full possibility of increased production will not be realized as long as the majority of the workers remain mere wage earners. *The majority must somehow become owners*, or at least in part, *of the instruments of production.*"

After the appearance of this announcement by a faction of the other religious body of the country, the Interchurch faction which had long urged that policy now insisted that the Interchurch World Movement should extend its influence and activities into the industrial field and that it should particularly interest itself in the human problems of labor. Less than a month later the Executive Committee of the Interchurch World Movement created the Industrial Relations Department whose general executive offices, according to the Interchurch official handbook, Part III, page 117, were:

Dr. (Now Bishop) Fred B. Fisher, Director.

Doubtless partly because of his eulogy of Bishop McConnell as a "radical Bishop" and his frequent similar use of the word "radical" at the time of the Interchurch World Movement activities, certain of Dr. Fisher's more conservative associates in the movement have characterized him as radical or leaning towards radicalism. A study of Dr. Fisher's published works, however, hardly seem to justify such a conclusion. Two of his three most prominent works, *Garments of Power, A Pathway for Mystics*, and *Gifts from the Desert* show his strong trend of thought towards what is known philosophically as "mysticism." "Mysticism," according to *Century Dictionary*, is:

"A form of religious belief which is founded upon spiritual experience *not discriminated* or *tested and systematized* in thought. Rationalism regards the *reason* as the highest faculty of man; mysticism on the other hand declares that spiritual truth cannot be comprehended by the *logical* faculty."

This rather than any actual radical point of view seems to be characteristic of Dr. Fisher's type of thinking.

In another volume entitled, *Ways to Win*, Dr. Fisher strongly advocates the entrance of local religious organizations as such into politics and particularly advocates that local ministers attempt to make themselves arbitrators in strikes and other industrial and social controversies and attempt to use the influence of the church to force an acceptance of such arbitration. Such theories may be questioned as to their practicability or soundness but they are hardly radical in the commonly accepted sense of the term.[1]

Mr. Robert W. Bruere, Superintendent Research Division.

Mr. Bruere is a graduate of Washington University, St. Louis, and was for a time a special student at the University of Berlin. He was a prominent member of the Intercollegiate Socialistic Society. He has long been associated with the Rand School of Social Science, where he has been a lecturer on American Literature. Mr. Bruere has also been conspicuously associated with other extreme radical

---

[1] "I should call Fisher an 'instinctive radical.' His first impulse on any question would be to the radical point of view. This would be apt to be modified later whenever he really sat down to think the thing out But his snap judgement on any matter would almost certainly be radical."   S. W.

"Fisher is a mystic in the same sense that practically all Methodists are mystics. An element of it is inseparable from the creed. Personally Fisher is one of the least mystical of all high Methodist clergymen."

J. E. C.

movements.   He has published several articles over his own name in the *New Republic* defending the I. W. W. and two particularly radical articles in the *Nation* of February 21 and 28, 1918.   When Mr. William D. Heywood and other members of the I. W. W. were being tried by the government for conspiracy to urge and assist the evasion of the draft laws and particularly for assisting 10,000 drafted men to evade, for which they were convicted and are now serving prison sentences or are fugitives from justice, Mr. Bruere was conspicuously active in raising a defense fund for them, even going to the extent of signing his name to an advertisement applying for such funds published in the *New Republic*, June 22, 1918.   Mr. Bruere was one of the founders and is the director of the Bureau of Industrial Research, which organization the Interchurch Report states furnished the "technical assistance" and part of the "evidence" and the direction of the "staff of investigators" on which "assistance" and "evidence" the Report as analyzed in part one of the present volumes was based.

Moreover there is no question that many of the leading officials of the Interchurch Movement knew these facts as to Mr. Bruere's activities and points of view.   During the time the question of whether the Steel Strike Report should or should not be published was being discussed by Interchurch officials several members of the National Civic Federation (of which, Mr. Samuel Gompers is vice-president —indicating at least that this organization was not working in the interests of the Steel Corporation) brought Mr. Bruere's conspicuous radical record particularly to the attention of various such Interchurch officials.   They were emphasized again in a special conference held between Mr. Ralph M. Easley of the Civic Federation and members of the Interchurch Commission of Investigation which had direct charge of the Steel Strike investigation and Report. Finally several weeks later (July 10, 1920) Mr. Easley wrote one of these members in part as follows:—

"We also at our interview discussed Mr. Robert W. Bruere, of whom you spoke in the highest terms, saying, in effect, that, if you were going to organize any big industrial movement, he would be the first man to whom you would go for advice.

"From your enthusiastic endorsement of that gentleman, I assume that you are not thoroughly conversant with his keen sympathy and association with that disloyal band of cut-throats, the Industrial Workers of the World, or with his efforts to raise a defense fund of $50,000 to fight the United States in the trial of these men at Chicago for treasonable and seditious conduct, for which conduct, in spite of the money raised by Mr. Bruere, they were convicted and sent to jail. Also, I cannot believe that you have read his notorious I. W. W. defense, 'On the trail of the I. W. W.,' written for Oswald Garrison Villard, that equally notorious pro-German pacifist and warm defender of all radical movements. . . .

"As you doubtless know, *The New York Call* is an official organ of the Socialist Party and enjoys the distinction of being denied the use of the mails by our government because of its peculiar seditious character. . . .   As recently as July 4, *The New York Call* announced a series of articles by Robert Bruere in the following language:

"'This is the first of a series of articles by Robert W. Bruere, which will appear weekly in *The Call* hereafter.

"'Bruere is a publicist of international repute. His impartial analysis of the I. W. W., published during the war in a local paper, was generously recognized as a notable contribution to the literature of labor in this country. Bruere is now connected with the Bureau of Industrial Research in this city, and has been added to the staff of special writers of the Federated Press, whose services *The Call* presents exclusively in New York.'"

In the index to Part I (page 38) of the New York State Legislative Investigation on Radicalism appears the following:

Bruere, Robert W.

Mr. Bruere's official position and title as printed in the official handbook of the Interchurch World Movement is "*Superintendent of the Research Division of the Industrial Relations Department.*" Thus he and Dr. Fisher occupied the two most important executive positions in the department which originated the investigation of the steel strike, and under whose authority the investigation was conducted.

Entirely in addition, however, to the fact that these men were at the head of this department, the very fact that radicalism's chief interest today is in the industrial field made it inevitable that not only whatever radical elements there were within the Interchurch Movement itself but that radical influences in genenal should concentrate their attention on this phase of Interchurch activity. As a matter of fact this department rapidly became the center of a coterie of radicals and near-radicals whose influence, and the danger of that influence to the Interchurch Movement, soon became a subject of such comment and concern that Mr. Raymond Robins—certainly himself far from a conservative—made the strongest representations to Interchurch officials in regard to this danger to the Industrial Department and the Movement.   Mr. Tyler Dennett also strongly urged in a memorandum to Dr. S. Earl Taylor the creation of a special "Department of Intellectual Resources" partly for the purpose of offsetting this obvious tendency of the Industrial Department.

CHAPTER II

THE resolution whose adoption led to the Interchurch World Movement's Investigation of the Steel Strike was presented by Mr. John M. Glenn, director of the Russell Sage Foundation, and a sound and able sociologist, at a meeting called by the Industrial Relations Department of the Interchurch World Movement and held in Hotel Pennsylvania, New York City, October 3, 1919.

It was the expressed intention of the Industrial Relations Department that the gathering at this meeting, which was to consider industrial questions, should be representative of employer and labor and public interest. Invitations to the meeting were sent out with this end in view. An unfortunately large number, however, of business men who were invited to represent the employer interest, and of the more prominent conservative men invited to represent the public interest, did not find time to attend or attended only part of the long session. As a matter of fact, therefore, the meeting actually consisted of a preponderance of representatives of labor interest and of the less conservative representatives of public interest. This fact, irrespective of any definite plan on the part of the Industrial Relations Committee, naturally and inevitably influenced the proceedings at the meeting.

Before Mr. Glenn's motion the Steel Strike had been the subject of vigorous debate. Speeches had been made, depicting in vigorous terms the alleged horrors and injustices of the strike, and condemning the United States Steel Corporation for its general policies and especially its refusal to institute the proposed "collective bargaining." A resolution was being offered which included the demand that the steel strike be investigated and reported on with the apparent thought that it would be promptly condemned. At this point Dr. Jeremiah Jenks, Research Professor of Government and Public Administration of New York University, who had been sitting in the meeting as an invited representative of public interest, was leaving the hall. Realizing, however, the spirit of the resolution just offered and the obvious belief of the man presenting it that such an investigation could be made and a verdict returned in a few hours or days, Dr. Jenks paused at the back of the hall, and when it appeared that the resolution of this nature was actually about to be put to a vote, he obtained recognition from the Chairman and stated that from his own experience he was convinced that any adequate investigation of such a widespread social movement as the steel strike would require an appropriation of many thousands of dollars, an adequate force of experts and at least six months' time. Dr. Jenks further stated that if any casual investigation were made or any snap judgment passed the good faith of the whole Interchurch World Movement would be subject to question and the success of the movement itself jeopardized.

The proposer of the former motion immediately replied that in his opinion "it didn't require either much money or time for such a body of men to decide a moral issue such as was represented in the Steel Strike," and he repeated his motion, that included both an investigation of the Steel Strike and a condemnation of the steel companies.[1]

It was at this point that Mr. Glenn, the Director of the Russell Sage Foundation, offered the formal resolution that

[1] This statement has been carefully reviewed by Dr. Jenks and much of it is in his own phraseology.

the meeting should authorize, and a special committee be appointed to conduct, an investigation of the steel strike. This resolution was put to a *viva voce* vote by Bishop McConnell, chairman of the meeting, and declared unanimously adopted.

The resolution itself was according to Mr. Glenn's best recollection substantially as follows:

"The Industrial Relations Conference recommends that a committee be appointed by the Executive Committee of the Interchurch World Movement to investigate the Steel Strike and other current industrial disturbances from the standpoint of the moral and ethical principles involved."[1]

In the Interchurch World Report on the Steel Strike (page 6, lines 8–11) it is stated that "The Conference *rejected* a resolution condemning one party to the strike for refusing to adopt the principle of collective bargaining." As a matter of fact, however, a resolution condemning the steel companies for not accepting collective bargaining had been presented before Mr. Glenn's motion and had been put to a vote and declared by the chairman to be unanimously carried. The result was that the meeting at this point was officially on record as condemning the steel companies in advance on the major issue of the steel strike which was about to be investigated.

Mr. John H. Walker, President of the Illinois Federation of Labor, however, immediately arose and pointed out that in view of the fact that the meeting had now adopted a resolution to investigate the steel strike, this previous resolution condemning one party in advance before the investigation might tend to prejudice public opinion as to the fairness and impartiality of the investigation. He, therefore, moved that the resolution condemning the companies

[1] This meeting also appointed a special "Findings Committee" to draft statements and definitions of these "moral and ethical principles." The report of this Committee is referred to later.

in advance be rescinded and stricken from the minutes. This resolution was put to a vote and carried.[1]

The remainder of the meeting was largely taken up by an extended explanation by Mr. Glenn E. Plumb of the "Plumb Plan" for government ownership of the railroads. At the end of Mr. Plumb's discussion, a resolution was offered and numerously seconded that the meeting declare in favor of the Plumb Plan for government ownership of the railroads. The chairman, however, ruled to refer this resolution to a special committee. Many objections were made to this ruling which insisted that the resolution be put to a vote, but the chairman ruled such objectors out of order.

In considering these facts, however, it must be carefully borne in mind that the particular composition of this meeting was not principally the fault of the Industrial Relations Department and certainly not of the Interchurch World Movement, but was due chiefly to the fact that many of the invited representatives of other interests were not present. It must be borne in mind also that the officers of the meeting were only able in a limited way, even if they wished, to control the actions of the meeting.

On the other hand no honest inquiry into conditions sur-

[1] Mr. Went and Mr. Reynolds state that there is no question about this fact and it was their particular official duty to keep in the closest touch with what went on at this meeting. Mr. Went states that this fact was plainly emphasized in his notes on the meeting and that he and Reynolds talked this point over in detail immediately after the meeting. Mr. Bronson Batchelor entirely corroborates Mr. Went on this. When the point was first taken up with Mr. Reynolds, he refused to commit himself at all until he knew exactly how his statement was to be used. After he had read the entire present analysis, he fully confirmed Mr. Went's and Mr. Batchelor's statement. He stated that before the meeting he had been asked to take special charge of the publicity work of the Industrial Relations Department but that after the Hotel Pennsylvania meeting and particularly because of the way the resolution first to condemn the steel companies and then to investigate the steel strike was handled, he immediately went to Dr. Fisher, discussed the subject with him and resigned his connection. Because of his great

rounding the acts and results of this meeting can pass by
certain further facts for which the officers of the Industrial
Relations Department were entirely responsible.

The spirit and actions of any meeting are naturally very
largely influenced by the speakers at the meeting and particular speakers for any given meeting are as a matter of
course chosen with this in view. Who the principal
speakers were at the Hotel Pennsylvania meeting was entirely in the hands of the Industrial Relations Department.
In addition to Mr. Plumb who spoke for government ownership of the railroads, the principal speakers were:

Mr. Julius Hecker.

Mr. Hecker was during part of the war a Y. M. C. A.
worker in Europe. But after a full hearing when he was
given every opportunity to clear himself, his passports were
cancelled by the State Department and the Y. M. C. A.
ordered to recall him and the Department refused him the
use of an American passport for further travel abroad during the war because of his pro-Bolshevistic activities.

Mr. Hecker said at a weekly conference of the clergy of
the Methodist Church held at 150 Fifth Avenue, June 7,
1919:

"There are a good many folks and some Methodist ministers who
oppose Bolshevism because they do not know anything about it. . . .

---

interest, however, in the success of the movement as a whole, he accepted the position of Superintendent of the Religious Press Division.

In regard to the official connection of these gentlemen with the Hotel
Pennsylvania Conference, Mr. Craig says:

"Tyler Dennett was in personal charge. Reynolds was in charge of
publicity material for the religious press. Craig (he himself) was in charge
of preparation of immediate copy for the daily press. Went, Reynolds
and others handled the running report from the conference room.
Chiquoine handled material for the Press Associations (A.P., etc.) No one
of these except perhaps Dennett could have complete personal knowledge
of all that happened, but Went and Reynolds probably had more than
the others. Batchelor had no official connection whatever with the
publicity department at the time. If he was there, it was as a
spectator."

We in the United States are *not yet* prepared for Bolshevism and therefore we will be obliged to handle *our revolution* in a different manner . . . But that it (our revolution) is coming there is no doubt."

This quotation is typical not only of Mr. Hecker's speech at this meeting as it was quoted and analyzed in the *National Civic Federation Review*, July 10, 1920, but was typical of the ideas for which by all his words and acts Mr. Hecker conspicuously stood.

In the index of the New York Legislative Investigation on Radicalism under the name Hecker, Dr. Julius F., appears "Methodist and Revolutionary Socialist, pages 1137–1138."

John Walker, President of the Illinois Federation of Labor.

Mr. Walker's closest official associate was Mr. John Fitzpatrick, chairman of the special committee which organized and conducted the Steel Strike.

Mr. Frederick C. Howe.

Mr. Howe was former Commissioner of Immigration at the port of New York. After wide newspaper criticism because of his unauthorized releasing of radicals held for deportation by the Department of Justice, and a Congressional investigation after which he was bitterly condemned on the floor of the House by members of both parties for neglect of duty and extreme radical activity and a resolution offered to withhold his salary he resigned. (See Record of the 66th Congress, pages 1522, 1523.)

Mr. Howe is also a correspondent of the Federated Press which will be described later and he is also listed as a well-known radical by the New York Legislative Report on Radicalism.[1]

[1] "There were also one or two mildly conservative speakers; I forget their names but it might be well to mention them."   S. W.

"Give full list of invited speakers."   J. W. J.

"Why not give a full list of makers of such speeches?"   H. C. R.

None of these gentlemen however could furnish such a list and the author has been unable to obtain it elsewhere.

These opinions and acts of all these speakers were conspicuous and widely known and could not but have been known to the Department of Industrial Relations when it invited them to speak before the Hotel Pennsylvania meeting. They were of course known to Mr. Robert W. Bruere, "Superintendent of Research" of this Department.

However, the steel strike investigation was not in the hands of this meeting; nor was the committee to investigate the steel strike appointed by this meeting.

To what extent if any, therefore, the type of speakers who were officially chosen to address this meeting and the actions and the spirit of this meeting itself can be regarded as being significant remains to be determined in relation with other facts as to the investigation and the Report.

In addition to passing the resolution to investigate the steel strike the Hotel Pennsylvania meeting also appointed a special "Findings Committee" which was to draft a statement as to the "Moral Principles Involved in Industrial Relations." After a very extensive debate and the coöperation of other committees, a set of "Findings" was presented and accepted by this meeting. The seemingly radical nature of many sections of these "Findings" which, though in vague terms, condemn the present industrial system, and recommend various notorious radical panaceas, created the widest discussion in the meeting and in the newspapers at the time. Dr. Jenks, however, who was called into consultation by this "Findings Committee" says that the members of the Committee themselves did not interpret certain sections of these Findings as many others interpreted them and as they are at least plainly capable of being interpreted. Mr. Craig and Mr. Went both strongly emphasize that no such committee could, as these "Findings" assume to do, officially commit the Interchurch World Movement. The fact, however, that these "Findings," in a somewhat modified form, were later published over the official imprint of the Interchurch World Movement as Pamphlet No. 178 II, 10 November, 1919, and are extensively reproduced on page 44A of the official handbook of the Interchurch World Movement is admitted by Mr. Craig to be an official "ratification of them in fact if not precisely in law."

On page 332, Volume II, the Interchurch Report in discussing the authorization of its attempted mediation with Judge Gary, quotes:

"The Findings Committee recommends to the Industrial Relations Department . . . that it make careful and thoroughgoing investigation of the strikes in the steel industry . . . likewise that the Department be requested . . . to use their offices in trying to bring about a joint conference and a settlement of this dispute by mutual agreement."

This certainly indicates that the actual Commissioners of Investigation of the Steel Strike considered that they held a direct mandate from the Hotel Pennsylvania meeting and its "Findings Committee."

CHAPTER III

THE SPECIAL "COMMISSION OF INQUIRY" WHICH INVESTI-GATED AND REPORTED ON THE STEEL STRIKE

IMMEDIATELY after the Hotel Pennsylvania meeting at which the resolution to investigate the steel strike was adopted, there was appointed by the Executive Committee of the Interchurch World Movement a special "Commission of Inquiry" which was to have direct charge of investigating the steel strike and preparing the Strike Report.

The fact that this special "Commission of Inquiry" thus had direct charge of the Steel Strike Investigation and the writing of the Steel Report and that they signed the report as members of the Commission and as individuals undoubtedly makes it most pertinent to inquire closely into its personnel.

Facts and quotations carefully verified which tend to show the fundamental point of view of each member of this commission are summarized herewith in connection with the name of each commissioner.

The point already emphasized, however, must be carefully borne in mind, that facts in regard to the personal point of view of the investigators can only be regarded as of problematical value and can have no real weight except in connection with facts as to other dominant influences in the investigation and preparation of the report.

"The Commission of Inquiry" consisted of:

Bishop Francis J. McConnell (Methodist), *Chairman.*
Bishop McConnell when introduced before the Hotel Pennsylvania meeting by Dr. (now Bishop) Fred B. Fisher, Director of the Industrial Relations Department, was referred to as "that strange combination, a radical Bishop."
In Bishop McConnell's address to that meeting, he is quoted in the *Christian Advocate* (November 13, 1919) report on his speech as *saying,*

"Whatever we do, we must keep alive in the church the spirit of prophetic radicalism . . . a man had better say 1000 wild things and get some good truth uttered, etc."

In connection with which statement the *Advocate* said:

"'To say a thousand wild things in order to get some good truth uttered' will seem to most people an entirely inadequate justification of the liberty of prophesying which the agitators now so copiously enjoy."

These quotations are in no sense chosen for emphasis because of the appearance of the word "radical" but because they briefly epitomize the whole spirit of his speech as summarized and commented on in an official publication of his own denomination. Moreover, many of Bishop McConnell's fellow-workers, all officially connected with the Interchurch World Movement and all of them ostensibly friendly to him, speak of his point of view in terms, the mildest of which are that he is "extremely liberal" or that he is "one of our most extreme thinkers."
Bishop McConnell's strong leaning towards radicalism is, moreover, quite plain from a study of his own published works.
His chapter on "Individualism" in his book, *Theology and Public Opinion* (1920) makes it clear that he does not wholly accept the basic philosophy of socialism.   In a number of sections in his book, *Democratic Christianity*, he defends Socialism from the charge of being basical atheistic and refers to those who support the present "capitalistic" system as opponents.   He does not declare plainly in favor

of socialism and states that socialism will have to be "Americanized" before it can become acceptable to America, but these chapters leave no doubt that he is at least a very "Near" socialist.

He concludes this discussion with the statement (page 54) that:

"In the march towards the larger democracy the church is more likely to sympathize with such movements as the British Labor Party."

It will be remembered also that the Interchurch Report points frequently to labor conditions abroad as an example to American industry.

The general principles of the British labor party are, of course, well known.

This party strongly supported the striking British coal miners who declared that if the government did not yield to their demands they would destroy the British coal mines and ruin the country with themselves, and whose official leaders openly stated: "If we go down to defeat the Nation will go with us."

Although this party has recently, after its investigation commission visited Russia, repudiated Sovietism as developed under Lenine, it had previously strongly supported Russian Sovietism and still definitely maintains socialistic views of only a slightly milder character.

In fact Foster spends pages 263, 264 and 265 of *The Great Steel Strike* in showing that the British Trade Union Movement, of which the British Labor Party is merely the political manifestation, is a model to the whole radical world of effective radicalism.

Bishop McConnell who holds and recommends such principles to the American Protestant Church was not only the chairman of the Commission of Investigation of the Steel Strike but by common consent its most influential member.

Dr. McConnell has recently been transferred from

Denver and made Bishop of the Pittsburgh district which includes the great industrial section of western Pennsylvania.

Dr. Daniel A. Poling (United Evangelical), *Vice-Chairman*

Dr. Poling is associate president of the International Society of Christian Endeavor and evening preacher at the Marble Collegiate Church on Upper Fifth Avenue, New York City. In addition to his membership on the Commission, Dr. Poling was a member of the General Committee of the Interchurch World Movement. Dr. Poling had been formerly regarded as a "Moderate" in his economic views, but after Dr. Fisher retired and he became active head of the Industrial Department it is generally stated that he seemed to become entirely committed to the point of view and policies represented by Robert W. Bruere and his Bureau of Industrial Research group.

Mr. George W. Coleman (Baptist).

Mr. Coleman is head of the Open Forum in Boston and has long been one of those who most strongly advocated that the Church should make a more definite and special appeal to the laboring classes. Mr. Coleman himself, in a speech before the Congregational Club of Worcester (Mass.) on March 14, 1921, said:

"To me one of *the most significant facts in this strike as a man interested in the church* . . . what a burden it has been upon me many a time to find everywhere the working man's organization looking upon the church as prejudicial to his interests, when I know what was in the hearts of the ministers. That is the attitude for years which labor has had toward the church. When I was called to New York to attend a special meeting of the steel strike commission, to listen to Mr. Fitzpatrick, one of the leaders of the strike, I was amazed when I got to the office of the Interchurch Commission, to have that man sit down and tell us the message he brought from 24 International Unions. The majority of the strikers were men of the Greek and Roman Catholic Churches, and Mr. Fitzpatrick himself was a devout Roman Catholic; yet he came representing all those men in their great struggle when everything they valued in life was at stake, they came to a body of

Protestant Churchmen and said through this representative of theirs, 'Gentlemen, I am commissioned in behalf of the strikers to put our case in your hands without any limitation or reservation.' . . . I said, This is a Blessed day I have come to see, when a great body of strikers have come to have enough confidence in a body of churchmen to trust us to do the right thing."

Dr. Nicholas Van Der Pyl (Congregationalist).

Dr. Van Der Pyl's views on economic and social questions do not appear to be a matter of printed record.

Dr. Alva W. Taylor (Disciple) is stated by a close associate to be a liberal in his theological views but a moderate in his views on economic questions.

Dr. John McDowell (Presbyterian).

Dr. McDowell is a preacher of the Evangelical type of vital appeal and power.   He is a strong admirer of Dwight L. Moody, the great American Evangelist of the last generation, and has written an effective appreciation of Mr. Moody's life and work.   Dr. McDowell in his own statement of his economic and social point of view, made expressly for the present analysis, said:

"I read my Christianity into my economics, not my economics into my Christianity.   The Social question as I see it from the Christian point of view is not one of system, it is one of spirit.   It is not a question of method but of motive.   The primary need therefore of the Social world and the industrial world is the Christian spirit in all human relations."

As to radicalism he said:

"I welcome to this country any man who wants to enjoy our freedom and our opportunities.   I should make it possible for him to know our ideals and our institutions.   But if such a man after entering our land and having the opportunity of knowing our ideals and institutions as embodied in our Constitution persists in denying our ideals and defying our institutions, I am in favor of deporting him at once.   We must make every individual in this land understand that this is a government of law and lawful processes."

Mrs. Fred Smith Bennett, Chairman of the Home Missions Council, Presbyterian Church.

Advisory Members.

"Those who did not take active part on the Investigation but signed the Report after examination of the evidence."

Bishop Melvin Bell.

Bishop Charles D. Williams (Episcopal).

Bishop Williams has been generally spoken of as the most definitely radical member of the Commission of Inquiry. Statements from his sermons have been frequently widely quoted in the newspapers as extremely radical. He made statements in a sermon in St. John's Cathedral in the spring of 1921 which were not only emphasized by the newspapers as extremely radical but which the present Bishop of New York felt it necessary to repudiate in a public statement the following Sunday as not representative of the attitude of the Episcopal Church.

For these reasons particular attention has been given to the economic point of view of Bishop Williams and a large number of his public sermons and writings have been carefully reviewed. In a sermon delivered a number of years ago on the subject, *The Gospel of Democracy* in which he particularly stated at length his point of view in regard to modern economic subjects, and in several other sermons, Bishop Williams made such statements as the following:

"That class consciousness hinders every effort for better things." Yet class consciousness is the very foundation of all radicalism.

"Socialism would fix every particle immovable in one dead level," he states and adds: "I cherish no fool's vision of an impossible society wherein everybody shall stand upon one absolute dead level of dreary uniformity." This constitutes a definite condemnation of a basic doctrine of socialism.

Under the heading, "What is the duty and obligation of the working man?" Bishop Williams says:

"Do you ever use the vast power which your (labor) organization gives you ruthlessly, lawlessly, tyrannously, simply to advance your own interests at the expense of right and justice? . . . Do you . . . skimp your job, do dishonest or slovenly work, when the eye of the foreman is not directly upon you, or when the demand for labor, in times of prosperity is so great that you are reasonably sure of your job? . . . Do you do efficient service only when the difficulty of getting and keeping a job makes it particularly prudent to make a good record? If so then you are just as much a sinner against the Christian ideal of society as the robber baron on Wall Street."

Certainly inefficiency of production, as widely practised by labor and indirect sabotage as practised by radicals, could hardly be more vigorously condemned.

Bishop Williams bitterly condemns the "idle rich" and the "four hundred" but equally sternly condemns the "half-baked, ill-trained enthusiast or fanatic," which he goes on to describe in terms which make his reference to average radicals entirely clear. He condemns "industrial parasites" and "idle holders of privilege" but continues:

"(society) could not for a moment do without its producers whether they are . . . *captains of industry* or horny-handed toilers."

On the other hand through a period of years Bishop Williams has been denouncing our whole industrial system, not merely for its incidental failures or weaknesses which most right-minded men see and which the wise leaders of industry itself have long been making serious efforts to correct, but as a system that is in itself "manifestly unjust and intolerable," whose chief characteristic as Bishop Williams seems to see it is that the wealth produced by the workers is "largely absorbed by a lot of social parasites."

Formerly Bishop Williams states that he was a Single Taxer and the basis on which he would inherently change the modern industrial system was doubtless the theories of Henry George.

In more recent speeches and sermons as they have been publicly quoted, Bishop Williams seems to have become even more convinced of the inherent and basic injustice and wrongness of our whole industrial system and demands that that system be changed by the "democratization of industry." He said in a sermon in Grace Church, New York City, on July 20, 1920:

"We have gone through all the stages of owner and slave, lord and serf, employer and employees. The next step is a co-partnership consisting of employer, employee and the public, the public coming in to regulate both and see that justice is done and that the consumer does not suffer."

Whether or not this statement is radical depends on the definition of the terms he uses—and he does not define them. Judge Gary himself has encouraged 100,000 of his employees to buy stock in their company and thus become co-partners in the steel industry; and he has at least several times referred to such stockholding employees as "partners in the industry." Also Judge Gary, the year previous to this sermon of Bishop Williams, publicly stated his belief that the public, through a special governmental commission, should regulate both the employer and employee in order to see that justice is done to all.

In this same sermon Bishop Williams bitterly denounces Bolshevism as "the enemy of democracy."

Bishop Williams may have the same point of view as all radicals in his overemphasis of the weakness of the modern industrial system and his failure to realize that many of those weaknesses are due not to the system but to inherent weaknesses in average human nature. Unquestionably he is also entirely unfair, and uninformed, when he insists continually on laying most of the troubles of industry to the "social parasites," "the idle holders of privilege" and "the reactionaries" which he seems to feel are the type of men who are largely in control of American industry today. The frequent expression of such a point of view in immoderate language, doubtless often sounds like radicalism—may, according to the definition put on his terms, border on radicalism, and coming from such an able religious leader is undoubtedly grist to the mills of radicalism. But no one who fairly analyzes Bishop Williams' chief public utterances, including his definite strong denunciations of socialism, and Bolshevism—the strongest condemnation of class consciousness, sabotage, of loafing on the job, and of using labor's organized power for selfish class interest—can fairly classify Bishop Williams as an economic "radical" as that term is used and meant today.

Bishop Williams' extreme and doubtless unwarranted prejudice against what he calls the "reactionaryism of the employer class" and his belief in the *inherent* injustice and wrongness of our modern industrial system may very possibly have prejudiced his point of view in the investigation of the steel strike. But his expressed views as a whole clearly indicate that he would not knowingly approve the economic theories which are actually, though covertly, advanced by the Report on the Steel Strike and it is inconceivable that he should knowingly approve the types and methods of many arguments there used to advance those theories.

CHAPTER IV

THE Interchurch Report begins its Foreword by stating:

"This volume presents the summary of industrial facts *as drawn from all data before the Commission and adopted as the Report of the Commission. . . .*"

"Another volume will be required for the supporting reports and exhibits by the staff of field investigators: George Soule, David Saposs, Miss Marian D. Savage, M. Carl Wisehart, and Robert Littell. Heber Blankernhorn had charge of the Field work and *later acted as Secretary to the Commission.*"

On page 6 it says:

"Those parts of the evidence obtained directly by the Commission were secured through personal observation and through Open Hearings held in Pittsburg in November, supplemented by inspection trips in Western Pennsylvania, Ohio, Indiana, and Illinois. More technical and detailed data were obtained by a staff of investigators working under a field director *from the Bureau of Industrial Research of New York.* Other evidence was obtained directly by the Bureau of Industrial Research, by the Bureau of Applied Economics in Washington, by a firm of consulting engineers (unnamed) and by various other organizations and technical experts (unnamed) working under the direction of the Commission."

In its Foreword to Volume II the Interchurch Report says:

"The field investigation lasted from the second week in October, 1919, to the first of February, 1920. . . . In January, February and March

27   417

the Commission from its own records *and the investigators' reports formulated* the Report on the steel strike. . . .

"This second volume is the work of the *investigators* first submitted to the Commission *during the investigation*, then resubmitted for revision to the members of the Commission from December, 1920 to May, 1921 and ordered printed as accepted with the introductory notes of the Secretary as Editor. Primary responsibility for the present Report (second Volume) rests with the signing investigators; *the Commission holds itself responsible for the use made of these reports in preparing the Steel Report* (1st Vol.). . . .

". . . As in the case of the first volume the supplementary reports were made with the technical assistance of the Bureau of Industrial Research. To members of the Bureau the Commission is further indebted for seeing this Volume through the press."

The Interchurch Report on the Steel Strike then was *"formulated"* by the Commission from its own records *and the investigators' reports.* It is "the summary of industrial facts *as drawn from all data before the Commission. The Commission holds itself responsible for the use made of these reports in preparing the Steel Report."* This all plainly indicates the degree to which the Interchurch Report is based on the work of these "outside field investigators and technical assistants."

Again, "those parts of the evidence secured directly by the Commission were obtained through open hearings *in November"* and "by inspection trips in western Pennsylvania, Ohio, Indiana and Illinois."

The Interchurch Report itself states that the Commission began "formulating the Report in January." The Commission was engaged at least from November 27th to December 5th in attempting to mediate with Judge Gary and the Commission seems to have been in touch with Judge Gary for at least a week after this. The Commission or its members are otherwise mentioned as being especially occupied in other various ways during this period. In other words while the Field Investigations are specifically stated to have lasted from October till February, the Interchurch Commission itself merely held open hearings in November

—for about two weeks. It is plain, therefore, that the great bulk of the data on which the Interchurch Report was based was gathered by the outside Field Investigators.

The Interchurch Report itself says (page 9): "The statements and affidavits of 500 steel workers carefully compared and tested, *constitute the rock bottom of the findings.*"

Ten of these statements and affidavits appear on pages 213 to 218 of the Interchurch Report. They are the only group appearing in the main volume. The dates range from February to August, 1919, from two to nine months before the Interchurch investigation was even proposed.

Forty-one such statements and affidavits are reproduced on pages 179 to 219 of Volume II. These are, except for a few isolated statements all the "rock bottom statements and affidavits" which appear in this volume. Of these 41, 16 are affidavits and 25 unsworn statements. Of the 16 affidavits, 9 show notary's dates of October 3d or earlier—before the Interchurch investigation was even proposed. The other 7 affidavits all show notary's dates of October 11th or earlier—before the first Interchurch investigator was sent into the field.

Of the 25 unsworn statements—which, however, the Interchurch Report itself continually refers to as "affidavits" —11 show dates of September 30th or earlier—before the Interchurch investigation was proposed, and 4 show dates of October 8th or 9th—before the first Interchurch investigator was sent into the field.   Ten statements, however, show dates of October 17th to November 11th, during which time "the staff of field investigators" was in the field. But of these 10 only 3—numbers 27, 28 and 38 in the order they are published—show dates after November 1st when the Interchurch Commission itself went into the field. Two of these statements are especially emphasized to have been made to "Commissioner Coleman."

Of the "500 rock bottom" affidavits and statements then, on which the Interchurch Report states it is based, as far as they are published, these 3 are all which the Inter-

Four statements not *three* bear dates later than Nov. 1st.

church Commissioners themselves could have been in any way directly responsible for. All the actual affidavits published and all the other statements were either collected by the outside investigators or came through some other source. As a matter of fact, as already explained, they were practically all borrowed from the propaganda affidavits and statements previously collected by or for James H. Maurer, the notorious radical labor leader who signed himself to the Soviet authorities as "representing 300 radical groups in 42 states."

Again of the most important chapters of the Interchurch Report itself, those in regard to hours and wages consist largely of "statistics" or are built largely on "statistics" and similar "technical data"; and as the chapters on "Bolshevism" and "Organizing for Conference" show the most intimate technical knowledge of radicalism, labor politics and similar highly specialized information, it must be presumed under the circumstances that the basis for all these chapters was largely furnished by these outside "technical assistants." As to the chapter on "Social Consequences" considerable portions consist of long verbatim quotations from sections of the 2nd Volume which are specifically signed by these outside investigators. In other words, aside from the Introduction and Conclusion, and possibly one chapter, the whole Interchurch Report seems from the very nature of the case to be chiefly based on the contributions of the outside "investigators" and "technical experts."

The New York Legislative Investigation of Radicalism specifically credits the Interchurch Report to these outside assistants. The Continent, the leading Presbyterian denominational periodical, credits the whole document to the outside "technical assistants" and says that to call it a Church investigation "was and is preposterous."

When the strike leaders, according to Mr. Foster in his Great Steel Strike (page 157), became so impressed by the scientific methods manifested by the Interchurch Investigation that they decided to have the Interchurch Movement try to mediate the strike with Judge Gary, Mr. Foster states that the arrangements were made, not with the Commissioners but with Mr. Blankenhorn. The Interchurch Mediation Committee's report back to the strike leaders after the attempt at mediation is signed by Mr. Blankenhorn. Moreover throughout the many references variously made by the strike leaders to the Interchurch Investigation, such references were almost invariably made to members of the outside body of assistants rather than to the Commissioners of Inquiry.

In other words all the evidence—that in the Interchurch Report itself, as well as that from outside sources,—points so conclusively to the fact that these outside investigators and "technical experts" played such an important, if not leading, part in the preparation of the Interchurch Report on the Steel Strike—the further evidence yet to be considered shows that they played such a dominant part in the preparation of the Interchurch Report—that it is correspondingly important to inquire in detail as to just who and what these outside "investigators" and "technical experts" were.

The "staff of field investigators" is stated in the Introduction to the Interchurch Report to have consisted of:

Mr. George Soule.

In its Foreword to Volume II, on page v, the Interchurch Report says:

"George Soule, Editor and writer on industrial research for many publications; author of War Department Report on Industrial Service Section of Ordinance Department; co-author with J. M. Budish of *The New Unionism.*"

This statement by the Interchurch Report, however, fails to indicate the nature of Mr. Soule's interest in "industrial research," or the type of the "many publications" for which he has been editor and contributor, or the lines along which he has written.   It does not suggest that his book, *The New Unionism*, which has already been extensively quoted in the present Analysis is a glorification of the Amalgamated Clothing Workers and their new type of radical unionism to which the Third International of Moscow has recently turned over the leadership in the American radical movement.   It gives no hint that Mr. Soule's writings consist almost exclusively of radical propaganda, often of the most open and pronounced kind.   Mr. Soule's periodical contributions for 1920—the year the Interchurch Report was written and published—were, as far as they can be discovered, in full as follows:

(1.) "LIBERAL TACTICS AGAIN." *New Republic, March 3, 1920.* This is an impassioned appeal, in the form of a letter to the public, in which Mr. Soule in addition to insisting that—

"There is no solution of the Railroad problem but something like the Plumb plan.   There is no solution of the coal problem but nationalization of the mines,"

urges votes for the Farmer-Labor party.

(2.) "THE RAILWAY MEN GET ACTION." *Nation, April 24, 1920*—which ends as follows:

"Disillusionment with *political action* (i.e., the need for industrial action), sudden, unheralded *general strikes*, industrial and interindustrial coöperation (i.e., the radical One Big Union), secret organization along Soviet lines, suspicion and hostility toward the organs of the Bourgeoise (i.e., government), 'proletarian discipline' (i.e., police)— these things characterize the movement of the workers the world over . . . they are the logical result of the situation in which the workers (i.e., 'transport workers of New York') have found themselves."

(3.) "THE CASE AGAINST INJUNCTIONS." *Nation, May 1, 1920*—is an emphasis of the workers' need of, and a glorification of, radical industrial unionism, as represented by the Amalgamated Clothing Workers, of which he says:

> "The Amalgamated is avowedly a *socialist* union and will not conceal the fact that it aspires to the elimination of the control of the private owner over industry"

—and which he again refers to as:

> ". . . the Amalgamated which represents the most advanced and successful union practice, not only in its relation with the employers but in its *attitude toward industrial problems* (which is expressly syndicalist, and) its constructive, *socialist* philosophy."

(4.) "THE TRANSPORTATION BREAKDOWN." *Nation, July 3, 1920*—which constitutes an appeal to the railroad workers against A. F. of L. craft unionism and in favor of industrial unionism like that of the Amalgamated Clothing Workers, which are specifically held up as an example.

(5.) "THE GREAT WOOLEN STRIKE." *Nation, Augus 14, 1920*—which ends with an attack on the present industrial system and particularly the wage system. This is the mildest article in the group.

(6.) "THE BUILDING SCANDAL." *Nation, November 17, 1920*. Beginning with a very justifiable attack on Brindellism, this article makes a strong appeal to the workers for "union democracy" like that of the "men's clothing workers" (i.e., the Amalgamated Clothing Workers). It denounces "private profits and private control" of the building industry, which Mr. Soule insists should be *state controlled*, without profits, and emphasizes that this platform has already been recommended by the local Farmer-Labor Party.

(7.) "LABOR'S IMPENDING BATTLE." *New Republic, November 17, 1920*. This is throughout a stirring appeal to labor to organize *industrially*, again holding up the Amalgamated Clothing Workers as an example, and also offering as

an example to American workers the "*industrially organized*
National Union of Railwaymen of Great Britain*," which it
will be remembered Foster in his *Great Steel Strike* holds up
as an example to American radicals.

These 1920 articles are also typical of Mr. Soule's
magazine contributions for 1919, 1921 and 1922.

The New York Legislative Investigation of Radicalism
speaks (page 1138) of

"George Soule, whose radical viewpoint may be gathered from (his)
association with Mr. Evans Clark under the direction of Ludwig C. A.
K. Martens, Head of the Soviet Bureau in the United States, (his) connection also with the Rand School of Social Science and certain revolutionary labor organizations."

After spending thirty pages presenting copies of letters,
propaganda documents and other various appeals to American workmen made through various American radical
organizations or periodicals by the Russian Soviet, and presenting detailed proof that Ludwig C. A. K. Martens was
the official Soviet representative through whom that propaganda was being put out, the New York Legislative Inves-
gation of Radicalism, on page 655, names the personnel of
this Soviet Propaganda Bureau in part as follows:

". . . Boris Leonidovitch, Tagueeff Rousttam Bek, Ella Tuch,
Rose Holland, Henrietta Meerowich, Rose Byers, Vladimir Olchovsky,
Evans Clark. . . ."

shortly after which appears the statement:

"In dealing with the subject, the Committee has found it necessary
to withhold from the report much of the evidence which has come into
its hands for the reason that it may be necessary to employ it in criminal
prosecution."

For at least the last year, Mr. George Soule and Mr.
Evans Clark have occupied the same office, Room 710,
1 Union Square, New York City, where they are both now
"Directors" of an organization known as the Labor Bureau.

On the back page of the April 9, 1921 issue of the New York *Call*, an official radical publication—of which incidentally Mr. Evans Clark is Labor Editor—appears a three-column article by Mrs. George Soule, known in radical Circles as Esther Norton, which contains the following:

"Magon, Debs, Haywood and hundreds of others gave up their liberty. They did it for us. It is our fight. What will we do to carry it on? . . .

"We can delay no longer. We can be satisfied with half-hearted attempts no longer. Now is the time for every worker to prove his sincerity to the labor movement by doing all in his power to help get the political prisoners, the class-war prisoners out of jail.

"Whatever your group, I. W. W., A. F. of L., Amalgamated, Communist, Socialist, Farmer-Labor, Left Wing, Right Wing, Center or Advance Guard—whatever you call yourself, get into line."

Mr. David J. Saposs.

The Foreword, Volume II, Interchurch Report, page v, says:

"David J. Saposs, Research Assistant to Professor John R. Commons co-author with Commons and Associates of History of Labor in the United States; special investigator U. S. Commission on Industrial Relations; Expert Bureau of Statistics New York State Department of, Labor; Industrial Investigator Carnegie Corporation Americanization study."

The New York Legislative Investigation of Radicalism lists Mr. Saposs as a "radical connected with steel strike investigation by Interchurch Movement"—"associated with Ludwig C. A. K. Martens, Russian Soviet representative to America; associated with Rand School."

Mr. Saposs' name also appears on the Bulletin Board at Number 1 Union Square as occupying Room 710 with Mr. Evans Clark and Mr. George Soule. It is understood that he represents their "Labor Bureau" in Chicago.

Mr. Saposs has been—whether he is now or not is not known—educational director of the Amalgamated Clothing Workers,[1] of which Committee Mr. William Z. Foster is an

[1] This committee is understood to be technically a separate organization from the A. C. W. Union.

official lecturer.   Mr. Saposs is also one of the incorporators of the radical magazine, *The Socialist Review.*

In the first November, 1919 issue of the *Survey* is an article by Mr. Saposs eulogizing both Mr. Foster and Mr. Fitzpatrick, the two chief steel strike leaders, in the highest terms and going into the special technical organization of the strike itself. Articles for this issue are due in the editor's hands three days before the appearance of the magazine (or about October 30th), at which time Mr. Saposs had been in the field about two weeks as an "impartial" investigator of the Steel Strike. His article, therefore, wholly sympathetic and partial to one side, was probably written just when he was beginning his "impartial" investigation. If it was, on the other hand, written before this, this fact lends color to a widely alleged fact, namely, that Mr. Saposs was an active worker on the side of the steel strikers till called upon to help investigate the steel strike.

Miss Marian D. Savage.

Miss Savage is a teacher of English literature at Wellesley College.

Mr. M. Karl Wisehart.

Mr. Wisehart has been a writer of fiction and popular articles on novel phases of science for the *American Magazine* and the *Century Magazine;* which magazines, in contrast to others mentioned in this chapter, are unquestionably thoroughly American.

Mr. Robert Littell.

Mr. Robert Littell who was employed to assist in obtaining the "more technical and detailed data" for the steel strike investigation in 1919 was a member of the Class of 1918 at Harvard College. At the end of the steel strike investigation, Mr. Littell became associated with his father in the editorial department of the *New Republic.*

Mr. Heber Blankenhorn.

On page 4 of its Foreword the Second Volume of the Interchurch Report says:

"The Commission was particularly fortunate in its Secretary, Heber Blankenhorn, member of the Bureau of Industrial Research, formerly Captain U. S. A. attached to the General Staff at Washington; then at general headquarters of the A. E. F. in France; later attached to the Peace Commission. He had charge of the Field investigation and investigators."

During the war, Mr. Blankenhorn was "Captain, Military Intelligence Department," which department had charge of spy and propaganda activities. Mr. Blankenhorn's own work was creating and directing propaganda to the German soldiers and working classes. It was well known, of course, that the Socialist revolution was at that time making strong headway in Germany, and in so far as they could further this movement, the Allied Intelligence Departments would assist in breaking down German's military spirit and power. Mr. Blankenhorn's associate in his propaganda work was Mr. Walter Lippman of the *New Republic*. Mr. Blankenhorn's work during the war was, from all accounts, most efficient and fully justified his reputation as a most clever and effective propagandist. The plan, for instance, which is generally credited to him personally, of sending tickets in immense numbers over the German lines by balloons, which tickets guaranteed to each German soldier who kept and presented one when he was captured, food and kind treatment, was widely spoken of as one of the cleverest "stunts" in its subtle psychological appeal of all such allied propaganda efforts.

In regard to Lippman's work before going to France the anarchist, Roger Baldwin, wrote Manley Hudson (New York Legislative Investigation of Radicalism, page 1087):

"Lippman and Frankfurter are of course out of that particular job now [war office] and I have to depend entirely on Keppel."

Just after this Mr. Baldwin was sent to prison for a year for personally carrying out the principles of his "anti-draft" propaganda in connection with which work he had been, according to himself, depending on Lippman and Frankfurter. Mr. Blankenhorn both before and after this had been closely associated with Roger Baldwin and his work. As a matter of fact, since the Interchurch Investigation Mr Blankenhorn has been most of his time working under Mr. Baldwin's co-worker, Louis P. Lochner, in an organization which is largely an offshoot of Mr. Baldwin's main radical activity.

After Mr. Baldwin's release from prison, he reorganized (as outlined in Chapter XXIV of the present Analysis and the New York Legislative Investigation of Radicalism, Chapters VII, VIII and IX, and pages 1979 to 1999) his wartime radical activities into a "propaganda organization" known as the American Civil Liberties Union, to work "chiefly in coöperation with labor unions and radical political groups" to combat laws against "criminal syndicalism," "criminal anarchy" and "sedition." The "National Committee" of this organization is largely made up of such well-known radicals as Chrystal Eastman, John A. Fitch, William Z. Foster, Morris Hillquit, James H. Maurer, Scott Nearing, Rose Schneidermann, etc., etc.

At about the same time there was also organized by the same general interests and partly by the same men the "Federated Press." Mr. Baldwin has acted as spokesman for this organization and Mr. Louis P. Lochner—who with James H. Maurer, Scott Nearing and others, in the cablegram already referred to, to the Russian Soviets, signed themselves as representing "300 radical groups in 42 states"—is the chief executive officer.

The Federated Press is described by its representatives as an "international labor-news service" organized in America because "America seemed the only country that has the facilities and the money to establish such a bureau."

Its purposes are twofold: first, "the spreading (in America) of news relating to the revolutionary progress in foreign countries and in general (of) a propaganda nature," and, second, to furnish American labor news to foreign radical papers and organizations.

The connection between the Federated Press and leading radicals of Russia and other European countries—as described in detail by Mr. E. J. Costello, who was sent abroad at the instigation of "one branch of the Soviet government service" for the purpose of establishing such connections and was deported from England while carrying out this mission—is published in the New York Legislative Investigation of Radicalism, pages 1993-1999.

On the back cover of the *Nation* of March 30, 1921, appeared a full page advertisement of the Federated Press. This advertisement features by name 17 special correspondents. The first five in the order they appear, with a list of some of their radical activities, as given by the New York State Legislative Investigation of Radicalism, are as follows:

Paul Hanna—Publicity agent I. W. W.

Laurence Todd—Civil Liberties Bureau—I. W. W.

Scott Nearing—Indicted under Esponage Act; Rand School; Civil Liberties Bureau; Federated Press.

Frederick Howe—American Civil Liberties Union.

Carl Sandberg—Finnish Red Government.

Among these specially featured "special correspondents of the Federated Press appears the name of Mr. Heber Blankenhorn—and a few months later that of Mr. William Z. Foster.[1]

Of a number of the most radical magazines obtainable

[1] The official report—now in the possession of the American Government—of the secret Communist Convention of August, 1922, to the Communist officials in Moscow says:—

"*Everywhere we support the labor press, urging unions to stand with the Federated Press.*"

such as the *New York Call, Chicago News Majority, Daily Free Russia, One Big Union Monthly*, I. W. W. official organ, etc., etc., all contained in the most recent issues that could be obtained, April 9th, from 3 to 7 articles signed by the Federated Press.

Again an appeal has recently been made in behalf of an organization known as "The Church Socialist League" with headquarters at 118 East 28th Street, New York, for $15,000 funds to "carry on Christian Socialist propaganda." This organization states as part of its "formulated program":

"We are not reformists trying to patch up an outworn garment, but REVOLUTIONISTS, striving for a complete revolution of our economic and social order."

In the list of "Executives and prominent members of the League" appears the name "H. Blankenhorn, field investigator for the Interchurch World Movement, N. Y. C."

OTHER TECHNICAL ASSISTANTS

In addition to these outside individuals who acted as "technical experts" to the Interchurch Commission of Inquiry two organizations are mentioned by name as having "obtained directly" "other evidence." These were:
The Bureau of Applied Economics in Washington, D. C.

This organization is referred to on page 6, line 23, of the Report as a source for data for the Steel Report. What this data consists of is not mentioned but as has been emphasized the Interchurch Report in its arguments as to steel wages and working hours in other industries in one place ignores, in another contradicts, and in others states conclusions the opposite of those shown by the detailed published statistics of this organization.

The Bureau of Industrial Research.

Under the heading "Socialist Propaganda in Educated Circles," the New York Legislative Investigation of Radicalism (page 1120) says:

"A so-called Bureau of Industrial Research . . . describes itself as being organized to promote sound human relationship in industry. . . . This organization coöperates with the New School for Social Research which has been established by men who belong to the ranks of the *Near-Bolshevik Intelligentsia*: some of them being too radical in their views to remain on the faculty of Columbia University."

Its officers as there given are—
Robert W. Bruere—Director.
Herbert Croly—Treasurer.
Ordway Tead.
Henry C. Metcalf.
P. Sargent Florence.
Leonard Outhwaite.
Carl G. Kersten.
Mary D. Blankenhorn."

"LIBERAL" AND RADICAL PUBLICATION

A number of the special investigators and technical experts who are at least chiefly responsible for the Interchurch Report on the Steel Strike have been specifically mentioned as contributors on radical subjects to various magazines mentioned by name. As a matter of fact practically all the individuals and members of organizations who thus assisted the Commission of Inquiry are contributors on various subjects to this same group of periodicals whose names are perhaps better known than their particular nature and policy.

Some of this group of publications are self-admittedly radical. Others adopt the camouflage which radicals so frequently adopt of maintaining an outward pose of being merely "liberal." In regard to this whole group of magazines the following may be noted:

The *Nation* is one such magazine which assumes before the public to be merely "liberal." The following excerpt of a letter written by Arthur C. Calhoun on July 29, 1919, and quoted by the New York Legislative Investigation of Radicalism (page 1114) indicates clearly what, among its own circle, it is admitted that policy of the *Nation* really is. This letter in part said:

"Beals was here last week. He is pushing the *Nation.* Says the circulation has quadrupled since they became Bolshevik."

Prof. Beals is listed by the New York Legislative Investigation on Radicalism (page 1114) as an ex-Professor and "open Bolshevist," while Prof. Calhoun as an important member of "The Tri-State Coöperative Society of Pittsburg, which promotes the production and distribution of Red propaganda." The editorial department of the *Nation* states that Charleton Beals was not officially connected with the *Nation* but has done a great deal of work for them.

Again in the June, 1920 issue of *Freedom,* published by the Ferrer group of Anarchists at Stelton, N. J., appeared the following:

"Beginning with this issue *Freedom* will appear under the Editorship of Harry Kelly, etc. . . . It may be asked, 'Why another paper, when the broadly libertarian and revolutionary movement is so ably represented by socialist publications like the *Revolutionary Age, Liberator, Rebel Worker, Workers World* and many others, and the advanced Liberal Movement by *The Dial, Nation, The World To-morrow* and to a lesser degree, the *New Republic* and *Survey?*' These publications are doing excellent work in their several ways, and with much of that work we find ourselves in hearty agreement. *They are,* however, *liberal in the best sense of the word, Bolshevik, or Socialist* and we are none of these, *even if we look with kindly eye on all of them. We are anarchists.*"

CHAPTER V

COMPOSITION AND AUTHORSHIP OF THE INTERCHURCH
REPORT

THE Interchurch Report on the Steel Strike in its preface states the history of the preparation and adoption of the Report as follows:

"CHRONOLOGY OF THE INVESTIGATION

Field Investigation..............October, 1919, to February, 1920
Mediation Effort................November 28 to December 5, 1919
Report adopted unanimously by the
  Commission of Inquiry.........:.March 29–30, 1920
Report received by the Executive
  Committee of the Interchurch
  World Movement..............May 10th
Recommended for publication by
  sub-committee of the Executive
  Committee....................June 25th.
                    Personnel
        Dr. Hubert C. Herring (Congregational)
        Bishop James Cannon, Jr. (Methodist South)
        Mr. Warren S. Stone (Congregational)
Adopted unanimously by the Execu-
  tive Committee of the Interchurch
  Movement...............June 28, 1920."

This official chronology is obviously intended only as a meager outline of the most salient facts in connection with the investigation and their dates. It makes no mention of the methods of procedure of the investigation—how much of the actual investigating was done by the Commission of Inquiry and how much was left to the outside "field investigators"—as to whether the "500 rock-bottom" affidavits, on which the Report states it is based, were obtained in testimony before the Commission itself or were merely obtained by the outside field investigators individually and presented later to the Commission of Inquiry—as to whether or not the testimony of the witnesses who made these affidavits were subject to any cross-examination to test or bring out the full value of their testimony—as to whether the Report itself was written by a member of the Commission of Inquiry or compiled by different members, with or without the assistance of the outside field investigators, or whether it was written by one or a group of the outside field investigators—or in regard to any fact as to its methods of being organized for presentation to the public— all of which facts would seem to be pertinent to a determination of the soundness of the method of investigation and the accuracy of presenting the results of the investigation.

In regard to the small group of 41 of these "500 rock-bottom affidavits" published in the Second Volume, the Interchurch Report admits that they were at least partly obtained, and the affidavits themselves show they were chiefly obtained, and composed by or for James F. Maurer who signed himself in now published correspondence with the Russian Soviets as "representing 300 radical groups in 42 states." These were not only plainly not subject to cross-examination or otherwise tested for accuracy but they are largely exclamations, descriptions, insinuations, often self-evidently coloured to seem to make sensational allegations which they actually do not make at all, and otherwise obviously composed for propaganda effect and as a matter of fact were originally used for propaganda purposes. That the Interchurch Report also offers such statements and affidavits as bona fide evidence after their own authors had under oath and cross-examination publicly repudiated all the substantial parts of them has already been shown in detail.

Moreover, although the facts as to the authorship of the Interchurch Report were immediately, and have been a number of times since, much discussed and inquired into, members of the Commission of Inquiry have refused to state the authorship beyond denying that certain alleged authors wrote the Report.

A Reverend Victor Bigelow, pastor of a Congregational Church in Andover, Massachusetts, in a debate in regard to the fairness of the Interchurch Report, with Mr. George W. Coleman, one of the members of the Commission of Inquiry, held before the Worcester Congregational Church, March 14, 1921, and of which the author was able to obtain a stenographic report, asked Mr. Coleman point blank who wrote the Steel Strike Report.   Mr. Coleman replied:

"We wrote it positively.   It was not written by any man.   No man lives today who can claim he wrote that Report."

Just how far this statement may be regarded as being technically within the truth will be pointed out in detail later.

A little later in the same speech, after enumerating who he means by "we"—that is, the members of the "Commission of Inquiry"—Mr. Coleman continued:

"Many of them (Commissioners of Inquiry) had not seen each other before.   They came from different parts of the country, from 8 different denominations.   They went right to work gathering information and gathering testimony.   We did not know where we were coming out exactly until we sat down to write our report—and wonder of wonders nine people representing 8 different denominations, coming from different parts of the country, *each of them with the interests of his own denomination at heart*, all agreed.   Did you ever hear anything like that in church affairs?"

And he says again:

"It (The Interchurch Report) stands as the report of organized Protestantism of North America as represented by the Interchurch

World Movement, giving it the fullest consideration and finally putting their O. K. and approval on it."

The fact that the Commission of Inquiry that signed the Report have thus chosen to take the attitude, both in the Report itself and in answer to inquiries in regard to it, of refusing to discuss its authorship beyond Mr. Coleman's very general statement that they all wrote it, or to discuss in any lengthy detail the methods adopted in making the investigation and preparing the Report—make it ´correspondingly difficult to obtain any very complete evidence on these points.

The following facts, however, appear from the following evidence:

Mr. Coleman said further, in the same Worcester speech:

" When I was called to New York to attend a special meeting of the steel strike commission, to listen to Mr. Fitzpatrick, one of the strike leaders," etc., during which meeting Mr. Coleman states that Mr. Fitzpatrick said, "Gentlemen, I am commissioned in behalf of the strikers to put our case in your hands without any limitation or reservation."

Mr. Coleman's previous statement that when the members of the Commission got together they went immediately to work "gathering information and gathering testimony," taken in connection with the phraseology of this statement, indicates that one of the first acts of the Commission of Inquiry was to thus discuss the investigation with Mr. Fitzpatrick, President of the Strike Leaders Committee, who during the discussion stated that he put the strikers' cause "without limitation or reservation" in the hands of the Commission of Inquiry.

Mr. George Soule who is the first mentioned (Interchurch Report Index) of the outside "staff of field investigators" states that he was put in immediate charge of the Pittsburg field work of the investigation and that he, followed shortly by Mr. David Saposs proceeded at once to the Pittsburg district with certain definite plans for making the investigation. He first approached certain officials of the subsidiary companies of the U. S. Steel Corporation, stating to them the fact and purpose of the proposed investigation, asking for relevant facts and figures and suggesting that the privilege of access to the books and records of the company and introductions to local superintendents be granted him.   Mr. Soule states that these requests were not in any case complied with and that they got a minimum of the information they desired from the local steel companies.   He then approached the strike leaders with the same request with which the strike leaders willingly complied, putting all their books and records at the disposal of the Interchurch Investigation and giving introductions to local leaders which admitted to all strike meetings.

Later— Mr. Soule does not recollect the exact time— members of the Commission of Inquiry spent "some time" in the Pittsburg District and held "hearings" before which all persons in the community having knowledge of the situation, who could be induced to testify, including clergymen, government officials, industrial experts, neutrals and many of the strike leaders and strikers and strike sympathizers testified, of which testimony a complete record was made.   Certain steel officials were requested to appear also before the Commission to give testimony.   They suggested, however, that they would prefer to meet the members of the Commission of Inquiry in their own offices. Several such interviews were arranged but at the request, according to Mr. Soule, of these steel officials, no records were made during such conversations of what was said.   Immediately thereafter all members of the Commission present recorded their memories of the interviews.[1]

Both the Interchurch Report and Mr. Soule also state that the Commission of Inquiry similarly visited certain other strike areas and Mr. Coleman names these as Johnstown and Chicago.   The Interchurch Report itself mentions without detail Ohio, Indiana and Illinois.

[1] This section in its present form has been revised by Mr. Soule so that a large part of it is in his own language.

The Chronology of the Investigation in the index of the Interchurch Report mentions "a Mediation effort Nov. 28th—Dec. 5th, 1919."

Mr. Foster in his book, *The Great Steel Strike*, furnished the only available evidence of the nature of this attempt at Mediation until the second Interchurch volume appeared nearly two years later.   He says (page 157):

"Consequently John Fitzpatrick, Chairman of the National (Strike) Committee, put before Mr. Blankenhorn a plan for the settlement of the strike by mediation. Mr. Blankenhorn felt however that it might be better to recommend that the Commission move independently rather than as merely representing the strikers."

Mr. Foster then devotes the next three pages to giving details in regard to the plan which was originated by the strikers but presented to Judge Gary as coming from the Interchurch Commission, in which it was proposed that the "Commission set up a permanent mediation body to bring about a conference between employers and employees in the steel industry."   In other words, the Commission of Inquiry thus proposed to Judge Gary as their plan what was actually the plan of the strike leaders that Judge Gary yield at this time and grant the "conference" which was the express chief issue in the whole strike.   The memorandum to Mr. Fitzpatrick, containing the statement of Judge Gary's refusal to agree to this plan, was signed by Mr. Blankenhorn and dated December 6th.   The Interchurch Report's own account in Volume II while more detailed and from a different point of view is substantially the same.

In the meantime, however, Mr. Soule had been assigned to a special investigation of conditions in regard to the refusal of authorities to allow strikers' meetings.   As Mr. Soule gave his chief attention thereafter to this special work, being succeeded by Mr. Blankenhorn as head of the general field work, he is less familiar with the lines along which the latter part of the general investigation was conducted and is only generally familiar with the facts as to the preparation of the main report itself.   All the facts available however, and the plain statement of the Interchurch Report itself show, as already emphasized that the whole investigation was carried on almost entirely by the staff of outside "field investigators" under the direction of Mr. Blankenhorn.

There can be no question that Mr. Heber Blankenhorn was also the actual author of the Interchurch Report.   The Interchurch Report states that he "had charge of the field work and *later* (*i.e.*, during the preparation of the Report) *acted as secretary to the Commission.*"   Mr. Blankenhorn is a writer by profession and his position as secretary would make him the logical author if any one man was to be the author.   The fact, definitely emphasized by the Interchurch Report, that he was "Editor" of its second volume and that he signed the various introductions, etc., to each section is doubtless also significant.   A comparison of the very distinct individual literary style of the Interchurch Report with the style of these sections of Volume II and with other writings of Mr. Blankenhorn offers a type of evidence which is accepted by our courts, that Mr. Blankenhorn is the author.

Moreover, any careful examination of the published works of various members of the Commission of Inquiry will also show plainly that the Interchurch Report is written with a style and vocabulary and particularly with a unique sentence structure, which is strikingly different from that employed by any of these Interchurch Commissioners in their own published works.

Part One of this analysis described the nature and sources of the "evidence" collected by the "technical assistants." It emphasized the means employed in extracting figures from government statistics and bits of testimony from the Senate report to produce impressions or force conclusions diametrically opposed to those arrived at by the government statisticians and by the Senate Committee from *all* of the figures and *all* of the testimony available.

It is, of course, conceivable that the Interchurch Commissioners of Inquiry themselves might have accepted this kind of "evidence" from their "technical assistants" or others in whom they had confidence and written a report around it in good faith.

But, as already pointed out, "evidence" throughout the Interchurch Report, including much that is in itself entirely innocent, is led up to and surrounded by context which seems to give it a meaning that the "evidence" itself does not possess. Arguments, which have no substantial basis in the evidence submitted with them, are built upon insinuation or misleading statements, the clever coupling of unrelated facts, and similar devices calculated to deceive.

It seems utterly inconceivable that any of the distinguished Christian leaders who signed the Interchurch Report would, even if they could, handle the "evidence" submitted by their "technical assistants" in the adroit manner exhibited by the Report for the purpose of producing impressions and forcing conclusions. Aside from other considerations, it would have required an unity of thought, purpose, and disposition, which it would have been difficult, if not impossible, to secure.

Mr. Blankenhorn, on the other hand, served during the war, as an officer in that branch of the service which demanded the highest type of ability in creating and disseminating effective propaganda; and since the war he has been openly working with William Z. Foster, whom the Interchurch Report particularly eulogizes, and with other radicals, as a professional propagandist in a notorious radical propaganda organization which the Interchurch Report twice goes out of its way to advertise, and whose propaganda is directed to advance at least the same general theories for which the Interchurch Report consistently argues.

Mr. Bronson Batchelor, Mr. Stanley Went, the original editor of the Interchurch Report on the Steel Strike, and Mr. Harold C. Reynolds, all three state not only that it was a matter of commonest knowledge among all those in touch with that part of the work of the Interchurch World Movement but that they know of their own personal knowledge that Mr. Blankenhorn wrote the Report.

Two of Mr. Blankenhorn's close personal associates state that he has said repeatedly to them or in their presence that he wrote the Interchurch Report on the steel strike going into details as to how and why he wrote it as he did.

Dr. William Hiram Foulkes, Chairman of the Executive Committee, which finally passed on the "Steel Report," discussed the Interchurch Report as a product of Mr. Blankenhorn's authorship without questioning the fact as to such authorship. In his conversation with Dr. McDowell, member of the Commission of Inquiry, the writer brought up the subject of Mr. Blankenhorn's authorship of the Interchurch Report. Dr. McDowell stated that:

" Mr. Blankenhorn was Secretary of the Commission and as such he prepared certain parts of the Report, which were laid before the Commission for their review and approval. The Commission passed on (the) Report as a whole after several careful reviews of its contents."

This statement by Dr. McDowell, was given only after he had inadvertently made a much broader admission. It was most carefully formulated. The phrase "prepared certain parts of the Report" may mean that Mr. Blankenhorn "prepared" all the Report except the "Findings," "Recommendations," and certain other brief sections which are known to have been prepared by others, or it may mean less than this. Dr. McDowell refused to be specific.

Again in a signed statement (published in full below), Mr. Tyler Dennett, Director of the Publicity Department, to whom the Report was submitted for editing, and who read the manuscript carefully with this end in view, refers to the Report as having been published "*substantially as Mr. Blankenhorn wrote it.*" But he added at the time and emphasized later that in his opinion Mr. Blankenhorn's authorship consisted largely of compilation—this opinion

Mr. Dennett's statements accompanying his signed statement were not approved by him in their present form before publication.

being based on the inferior literary quality of certain parts of the manuscript. Mr. Went, to whom Mr. Dennett turned the manuscript over to edit, also emphasizes the inferior literary quality of certain parts of it. This would obviously seem to preclude the possibility that any of the Interchurch Commissioners themselves could have prepared the material from which Mr. Blankenhorn is thus thought to have "compiled" these sections or have materially changed the Report after it was written and before it was edited.

In regard to the editing of the Interchurch Report, Mr. Dennett stated:

"A copy of the Report on the Steel Strike in its original form was put into my hands in the latter part of May (1920) as part of the regular routine of my office, for the purpose of editing and publicity. The manuscript was turned over to Mr. Stanley Went for this purpose. Later, the Report was edited without reference to Mr. Went's work by Mr. James E. Craig.

"In regard to the editing of the Steel Strike Report this consisted chiefly of changes in literary style and the elimination of statements which the editors did not believe to be warranted by the evidence presented. Otherwise the Report was published substantially as Mr. Blankenhorn wrote it. No facts or statements essential to the general conclusions were eliminated. The editors made no attempt to pass on the merits of the evidence presented."

Between the date that the "Report (was) adopted unanimously by the Commission of Inquiry, March 29-30, 1920," according to the Interchurch Report "chronology," page 5, and "after several careful reviews of its contents" according to Dr. McDowell, and the date of its being edited, the Report was "received by the Executive Committee of the Interchurch Movement, May 10." This was at a meeting at Columbus, Ohio. During the day the Executive Committee had discussed the fact that the April financial drive and second supplementary financial drive which had immediately followed it, had failed and that the Movement faced the necessity of liquidation. At a dinner conference at which Dr. Foulkes presided, and at which Bishop McConnell, Mr. John D. Rockefeller, Jr., and Mr.

Tyler Dennett, in addition to the members of the Executive Committee, were present, copies of a summary of the Report on the Steel Strike, corresponding in general to the Introduction in the volume as published, were circulated and Bishop McConnell urged that the Report be accepted for publication. This meeting appointed a sub-committee, consisting (Interchurch Report chronology, page 5) of Dr. Hubert C. Herring, Bishop James Cannon, Jr., and Mr. Warren S. Stone, to go into the subject in greater detail. The copies of the Summary were not left in the hands of the Committee members present but were collected after the meeting.

Some ten days later the complete Steel Strike Report manuscript was sent to Mr. Tyler Dennett's department "for the purpose of editing and publicity." After reading the manuscript carefully himself Mr. Dennett, as already stated, turned it over to Mr. Stanley Went for editing. Mr. Went was engaged in this work from the latter part of May until the middle of June.

On June 17th Mr. Went returned Mr. Blankenhorn's original draft to Mr. Tyler Dennett accompanied by the memorandum which has been reproduced in part in the Foreword of the present Analysis in which Mr. Went condemned the bias of the Report as "so patent that it would make it a comparatively easy matter to discredit the entire Report."

He stated further in this memorandum that he had edited the Report as lightly as seemed compatible "with the end in view," "that end as, I understand it, was to present the Report in a form which should give the least possible impression of bias on the part of the investigating committee." He states that he did not follow his own feelings in the matter but rather had "leaned over backwards in a desire to present the case of the Commission as much as possible in the way the *original writer* thought it should be presented."

Mr. Went states that two further reasons why he did not

attempt to go beyond this in editing the Report were because he considered that any adequate editing would require almost complete rewriting and because he doubted whether the Report even with any amount of editing would be allowed by the higher officials of the Interchurch World Movement to be published.

Mr. James Craig who did the final editing with "another gentleman" under the authority of Dr. Poling, states that Mr. Went's complete editorial notes and comments on the Report were turned over by Mr. Dennett to him. Mr. Craig states further that in order not to be in any way influenced in advance, he did not refer to Mr. Went's notes until after he had gone over the Report and formed his own opinions. He states that his own personal opinion in many respects was the same as that of Mr. Went but that as it had been decided by his superiors to publish the Report he did not allow his personal opinion to enter into the matter. Mr. Craig has made a specific statement on this whole subject as follows:

"Mr. Went began some preliminary editing but this work was stopped because of the financial collapse of the Movement following the unsuccessful financial campaign, April 25th–May 2nd. Whether the Report should be published or not was bound up very largely with the equally vexing question of whether the Movement could continue any activity. It was finally agreed to disband the organization except for enough people to wind up affairs. The entire publicity department was discharged except myself. I was retained because I had been doing some special work for Dr. Cory, Dr. Poling and Dr. Diffendorfer in connection with the supplementary effort to raise money. When it was decided to continue the work on the Steel Report and when sufficient funds were in hand for that purpose I was asked to outline a publicity plan and to prepare the manuscript of the Report for publication. My personal economic views did not enter into the matter at all. This is the more evident from the fact that my own views in general accord with those of Mr. Went. I approached the task from the viewpoint of a conscientious newspaper copy editor, trying to do a high-grade technical task, in which I was looking after the interests of my employer. My employer was and had been for more than a year previous to this the Interchurch World Movement."

The fact above emphasized by Mr. Craig, that the two financial drives in April and May so failed to raise the needed amounts of money that the whole Interchurch Movement began a liquidation in which it not only abandoned all the fundamental objectives for which it had been organized, but the great bulk of the work which it had already done, raises the question that has often been discussed in inner-Interchurch circles as to why, under such circumstances, the Steel Strike Report was practically the only activity carried forward and how, under these circumstances, the money was found for this purpose.

The author made particular effort to get the facts as to how and where under the circumstances the money was found for completing and publishing the Interchurch Report, including the Second Volume. Three gentlemen, intimately associated with the Movement, told the author that shortly before the Report was published, Mrs. D. Willard Straight donated $50,000 to the Interchurch Movement with the express provision that the money was to be used in the Industrial Department only. They stated that it was generally believed in the inner circles of the Movement that the Report was completed and published with this money. They also stated, however, that as they were not in a position to substantiate the detailed accuracy of their understanding, they did not wish to be personally quoted.

Mrs. D. Willard Straight is well known as the financial backer of the *New Republic*, and more recently of *The New Student*, an inter-collegiate magazine through which *The World Tomorrow, Nation, New Republic, Bureau of Industrial Research, Civil Liberties Union*, etc., group are making a specialized effort at radical propaganda among American colleges. During the widespread campaign of radical agitation built around the Sacco-Vanzetti murder trial, as part of which agitation Spanish radicals attempted to blow up the American Embassy, Mrs. Straight, according to numerous published statements, gave $2,500 to the Sacco-Vanzetti defense fund. In fact Mrs. Straight is so well known as a financial supporter of various radical activities that when the New York Legislative Investigation of Radicalism, on page 1097, publishes correspondence relating to Mr. Roger Baldwin's sending Chumley, the collector for the I. W. W. to Mrs. Straight, it obviously does not even regard it as necessary to comment on her status in the matter.

After the liquidation of the Interchurch Movement, many of its records were turned over to the New York Federation of Churches.   Reverend H. J. Laflamme of that organization is one of a large number of former Interchurch Movement officials who apparently believe that in view of the fact that the Interchurch activities were made possible through millions of dollars of public contributions the public certainly has a right to know the facts in regard to at least the most conspicuous of such activities.   As a result of his investigation of the records in his possession, Mr. Laflamme on August 11, 1922, wrote the author as follows:

"Mrs. D. Willard Straight's $50,000 was given before May of 1920 and to be used in the Industrial Department only.   Beyond this I have no record or knowledge."

This concrete evidence seemed strongly to substantiate the above mentioned statements of various Interchurch officials.   A further search, however, of the Interchurch records on this subject by Mr. Laflamme shows that no part of Mrs. Straight's $50,000 pledge was ever paid at least into the regular channels of the Interchurch Movement.   Obviously then either, (1) Mrs. Straight refused to pay a pledge she had made, which seems highly improbable in itself and particularly improbable in view of the fact that the work for which this pledge was thus understood to be specifically given was carried out not only by the publication of the original Interchurch Report but by the publication after months of further work of a second Interchurch Report; or (2) this contribution was paid to individual officials of the Interchurch Movement who never accounted for it to the Movement—which seems entirely improbable, or (3) by some special arrangement its payment was transferred to the outside group associated with the Bruere-Blankenhorn Bureau of Industrial Research who were actually chiefly responsible for the original Interchurch Report and admittedly responsible for the second Interchurch Report.

This latter information from Mr. Laflamme and the three alternatives it presents was discussed with the three gentlemen above referred to. They believed that it tended to confirm their former understanding. A fourth man, however, in perhaps the best position of all to know the facts, but who also would not be personally quoted, stated that money had already been provided to complete the Interchurch Report; that Mrs. Straight's pledge of $50,000 was to cover the expenses of work to be done by the Industrial Department in the following year, and that as the Movement, and so the Industrial Department, was discontinued, and the work not carried through, Mrs. Straight did not pay this pledge at all. He was asked if he knew that Mrs. Straight did not pay this money directly to the Bureau of Industrial Research and if not where they got the money to carry on the work necessary to the publication of the second Interchurch Report. He replied that it is well known that Mrs. Straight regularly supports the Bureau of Industrial Research.

Evidence from anonymous sources which also perhaps involves a certain amount of opinion, is, of course, not very satisfactory. In the present instance, however, all this part of the evidence may be entirely left out of consideration, and there still remains, as matters of specific record, the following facts. Although the Interchurch Movement had failed to obtain the money to carry out the fundamental religious work for which it was started and was abandoning such fundamental religious work, much of which it had well on towards completion, it did complete and publish the Interchurch Report. This Report, in spite of the fact that it was published with full knowledge of the financial condition of the Movement, refers in several places to the intention of preparing and publishing further reports, which would of course involve much further expense. A large further Report was prepared and published over a year later. When the financial future and so the continued existence of the Interchurch Movement was in doubt, Mrs. Straight, whose contributions to radical and "liberal" movements are notorious, pledged $50,000 "to be used in the Industrial Department only." This is the Department which originated the Steel Strike investigation and of which Mr. Robert W. Bruere—whose Bureau of Industrial Research was the technical adviser and furnished the investigators and the author for the Interchurch Report—was Superintendent of Research,—"research" being the chief function of this Department. Whether, therefore, the particular $50,000 thus pledged, went through some Interchurch channel or to the Bureau of Industrial Research direct, to pay for the completion and publication of the two Interchurch Reports, or whether, because of the fact that the same Bruere-Blankenhorn group had to function nominally as the Bureau of Industrial Research instead of nominally as the Interchurch Industrial Department, in the preparation and publication of the second Report, this particular $50,000 was not paid, it is at least entirely clear that these Reports are of a nature and represent a point of view which radical interests stood ready to pay $50,000 to have carried on.

On June 25th, just a week after Mr. Went turned the edited document over to Mr. Dennett, the Interchurch Report was recommended for publication by the sub-committee of the Executive Committee appointed May 10th.

The Preface of the Interchurch Report itself states that the Report was "*adopted unanimously* by the Executive Committee of the Interchurch World Movement on June 28th"—three days later.

According to the official handbook of the Interchurch World Movement, page 109, the Executive Committee consisted of:

John R. Mott, Chairman.

Mr. Mott is General Secretary of the International Committee of the Y. M. C. A. and has for years been a religious leader of world reputation. Dr. Mott's continuous absence from the city, on account of his health, made a personal interview impossible but his secretary has stated for him that Dr. Mott left for Europe before the final consideration of the Steel Investigation Report by the Executive Committee and had never seen the Report before its publication.

William Hiram Foulkes, Vice Chairman.

On Dr. Mott's resignation and departure for Europe Dr. Foulkes became automatically Chairman of the Executive Committee and acted in that capacity throughout all the final discussion of the Interchurch Report on the Steel Strike. Dr. Foulkes, because of this official position, was the first person—other than Mr. Batchelor and Mr. Went whom the writer knew personally—with whom the writer discussed the question of the publication of the present analysis of the Interchurch Report.

Dr. Foulkes stated at once that he had voted to accept and publish the Report at the time because of the very high regard and confidence in which he held and still holds certain members of the Commission of Inquiry. During the first conversation of over two hours, many of the points discussed in the present analysis were gone over, during which Doctor Foulkes stated repeatedly and in no uncertain terms that he had been forced to change his opinion in regard to the merits of the Interchurch Report. He particularly emphasized the obvious influence on the Report of the men who were employed as investigators and technical experts. He also proposed a program of action in the preparation and presentation of the present analysis which has already been discussed in the Introduction to the present volume.

29

In October the complete original manuscript of the present analysis was placed in the hands of Dr. Foulkes, and one or two brief conferences held on the subject.   In the present section of this original manuscript appeared a number of quotations from Dr. Foulkes, taken from the writer's memorandum made immediately after the first lengthy conversation with him.   Early in November the writer received the following letter from Dr. Foulkes:

"November 1, 1921.

"My dear Mr. Olds:

"I fear that my frequent absence from the city may interfere with further conference with you relative to the material which you have kindly submitted to me for my review.

"I find, as I begin to read your manuscript, that it deals with so many alleged facts and conclusions which are out of the range of my observation and knowledge that it does not seem wise for me to attempt to pass any detailed judgment upon the statements you have made.   I do not understand, indeed, that you desire to have my general judgment but I am writing specifically in order that there may be no misunderstanding.

"I note also in Section 6, page 13, your brief statement concerning your impression of the interview you had with me.   I do not have quite the same memory of that conversation that you appear to have.   I do not recall stating what you have quoted me as stating 'that there is no question that the Steel Strike Report was put over on the Interchurch World Movement'—'that Radicals were undoubtedly behind the Report and turned the situation to their own advantage.'   What I recall as saying is that I feared from what I had heard, after the investigation had been made, that some of the actual investigators were not as unprejudiced as they should have been and that personally representing one side of the controversy their testimony was, therefore, liable to be discounted.

"For me to assert that they are Radicals, that the Report was 'put over' and that these men turned the situation to their own advantage, is a conclusion to which I do not care to be committed.

"Very sincerely yours,

"(Signed)   William Hiram Foulkes."

William B. Millar, Secretary.

Dr. Millar's office stated:

"Dr. Millar was laid aside by a very serious illness at the Atlantic City Conference of the Interchurch World Movement in January, 1920, and took no further active part in the affairs of the Movement."

and Dr. Millar himself later wrote in regard to the Steel Report:

"I was taken sick before the report of this Committee and never got back into the work at all."

George M. Fowles, Treasurer.

Dr. Fowles was Treasurer of the Interchurch World Movement and a member of other important committees as well as the Executive Committee. He is also treasurer of the Methodist Foreign Mission Board. Dr. Fowles said at once:

"You can put me down as having voted for the Interchurch Report. I know others are going back on the Report but I voted for it and I am going to stand by my guns till it is proved the Report is wrong." When asked if he had read the Report before his vote, he replied that he had. When it was suggested to him, however, that he doubtless had not compared the evidence with the original sources, and a number of instances of the manipulation of statistics and the expurgation of testimony that made the evidence in the Report very different from the real evidence itself was specifically called to his attention, he said of course he had not gone into that becuase they had hired the best technical experts on such subjects—that they had hired Robert Bruere's Bureau of Research and that he had the greatest confidence in Mr. Bruere and his organization. When some of the facts already stated herein, in regard to Mr. Bruere's extreme radicalism, were presented, he replied that he himself didn't believe in radicalism at all and that he didn't believe in the autocratic policies of the Labor Unions either, but that he had the greatest confidence in Mr. Bruere.

Dr. Fowles asked in turn whether it was true, "Yes or No," that the steel workers or at least most of them had to work 12 hours a day and 24 to 36 hours every so often. This impression, that practically all the steel workers were forced against their will to work 12 hours and frequently the 24-hour day, seems to be general among Interchurch officials and is the reason assigned in almost every case for those who did favor it, having favored at the time the publication of the Interchurch Report. When these allegations were denied, Dr. Fowles again said he would not accept such inaccuracies as were pointed out without going over such questions with Mr. Bruere and getting his side of the case.[1]

S. Earl Taylor, General Secretary.

Dr. Taylor has been continually in Arizona during the last several years and could not be interviewed   It is understood, however, that he approved the Report.

Robert Lansing, Chairman, General Committee.

Mr. Lansing was at the time Secretary of State. During the entire period in which the Interchurch Report was written and discussed Mr. Lansing was in Paris as a member of the American Peace Commission. On June 28, 1919, the date on which it is stated the Executive Committee *"adopted unanimously"* the Interchurch Report on the Steel Strike, Mr. Lansing was signing the Peace of Versailles.

Fred B. Smith, Vice Chairman, General Committee.

Mr. Smith, who is connected with the Johns-Manville Company, stated that he never read the Report and knew nothing about it. When certain of its more glaring errors and misstatements, as pointed out in Part I of the present analysis, were called to his attention, he stated that he "regarded the Report on the Steel Strike as dead and buried" and that he had "no more interest in it now than in some Egyptian hieroglyphics in a college library."

When it was further pointed out to him that irrespective of that fact these statements had been published to the world and were still being circulated as being "adopted unanimously and approved" by the Executive Committee of which he was a member, and he was asked whether or not he had so approved and adopted them at the time he said

[1] Due to Dr. Fowles' long absence abroad it has been impossible to submit the above to him for his final correction or approval.

he was a member of the General Committee, not the Executive Committee. When his name was pointed out to him as appearing on the official list of the Executive Committee he stated that he remembered the question of publishing the Report had been brought up one morning out at Cleveland while members of various committees were at breakfast together. He said that he personally at the time was discussing matters connected with another committee—that the Interchurch Report might have been approved—as a matter of fact it must have been approved or it wouldn't have been published.[1]

The Interchurch Report on the Steel Strike was doubtless "approved unanimously" by *some part* of the Executive Committee at the June 28th meeting, which was held at 150 Fifth Avenue, New York City. But that it was not "approved unanimously by the Executive Committee" is plain.

In the official Handbook of the Interchurch World Move-

---

[1] Although the writer had a formal letter of introduction to Mr. Smith, it required repeated efforts over a period of months to obtain the interview of which the above, written immediately after that interview is the substance. Repeated efforts were also made before publication to submit the above passage in regard to that interview to Mr. Smith for his approval or correction. Finally, on the afternoon of September 13th, it was submitted to and read by Mr. Smith's secretary at his office, 271 Madison Avenue. His Secretary made an appointment, subject to confirmation by telephone, for the writer to see Mr. Smith personally the following day. The next morning (the 14th) Mr. Smith personally spoke to the writer over the telephone. He asked the nature of the statement and was told that it was in substance that he had not read the Report before its approval and publication. He replied that he had a copy in his library "this minute" and had read it and stated that he would not be quoted in any way in regard to the Interchurch Report and demanded that the writer agree not to quote him in any way in regard to the previous interview. The writer attempted to explain the reason for, and the nature of, the quotation but Mr. Smith interrupted insisting that the former interview was a private conversation which the writer had no right to publish without his permission and stated that if he was quoted in any way, shape or manner, he would "make a noise that you can hear from here to Fifth Avenue." The writer insisted that the matter was not of a private na-

ment (page 109) the names of the above seven gentlemen are prominently listed down the center of the page with their full titles. Obviously it was the national and international standing of certain of these gentlemen which made their supposed "unanimous approval" of the Report a big factor in its general acceptance. Their statements at this time quoted above are correspondingly significant.

The sixteen other members of the Executive Committee, the official Handbook lists in double columns and without titles and in alphabetical order. These men and women, however, are so widely scattered as to address, and investigation by correspondence on such a subject is so unsatisfactory, that no effort has been made to ascertain how much further less than "unanimous" the approval of the Interchurch Report by all the Executive Committee actually was.

Moreover, it is to be noted that in the Foreword to the Second Volume, published from three to six months after the foregoing interviews had been had and brought to the

---

ture and did not concern merely Mr. Smith's personal wishes, but that on the contrary, as Mr. Smith had already committed himself or allowed himself to be committed as officially supporting the subject matter of the Interchurch Report and approving its wide publicity, and as the alleged unanimous approval of Mr. Smith's committee had been used as part of that publicity, . . . The writer was not allowed to finish but was interrupted with the statement that he could doubtless understand plain English and that he (Mr. Smith) was stating in plain English that he was not to be quoted in any way, shape or manner and that if the writer did quote him he would get into trouble.

Mr. Tyler Dennett later talked to Mr. Smith in regard to modifying this statement for publication and at Mr. Dennett's suggestion the author made another but unsuccessful attempt to see Mr. Smith. The author regrets publishing a statement which obviously Mr. Smith made without due consideration. He has made every effort to have it modified by Mr. Smith's more careful recollection. Under the circumstance, however, of Mr. Smith's refusal to modify it and his threat the author is left no alternative but to publish the statement as originally given.

attention of the present Interchurch Executives, the Interchurch Report changes its statement that it "was *adopted unanimously by the Executive Committee of the Interchurch Movement*" to the statement that "*at its session of June* 28th the Steel Report was adopted unanimously by the Executive Committee, *all members having been informed of the calendar for the day.*"

The final preparation of the Interchurch Report for publication was placed in the hands of Mr. James E. Craig and "another gentleman," acting under the direction of Dr. Poling, the understanding being, according to Mr. Craig, that Dr. Poling was to decide any matters on which he (Craig) and the "second gentleman" could not agree. There were certain matters in connection with this final editing on which obviously the greatest secrecy was enjoined. Mr. Craig was entirely willing to state his own connection and that of Dr. Poling with the work but he would not state for publication the name of the "second gentleman," without the permission of Dr. Cory, which permission though several times asked for was not given.

This second joint final editor of the Interchurch Report was Mr. Robert W. Bruere.

SUMMARY OF PART TWO

FROM a careful analysis then of the chief circumstances which led up to the Investigation of the steel strike by the Interchurch World Movement and its Report on that strike, these facts appear:

First: The Interchurch World Movement was projected at a time immediately following a great world crisis in which the minds of a great proportion of all peoples were in a particularly abnormal state. It was inevitable that many extreme theories should be advanced and agitated in such a movement in 1919.

Second: The proposition that the Interchurch World Movement should especially and directly interest itself in the industrial problems of the day, and interest itself particularly in the great human problem of the relation between capital and labor, is entirely natural and the decision to establish a special Department of Industrial Relations to study such problems was entirely logical even though the basis on which this department was organized did not prove to be sound or wise.

Third: Because industrial relations and particularly relations between employer and labor constitute the point at which practically all radicals and revolutionary theorists insist our basic institutions should be changed and our economic system be revolutionized, it was inevitable that all such radicals and theorists should at once concentrate their interest and attention on this particular phase of proposed Interchurch activities.

Fourth: The first prominent activity of the Department of Industrial Relations was the calling of a special meeting at Hotel Pennsylvania to consider industrial problems, at which the most important speakers were Glen E. Plumb, the advocate of government ownership of railroads; John Walker, President of the Illinois Federation of Labor; Mr. Julius Hecker whose passports were cancelled by the State Department because of extreme pro-Bolshevistic activities, and the notorious Mr. Frederick C. Howe who resigned as Commissioner of Immigration after he had been investigated and strongly condemned by a Congressional committee for his radical activities.

This meeting at Hotel Pennsylvania voted to condemn the steel companies and then voted to appoint a special committee to investigate the steel strike.   It was only after it had been pointed out that the vote to condemn might prejudice the acceptance of the verdict of the investigation that the vote to condemn was rescinded and ordered stricken from the minutes.   This meeting also appointed a committee, "to formulate and give expression to principles and policies of industrial relationships"; and adopted the report or "Findings" of this Committee which are clearly capable of being interpreted as radical.

Fifth: There is no question however that at least some effort was made by other officials of the Interchurch Movement to counteract this tendency towards radicalism. Thru their efforts the "Findings" adopted by the Hotel Pennsylvania meeting were considerably softened before they were published and in the appointment of the special Commission of Inquiry to investigate the steel strike the Executive Committee appointed members, against most of whom no charges of real radicalism can be successfully argued.

Sixth: A far more important point however than the particular shade of belief which may or may not have influenced this Commission of Inquiry in their investigation of the steel strike is the fact that the Commission consisted predominantly of men who not only had had no experience with industrial problems but whose whole experience had been in spiritual leadership, in enthusing and inspiring men's minds and imaginations—which experience requires a supreme development of quite opposite mental and emotional qualities from those required for a careful analysis of intricate material facts or a judicial determination of the merits of the complicated interplay of politics which characterize any great industrial conflict. The fact that the Commission of Inquiry immediately employed, or had employed for them, all the outside "technical assistance"— the fact that except for the evidence accumulated in the comparatively few days they themselves spent in the strike area, the evidence on which they based their conclusions was prepared and submitted to them by their various "technical assistants," indicates their own wise realization of the importance of a very different kind of experience than their own. The further fact that it must be regarded as impossible that this Commission of Inquiry itself could have ingeniously expurgated printed testimony and cleverly manipulated and fabricated statistics to attempt to show the opposite of the actual truth indicates how much they must have relied on outside "technical assistants."

  Seventh: There can be no question however of the radicalism of all the most important outside "technical assistants." The dominant members of the staff of field investigators have conspicuous public records as radicals. They are found immediately on investigation to be friends and associates of Foster—fellow-workers with Roger Baldwin for the type of "civil liberties" campaign for attempting to carry out which he served a year in prison—officially connected with the Rand School—prominent official members of committees or organizations in which they are fellow-workers with other prominent radical leaders—and chiefly officially engaged in furthering the new type of revolutionary unionism represented by the Amalgamated Clothing Workers to which the recent Soviet International at Moscow has transferred the former I. W. W. leadership in the American Radical Movement.

Eighth: There seems little question that this type of outside "technical assistance" not merely furnished the detailed technical data but so arranged the evidence—from which one such outside "technical assistant," who was Secretary of the Commission, wrote the Report—that the Commission of Inquiry, with its own lack of experience in such matters and its confidence in its outside "technical assistants," accepted and approved this evidence and later accepted and approved the Report in entire good faith.

Ninth: Two field investigators, both prominent radicals and notoriously committed to Labor's side on all modern industrial questions, initiated the actual investigation.

Mr. Soule states that his plans contemplated an entirely impartial investigation of the facts but that the steel companies would not coöperate with him by giving him the facts. It is a matter of public record however, as already shown in detail, that not only Mr. Soule but his assistant Mr. Saposs both condemn the modern industrial system and believe that industry ought to be turned over to the workers. These men then with this point of view, and working almost exclusively with the strikers not only themselves prepared much of the evidence, but obviously set the stage for the obtaining of such evidence as the Commission itself obtained when it visited the strike area.

Tenth: Such investigation as was made by the Commission itself in the strike area consisted chiefly of:

A. Conversations held with steel officials in the offices of the officials—because "the officers refused to attend the formal 'Hearings' set up by the Interchurch Commission" —of which conversations stenographic reports were not permitted and from which the Commissioners seem to have got little satisfaction, and which doubtless tended to prejudice them still further against the steel companies; and

B. The "Hearings" in which strike leaders and witnesses for the strike leaders furnished the chief evidence or at least practically the only evidence used.

It must be remembered that such "Hearings" were held in the midst of a bitter industrial conflict when the minds of all the parties involved were warped by the most extreme partisanship. Under such circumstances it would have required a very great degree of judicial impartiality and judicial experience and very careful cross-examination to get at the real facts. It must be remembered that the Commission's own investigators in whom it showed it had the most implicit confidence but who were entirely committed to labor's side and who had been working on the closest most friendly terms with the strike leaders—were doubtless the men who produced the witnesses before the Commission. Except for possibly three statements, all the "rock-bottom affidavits," on which the Commission admits it formed its judgments and on which the Report was written, were, as far as they have been published, the products either of these outside investigators or of their notorious fellow-radical, James H. Maurer.

Eleventh: Again during the conferences in New York when all the evidence that had been collected was gone over, as Mr. Coleman describes, in order to "find out where (they) were coming out" the situation held the same potentialities and doubtless worked out in exactly the same way.

As the great mass of evidence—hundreds of affidavits, statements, excerpts of testimony, figures and tables—was being considered and passed on by the Commission, it was obviously the simplest matter for whatever "technical assistant" prepared the cleverly manipulated tables or the carefully expurgated evidence to have such matter approved and its conclusions accepted. For doubtless already largely convinced in favor of the strikers by the overwhelming proportion of testimony presented by the strikers before their "Hearings" in the strike area, it was perhaps not to be expected that men without wide experience in analyzing evidence should have even thought, when tables of statistics were presented to them by their own supposed experts, to take the time and trouble to go back of those tables and statistics to the sources from which they came or to have compared excerpts of testimony similarly submitted with the full contexts of the original, or have done otherwise than accept at face value the large amount of various "evidence" presented to them.

Twelfth: On the basis of this evidence which may thus easily have led the Commission of Inquiry, as Mr. Coleman states, to unanimous agreement as to at least the general nature of the Report, Mr. Blankenhorn, a conspicuous pronounced radical, who was Secretary to the Commission, wrote the Report itself, including a far greater amount of insinuations, misleading statements and false implications than even the present Report contains.

Thirteenth: After the Report was thus written and 8 typewritten copies had been circulated among the Commissioners and other members of the Interchurch World Movement, the Report was turned over to Mr. Stanley Went "to edit and take out the appearance of bias"; this editing however consisted chiefly merely of the striking out of certain more flagrant, obviously unwarrantable statements. In his official memorandum of June 17th with which he returned the edited manuscript, Mr. Went strongly condemned the obvious bias of the whole Report.

Fourteenth: The "Findings," a group of milder and more generalized conclusions, were in the meantime added by a sub-committee. On May 10th these added "Findings" were approved by the Commission of Inquiry and the Report turned over to the Executive Committee of the Interchurch World Movement for its approval. After six weeks, during which, according to all reports, there was much very serious argument as to whether or not the Report should be published, the Report itself says it was "unanimously approved" by the Executive Committee.

As a matter of fact however of the 7 most featured and doubtless leading members of the Executive Committee, four not only never approved the Report but never read or even saw it before it was published, and at least one more approved it without reading it. The Report was then finally edited and prepared for publication by Mr. James E. Craig and Mr. Robert W. Bruere.

Fifteenth: Nothing could be plainer than the dominant influence in the Interchurch investigation and Report of this notorious radical Robert W. Bruere—whose record is described on pages 396 to 399 of the present analysis—member of the "Federated Press" which secret reports to Moscow authorities, recently seized by the government, show is backed by the No. 1, unlawful branch of the ultra-revolutionary Communist Party, etc., etc. Mr. Bruere was Superintendent of Research of the Industrial Department of the Interchurch Movement, which department initiated the Steel Strike investigation. He was Director of the Bureau of Industrial Research whose name is formally signed to the Interchurch Report on the title page as technical assistants. The "staff of field investigators," on the results of whose "investigations" the Interchurch Report is stated to be largely based, and is provably chiefly based, worked under a "field director" (Mr. Blankenhorn) *"from the Bureau of Industrial Research."*

This same employee or partner of Mr. Bruere, as "Secretary to the Commission," actually wrote the Interchurch Report. Finally after the first editor selected by the Interchurch officials had strongly condemned the "obvious bias" of the Report, the Report was turned over for final editing to Mr. Craig, acting only as a copy editor, and Mr. Robert W. Bruere.

Moreover, when a year and a half after the Interchurch Movement was forced by its financial failure to abandon the fundamental religious work for which it was created the second Interchurch Report nevertheless appeared, this volume is stated in its own preface to be edited by and "seen through the Press" by the Bruere-Blankenhorn Bureau of Industrial Research.

The basic aim of Part Two of the present analysis is, as stated, to determine what men and interests are responsible for the Interchurch Report being as it is and what it is— not because a determination of such facts will in any way modify conclusions as to the Report itself but in order that men who are not actually responsible may not be made to appear responsible for the Report.

It has already been emphasized that the details in regard to the preparation of the Report are not always clear or undisputed. But while for reasons emphasized in the "afterword" of the present volume, such details are desirable, and an effort has therefore been made to present them as fully and clearly as has, under the circumstances, been possible, all such details may be entirely dispensed with and it still can be established beyond reasonable doubt that neither the Interchurch World Movement nor the Interchurch Commission of Inquiry are more than negatively responsible for the Interchurch Report being the kind of document it provably is.

For, irrespective of all such details, these main facts stand out.

I. The nature of the Interchurch Report itself as analyzed herein.

II. The type of men who constituted the Interchurch Commission of Inquiry.

III. The fact that this Commission employed or had employed for them, certain outside "technical" advisers, assistants and "investigators"; the fact as to who these men were,—which is a matter of published Interchurch record; and the facts as to what the most prominent of these men are—which is a matter of widespread public record.

Given merely these facts, from the very nature of the case, only one of two conclusions is reasonably possible. Either:

First: the Commission of Inquiry itself was actually the creator of the Report—itself collected the evidence, weighed the evidence, and prepared the evidence for submission to the public in the Report, and the various "technical experts" actually played only a subordinate rôle in the investigations, and Mr. Blankenhorn, as author, merely did the mechanical work of assembling and putting together the evidence and expressing the point of view for which the Commission itself is actually responsible.

If this is true then these nine nationally prominent Christian leaders who made up the Commission of Inquiry, who were appointed to and state that they did make an impartial investigation, not only deliberately refused to consider all the conspicuous evidence on one side—not only warped much general evidence by a careful expurgation of all the facts that were not favorable to one side—not only filled the Report with misleading insinuations and misleading phraseology in order to give false impressions that no twisting of the real facts could have given, but also they either possessed, or gained within a comparatively few weeks' time, an intimate technical knowledge of the various philosophies and aims of the various radical schools, including a fluent knowledge of technical radical phraseology and slang, and finally in the same comparatively few weeks they gained such an intimate knowledge of the technicalities of wage rates and classifications and schedules of working hours throughout industry, and a vast variety of similar highly specialized technical knowledge, that they could and did separate and manipulate and otherwise falsify and fabricate intricate statistics so cleverly as to make them seem to show the opposite of what the figures really do show.

Such a conclusion is obviously beyond the realm of reasonable possibility.

The obvious and only alternative to this conclusion, is the conclusion adduced from the known facts by the present analysis, as follows:

Second: That the "technical assistants" whether or not the Commission of Inquiry knew it at the time or realize it now, were chiefly made up of conspicuous radicals entirely committed in advance to one side of any labor controversy and always under all circumstances working for one end in industry;

—that these technical advisers, having gone into the strike area in advance and working with the strike leaders, either deliberately or because of inherent bias, brought to the attention of the Commission of Inquiry evidence only or chiefly favorable to the strikers, which together with the fact that the steel officials refused to consider this investigation seriously, resulted in bringing only one side of the case to the Commission's attention;

—that when the great mass of evidence thus collected by the technical advisers and the Commission of Inquiry in the field together with tables and statistics which were compiled by these same or other technical advisers was assembled for analysis for a final determination of the Report, the Commission of Inquiry because of their confidence in their technical advisers never thought of going back of the testimony and the facts and tables as submitted, to analyze and check them with their original sources but accepted such evidence at its face value and formed final conclusions as to the nature of the Report accordingly;

—that, having thus been led to reach their conclusions as to the general nature of the Report, the Commission of Inquiry easily accepted those conclusions substantially as Mr. Blankenhorn stated them in the Report;

—that such directors or other members of the Interchurch World Movement as approved the Interchurch Report, did so, because they too, perhaps naturally under the circumstances, accepted the alleged evidence it contained at face value and because also of their confidence in the Commission of Inquiry;

—that therefore, irrespective of what the Commissioners of Inquiry may honestly believe, the whole investigation and Report, far from being actually the product of conscientious Christian thinking, was the result of the flagrant manipulation of circumstances and evidence by the Commission's radical "technical" advisers and assistants and "investigators."

AFTERWORD

THE Interchurch Report on the Steel Strike signed as it is by nine prominent religious leaders and underwritten by the Interchurch World Movement, has undoubtedly been widely accepted at substantially its face value, by a large part not merely of the religious world, but also of the general public. Numerous reviews of it have appeared in the public press in which the reviewers, although discounting those portions dealing with facts within their particular knowledge, have nevertheless accepted the Report in general at its face value. Inquiry has revealed that many statisticians, economists and other men of high professional standing, though conscious of many inaccuracies and fallacies in the Report, have nevertheless been much impressed by the way its conclusions are seemingly supported by facts and statistics alleged to be from authoritative sources. These gentlemen, impressed by the statistical knowledge and methods displayed by the Report, have accepted many of its conclusions accordingly.[1] This at least partial acceptance of the Report by such competent authorities indicates the probability, repeatedly emphasized by some of those connected with the preparation of the Report, that the Report is widely accepted and used by educational institutions as a text-book on modern industrial problems. These facts alone amply justify the publication of the present analysis.

Beyond all facts as to the merits of the Interchurch Report itself, however, or as to its use, is the fact that it is a representative document—a conspicuous typical example of

[1] There have, however, been several very significant exceptions.

467

a new type of propaganda which is being more and more widely used and whose motives and methods as well as whose merits should therefore at least be recognized and understood by the public.

The application of artificial power to the production of the world's needs during the last 140 years has worked astonishing changes. In 1340 the population of England and Wales was about 4,000,000. In the following four centuries it increased to about 6,000,000 or about 50%. But in the next one and a half centuries under the modern industrial system it increased to 32,000,000 or 500%. In the one thousand years between Charlemagne and Napoleon the population of what is modern Germany reached 24,000,000. In one hundred years under the industrial system it jumped to 70,000,000. In the two centuries before 1810 our own population reached 10,000,000. One century of industrialism permitted the multiplication of this to 110,000,000.

It has already been pointed out that in terms of the purchasing power of wheat flour, the American skilled worker today receives three times as much as he did in 1850. As regards comparative housing conditions, so liberal an historian as Mr. Hendrik Van Loon emphasizes dramatically what any competent history will show, that the European of the pre-industrialism period lived "in miserable hovels compared to which a modern tenement stands forth as a luxurious palace." That industrialism has made commonplace among every class of our population innumerable contrivances of comfort undreamed of in the days of our forefathers is known to every child who has listened at the knees of his grandfather. Our ever increasing educational institutions, hospitals, libraries, newspapers, facilities for travel and other broadly human advantages which those in every walk of life enjoy today, have been made possible chiefly by the surplus of capital and extra leisure which the modern industrial system has created.

But principles of social conduct and habits of thought move slowly. They have not changed with the phenomenal rapidity with which industrialism has changed actual living conditions. Moreover the fundamental, and by and large the valuable human characteristic persists that the more most people get the more they want. The very extent, therefore, to which the industrial system has advanced, improved and tended to equalize living standards, seems only to have intensified the demand that this advanced improvement and equalization shall be carried on still more rapidly. The problems to which these facts have given rise are becoming our dominant political issues today. The principles of liberty and the rules of conduct anciently established and cherished by many generations, may or may not be entirely sufficient to solve all such problems. There justly exists much difference of opinion upon this point. So far as such opinions are honestly held, so far as we frankly face the problem of how far we can afford to endanger the principles upon which we have obtained our present real advantages, and so far as arguments advanced in support of these opinions are based on honest interpretation of known facts, all such opinions may prove of constructive value. But many opinions as to the need of fundamental changes to-day, whether honestly held or not, are certainly not being advanced on their merits. On the contrary, they are adroitly presented and covertly advanced to hide the fact that they actually involve the "burning of the barn to get rid of the rats"—their sponsors cherishing the hope that the fire can be well started before those whose assistance is being sought in setting it are aware of what they are helping to do.

Radical criticism of industrialism undoubtedly takes its initial impetus from Carl Marx, the father of modern socialism. Marx made the definite and sweeping prediction that the industrial system would inevitably operate to reduce the living standard of all workers until it was established on a mere subsistence level where it would be arbitrarily maintained. Upon this prediction Marx built an elaborate theory for the revolutionization of the ownership and management of all industry and of all government. But his theory still contemplated the principle of government by majority in the interests of all. The subsequent development of the industrial system has completely refuted the fundamental prediction of Marx. With the passing of the premise of his prediction has passed Marxian idealism and the notion of a democratic administration of industry by the state in the interests of all the citizens. Modern radicalism is advocating the seizure without compensation of the different industrial units by the particular workers engaged and their operation in the interests of those workers. Under this system the industry, not the community, becomes the unit of interest; men are divided against each other according to their occupations rather than bound together according to the interests of the community in which they live, and the only persons who are permitted to express an opinion, to vote or to receive consideration, are the manual workers and their self-constituted attorneys and representatives.

No one realizes more clearly than the radicals that no majority of Americans would ever adopt or willingly permit such a programme of plunder and class chauvinism to be carried out. Radicalism's programme, therefore, is admittedly based on force strategically applied by a united minority against a majority they hope to deceive and divide. The primary effort of radicalism,—to build its active fighting minority of industrial workers through capitalizing discontent, preaching class hatred, appealing to envy and greed and maligning public officials and courts and government,—is more or less open and recognized. Its secondary effort, however, to deceive and disunite the general public, to confuse economic and political issues and to disrupt or dissipate every constructive economic effort depends for its success upon its more or less complete concealment.[1]

[1] The Executive Committee of the Third International in 1921 reaffirmed the principle:
" We talk in two languages, that which we talk to the bourgoisie we fool them with, that which we talk to the world proletariat is the truth."

For the achievement, therefore, of its secondary effort, radicalism changes its appearance and appeal—its red becomes pink or "merely liberal" and its programme of hate and plunder becomes one of "sympathy" and "idealism." In this guise radicalism has created various and widely distributed organizations to carry its propaganda to the general public. Among the most prominent of these are the Rand School of Social Science, the Bureau of Industrial Research, organized by Mr. Robert W. Bruere, a teacher of literature in the Rand School until this school was being made conspicuous through government attack; the American Civil Liberties Union, posing as interested merely in protecting the constitutional guarantees of freedom of speech and assemblage but actually radicalism's legal department and one of its most important and effective propaganda organizations. The function of these and similar bureaus, schools and leagues is to prepare "statistics," "data," "legal" arguments and other allegedly scientific material for the use of radical propagandists.

But the usefulness of such organizations wears off as time reveals their true nature. Radicalism therefore, has more recently resorted to the device of applying to existing social and economic institutions the programme already applied to craft unionism of "boring from within," in the attempt to get such control of non-radical organizations as will permit their use as media for radical propaganda.

Radical "boring from within" does not, of course, mean the attempt to convert all the members of the organization subjected to this operation to the extreme radicalism of the "borers." Its purpose is generally served if it can tinge enough members or officials with sufficient "liberalism," or sufficiently play upon their idealism or sentimentalism to secure their support or acquiescence in furnishing the members of the organization and their followers with such propaganda as the borers in each case deem wise. In this way radicalism's operations are better cloaked, while it obtains what support it needs from great groups of individuals who would not conceivably work for or accept its basic program.

The means by which such "boring" is instituted and carried on vary, of course, with circumstances. The management of the modern variety of social and particularly religious organizations, created to interest or inform the public in social or economic questions, is frequently in the hands of men whose chief qualification consists of the ability to make effective emotional appeals that will arouse public interest in their work—a type of ability which is not always accompanied by the power of clear analysis or impartial judgment. Such a situation may often be readily capitalized by the clever radical "borer" who, because of his connection with some so-called "industrial" or "economic" bureau or school, created and so named for the particular purpose of giving prestige to such radical activities, is able to insinuate himself into the organization in the guise of an "economic" or other "technical" expert.

Again the problem of raising money is often one of the most important and pressing which has to be faced by the type of organizations under discussion. The individual or group therefore, which can devise successful ways and means to this end may hope to become correspondingly influential in the activities which such money supports. It is a matter of record, as has already been noted, that a $50,000 pledge was obtained from a notoriously radical source to finance the activities of the Interchurch Industrial Department. It is also a matter of record that advertisements have appeared from time to time in radical and "liberal" publications offering to furnish financial plans to social and church organizations. Such facts indicate how keenly alive radicalism is to the value of this method of making its influence felt.

The method of controlling the agents of radicalism and their "boring" activities in various types and widely scattered organizations is entirely clear from the casual study of the lists of officials of such organizations. It is a familiar method. It is what is popularly known as the "community of interests" system, operating through "interlocking directorates." The radical directors of ultra-radical central organizations serve as directors and officers with less radical and even conservative directors in a much wider group of "liberal" organizations, while the most intimate of their fellow directors in such organizations in turn serve as directors or officers in a still wider group of more "merely liberal" organizations. Again we have an excellent example in the Interchurch Report itself. Mr. Foster, the hero of the Report, is a member of the No. 1 Communist governing organization, in constant touch with Moscow. As member of the Federated press he is in constant touch with Mr. Blankenhorn, who wrote the Interchurch Report, and Mr. Bruere, the head of its technical assistants. Blankenhorn and Bruere in turn, in their Bureau of Industrial Research, are in touch with the trade unions, social organizations, college socialist societies, and the like, to which they supply data and material. Through common membership in the National Committee of the American Civil Liberties Union, Foster is in active touch with James A. Maurer, who furnished most of the Interchurch "rock-bottom" affidavits, and Maurer in turn is president of the Pennsylvania State Federation of Labor, a subordinate organization of the American Federation of Labor. Through the same organization Foster is in touch with Baldwin whose assistants are seeking from the courts a new interpretation of the principles of freedom of speech, of the press, and of assemblage, which will destroy the power of the Government to protect itself and its citizens against propaganda for the overthrow of our government by force and violence.

Through its control, thus secured and maintained and directed, of an ever increasing number of organizations, which profess to represent, and are accepted by the general public as representing, some religious or broadly social work, radicalism is today carrying on an "under cover" propaganda campaign which is as far reaching as it is generally unsuspected. Thus radicalism is continually presenting to the public as sound bases for public opinion and action all manner of "social programs" which as a matter of fact are merely clever compositions of sentimental plausibilities and idealistic sounding sophistries designed to confuse the real issues involved and breed distrust of those who are honestly attempting to meet and solve those issues on a workable basis. Thus it is continually determining the selection of lecturers and subjects to which the widest variety of audiences in all parts cf the country listen without the least suspicion that they are actually listening to organized propaganda. Thus it controls the writing and distribution of innumerable articles, bulletins, pamphlets, supposedly expert reports and allegedly statistical studies on the widest variety of subjects of popular interest, often presented in the most impressive scientific guise, but actually ingeniously contrived to misrepresent the real facts, to confuse the true issues, to insinuate distrust in our institutions, or subtly lead up to some radical conclusions.

Moreover it is a recognized fact—and one which such propaganda is built to take advantage of—that under ordinary circumstances correction and disproof can seldom hope to catch up with sensationally stated and cleverly propagated misinformation.

That the Interchurch Report is typical of this general radical "under-cover" propaganda with which, in all manner of disguises, the country is today being broadcast, is plain from the comparison of arguments, conclusions and even phraseology already made, and from the fact that it was actually prepared by the representatives of the same organizations which are at least ultimately responsible for this general campaign. But the Interchurch Report is more than merely typical. From its inception, in which the radicals had such a prominent part, the Interchurch Steel Strike Report offered the possibilities of having their "under-cover" propaganda underwritten and circulated by what promised to be the most influential religious organization in American history. The "borers" in this case consisted not merely of the immediate representatives of one particular radical group, as is usual, but of some of the ablest representatives of the most important interlocking radical groups. Their success was such that they had the preparation of the Report substantially in their own hands. With such an incentive and such an opportunity it is inconceivable that these men should have made the Interchurch Report less than the best and strongest possible argument of its kind.

Moreover the Interchurch Report on the Steel Strike deals on such an extensive scale with a subject of such recognized public importance; its arguments and conclusions have been brought so sensationally to public attention and so reaffirmed not only by those who are responsible for this Report but by the widest variety of radical and "liberal" leaders and groups, that it cannot—as does the bulk of similar, but less individually conspicuous propaganda— evade a reckoning with the truth.

The primary motive of the present analysis is the hope that such a critical examination as is here presented, of the actual merits of such arguments and of the methods by which they have been propagated, in the case of this most conspicuous example, may make it easier for the average American to recognize and judge such propaganda in whatever guise he may meet it. It is particularly hoped that such exact and detailed citations, as are here given, of the original authorities on which such arguments are alleged to be based, and to the other pertinent evidence, may both offer the incentive, and make it easier, for those who may be interested in modern "liberalism" to investigate fully for themselves the actual merits of the most prominent product of modern "liberalism."